CONSTITUTIONALISM IN TRANSFORMATION: EUROPEAN AND THEORETICAL PERSPECTIVES

Edited by Richard Bellamy
and Dario Castiglione

BLACKWELL
Publishers

ISBN 0-631-202501

First published 1996

Blackwell Publishers
108 Cowley Road, Oxford, OX4 1JF, U.K.

and

238 Main Street,
Cambridge, MA 02142, USA.

British Library Cataloguing in Publication Data
A catalogue record for this book is available from the
British Library

Library of Congress Cataloguing-in-Publication Data
A catalogue record for this book is available from the
British Library

Printed in Great Britain by Page Bros, Norwich

This book is printed on acid-free paper

CONTENTS

Acknowledgements

These essays were first discussed at a workshop at the University of East Anglia, where Richard Bellamy was then Professor of Politics, in September 1995. We are grateful to the Political Studies Association, the British Academy, the Economic and Social Research Council and the University of East Anglia for providing financial support for this event. We would also like to thank Michael Moran, the editor of *Political Studies*, both for inviting us to edit this special issue and for his advice and comments with regard to its contents. Vital secretarial assistance was provided by Mrs. Anne Martin and Mrs. Vicki Blundell at UEA and Exeter respectively. This volume forms part of a research project on 'Principles and Languages for the Constitution of Europe' directed by Richard Bellamy and Dario Castiglione, for which they have been awarded an ESRC Project Grant (R000221170).

R.P.B.
D.C.

Introduction: Constitutions and Politics

RICHARD BELLAMY AND DARIO CASTIGLIONE

Constitutions play a vital role in politics. With a few honourable exceptions, however, contemporary political scientists and theorists have paid them remarkably little attention. Apart from a periodic interest in electoral laws, voting systems and the relative merits of parliamentarism and presidentialism, the profession has treated the study of constitutions as at best an irrelevance and at worst misleading, providing no guide to the genuine operations of politics. Amongst British academics, this lack of interest has often been attributed to the peculiarity of the country's own unwritten constitution. But this attitude is equally common in countries with a strong constitutionalist tradition – one need only think of the American behaviourist school. This relative indifference to constitutional issues amongst the political studies community would appear to result from a number of more general factors, therefore, that derive from certain prevailing conceptions of the discipline.

By and large, political scientists view constitutions as idealistic and, as a consequence, insignificant. They have regarded them as formal legal frameworks bearing little or no relation to the real workings of the political system such as the influence of government and the administrative machine, or the clash of interests and political cultures within a nation. After all, they point out, many repressive regimes have had written constitutions offering all kinds of formal protection for individual and collective rights. But these provisions proved totally worthless because the constitutional documents within which they appeared had no influence on, and largely misdescribed, the actual exercise of power in those countries. Seen in this light, constitutions appear to be either the unnecessary adornments of good regimes that work well for totally unrelated reasons, or the means whereby bad regimes are provided with a spurious legitimacy. Political theorists, in contrast, have often ignored constitutions because they have considered them too empirical and the preserve of mainly legal, historical and sociological scholars. They have found the institutional, cultural and positive characteristics of constitutions difficult to integrate into their more abstract discussions of justice and power, self-interest and collective choice.

This volume challenges these rather narrow conceptions of the discipline of politics, revealing in the process the political significance of constitutions. Constitutionalism offers not only a mutually beneficial point of contact between the descriptive and the prescriptive branches of political studies, it also relates politics to other fields of enquiry. To this end, the editors have invited contributions from jurists, sociologists and economists as well as from political scientists and theorists and historians of political thought. This interdisciplinary endeavour illuminates how politics requires certain normative and social preconditions that constitutions strive, with varying degrees of success, to

embody. However, a number of contributors are equally concerned to demonstrate how constitutions in their turn employ the resources of politics both to
establish and sustain themselves. Democratic institutions that balance a variety
of social forces and encourage a certain quality of political debate are as much a
part of the constitution as formal legal provisions concerning rights and judicial
review. In this way, we hope to have broadened not only our understanding of
politics, its presuppositions and its mode of operation, but also our notion of
constitutionalism.

The times are propitious for a reconsideration of constitutionalism. Current
interest in constitutions has been stimulated above all by the post-1989
developments in Eastern Europe and the constitutional challenge posed by the
European Union in the West. As in post-fascist Europe, the constitution-
making process in the former Eastern bloc has been mainly characterized by the
'negative' task of rejecting the previous regimes and what they stood for.
Constitutional democracy (often unreflectively pronounced in a single breath) is
now seen as the sole legitimate political regime. Paradoxically, however, the
ideological success of constitutional democracy in the East comes at a time
when many of its fundamental principles are being called into question in the
West. The European Union has highlighted the inadequacies of certain key
concepts of constitutional and democratic thought outside the context of
relatively homogeneous nation states, such as the sovereignty of the people and
the link between citizenship and rights. Rethinking the constitution is thus part
of a more general re-assessment of *fin de siècle* politics as international globalization without and multiculturalism within take it beyond the boundaries of
the sovereign nation state.

This volume explores a number of aspects of this transformation of constitutionalism, with special reference to the European situation. Section one traces
the historical transformation of the meaning of constitutionalism. Dario
Castiglione and Richard Bellamy contend that the essentially liberal legalistic
conception of a constitution as a formal framework of rights is a relatively
recent invention. In the past, constitutions represented the form of government
and emphasized the role of politics as the art of balancing, reducing and
managing conflicts. They advocate a return to this more political and
republican understanding of constitutionalism – a theme picked up in section
four.

Section two looks at the way constitutions are being transformed within a
number of West European states. Luigi Ferrajoli, Tony Prosser, Jeremy
Jennings, and Howard Caygill and Alan Scott examine the developing tensions
between constitutionalism and democracy as manifested respectively in Italy,
Britain, France and Germany. In each case, they note how the relationship
between the two reflects the particular constitutional tradition of the country
concerned. Thus, Ferrajoli argues that the rise to power of a major media
magnate and financier, and the close links between his party and his commercial
empire, threatens not only the separation of public and private interests
intrinsic to all forms of liberal constitutionalism, but also strikes at the anti-
majoritarian and, given the electoral pact with the National Alliance, antifascist principles of the Italian constitution. Prosser, in contrast, maintains that
the majoritarian reading of democracy is a peculiarity of the British state and its
personal conception of sovereign power. He believes this view is rightly being
undermined by a rights-based theory of democracy as a result of Britain's

membership of the European Union. Jennings notes a similar tension between popular sovereignty and rights as championed by the French republican and liberal traditions respectively. He observes that the presence of a significant immigrant population has problematized the idea of the nation invoked by the former and rendered ever more urgent a move towards the latter. However, Caygill and Scott show how this liberal constitutionalism is not without problems of its own. The multicultural subversion of liberal pretensions to universality is sometimes portrayed as solely the product of aboriginal or immigrant communities disturbing the cultural homogeneity of advanced Western nation states. Caygill and Scott's discussion of the Bavarian crucifix order and the clash between Catholic and Protestant cultures within Germany reveals this to be a problem that can arise between well-established Western traditions as well. They describe how each group made a claim to the authority of liberal democratic principles to justify their nevertheless conflicting positions in this case. Placing majoritarianism to one side, they maintain a fundamental tension persists between the universalism of the rule of law and the particularist concerns voiced through democratic politics, and that certain issues may only be resolvable in terms of the latter.

Section three starts by exploring how the European Union has transformed constitutional thought. Joseph Weiler argues that insufficient attention has been paid to the need to create a European Demos if the institutions of the European Union are to have legitimacy in the eyes of those whom they govern. However, one cannot transfer the conceptions of citizenship and popular sovereignty characteristic of nation states to the very different context of the European Union – a point also made by Ulrich Preuß in his chapter. Rather, a way has to be found whereby individuals can possess a variety of political and cultural identities. Neil MacCormick contends that this project involves combining the ties of ethnicity, religion and nationalism with a liberal respect for persons, a compound he believes has been made possible by the weakening of state sovereignty entailed by the European Union. Regrettably, no such development appears to be occurring in the new regimes emerging in Eastern Europe. Quite the contrary, an illiberal ethnic nationalism has all too often been linked to both a narrow account of state sovereignty and a majoritarian view of democracy, with dire consequences for the rights of those minorities that remain. As Istvan Pogany comments in his detailed survey of these events, constitution making has rarely involved a genuine transformation of the constitutional culture and politics of these regimes. Instead, they have remained somewhat formal documents that fail to connect with the underlying social and political realities of the systems they are intended to regulate.

In the fourth and final section, contributors explore how such legal formalism might be overcome through an examination of the institutional mechanisms employed by a constitutional regime. To varying degrees, they advocate a move away from the currently dominant legalistic paradigm back to the political conception of constitutionalism outlined in the opening section of the volume. Stephen Elkin's chapter links up directly with Bellamy's in this respect, offering an update of the Madisonian idea of a constitution described there. Geoffrey Brennan and Alan Hamlin investigate the ways these political strategies might nevertheless use various forms of reasoning normally associated with economics in order to motivate support for the public interest. Finally, Robert Goodin and Judith Squires look at institutional solutions to the incorporation of radically diverse social groups within a single polity. Goodin argues a mixed commonwealth may be reached not by striving for approximations to some ideal but by opting for second best – a technique he too adapts from economic theory. However, he concludes that there is only so much difference that it is either reasonable or practicable to seek to recognize. Squires traces how theorists of difference have gradually come to a similar conclusion. As a result, they have exchanged their initial antagonism to liberal constitutionalism for a desire to reform it in order to accommodate their concerns, looking in particular to new kinds of representation. On closer examination, the dialogic forms of democracy they once advanced as alternatives to liberal democracy, turn out to presuppose the very rights liberal constitutions typically uphold.

Like other contributors to this volume, Squires believes that liberal rights-based constitutionalism and republican democratic constitutionalism are in many respects complementary rather than opposed traditions. Where the contributors tend to divide is over how best to combine the two so as to offer plausible political means capable of meeting the demands of today's complex and pluralistic societies. Whilst some stress the first, others emphasize the second. All insist, however, that political scientists and theorists can only play a constructive role in shaping the politics of the future if they take constitutions more seriously than at present.

The Political Theory of the Constitution

DARIO CASTIGLIONE[1]

Our current understanding of what a constitution is largely depends on the constructions which nineteenth-century constitutionalism placed upon it, locking the constitution into a series of complex relationships with liberal views of the modern nation state, parliamentary democracy, the rule of law and the market economy. As a political doctrine, constitutionalism is a modern invention. It comprises those theories which offer a series of principled arguments for the limitation of political power in general and of government's sway over citizens in particular. In the course of the last two centuries, these limitations and their underlying principles have been partly embodied in the institutions and practices of the modern constitutional state. Constitutions have therefore been presented as the centre piece in the strategy for the limitation of power. They have often been invoked in order to legitimize, regulate and keep under control the powers that be, and regarded as the best means for the recognition and protection of the rights and liberties of the citizens.

This interpretation of the modern constitutional state is correct in as far as it goes. Indeed, since ancient times there has been an intimate connection between the constitution and the idea of curbing human power. However, in emphasizing the *negative* limits imposed by constitutions, the contemporary view mistakenly takes the part for the whole.[2] In this essay I wish to offer a critical and more comprehensive understanding of the political theory of the modern constitution. I am also assuming that a 'political theory of the constitution' has at least three different objects: namely, the constitution as a political concept, constitutionalism as an ideological construction, and the constitutional state as a modern political formation. These have been too often confused with one another. Such a position is both historically and analytically untenable. The rest of this essay will mainly deal with the first two issues; but in the conclusion something will be said on the modern constitutional state and the challenges that lie ahead.

The Idea of the Constitution

A constitution, according to Thomas Paine, is not a 'thing' in name only, but also 'in fact' – it can be produced 'in a visible form' and quoted 'article by

[1] I am grateful to the participants in the Norwich workshop for their comments on an earlier draft of this essay, in particular to Richard Bellamy for advice and discussion at various stages of its preparation, and to Catherine Armstrong for her help with the final version.
[2] For a recent discussion of 'negative' and 'enabling' constitutionalism, cf. S. Holmes, *Passions and Constraint. On the Theory of Liberal Democracy* (Chicago, University of Chicago Press, 1995), chs 4–7; see also R. Bellamy and D. Castiglione, 'Constitutionalism and democracy: political theory and the American constitution', *British Journal of Political Science* (forthcoming).

article'.[3] Paine's distinction – whose meaning is obvious within the context of his polemic against *immemorial* constitutions – gives rise to two possible misconceptions. By assuming an essentialist definition of the constitution – the 'thing' in the form either of a material document or of the more abstract rules/ form of the state – one risks pre-empting philosophical discussion.[4] By taking a semantic approach – treating the 'constitution' and the correlated semantemes in the main European languages merely as lexicographic objects – one may fail to engage in the philosophical argument altogether. The approach here adopted instead views the constitution as a complex political *concept* – the product of stratified socio-historical *conceptions* – which I shall discuss analytically, rather than by a reconstruction of the historical development of the conceptions themselves.

According to a standard definition, the constitution is both the act and/or the norms that constitute a political body, and the structure and/or characteristics that define a constituted political body. This set of meanings suggests that the idea of a constitution, as the fundamental 'rule' of the state, involves both constitutive and regulative functions.[5] Each function is also open to a variety of constructions, depending respectively on whether a constitution is meant as the basic norm or the basic order of a society. Although these two dichotomies – of normative and descriptive meanings on the one hand, and constitutive and regulative functions on the other – remain the fundamental distinctions according to which ideas of the constitution can be classified, I believe they both need supplementing.

The Meanings of the Constitution

General classifications of the meanings of the constitution have no more than a heuristic value,[6] so the classification proposed here is intended only to elicit the political ideas which each meaning expresses. From this perspective, we can distinguish between four general meanings of the constitution, referred to here as the positive, the absolute (either in the normative, the positivist, the voluntarist, or the organic sense), the functional and the instrumental. I take the interpretations of the constitution underlying these meanings to be clearly distinct and, so to speak, autonomous.

The positive meaning of the constitution is the most obvious one, but no less controversial for that. Paine's reference to the constitution as a 'thing . . . in fact'

---

[3] T. Paine (B. Kuklick, ed.), *Political Writings* (Cambridge, Cambridge University Press, 1989), p. 81.

[4] Cf. K. Loewenstein. 'Reflections on the value of constitutions in our revolutionary age' in A. J. Zucher (ed.), *Constitutions and Constitutional Trends since World War II* (New York, New York University Press, 1951), p. 193.

[5] Cf. D. Castiglione, 'Contracts and constitutions' in R. Bellamy, V. Bufacchi and D. Castiglione (eds), *Democracy and Constitutionalism in the Union of Europe* (London, Lothian Foundation, 1995), pp. 64–5 and 69.

[6] For other classifications, cf. C. Schmitt, *Verfassungslehre* (Berlin, Duncker and Humblot, 1928), ch. 1; C. Mortati, 'Costituzione' in *Enciclopedia del Diritto* (Milano, Giuffrè, 1962), vol. XI, pp. 133–233; C. J. Friedrich, *Constitutional Government and Democracy* (Boston, Ginn, rev. ed., 1950), ch. 7; N. Bobbio and F. Pierandrei, *Introduzione alla Costituzione* (Bari, Laterza, rev. ed., 1980), pp. 17–9; G. Maddox, 'Constitution' in T. Ball, J. Farr and R. L. Hanson (eds), *Political Innovation and Conceptual Change* (Cambridge, Cambridge University Press, 1989), pp. 50–67; M. Dogliani, *Introduzione al diritto costituzionale* (Bologna, il Mulino, 1994), ch. 1.

points at important formal characteristics of modern written constitutions. Since the end of the eighteenth century these have become fundamental charters, with both symbolic and normative functions, according to which the basic political structure of society is given form and a certain stability. Their widespread diffusion depended on a number of political and ideal features of the positive constitution corresponding to parallel developments in modern politics and society. On the one hand, constitutions came progressively to be identified with written statutes and charters of rights through which monarchical power recognized the liberties of the citizens and their participation in public affairs. The demand for a written constitution therefore assumed a particular political meaning transcending its formal properties.[7] On the other hand, the written quality of the constitution corresponded to the diffusion of more voluntarist (in opposition to traditionalist) and constructivist (in opposition to naturalist) attitudes to the regulation of human affairs,[8] and also to general processes of rationalization and positivization of the law.[9]

The positive meaning outlined here clearly implies the rejection of certain ancient and traditional conceptions of the constitution, because, as Paine suggested, these lacked important formal characteristics that made them publicly recognizable as such. But, once the positive meaning of the constitution is divested of its polemical (and historically contingent) substance, the concept becomes both overformal and relativistic. Indeed any document having the required formal characteristics, regardless of its content, efficacy or legitimacy, may be considered a constitution. If this were so, all states where the machinery for and procedures of government were fixed on paper should be counted as constitutional. Clearly then, the positive meaning of the constitution must be dependent on some other meaning to prevent it from becoming trivial.

This more fundamental meaning of the constitution is generally, though not necessarily, supplied by making reference to an absolute concept of the constitution. The use of 'absolute' does not indicate any trascendental quality, but the sense in which the constitution itself provides the basis for a normative order. In its absolute sense, the constitution, or the constitutional meta-text,[10] needs to be distinguished from individual constitutional laws and even from the sum of them.[11] As the source of legitimacy, it must possess a certain unity and an internal coherence, so that appeals to it may be meaningful and capable of carrying conviction.[12] The purely formal characteristics of a constitutional text – such as its written form, its aggravated amendment procedures, etc. –

---

[7] Schmitt, *Verfassungslehre*, ch. 1, para. 2.

[8] Cf. G. Rebuffa, *Costituzioni e costituzionalismi* (Torino, Giappichelli, 1990), pp. 34–54; P. W. Kahn, *Legitimacy and History. Self-Government in American Constitutional Theory* (New Haven & London, Yale University Press, 1992), ch. 1; L. Ferrajoli, 'Democracy and the constitution in Italy', in this volume. On the relationship between constitutions and contractarian thinking, see Castiglione, 'Contracts and constitutions', pp. 63–67.

[9] Cf. U. K. Preuß, 'The political meaning of constitutionalism' in R. Bellamy (ed.), *Constitutionalism, Democracy and Sovereignty: American and European Perspectives* (Aldershot, Avebury, 1996), pp. 13–8.

[10] Cf. Mortati, 'Constituzione', pp. 144–5.

[11] Cf. Schmitt, *Verfassungslehre*, ch. 1, para. 2.

[12] Cf. P. Häberle, 'I diritti fondamentali nelle società pluraliste e la Costituzione del Pluralismo' in M. Luciani (ed.), *La democrazia alla fine del secolo* (Bari, Laterza, 1994), pp. 96–121; P. Häberle, *Die Wesensgehaltgarantie des Art. 19 Abs. 2 Grundgesetz* (Heidelberg, Müller, 3rd rev. ed., 1983), ch. 1; and Ferrajoli, 'Democracy and the constitution in Italy', in this volume.

cannot by themselves be the basis for such a coherent normative order, so that the constitution must either have or stand for some more substantive norm-engendering principle.[13]

If, as argued, the absolute meaning of the constitution depends on some ethical or meta-ethical preconception, there are a great many forms which this meaning can take. On the whole, there are three main grounds upon which the constitution can be said to obligate, depending on whether appeals are made to normative, voluntarist, or organic ideals. Normative conceptions consider the constitution as a fundamental norm upon which the whole organization of socio-political life must ultimately depend. Although the philosophical justification of the basic norm may rest on widely different principles (natural law, utility, liberty, equality, democratic ideals, or a mixture of these), the overall emphasis of this conception lies in treating the constitution as a superior law in both its form and its internal compulsion.[14] A variant of this normative conception is the positivist interpretation of the basic norm (to be distinguished here from the positive conception of the constitution outlined above), according to which its content is understood not as a general ethical principle or body of principles (these can 'influence' legislators or function as their 'motives'), but as the very binding force of the basic norm as a legal norm (the principle of legality).[15]

Voluntarists also consider the constitution as a basic norm, but stress the existential origin of the norm itself in the will of the subject of the constitution, so that they rest the legitimacy of the constitutional system on the interests and intentions expressed in the original act or decision from which the political association emanates. The founding moment itself can take various forms, from a contract between 'naturally' independent individuals or groups, to an act of subjugation of the entire community to the will of either the sovereign or a dominant group within the community.[16]

Those who subscribe to the organic approach, consider the constitution as the 'living' expression of some more fundamental principle of civil co-operation.[17] Even though the organic approach depicts the constitution as something already in existence,[18] this is nonetheless a normative construction in so far as it commands respect because it grows out 'of the habitual conditions, relations, and reciprocal claims'[19] of the people of a country.

The organic conception bears some relation to the functional meaning of the constitution, in that they both exploit the fundamental constitutive/regulative ambiguity of the concept. In its functional meaning, the constitution can be seen either as framing the regular powers of a society and of its political system or as

---

[13] Cf. H. Kelsen, *Introduction to the Problems of Legal Theory* (Oxford, Clarendon, 1992), pp. 61–2.

[14] Cf. G. Zagrebelsky, *Il diritto mite* (Torino, Einaudi, 1992), chs 1 and 6; Häberle, *Die Wesensgehaltgarantie*; and M. Fioravanti, 'Quale futuro per la "costituzione"?', *Quaderni Fiorentini. Per la storia del pensiero giuridico moderno*, 21 (1992), 623–37.

[15] H. Kelsen, *General Theory of Norms* (Oxford, Clarendon, 1991), pp. 116–7.

[16] Cf. Schmitt, *Verfassungslehre*, ch. 1, para. 8; A. Negri, *Il potere costituente. Saggio sulle aternative del moderno* (Varese, Sugarco, 1992), ch. 1.

[17] Cf. W. Bagehot, *The English Constitution* (London, Oxford University Press, 1961), p. 259; G. W. F. Hegel (T. M. Knox, ed.), *Philosophy of Right* (London, Oxford University Press, 1967), p. 291.

[18] Hegel, *Philosophy of Right*, p. 178.

[19] E. Burke, *Reflections on the French Revolution* (London, Dent, 1955), p. 281.

mirroring them. Indeed this ambiguity is central to any conception of the constitution purporting to find a proper equilibrium between change and continuity. But the central idea invoked by the functional meaning is that of regularity. The constitution, in its functional sense, is therefore the general pattern according to which a society is ordered. Traditionally this pattern has been identified with the political form of the state, but since 'political' here means the distribution and balance of power at large, the functional meaning can refer to either the structure and institutions of political governance or the general balance of power and 'property' within society.

If the functional meaning plays down the normative content of the constitution by looking at it as the basic 'order' of society; the instrumental meaning of the constitution achieves the same result by subordinating the constitution to some 'external' principle. In the instrumental sense, the constitution is only the framework of the state.[20] This, however, is considered as a simple means for the achievement of autonomously established ends. Naturally, nothing excludes that these ends and their supporting principles may be fixed in the constitutional document and adopted as the proper ends bearing upon the framework of the state and the 'plan of government'. In this sense, there would seem to be little difference between the instrumental and the normative meanings of the constitution. But there remains an essential difference in that the constitution, in its instrumental sense, is not properly conceived as the 'expression' of the basic norm, but simply as its instrument – not the supreme law, but a 'superstructure' for the maintenance of an independent normative order.[21] As von Humboldt wrote,

> the State constitution and the national community ... should not be confused. While the State constitution ... sets the citizens in a specific relationship to each other, there is another which is wholly distinct from this ... the free cooperation of the members of the nation ...[22]

The Functions of the Constitution

This brief analysis demonstrates the great variety of 'things' that may be understood by the term constitution. This may be a document; the embodiment of either a norm, a command, a subjective will, or a practice; the organized form of a political society; or, finally, a series of devices through which independent normative principles are given institutional support within the political community. Although, as already suggested, these meanings often overlap in constitutional practice, at a philosophical level most of them appear to be mutually exclusive. This fact has not always been wholly appreciated, for different conceptions of the constitution seem at least to agree on its purpose. Indeed, what a constitution *is* can hardly be distinguished from what a constitution *does*. In very broad terms, a constitution *constitutes* a political entity, establishes its fundamental *structure*, and defines the *limits* within which

---

[20] Cf. W. von Humboldt (J. W. Burrow, ed.), *The Limits of State Action* (Indianapolis, Liberty Fund, 1993), p. 3.

[21] Cf. F. A. Hayek, *Law, Legislation and Liberty*, Vol. 1, *Rules and Order* (London, Routledge and Kegan Paul, 1982), p. 134; for a similar instrumental conception, see J. Rawls, *Political Liberalism* (New York, Columbia University Press, 1993), pp. 227–30.

[22] Humboldt, *The Limits of State Action*, p. 137.

power can be exercised politically. This is a purely analytical distinction, for these three functions cannot easily be distinguished, so that it is often difficult to associate them with separate parts of a constitution.

Turning to the content of the distinction, constituting a polity is the act of giving origin to a political entity and of sanctioning its nature and primary ends (if only the minimal one of social co-operation in order to ensure individual self-preservation). This function can be seen as the result of the voluntary and possibly rational act of either separate individuals, 'natural' communities, or corporate persons. However, it can also be identified as the organic and natural result of traditional ways of doing things. In Bolingbroke's remark that the proper meaning of a constitution is the 'assemblage of laws, institutions and customs ... according to which the community hath agreed to be governed',[23] the emphasis is not on the fact that the people may have *originally* agreed on a 'general system' of laws, institutions and customs, but that these have progressively come to represent that 'general system' which people value as their own way of administering public affairs. The constitutive function, according to which the constitution defines a people and its way of life, can therefore result either from an original and voluntary agreement or from the process of identification with a given group, its customs and traditions.

The second main purpose of a constitution is that it gives *form* to the institutions and procedures of governance (in its broadest sense, comprising the legislative, administrative and judicial functions) of a political community. Here the 'assemblage of laws, institutions and customs' defining a social union is not seen as the provider of a common identity, but as the functional division of competences and powers within the community according to certain objectives and values. The classical way of posing the problem of the *structure* of the political community is that of establishing the general division between the rulers and the ruled. This implies a number of things such as the criteria according to which the division is to be established and maintained, the definition of the areas where collective decision making is either required or encouraged, the values to which rulers can appeal (substantive legitimacy) and the procedures that need to be followed (formal legitimacy) in order that decisions taken by the ruler have a fair chance of being effected. All this gives a certain order and regularity to the exercise of power, so that by establishing a 'structured polity' constitutions really become, in the words of Isocrates, the 'soul of the city',[24] as well as representing, as Montesquieu suggested, the fundamentals upon which the general spirit of the laws largely depends.[25]

The third main purpose of the constitution is to limit the exercise of power. Modern liberal constitutionalism insists that the clear definition of negative limits to the sphere of, and capacity for, government action and the normative restriction of political sovereignty are indeed the primary functions of constitutions. But this does not seem to follow from any particular property of the constitution in general. The more immediate way in which constitutions limit power follows rather from what has already been said with regard to its two other main purposes. On the one hand, power is personally, territorially

---

[23] *The Works of Lord Bolingbroke* (London, Frank Cass, reprint, 1967), p. 88; cf. also C. H. MacIlwain, *Constitutionalism: Ancient and Modern* (Ithaca, NY, Cornell University Press, 1958), p. 3.

[24] Quoted in Dogliani, *Introduzione al diritto costituzionale*, p. 37.

[25] Montesquieu (R. Derathé, ed.), *De l'Esprit des Lois* (Paris, Garnier, 1973), vol. I, book I, ch. 3, p. 13.

and, in principle, also temporarily limited by the creation (or the self-recognition based on customs and tradition) of a polity;[26] on the other, certain forms of power are *de facto* excluded by simply naming the principles, institutions and procedures which are properly political. The *constitutive* limitations of politics work in two ways. Firstly, they guarantee that there are areas of activity and social relationships not directly touched by politics itself, in so far as they fall outside either its scope or its reach. The extent of these protected areas does not here depend on an assessment of their intrinsic worth but on the role that the 'political' is given in determining the good or the just life, and, in more practical terms, on the means put at the political rulers' disposal. Secondly, the definition of the 'political' guarantees that political power is limited in so far as its normal workings are made regular and predictable. These two kinds of *de facto* limits to politics are closely related – though not identical in their justification – to the *negative* and normatively self-imposed limitations that liberal constitutionalism predicates. When both constitutive and negative limits are considered together, they represent the attempt to de-personalize political power, something which is usually done either by appealing to a superior order regulating the very excercise of power, or by devising social and political mechanisms through which no party or faction is guaranteed supremacy on all issues at all times.

Political Power: Limited, not Absolute

The variety of meanings which have emerged from the analytical discussion of the idea of the constitution reflects both a difference in interpretation as to the place of the constitution in relation to politics, and a diversity of views on whether the constitution has intrinsic or purely instrumental value. The analysis of its functions has also shown that behind the agreement on what a constitution does in general, there lie important differences in how it is seen to limit politics in particular. Indeed, constitutionalism's simple objective of restraining political power can be achieved in more than one way, implying different ideas of the constitution and different conceptions of the very nature of political power. Historically, the aspiration to make power impersonal has been the philosophical nub of disputes about constitutionalism. It is in this sense that the classical *topoi* of the relationship between the 'government of laws' and the 'government of men'[27] – a conundrum which both ancients and moderns have repeatedly strived to solve – captures the essence of discussions about constitutionalism. In view of the inner complexity and influence of Aristotle's own treatment of the subject, this seems a good point from which to start our own discussion of constitutionalism.

Government of Men, Government of Laws

There is a fundamental ambivalence in the classical formulation of this distinction, since it is often unclear whether it is intended as part of a normative

---

[26] Cf. Kelsen, *Introduction to the Problems of Legal Theory*, p. 100; and N. Bobbio, *Stato, Governo, Società* (Torino, Einaudi, 1985), p. 86.

[27] Since much of the discussion in this section is about the history of constitutionalism, I have kept to the traditional, gendered, terminology.

discussion on good government, or as an empirical criterion to distinguish between different forms of government. The same equivocation applies to *politeia* (the Greek concept that comes nearest to 'constitution'), which is often taken to mean the 'state as it actually is',[28] but also refers to political regimes with certain axiological characteristics. Indeed, as will be shown presently, the link between the two issues – the nature of *politeia* and that of the 'government of laws' – is more than superficial.

Before Plato and Aristotle, *politeia* implied a regime with laws, since these were considered to be an integral part of political orders founded upon both the equality of (*isonomia*), and the sharing of power between, citizens (*polites*). Democracy and oligarchy were such regimes, whereas monarchy, with its sole ruler, was rarely described as *politeia*, since it was 'a regime without laws'.[29]

Aristotle's own conception of *politeia* also rested upon equality. Political authority obtained only in associations formed by free and equal men, capable of ruling and being ruled.[30] A constitution was meant to establish that political order that best reflected the balance of equality (more properly 'proportional equality') in a community.[31] Political equality, as sanctioned by the constitution, was a form of justice, because, like any other form of justice, its virtue lay in binding people together.[32] *Politeia* was therefore a community where certain fundamental principles of political justice applied, this being nothing other than the congruence between the particular form of 'proportional equality' sanctioned by the constitution and that actually existent in the *polis*.

However, according to Aristotle, and contrary to previous authors, the normative element of the constitution was not embodied in an external law – whether divine, natural, customary, or positive – but in its correspondence with the nature and the very end of life in a *polis*. This teleological and organic conception of politics locks political equality and the constitution into a vicious circle; for, on the one hand, the constitution is meant to reflect the balance of equality between the citizens, while, on the other, the extent of citizenship depends on the constitution itself. Certain forms of monarchical government prove this circularity. Aristotle himself was inclined to count them as political on the basis of the principle of proportional equality, even though by this same principle monarchical rulers seem entitled to act despotically – as masters within the household – and not as political rulers.[33] In the first of the senses analysed here, therefore, the relationship that Aristotle established between the law (*nomos*) and the constitution (*politeia*) is equivocal, because the internal normativity of the idea of the *polis* risks dissolving the concept of political rule.

[28] McIlwain, *Constitutionalism: Ancient and Modern*, p. 26.
[29] J. Bordes, *Politeia dans la pensée grecque jusq'à Aristote* (Paris, Belles Lettres, 1982), p. 361. Even oligarchies, particularly those where power (*arché*) was not exercised according to ancient laws and customs, could be classified as tyrannical and therefore excluded from the general class of political regimes. Indeed, it was held that in tyrannical regimes at large 'there are no *politai*, but a tyrant and *idiotaï*' p. 318; cf. also Dogliani, *Introduzione al diritto costituzionale*, pp. 47–51.
[30] Aristotle (H. Rackham, trans.), *Politics* (London, Heinemann, 1967), 1252a, 1255b, 1277b.
[31] The intimate connection between equality and political constitution was proved *a contrario* by constitutional change (*metabole*), since this originated as an attempt (not always justified) to restore proportional equality within the political community (Aristotle, *Politics*, 1301b) either through a new constitutional form reflecting a different conception of equality or through a change in relative positions within the same constitutional form.
[32] Cf. Aristotle (G. C. Armstrong, trans.), *Magna Moralia* (London, Heinemann, 1947), 1194b.
[33] Aristotle, *Politics*, 1285b, but cf. also 1287a.

But there is another more specific sense in which the relationship between the laws (*nomoi*) and the constitution appears in Aristotle. As we have seen, for him the normativity of *politeia* was something clearly distinct from being a 'regime with laws'.[34] But can there be a constitutional regime without laws? Or, ought a constitutional regime also to be a 'government of laws'? Aristotle's solutions to these questions were complex. As with political rule, he maintained that legislation is also based on a certain equality between the citizens.[35] Aristotle made this point *a contrario*. Men of exceptional virtue and knowledge are like 'gods amongst men', who require no laws because they are a law unto themselves.[36] This makes equality a pre-condition for legislation as well as for the constitution (*politeia*). Even though *politeia* and a 'regime with laws' may not be identical, there is however a *prima facie* case for assuming that they are coincidental in conditions of broadly defined equality.

Having established the kind of relationship that holds between the laws and political rule, the nature of the more particular relationship which exists between rulers, as ordained by the constitution,[37] and laws can be examined. On this point, Aristotle was indebted to Plato. Under ideal conditions men should predominate over laws, which are indiscriminate over the motives and circumstances of human actions,[38] 'like an obstinate and ignorant tyrant'.[39] In normal circumstances, instead, the partial wisdom of written and customary laws is preferable,[40] since these are 'copies' of the 'truths' of the science of good ruling, which rulers themselves may lack.[41] To these arguments Aristotle added two other considerations. Laws are 'intelligence without passion', and so come close to the ideal of power exercised with reason and impartiality. Secondly, it is an oversimplification to think that in comparison to human governance laws are over-rigid, because both forms of rule need to be guided by some general principle. These arguments seem to offer respectively a negative reason, in support of the laws as checks upon the passionate element of human nature,[42] and a positive one, in stressing that both laws and political decisions must appeal to rationality and general rules.

The positive argument was further developed, and partly qualified, by Aristotle, when he suggested that those who support the 'government of laws' maintain neither that laws are infallible nor that they are completely impersonal; but that the real question they wish to address is one of sovereignty: who should decide (the one or the many) when the laws provide inadequate guidance for action.[43] Moreover, who is to establish the rightness of the laws themselves? For, Aristotle says, 'suppose ... that law is sovereign, but law of an oligarchic or democratic nature, what difference will it make as

[34] Aristotle recommends that laws should be made in the spirit of the constitution, *Politics*, 1289a.
[35] Cf. Aristotle, *Politics*, 1287a, where law (*nomos*) is also said to be order (*taxis*).
[36] Aristotle, *Politics*, 1284a.
[37] Aristotle, *Politics*, 1289a.
[38] Plato (J. Anna and R. Waterfield, eds), *Statesman* (Cambridge, Cambridge University Press, 1995), 294b; cf. also MacIlwain, *Constitutionalism*, ch. 2.
[39] Plato, *Statesman*, 294c; cf. aso Aristotle, *Politics*, 1286a.
[40] Plato, *Statesman*, 300e–301c.
[41] Plato, *Statesman*, 300c; and Aristotle, *Politics*, 1287a; cf. also MacIlwain, *Constitutionalism*, pp. 30–4.
[42] Cf. Aristotle, *Politics*, 1281 for a more pessimistic view.
[43] Aristotle, *Politics*, 1287b, and 1282b.

regards the difficulties that have been raised?'.[44] The difficulties to which Aristotle here refers are those concerning who is entitled to rule. Aristotle's qualified position was that, in general, the many have collectively more virtue, wisdom, and judgement than either the few or the single ruler. The 'government of laws' is consequently closely related to a constitution that confers political authority on the many, not in the sense that democracies constitute the 'governments of laws', but in the more subtle sense that those constitutions with a large citizenship are the most successful in both establishing rightful laws and supplementing them when necessary. This makes them the paradigm for regimes where power is exercised *politically*, that is according to both the constitution and the laws.

Although partially ambiguous, Aristotle's attempt to reconcile authoritative with rightful government remained a point of reference for successive discussions of the relationship between rulers and the laws. Laws should normally direct the actions of rulers, but ultimately depend on human judgement. Political justice, as the establishment of the 'right' constitution, is the fundamental pre-condition for such a reconciliation. Political power is not absolute both because, in its normal administration, it is limited by the laws and because it is *political* in nature – a power, that is, exercised on the basis of the principle of (relative) equality. These two senses of limits to political power – which in the previous section were referred to as the *negative* and the *constitutive* – were seized upon by subsequent authors and arguably form the two main paradigms, 'liberal' and 'republican', through which constitutionalism emerged as a modern political doctrine.

The Republican Constitution

The republican tradition, from Machiavelli to the late eighteenth century, took the Aristotelian lesson at its most sceptical, questioning the feasibility of having laws to govern men.[45] Rousseau, for one, thought that it 'is impossible ... to make laws that the passions of men will not corrupt'. Laws can compel and punish, but to be effective they need to 'reach men's hearts'. For Rousseau, as for Aristotle, good government is the combination of good laws with the good disposition of the body politic. Statesmanship consists in making such a combination possible by providing both 'a good and sound constitution ... under which the law holds sway over the heart of the citizens', and 'institutions that ... develop habits that abide and attachments that nothing can dissolve'.[46]

Kant stated the same problem in reverse. Sociability as a condition of human life makes 'man ... an animal who needs a master'. In such a condition, human beings are divided between their rational conviction that 'a law to impose limits on the liberty of all' is necessary, and their self-seeking nature, which makes them break that very universal law. What is needed is a superior authority, which ought 'to be just *in itself* and yet also a *man*. This is the most difficult of all

---

[44] Aristotle, *Politics*, 1281a.

[45] 'Putting laws over – Rousseau wrote – is a problem in politics that I like to compare to that of squaring the circle in geometry. Solve that problem correctly, and the government based upon your solution will be a good government, proof against corruption. But until you solve it, rest assured of this: you may think you have made the laws govern; but men will do the governing.' J. J. Rousseau (W. Kendall, trans.), *The Government of Poland* (Indianapolis, Hackett, 1985), p. 3.

[46] Rousseau, *The Government of Poland*, p. 4.

tasks, and a perfect solution is impossible. Nothing straight can be constructed from such warped wood as that from which man is made of.' The only thing that human beings can hope for is to establish a 'civil constitution' as an *imperfect* solution to the rational fool paradox.[47]

Standing at the end of the early modern republican tradition, both Rousseau and Kant saw the constitution as the centre-piece for the difficult accommodation of liberty and authority, of the 'government of laws' and the 'government of men'. The republican paradigm of constitutionalism offered three important insights into how this might be achieved: the special place of legislators; the mediating role of 'good orders'; and, finally, the principle underlying the separation of powers.[48]

As we have seen, Aristotle considered the impersonal nature of the 'government of laws' both an ideal advantage and a practical stumbling block, since sovereignty must surely rest with the rulers. The republican paradigm offers a way out from this dilemma by distinguishing rulers from legislators, and by attributing special qualities and an exceptional historical position to the latter. At first this would appear no solution at all, for the personal element of political power is, if anything, enhanced by the artificial image of a legislator. But ancient legislation was an amalgam of customs, laws, and constitutional order, so that, behind the figure of the legislator there lies a more naturalistic and organic interpretation of the origins of the state. Indeed, the advantages implicit in such an interpretation were not lost on those like Machiavelli, and before him Polybius, who interpreted the constitutional evolution of the Roman Republic as the product of both accident and prudence, and so considered its progress neither as entirely natural nor as the sole result of human foresight.[49]

But in the history of commonwealths there are also occasions when corruption calls for a new beginning. These are times, as Harrington commenting on Machiavelli remarked, when 'extraordinary' means are required since the ordinary ones have failed. In such instances, wise legislators should be prepared to take the sovereign power in their hands – an action, Harrington says, that has the full approval of 'any man that is master of reason', for the end is 'no other than the constitution of a well-ordered commonwealth'.[50]

Depending on the circumstances, the figure of the legislator may assume either the impersonal characteristics of ancient legislation and of the natural evolution of the constitution, or the very personal character of a founder and reformer. This duality seems to bring about a mixed interpretation of sovereignty similar to the one suggested by Aristotle. But with the diffusion of contractualist conceptions of politics, the republican figure of the legislator took on a new democratic and unitarian dimension. The constitution became the immediate result of the social contract,[51] and was placed in the hands of the

---

[47] Rousseau, *The Government of Poland*, pp. 45–6.

[48] For a full and more historically minded discussion of the importance of the idea of the separation of powers, cf. R. Bellamy. 'The political form of the constitution: the separation of powers, rights and representative democracy', in this collection.

[49] N. Machiavelli, *Discorsi sopra la prima deca di Tito Livio* (Milano, Rizzoli, 1984), book I, chs 2–9, pp. 64–88. Cf. also Bellamy, 'The political form of the constitution', this volume.

[50] J. Harrington (J. G. A. Pocock, ed.), *The Commonwealth of Oceana* (Cambridge, Cambridge University Press, 1992), p. 67.

[51] I. Kant (H. Reiss, ed.), *Political Writings* (Cambridge, Cambridge University Press, 1991), p. 73.

sovereign people.[52] But the people as a legislator (constituent power) was now distinguished from the people as the legislative power (constituted power). To the one, and to its 'extraordinary' representatives, belongs the extraordinary power to fix and reform the constitution; to the other, and to its 'ordinary' representatives, belongs rather the power of ordinary legislation.[53] This was also Paine's distinction between the nation in its *original* character and the nation in its *organized* character,[54] from which he clearly derived the other distinction between constitution and government and their respective origins and powers.[55] This elaboration of the distinction between rulers and legislators within the context of the modern democratic constitution makes for a kind of sovereignty that is personal and absolute in principle, but limited and subject to the rule of law in its practical and ordinary application.

The second element of the republican constitution, its emphasis upon 'good orders', suggests a different strategy for dealing with the alternative between the government of men and that of laws. For Machiavelli 'orders' were that complex of institutions regulating the distribution of power, of political rights and obligations within a commonwealth. In so far as they are the means through which laws are made and magistrates selected, 'orders' are meant to outlast both particular laws and governments.[56] In *Oceana*, Harrington warned against the advice both of the 'lawyers ... to fit your government unto their laws',[57] and of the 'demagogues': 'give us good men and they will make us good laws'.[58] They were both mistaken because they reversed the correct relationship between good 'orders', on the one hand, and good laws and good rulers, on the other, by making the latter the causes, and not the effects, of the former.

Montesquieu's own distinction between the 'nature' and the 'principles' of government partly echoed this conception.[59] He made the spirit of the laws depend on the 'fundamental laws', which are those from which the government derives its particular 'nature'. According to Montesquieu, the only form of government that lacks fundamental laws is despotism, because this has neither a structure of governance nor a depositary (*depot*) of the laws – all decisions being taken by either the despot himself or his *vizir*.[60] Indeed, despotism is a government which has no political nature and where there are no laws. By contrast, both republican and monarchical governments are regimes regulated by the distribution of political authority and by the action of the laws.

The republican emphasis on 'good orders' suggests a way of by-passing the stark alternative between the rule of men and the rule of laws. Fixing the laws and choosing the rulers are not the most fundamental operations of a political

[52] Rousseau, *The Government of Poland*, p. 57.

[53] Cf. E.-J. Sieyès, *Qu'est-ce que le tiers état?* (Genève, Droz, 1970), ch. 5.

[54] Paine, *Political Writings*, p. 82.

[55] Paine, *Political Writings*, pp. 174–80. One important element of the republican conception of the constitution is therefore the role that people play as both the *consituent* and the *controlling* power. The distinction between constituent and constituted power is at the basis of what B. Ackerman calls 'dualist democracy', although he wrongly assumes that this is peculiarly American, cf. *We The People. Foundations* (Cambridge, MA, Belknap, 1991), ch. 1.

[56] Machiavelli, *Discorsi*, book I, ch. 18, pp. 109–10.

[57] Harrington, *Oceana*, p. 41.

[58] Harrington, *Oceana*, p. 64.

[59] Montesquieu, *De l'Esprit*, vol. I, books II–III, pp. 14–35.

[60] Montesquieu, *De l'Esprit*, vol. I, book II, ch. 5, pp. 24–5.

society, since they both depend on the institutional machinery that the constitution itself is meant to put in place.

The third core feature of the republican constitution, the principle of the separation of powers, addresses the question of the nature of political sovereignty more directly. This principle is not exclusively republican, but historically it was originally meant to oppose monarchical theories of absolute power in the seventeenth and eighteenth century. The principle was clearly formulated in Harrington's rejection of Hobbes's ideas of liberty and sovereignty. According to Harrington, there are two forms of government; one, *de jure*, founded upon 'common right or interest' and the 'empire of laws'; the other, *de facto*, supported by the power of the sword.[61] Harrington criticized the *de facto* theory because he felt it to be mistaken on both the principles of power and authority. He dismissed the dependence of power on the sword as trivial, since military power is not self-standing: 'an army is a beast that hath a great belly and must be fed; wherefore this will come unto ... the balance of property, without which the public sword is but a name or mere spitfrog'.[62] He rejected the idea that authority, as an imposition on the liberty of the subjects, is everywhere the same, on two other grounds. Even taking reason to be nothing more than the simple rationalization of interest, there must be different degrees of reason, as there are of interest. The interest of mankind, being universal, must give rise to a superior reason, agreeable to all. Now, Harrington says, it is a simple matter of computation that the interest of popular government 'come[s] the nearest unto the interest of mankind', so it must also be true that authority in popular governments must be according to 'right reason'.[63] However, Harrington admitted that this argument only demonstrates the hypothetical superiority of popular regimes. In order for these truly to embody right reason, he proposes the application of the kind of perfect procedural justice that applies to the distribution of things, where one divides and the other chooses.[64] In political society, power should be divided in such a way that one body should debate and counsel and another make decisions, as in republican Rome, where laws were made '*auctoritate patrum et jussu populi*, by the authority of the fathers and the power of the people'.[65] Harrington's main republican principle of authority was therefore that no man should be legislator and judge in his own affairs.[66] In so far as this kind of authority is the closest to right reason, it will secure liberty and the government of laws.[67]

At the end of the eighteenth century, Kant made a similar case when he maintained that obedience to a civil constitution must accommodate the 'spirit of freedom', because 'each individual requires to be convinced by reason that

---

[61] Harrington, *Oceana*, p. 8.

[62] Harrington, *Oceana*, p. 13.

[63] Harrington, *Oceana*, pp. 21–2.

[64] Harrington, *Oceana*, p. 22.

[65] Harrington, *Oceana*, p. 24.

[66] According to Harrington, the orders of commonwealths should be organized in such a way that these 'be governments of the senate proposing, the people resolving, and the magistracy executing', *Oceana*, p. 32.

[67] 'If the liberty of a man consist in the empire of his reason, the absence whereof would betray him unto the bondage of his passions; then the liberty of a commonwealth consisteth in the empire of her laws, the absence whereof would betray her unto the lusts of tyrants,' Harrington, *Oceana*, pp. 19–20.

the coercion which prevails is lawful'.[68] He also agreed that this was only feasible in 'republican' states; but this consensus was qualified by his wish to distinguish between republics and popular governments, which, he maintained, belonged to two separate kinds of classification, one concerned with the forms of the state (either republican or despotic) and the other with the forms of government (the more traditional tripartition). Republican constitutions guaranteed freedom (qua men); dependence upon a common law (qua subjects); and legal equality (qua citizens).[69] The political embodiment of these principles was for Kant the separation of the executive from the legislative power, which he also described as the 'representative' principle: 'because one and the same person cannot at the same time be both the legislator and the executor of his own will'.[70] As with Harrington, Kant's principle of the separation of powers points to a conception of political power as something distinct from mere force, and that is ultimately based on appeals to fairness and rational arguments, both of which are essentials in societies where citizens are considered equals and worthy of equal consideration.

The Limited Constitution

The republican paradigm of constitutionalism outlined here rests on a conception of political power as intrinsically limited. This limitation is achieved by the articulation of sovereignty as constituent and constituted power, by its concrete embodiment in institutional mechanisms, and by a normative conception of political power itself. On the latter issue, however, there are important points of convergence with the liberal paradigm of constitutionalism. Kant's understanding of the link between the principle of the separation of powers and the (republican) principle of representation, for instance, graphically shows this convergence of approaches. From his own assumption that political representation is the best way of giving substance to the principle of the separation of powers, Kant concluded that 'of the forms of sovereignty, *democracy*, in the truest sense of the word, is necessarily a *despotism*'.[71] Contrariwise, the fewer the rulers, the greater the degree of representation in a society; so that, paradoxically, Kant justified the superiority of monarchical forms of government by appealing to 'republican' arguments. This shift of meaning from republicanism as a form of government to republicanism as a form of state mirrors the earlier development of the idea of monarchical sovereignty generally associated with Montesquieu, who described monarchy as that kind of regime where there are 'intermediate' bodies.[72]

For Montesquieu, contemporary forms of monarchical regimes represented the paradigm of moderate government, whose main features are the presence of laws (ensuring that people can actually do what the laws themselves allow them to),[73] and the separation of powers as a check upon the rulers' natural

[68] Kant, *Political Writings*, p. 85.
[69] Kant, *Political Writings*, pp. 99–100.
[70] Kant, *Political Writings*, p. 101.
[71] Kant, *Political Writings*, p. 101.
[72] Montesquieu, *De l'Esprit*, vol. I, books III and V. On the 'spatial' construction of representation in the *ancien régime*, cf. P. Violante, *Lo spazio della rappresentanza. Francia 1788–1789* (Palermo-Sao Paulo, Ila Palma, 1981), chs 1–2.
[73] Montesquieu, *De l'Esprit*, vol. I, book XI, ch. 3, p. 167.

temptation to abuse their own position (this guarantees what Montesquieu called constitutional liberty).[74] The moderation of monarchical regimes consists, therefore, in providing security for its subjects by posing external constraints on political power. Although these restraining functions, particularly those associated with intermediate bodies, are, so to speak, internal to the very nature of the monarchical regime, in other passages of *De l'Esprit des Lois*[75] Montesquieu suggested that limitations can be imposed on any constitution that is not despotic, so having the effect of transforming it into a moderate form of government by tempering its guiding principles.

The idea of a *limited* constitution was also central to Tocqueville's analysis of democracy in America. This needs to be distinguished from mixed forms of government, which Tocqueville himself considered to be chimerical.[76] In each particular government only one principle prevails. Limitation of power is more properly the effect of particular circumstances and manners, rather than the product of laws and institutional mechanisms internal to the constitution. This view accords with Tocqueville's own conception of the constitution of a state (*état sociale*) as the complex amalgam of orders, laws and customs.[77] The principle underlying the social constitution of America was that of equality and its prevalence throughout the institutions made America a democratic society.[78] According to Tocqueville, the only check on the dominance of the popular principle was the anti-democratic character of the American jurists (*legistes*), whose formation and tastes inclined them towards aristocratic principles and ideas,[79] and who, by their power of judicial review, restrained the omnipotence of the legislature and of the people at large, typical of democratic systems. The power of the jurists was not absolute, and did not change the central principle of American government, because the constitution itself was open to change and this power remained with the people. But the correction of democracy was important and, as Tocqueville suggested, the result not just of the institutional balance between powers, but of the social characteristics of the jurists as a countervailing power. That for Tocqueville this was so is also evident from his conviction that a similar power in the hands of the legal profession in Europe would produce very different results, in view of the close link between this group and the administrative machine of the state. In Europe, jurists did not represent an effective check, because they would, if anything, reinforce the power of the state over the individual.[80]

The paradigm of the limited constitution as identified here developed autonomously from the republican tradition. Its roots were in late medieval discussions of the relationship between governance and jurisdiction; and its political vocabulary partly derived from civil jurisprudence and early modern theories of natural law and natural rights. In general, it distinguished itself from the republican paradigm by its conception of the separation of powers and the administration of law as instrumental to the protection of individual rights, and by its emphasis on impersonal conceptions of political sovereignty. Its main

[74] Montesquieu, *De l'Esprit*, vol. I, book XI, pp. 165–201.
[75] Cf. Montesquieu, *De l'Esprit*, vol. I, book VIII, ch. 3, p. 125.
[76] A. de Tocqueville, *De la démocratie en Amérique* (Paris, Gallimard, 1986), vol. I, p. 377.
[77] Tocqueville, *De la démocratie*, vol. I, p. 96.
[78] Tocqueville, *De la démocratie*, pp. 104–6 and 265.
[79] Tocqueville, *De la démocratie*, p. 394.
[80] Rebuffa, *Costituzioni e costituzionalismi*, ch. 1, para. 4.

characteristics were the importance given to fundamental laws in the constitution of a state; the principles of the rule of law and the jurisdictional state; and the great emphasis placed on the idea of pre-political individual rights.

The appeal to fundamental laws over and above the political community was not simply meant as the inner regulation of political sovereignty, but as the fixing of a more general sovereignty of the laws (or of the constitution as a superior law), having the specific object of subjugating political will to a superior reason.[81] According to MacIlwain's historical reconstruction, the legalistic bias of this conception found its origins in Ancient Rome, in so far as Roman jurisprudence greatly contributed to the rationalization of the legal system and its autonomy from politics.[82] This Roman inheritance was of great importance for the challenge mounted in the middle ages to the idea of the prince as '*legibus solutus*'. The power of the ruler was indeed considered as absolute when referring to matters of government (*gubernaculum*), but was subject to the law and to the 'due process of law' in jurisdictional matters (*jurisditio*).[83] According to this interpretation, the real limitation of power does not follow from the establishment of mixed or balanced forms of government, but from the conferment of rights and privileges against the sovereign and in the separate administration of justice, so that magistrates may appeal to either customary laws or previous concessions and require the sovereign himself to respect the law. This appeal to an ancient constitution and immemorial laws is typical of constitutionalism before Montesquieu; but, with the encroachment upon ancient rights and privileges by the increasingly powerful sovereign, the constitutional limitations were applied to the very core of government in its administrative functions.[84] This is the beginning of modern constitutionalism of the liberal kind, which also originates from another shift in the conception of fundamental laws. These were no longer seen as the product of ancient tradition and customs, or justified on the basis of their derivation from divine law, but presented as the expression of a superior law both natural, rational and universal in character. The development of a modern natural law tradition contributed to such a shift, and Tocqueville, for one, made use of this conception of superior law as against democratic majoritarianism by suggesting that there is indeed a law of justice that applies to society in general, where sovereignty belongs to mankind as a whole. The laws and rights upheld in this society should naturally trump those which the majority in a particular political society wishes to enforce.[85] Liberal constitutionalism, therefore, embraces the sovereignty of the laws (or of the constitution as a superior law) over men and their machinery of government.

The other way in which liberal constitutionalism reinforced the idea of the sovereignty of the laws was by considering law and legal relationships as the core of the process of social integration. The separation of public and private law and the adoption of the latter as both the model for and the scope of the former were the two central elements of this strategy. The extreme

[81] Cf. MacIlwain, *Constitutionalism*, ch. 1.
[82] Cf. MacIlwain, *Constitutionalism*, ch. 4; and Dogliani, *Introduzione al diritto costituzionale*, ch. 3.
[83] MacIlwain, *Constitutionalism*, ch. 4.
[84] MacIlwain, *Constitutionalism*, ch. 5.
[85] Tocqueville, *De la démocratie*, vol. I, p. 375–6.

formalization of the idea of the rule of law, the autonomy of civil society and the naturalization of its principles (rights to property and freedom of contract), the dual image of the *Rechtsstaat* as, on the one hand, the representation of the whole legal system, and, on the other, as the personification of the state and its subjection to private law, are all parts of the same strategy of substituting the rule of law for political sovereignty.[86] It is in this sense that the real constitution of a society is considered to be neither the complex of its institutions nor the document establishing the form of the state and the structure of governance, but the legal system itself, whose central substantive concerns are the defence of traditional civil rights.

This takes us to the third feature of the limited constitution, the priority given to negative liberty. Both Humboldt and Constant, for instance, considered the freedom of the moderns to be rooted in individual pursuits unhampered – as far as possible – by state intervention. Humboldt remarked that individual security is tantamount to 'legal freedom', and that the monarchical state, where such a liberty seems best preserved, is – contrary to what happens in republics – only a means for the enforcement and protection of this form of liberty.[87] Humboldt also maintained that not all methods which are functional to the preservation of negative liberty seem to be congruent with it. Strengthening the power of the government offers some security against unwarranted oppression by others, but it also presents a threat to the liberty of individuals.[88] The cultivation of the spirit of the constitution is something better adapted to republics. In other societies, it risks weakening individualism, which Humboldt considered as the true source of modern progress.[89] It is therefore preferable for the constitution to be neutral on the character of the citizens. At most, it should contribute to inculcate in them the deepest regard for both the rights of others and the love for one's own liberty, whilst favouring the increase in their private interests. It is through these means that, according to von Humboldt, the limited constitution can effectively be established, so that 'man' is not sacrificed to the 'citizen', and his free development presupposed to any attachment to the political community and its constitution.[90]

Conclusion: the Modern Constitutional State and its Future

Republican and liberal constitutionalism represent two different conceptions of the constitution, and, more generally, of the nature of politics. Historically, the two paradigms were combined in ways which I have hinted at, but which I cannot explore here fully. Indeed, the modern constitutional state emerged at the end of the eighteenth century from the combined pursuit of both strategies in conditions dominated by a number of momentous transformations. Since there is no space here to pursue this line of argument, a brief outline may do.

[86] Cf. F. Neumann, *The Rule of Law. Political Theory and the Legal System in Modern Society* (Leamington Spa, Berg, 1986); E.-W. Böckenförde, *State, Society and Liberty. Studies in Political Theory and Constitutional Law* (New York and Oxford, Berg, 1991), chs 3–5; and M. Fioravanti, 'Lo Stato di diritto come forma di Stato. Notazioni preliminari sulla tradizione europeo-continentale' in R. Gherardi and G. Gozzi (eds), *Saperi della borghesia e storia dei concetti tra Otto e Novecento* (Bologna, Il Mulino, 1995).
[87] Humboldt, *The Limits of State Action*, pp. 49–50 and 84.
[88] Humboldt, *The Limits of State Action*, p. 135.
[89] Humboldt, *The Limits of State Action*, p. 48.
[90] Humboldt, *The Limits of State Action*, pp. 49 and 136.

At a socio-political level, the growing power of the nation state and its expanding capacity to determine and control the life of its subjects created the need for extra protection from the power of government and administration. This became even more imperative as a consequence of the autonomous development of a civil society and the democratization of social relationships in a 'disenchanted' world.[91] In these conditions, the modern constitution – in the form of a 'positive' and 'demoralized' superior law[92] – was conceived as the central guarantee offered by the constitutional state so as to make authority consistent with the 'spirit of freedom'. However, as mentioned at the beginning of this essay, since the nineteenth century the development of the constitutional state has increasingly been represented from a liberal perspective, so that the dominant view of constitutionalism sees this in mainly legal and rights-based terms.[93] But a more accurate representation of this historical development of the constitutional state may consider it as the institutional translation of three different guarantees. The core principles of a constitution, the political form of the state, and the rights of the individual – sometimes, but not always, listed in a separate bill of rights – function as a *principled guarantee*, establishing the rightful and legitimate objectives of the political community. The general organization and division of powers represent the *organizational guarantee*, so that the exercise of power is effective and corresponds to the proper ends of the political association. The third element of the modern constitutional state in democratic societies consists in the *representational guarantee*, by which citizens are guaranteed equal participation in the political body and a fair chance to pursue their own life and happiness.

These three guarantees represent the core of the modern constitutional state. But throughout this century they have been constantly eroded by new social and political developments, so that the kind of institutions and procedures which were appropriate to the regulation and limitation of political power in the past seem now inadequate. Although constitutional law and modern constitutions have partly reflected this change of circumstances, political theories of the constitution are still anchored to eighteenth- and nineteenth-century models. The question of the new 'generations' of rights and how to integrate them within a constitution;[94] the erosion of sovereignty and accountability posed by the existence of powerful autonomous powers within and without the state;[95] the reconfiguration of representation in modern politics dominated by mass

---

[91] Cf. J. Habermas, *The Structural Transformation of the Public Sphere: an Inquiry into a Category of Bourgeois Society* (Cambridge, MA, MIT, 1989); P. Rosanvallon, *Le sacre du citoyen. Histoire du suffrage universel en France* (Paris, Gallimard, 1992).

[92] Cf. Preuß, 'The political meaning of constitutionalism'; U. Preuß, *Constitutional Revolution. The Link between Constitutionalism and Progress* (New Jersey, Humanities, 1995).

[93] Cf. Hayek, *Rules and Order*, pp. 1–7.

[94] Häberle, *Die Wesensgehaltgarantie*; Häberle, 'I diritti fondamentali nelle società pluraliste'; E.-W. Böckenförde, *Staat, Verfassung, Demokratie. Studien zur Verfassungstheories und zum Verfassungrecht* (Frankfurt am Main, Suhrkamp, 1991); Böckenförde, *State, Society and Liberty*, chs 8 and 9; D. Grimm, *Die Zukunft der Verfassung* (Frankfurt am Main, Suhrkamp, 1991); R. Dworkin, *Taking Rights Seriously* (London, Duckworth, 1978); G. Peces Barba, *Los Valores Superiores* (Madrid, Tecnos, 1984); N. Bobbio, *L'età dei diritti* (Torino, Einaudi, 1990); L. Ferrajoli, *Diritto e ragione. Teoria del garantismo penale* (Roma-Bari, Laterza, 2nd ed., 1990), chs 13–14; Zagrebelsky, *Il diritto mite*, ch. 6.

[95] Böckenförde, *State, Society and Liberty*, chs 7 and 10.

parties and their bureaucracies, are only some of the challenges.[96] More generally, the very complexity of modern society poses a challenge to the unitary and sovereign nature both of the constitutional state in a given national territory and of the constitution as an overarching document.[97] These are new issues for which new political thinking is urgently required. To rediscover the ideological complexity of constitutionalism, particularly in its republican variant, and the philosophical polymorphism of the idea of the constitution is perhaps a small contribution towards that task.

---

[96] Cf. O. Kirchheimer, *Politics, Law and Social Change* (New York and London, Columbia University Press, 1969), part II.

[97] Cf. G. Burdeau, 'Une survivance: la notion de constitution' in *L'Evolution du droit public, études offertes à Achille Mestre* (Paris, 1956).

The Political Form of the Constitution: the Separation of Powers, Rights and Representative Democracy

RICHARD BELLAMY[1]

According to article 16 of the French Declaration of the Rights of Man and of the Citizen of 1789, 'A society where rights are not secured or the separation of powers established has no constitution at all'.[2] Together with representative government, which to a large extent was assimilated to the second, these two principles have defined constitutionalism, providing the chief means for combining the rule of law with government by fallible and occasionally sinful men.

In recent years, however, the first has come to predominate. Rights, upheld by judicial review, are said to comprise the prime component of constitutionalism, providing a normative legal framework within which politics operates. Political mechanisms, in consequence, have been ascribed a secondary role. Whereas rights supposedly provide the substantive aspect of the constitution, defining what the ends of a given polity are, the political dimension proper has been relegated to a set of formal rules describing who makes decisions and how, that simply supply the means for achieving these goals.[3] In this way, constitutionalism has come to mean nothing more than a system of legally entrenched rights that can override, where necessary, the ordinary political process.[4]

The doctrine of the separation of powers, in contrast, belongs to a tradition which conceives the constitution as a form of government.[5] From this perspective, the protection and realization of rights and the rule of law fall within rather than outside politics, and are matters of institutional design and the social character of the polity. The organization of government serves not simply to

---

[1] I am grateful to Terrence Ball, Dario Castiglione, Stephen Elkin, Michael Moran, Timothy O'Hagan, and John Zvesper for their comments on an earlier version of this paper.

[2] Article 16 of the Declaration of the Rights of Man and the Citizen 1789, as reproduced in English translation in S. E. Finer, V. Bogdanor and B. Rudden, *Comparing Constitutions* (Oxford, Clarendon, 1995), p. 210.

[3] For this formulation of the nature of the constitution, see Luigi Ferrajoli, 'Democracy and the constitution in Italy', this volume.

[4] Ronald Dworkin, for example, recently defined constitutionalism as no more than 'a system that establishes legal rights that the dominant legislature does not have the power to override or compromise', and remarks how 'constitutionalism so understood is an increasingly popular political phenomenon'. R. Dworkin, 'Constitutionalism and democracy', *European Journal of Philosophy*, 3 (1995), p. 2.

[5] As Maurice Vile notes in his *Constitutionalism and the Separation of Powers* (Oxford, Clarendon, 1967), p. 2, 'The doctrine of the separation of powers finds its roots in the ancient world', where, to the extent the idea existed at all, the constitution of the body politic, as in the human body, referred to its nature, character or form. On this last point, see C. H. McIlwain, *Constitutionalism: Ancient and Modern* (Ithaca, NY, Cornell University Press, 1940), ch. II.

control and limit the power of those who exercise it. As sovereignty has passed from monarchs to the people, the aim increasingly becomes to channel that power so that the values and interests represented by rights are promoted and identified with as well as safeguarded. Constitutional entrenchment and judicial review play an important part in this scheme, but a subordinate rather than the dominant one of today's largely legalistic conceptions of the constitution.

Amongst a number of contemporary legal and political philosophers, the United States Constitution has become the exemplar of rights-based constitutionalism.[6] This chapter suggests an alternative story. I shall argue that both historically and substantively liberal rights-based constitutionalism must be located within a more republican conception of the constitution as a system of politics.[7] I begin by analysing the main features and problems of the doctrine of the separation of powers, and its relationship to rights and the rule of law. I then survey the historical development of the theory. I note how it was first combined with organic theories of mixed government and the balancing of powers within the body politic, and then transformed by the view of political societies as a popular construct and incorporated within representative democracy. As we shall see, the identification of a discrete judicial power was late to emerge and its role a limited and comparatively minor one. For the founding fathers of the American republic, the central mechanisms for the identification and protection of rights were political rather than legal and linked to the democratic separation of governmental powers and the related mixing of social interests.

The Separation of Powers and Rights: a Preliminary Analysis

In his classic study, Maurice Vile has identified the following three components of what he calls the 'pure' doctrine of the separation of powers.[8] First, it argues that a functional distinction exists between legislative, executive and judicial acts. Second, it proposes the division of government into three corresponding agencies, and maintains that they must be kept distinct from each other. Third, and relatedly, it insists that there should be no overlap amongst the personnel who staff these agencies.

The underlying rationale of this proposal is that individuals or groups should not be judges in their own cause. The division between the three branches aims

---

[6] Ronald Dworkin is the clearest exponent of this view, e.g. *Law's Empire* (London, Fontana, 1986) and *A Matter of Principle* (Oxford, Clarendon, 1985). Recently, however, John Rawls would appear to have embraced a similar position, see *Political Liberalism* (New York, Columbia University Press, 1993), lecture VI.

[7] B. Ackerman, *We the People: Foundations* (Cambridge, MA. Belknap, 1991) and C. R. Sunstein, *The Partial Constitution* (Cambridge, MA, Harvard University Press, 1993), are among contemporary commentators who adopt a view of the American Constitution nearer to that advocated here than Dworkin, *Law's Empire* or Rawls, *Political Liberalism*. See R. Bellamy and D. Castiglione, 'Constitutionalism and democracy: political theory and the American constitution', *British Journal of Political Science*, forthcoming, for a critical comparison of these two groups of writers. The key historical discussion is of course J. G. A. Pocock, *The Machiavellian Moment: Florentine Political Thought and the Atlantic Republican Tradition* (Princeton, NJ and London, Princeton University Press, 1975). It is worth underlining that I do not treat liberalism and republicanism as exclusive categories, my aim is merely to place the emphasis on the latter and note how it frames the former. For a discussion of the ways liberalism and republicanism have overlapped historically see J. Isaac, 'Republicanism vs. liberalism: a reconsideration', *History of Political Thought*, 9 (1988), 349–77.

[8] Vile, *Constitutionalism and the Separation of Powers*, pp. 13–8.

to ensure that those who formulate the laws are distinct from those entrusted with their interpretation, application and enforcement. In this way, those who make the laws are themselves made subject to them. They have an incentive to avoid self-interested legislation and to frame it in general terms, so as to be equally applicable to all. These rules then guide the decisions of the executive and judiciary, who because they are similarly under the law also have good reason to act in an impartial manner. Although the three agencies of government are autonomous within this scheme, therefore, the legislature has a certain logical priority over the other two. This fact proves important for later elaborations of the doctrine.

Four benefits are said to accrue from this system.[9] First, arbitrariness in the sense of either using public power for private ends or acting on the basis of a momentary whim, is replaced with the stability of relatively fixed, open, clear and prospective laws, that are impartially administered and made to promote the common good. Second, individual freedom is promoted by the resulting ability to plan within a comparatively secure and predictable environment. Third, separating functions is said to bring the efficiency gains associated with the division of labour. In particular, the activity of the legislature is made less cumbersome as a result of devolving more short-term decisions to an executive branch capable of acting with greater coherence and dispatch. Fourth, this system secures the mutual accountability of the powers. Initially, the aim was to make the executive accountable to the legislature, but with time the chief problem became how to hold the legislature to account.

These mechanisms retain their relevance even if you regard rights as fixed elements of a higher law that are above politics. Although Locke, for example, conceived political society as but a means for the preservation of the Law of Nature, he advocated a form of the separation of powers as essential to its impartial codification and execution.[10] The role of government may not have been so much to make the law as to write it down and apply it, but Locke thought that the essential difference between political society and the state of nature was that in the second no individual can be both judge and executioner of the natural law.[11] It was this aspiration on the part of absolute monarchs that rendered their rule arbitrary, and, *pace* Hobbes,[12] effectively abolished rather than sustained civil society.[13] Even on this reading, constitutionalism depends less on the acknowledgment of natural rights *per se*, a matter that Locke was in any case more inclined to assert than to demonstrate, as on the existence of a form of government capable of giving them substance. Note too that Locke identified the legislature as the 'supreme' power, since it sets down the 'positive laws' and 'common rule' that are to be executed.[14]

---

[9] The following list differs in certain ways from, but is compatible with, the five reasons that have been given for employing the doctrine recorded by W. B. Gwyn, *The Meaning of the Separation of Powers: an Analysis of the Doctrine from its Origin to the Adoption of the United States Constitution* (The Hague, Martinus Nijhoff, 1965), pp. 127–8.

[10] J. Locke (P. Laslett, ed.), *Two Treatises of Government* (Cambridge, Cambridge University Press, 1988), *The Second Treatise of Government* (hereafter II), paras 143–4.

[11] Locke, *Two Treatises*, II, paras 87, 91.

[12] T. Hobbes, *Leviathan* (Cambridge, Cambridge University Press, 1991), chs 18 and 29.

[13] Locke, *Two Treatises*, II, paras 88–93.

[14] Locke, *Two Treatises*, II, paras 149–50, 20, 91. Locke, of course, only distinguishes legislative and executive power. In part, this is precisely because the judiciary exercises the subordinate role of executing rather than making law. However, it is clear that he fully appreciated the importance of

The separation of powers, however, suffers from a number of notorious and related problems, of which two are particularly important. First, there is the conceptual and practical difficulty of distinguishing the different functions.[15] When judges, for example, adjudicate on which rules do or do not apply in particular cases, they also often end up setting precedents that in effect constitute new rules. Similarly, officials frequently have to create rules in the course of implementing a given law that in turn come to take on a life of their own. Legislators, too, are inevitably concerned with how the laws they frame will be interpreted and applied to specific cases. Thus, each branch of government will find itself engaged in all three activities to one degree or another. The more complex the activities of government, the more interrelated they are likely to become.

Second, to the extent such functional separation is possible, its ability to limit the power of those controlling the various agencies will be undermined if all represent similar groups or interests. In such circumstances, it may not be enough for each arm to be run by different people since they might nevertheless collaborate to promote a shared partial interest rather than working for the common good.

It might be thought that these problems render the doctrine totally incoherent and unworkable, especially since, for reasons explored below, both are exacerbated in democracies. However, they were recognized fairly early on, and in a number of respects led to adaptations of the theory that modified the details of its operation whilst reinforcing its spirit. As we shall see, the doctrine was rarely applied in its pure form, but was always combined with elements of the related theories of mixed and balanced government that rectified its deficiencies. In particular, representation allowed democracy to become an aspect of, rather than a rival to, the separating of power.

Before turning to these developments, however, it is worth stressing that rights discourse cannot rise above these difficulties. If rights could be defined in non-contentious ways, their policy implications drawn with facility, and human beings trusted always to act with an angelic degree of rectitude and foresight, there would be no need for constitutional government. Unfortunately, none of these conditions obtain. Justifications for rights differ widely and give rise in their turn to disputes about what interests and values deserve special protection, who they apply to, the weight to be accorded them vis-à-vis other moral principles and social considerations, and how they are to be implemented in particular contexts. The constitutionalization of rights does not put an end to such debates – merely transposes them into somewhat scholastic arguments about the precise meaning of the form of words employed in a given charter.[16] These dilemmas relate directly to the issues of the making, adjudication and application of law, and the desire to guard against partiality or arbitrariness in the framing and execution of legislation. They also reflect a difficulty in isolating what has been called the 'higher' law, represented by certain basic universal

---

having the criminal and civil cases decided by 'known authorized judges' who are distinct both from the legislature and the executive (II, 20, 131, 136, 214).

[15] Vile, *Constitutionalism*, pp. 318–21.

[16] These difficulties are analysed in R. Bellamy, 'Citizenship and rights' in R. Bellamy (ed.), *Theories and Concepts of Politics* (Manchester, Manchester University Press, 1993), ch. 3; and J. Waldron, 'A right-based critique of constitutional rights', *Oxford Journal of Legal Studies*, 13 (1993), 18–51.

norms, from the ordinary concerns raised by particular cases and policies. The two increasingly interact, as the experience of established constitutional courts amply testifies.[17] In these circumstances, the worries raised by the separation of powers take on greater rather than less relevance. Both control and influence become harder to exercise in ways that do not appear crude, capricious or coercive. Such problems are not new, however, merely an intensification of processes that have bedeviled theorists of constitutional government since at least the sixteenth century. The development of the doctrine, to which I now turn, is highly instructive in this respect.

From Mixed Government to the Balanced Constitution

The *locus classicus* of the separation of powers is book XI chapter VI of Montesquieu's *The Spirit of the Laws*. As historians of the doctrine have pointed out,[18] the idea did not originate with him. Rather, he brought together a whole range of earlier thinking on the subject. Based on a discussion of the English Constitution, his account synthesizes the doctrine with three others: mixed government, the idea of a balance of power, and the theory of checks and balances. All four overlap to some degree but have disparate origins. Montesquieu's contribution turned on his combining them so as to avoid some of the problems with the 'pure' doctrine identified above.

To show how he achieved this synthesis, a brief survey of the three other doctrines involved is necessary. The theory of mixed government originated with ancient thought and the classification of different political systems on the basis of whether One, a Few or Many ruled. According to this argument, the three basic types of polity – monarchy, aristocracy and democracy – were all liable to degenerate into tyranny, oligarchy and anarchy respectively. This corruption stemmed from the concentration of power in the hands of a single person or group, which created a temptation to its abuse in arbitrary or self-interested rule. The solution, which received its canonical expression in book VI of Polybius's *Histories*, was to ensure moderation and proportion by combining or mixing various types.[19] As a result, the virtues of each form of government, namely a strong executive, the involvement of the better elements of society, and popular legitimacy, could be obtained without the corresponding vices.[20]

As Wilfried Nippel has remarked, Polybius's conception of mixed government did not involve 'normative ideas of a necessary differentiation of governmental functions'.[21] Its prime purpose was to ensure that the exercise of

---

[17] For an analysis of these difficulties with regard to the European Convention on Human Rights, see R. Bellamy, 'The constitution of Europe: rights or democracy?' in R. Bellamy, V. Bufacchi and D. Castiglione (eds), *Democracy and Constitutional Culture in the Union of Europe* (London, Lothian Foundation, 1995), ch. 11.

[18] Vile, *Constitutionalism*, p. 76; Gwyn, *Separation of Powers*, p. 100.

[19] See, in particular, Polybius (I. Scott-Kilvert, trans., F. W. Walbank, ed.), *The Rise of the Roman Empire* (Harmondsworth, Penguin, 1979), bk VI, chs 3, 4 and 10, pp. 303–5, 310–1. For a clear discussion of book VI, see F. W. Walbank, *Polybius* (Berkeley, University of California Press, 1972), ch. V.

[20] E.g. see the discussion of the Roman constitution in Polybius, *Rise of the Roman Empire*, bk VI, chs 11–18, pp. 311–8.

[21] W. Nippel, 'Ancient and modern republicanism: "mixed constitution" and "ephors" ', in B. Fontana (ed.), *The Invention of the Modern Republic* (Cambridge, Cambridge University Press, 1994), p. 9.

political power reflected the 'natural' balance of the different social classes and interests within the political 'body', and to provide mechanisms whereby each could check the other.[22] Nippel also rightly points out that,[23] although the Polybian version of the argument came to predominate, it diverged in important respects from the Aristotelian account. Aristotle had regarded kingship as the best form, and democracy as a corruption of what he called Polity. Unfortunately, he thought the ideal was almost impossible to obtain, and was highly likely to degenerate into tyranny, which was the worst possible option. Consequently, he had advocated Polity as the most generalizable form of government. This consisted of a mixture of two corrupt forms – democracy and oligarchy. Unlike Polybius, Aristotle had not considered that different political bodies should represent different groups and he had thought that citizens should be directly involved in government. His aim had been to employ devices, such as a combination of election and lot, to ensure a social mixture amongst the political officers. Whereas Polybius conceived mixed government as a balance of classes, therefore, Aristotle had interpreted it as meaning a mingling of them. He had believed that whilst democracy and oligarchy undermined the common interest by placing government exclusively in the hands of either those without means or those with them respectively, a Polity resulted when those with moderate wealth predominated and tempered the conflict between rich and poor.[24]

The importance of balancing social power was given especial emphasis by Machiavelli, whose *Discorsi* can in many respects be read as a radical version of the Polybian argument, obtained via an Aristotelian appreciation of an active citizenry. Continuing the organic imagery of the ancients, he observed that all political bodies contain two classes, the nobles (*grandi*) and the people (*popolo*), whose 'humours' (*umori*) or desires conflict. He contended that the prime advantage of the Roman 'mixed constitution' admired by Polybius was the balance it achieved amongst these two humours by dividing power between the respective classes. Indeed, he claimed that their discord, far from being destructive, had actively promoted 'all the laws made in favour of liberty'.[25] The republic had only collapsed when the economic struggle finally subverted this political balance and the patricians overthrew it in order to recover the privileges taken away from them by the Gracchi's attempt to enforce the Agrarian Law.[26]

Machiavelli's analysis involved a sociological insight that linked the relative merits of different political institutions or *ordini* to the social conditions – what he called the *materia* – of the polity in which they operated. 'Good laws' and 'good customs' were interdependent, and only 'extreme force', which had dangers of its own, could create the second through the imposition of the first.[27] He related the process of corruption and the attendant Polybian cycle of

---

[22] The issue is complicated by the fact that different governmental bodies did not necessarily represent different social classes. See in this regard Nippel's comments on the ephorate in the Spartan system in his 'Ancient and modern republicanism', pp. 8–10.

[23] Nippel, 'Ancient and modern republicanism', pp. 7–8, 9.

[24] See Aristotle (T. A. Sinclair, trans., T. J. Saunders, ed.), *The Politics* (Harmondsworth, Penguin, rev. ed., 1981), bk. III, ch. 7, 1279a22–1279b4; bk.IV, chs 2, 3, 8, 9, 1289a26–1290a13, 1293b22–1294b41.

[25] N. Machiavelli, *Discorsi sopra la prima deca di Tito Livio* in N. Machiavelli (S. Bertelli, ed.), *Il Principe e Discorsi* (Milan, Feltrinelli, 1960), bk. I, Ch. 4, p. 137.

[26] Machiavelli, *Discorsi*, bk. I, chs 37, p. 218.

[27] Machiavelli, *Discorsi*, bk. I, chs 17, p. 178.

constitutional change, that ultimately affected even mixed governments, to changes in society at large.[28] Differences in manners and the degree of equality between citizens were particularly important in this regard. Thus, republics were more suited to egalitarian societies in which there was a general concern for the common good amongst the citizenry, whilst principalities were more appropriate to conditions of social inequality.[29] Machiavelli disputed classic fears of the inconstancy and unreliability of the multitude. He believed that the greater equality of republics made the people more prudent, law-abiding and caused them to identify their interest more closely with the common welfare. In particular, there was a greater preparedness to bear arms and hence no need for mercenaries. These features rendered republican governments more stable and secure than principalities, in which the temptation to abuse one's power was greater.[30]

The republican interpretation of mixed government as involving a balance of social groups first entered English constitutional discourse to support the view that royal power should be limited by the nobility and the people.[31] It was deployed most forcefully in Charles I's *Answer to the Nineteen Propositions* of 1642, where it served to characterize the parliamentary system as combining King, Lords and Commons. The *Answer*'s authors maintained that 'the experience and wisdom of your ancestors' had 'moulded' a mixture 'as to give to this kingdom (as far as humane prudence can contrive) the conveniences of all three, without the inconveniences of any one, as long as the balance hangs even between the three estates . . .', and warned of the dangers of subverting this arrangement.[32] Following Polybius, this version of mixed government was treated more as a matter of historical development than design. It formed a natural response to the process of corruption, the *Answer* underlining the Polybian lesson that to disturb this hard won balance risked unleashing the 'vices' of 'tyranny . . . faction and division [and] tumults, violence and licentiousness' to which monarchy, aristocracy and democracy respectively were prone.[33] However, it was a dangerous argument to employ. Not only did it undermine the absolute authority of the king by suggesting that power was shared, as Filmer pointed out,[34] it was also open to the radical Machiavellian argument of Harrington.[35] He claimed that the mixed constitution was unstable precisely because it no longer reflected a social balance. The undermining of the feudal system and the gradual transferral of property, and with it military and political power, to the commons meant that the only stable political system was a republic in which property and military responsibilities were shared amongst them alone,

---

[28] Machiavelli, *Discorsi*, bk. I, chs 16–18, pp. 173–83.

[29] Machiavelli, *Discorsi*, bk. I, ch. 55, p. 258.

[30] Machiavelli, *Discorsi*, bk. I, ch. 58, pp. 261–6; bk. II, ch. 2, p. 280.

[31] For details, see Gwyn, *Separation of Powers*, ch. II; Vile, *Constitutionalism*, pp. 36–40; Pocock, *Machiavellian Moment*, pp. 361–6.

[32] *The King's Answer to the Nineteen Propositions*, 18 June 1642, in J. P. Kenyon (ed.), *The Stuart Constitution: Documents and Commentary* (Cambridge, Cambridge University Press, 1966), p. 21.

[33] *The King's Answer*, p. 21.

[34] J. Filmer, 'The anarchy of a limited or mixed monarchy' in J. P. Somerville, (ed.), *Patriarcha and Other Political Works of Sir Robert Filmer* (Cambridge, Cambridge University Press, 1991).

[35] See Pocock, *Machiavellian Moment*, p. 388, and Pocock's introduction to his edition of *The Political Works of James Harrington* (Cambridge, Cambridge University Press, 1977), pp. 15–42. Pocock describes Harrington (p. 15) as 'England's premier civic humanist and Machiavellian'.

rather than with the king and aristocracy.[36] Harrington's consequent advocacy of economic and institutional 'superstructures' capable of inducing civic virtue within a single social group proved important,[37] as we shall see, when it came to elaborating a democratic version of the separation of powers.

Unfortunately, Cromwell failed to seize the *occasione* to institute the Harringtonian republic. Nevertheless, the problem of controlling government in a society without distinctions of rank remained. It was these circumstances that helped to crystallize the essential elements of the modern theory of the separation of powers: namely, the notion that different agencies should perform distinct functions and the belief that the judicial branch especially should be independent. Lack of space prohibits an account of this history here.[38] Suffice it to say, that the struggle between King and Parliament,[39] the experience of the Long Parliament, and the setting up of the Protectorate,[40] all served in different ways to raise the issues of the respective roles, limits and relations of legislature and executive. Two points proved especially significant. On the one hand, it emerged that large assemblies were inefficient for the implementation of laws and policy. On the other hand, legislative functions should not be entrusted to those executing or judging violations of the law if legislation was to be made in the common interest, administered impartially, and officials held to account. A separation of legislative and executive powers appeared justified on both counts. Thus, the doctrine was a commonplace by the time of Locke's seminal analysis of the 'powers of government' in the *Second Treatise*, discussed in the last section.[41] By this time, however, the Restoration had occasioned its being reworked within the context of a view of the English constitution as a model of the 'balance' to be achieved in mixed monarchy. Although present in Locke and other writers, notably Bolingbroke,[42] this thesis only gained its paradigmatic form with Montesquieu.

Montesquieu began by enunciating some of the basic premises of constitutional government. Political liberty, he asserted, differed from self-defeating licence by requiring acceptance of the rule of law.[43] However, law and liberty went together 'only when there is no abuse of power'.[44] Since 'all experience proves that every man with power is led to abuse it', all power must be kept within bounds by so framing the constitution 'that power checks [*arrête*]

---

[36] Harrington, *Political Writings*, pp. 163–5.

[37] Harrington, *Political Writings*, pp. 171–4.

[38] See Vile, *Constitutionalism*, pp. 37–52; Gywn, *Separation of Powers*, chs III and IV.

[39] P. Hunton's *A Treatise of Monarchy* (1648) was of particular importance in this regard. The relevant sections are reproduced in D. Wootton (ed.), *Divine Right and Democracy: an Anthology of Political Writing in Stuart England* (Hamondsworth, Penguin, 1986), pp. 191–5.

[40] It was included in part in the 1653 *Instrument of Government* and later defences of the Commonwealth. The key text here is M. Needham's *The Excellencie of a Free-State* (1656), an extract from which appears as Appendix 1 of Gwyn, *Separation of Powers*, pp. 131–3.

[41] Many of the peculiarities of Locke's account arise from his adherence to the existing arrangements of the English constitution. See Vile, *Constitutionalism*, pp. 58–67, and Gwyn, *Separation of Powers*, ch. V.

[42] On Bolingbroke, see Vile, *Constitutionalism*, pp. 72–5. R. Shackleton, *Montesquieu: a Critical Biography* (Oxford, Clarendon, 1961), pp. 298–300 notes that, along with Locke, he was probably the most important influence on Montesquieu's conception of the English Constitution.

[43] C.-L. de S. Montesquieu, *De l'esprit des lois*, 2 vols (Paris, Garnier-Flammarion, 1979), I, bk. XI, ch. 3, p. 292.

[44] Montesquieu, *de l'esprit*, bk. XI, ch. 4, p. 293.

power'.[45] His innovation lay in modifying the idea of functional separation so that it operates as a check.

Montesquieu's initial description of the separation of powers followed the Lockean distinction between legislative and executive, the latter being further subdivided into internal and external affairs. However, he immediately restated the doctrine introducing this time a third 'power of judging'.[46] Although not the first to do so, this tripartite division only gained wide currency with Montesquieu. The vast majority of earlier writers had classified judicial power under the domestic duties of the executive, though they did argue that those who decided civil and criminal cases ought not to exercise other executive functions. He then drew not only the standard conclusion that uniting the executive and legislative endangered liberty by allowing a monarch or senate to make 'tyrannical laws in order to execute them in a tyrannical way',[47] but also argued that an even greater danger of oppression followed if the judicial power was united to either of the other two, or worse still all three came together in the same person or body.[48] His reasoning was that whilst the legislature was concerned solely with declaring 'the general will of the state' and the executive with 'nothing more than the execution of that general will', only the judiciary applied the laws to particular persons.[49] Consequently, the true definition of despotism was the uniting of this power with the other two.

Montesquieu did not believe that formal separation alone would allow each to check the others. Criticizing the Venetian republic, he observed that although the legislative, executive and judicial power were divided between the Supreme Council, the *pregardi* and the *quarantia* respectively, 'all these tribunals are formed from magistrates who belong to the same social estate, which virtually turns them into one and the same power'.[50] A material and procedural basis had to be given to the distinction, therefore.

Mixed government partially resolved this difficulty, since he considered that making the executive an hereditary monarch ensured its separation from the legislature. Departing, as he often did, from the reality of the English situation, he argued against ministers being taken from the legislature on the grounds that in this case 'the two powers would be united' and 'there would no longer be any liberty'.[51] This arrangement also served the efficiency aspect of the separation of power, 'because this part of government, which almost always requires rapid action, is better administered by one person than many'.[52] However, mixed government added an additional dimension by dividing the legislature between two assemblies – the one consisting of the nobles and the other of the representatives of the people. Separate representation for the nobility was warranted by the need to protect their distinct interests and views stemming from the advantages of 'birth, riches or honours'.[53] But bicameralism also operated as part of a checking mechanism. Montesquieu advocated that both

[45] Montesquieu, *de l'esprit*, bk. XI, ch. 4, p. 293.
[46] Montesquieu, *de l'esprit*, bk. XI, ch. 6, p. 294.
[47] Montesquieu, *de l'esprit*, bk. XI, ch. 6, p. 294.
[48] Montesquieu, *de l'esprit*, bk. XI, ch. 6, p. 295.
[49] Montesquieu, *de l'esprit*, bk. XI, ch. 6, p. 296.
[50] Montesquieu, *de l'esprit*, bk. XI, ch. 6, p. 295.
[51] Montesquieu, *de l'esprit*, bk. XI, ch. 6, p. 299.
[52] Montesquieu, *de l'esprit*, bk. XI, ch. 6, p. 299.
[53] Montesquieu, *de l'esprit*, bk. XI, ch. 6, p. 298.

the executive and the upper chamber should be able to check the power of the legislature by having the right of veto.[54] Likewise, he believed that the legislature should have the power to investigate how the executive officers had carried out the law and impeach them if found corrupt. But he thought the monarch ought to be distinguished from his 'evil counsellors' in this respect, otherwise his independence would be jeopardized.[55] These suggestions partially undermined a pure separation, since they gave the executive a negative share in legislation. However, they helped strengthen the weaker parts of the constitution against the growing strength of the legislature, whose wider and logically prior role of law-making made it the most powerful body and so the most in need of restraining from going beyond its remit.

Montesquieu's most novel argument in this regard was his reworking of the republican thesis that the best way of ensuring that legislation reflected the common interest was to have it made by the people. In a 'free state', he affirmed, 'every man who is considered a free citizen ought to be governed by himself. Hence the people as an estate ought to have the legislative power.'[56] However, this republican point did not lead to advocacy of republican forms of government. He criticized ancient direct democracy for confusing the power of the people with its liberty.[57] Such radical participation subverted the distinction between legislative and executive powers. Besides being unworkable in large states, even in small ones it involved many people in decisions they were 'unfit' to make. Representative democracy remedied these defects by introducing checks into the democratic process. It involved selecting only the more capable citizens and reducing those involved in debating public business to manageable proportions. It exploited the fact that people were better able to choose suitable candidates and, if necessary, reject them, than to propose laws.[58] As Harrington had noticed, this division between proposers and resolvers could offer a perfect procedural guarantee of fairness.[59] A further check against class-based legislation was provided by organizing constituencies geographically rather than according to estates, thereby removing the case for mandation.[60] Finally, in book XIX chapter 27 Montesquieu introduced a related social foundation to the constitution in the customs of a free people. The habit of saying and thinking what one liked, led citizens to divide into parties supporting either the legislature or the executive. Self-interest motivated those favoured by the executive to support it, those with nothing to hope for to attack it. The effect of liberty, he contended, was for citizens always to favour the weaker side. The jealousy of the people and their representatives in the legislature was in this respect the surest way to check the executive.[61]

This fusion of the separation of powers and mixed government produced a socially and politically balanced and mutually checking constitution. Although such an arrangement might lead to 'inaction', he claimed the 'necessary

[54] Montesquieu, de l'esprit, bk. XI, ch. 6, pp. 298–9.
[55] Montesquieu, de l'esprit, bk. XI, ch. 6, pp. 300–1.
[56] Montesquieu, de l'esprit, bk. XI, ch. 6, p. 297.
[57] Montesquieu, de l'esprit, bk. XI, ch. 2, p. 292.
[58] Montesquieu, de l'esprit, bk. XI, ch. 6, p. 297.
[59] Harrington, Political Works, pp. 172, 174.
[60] Montesquieu, de l'esprit, bk. XI, ch. 6, p. 297.
[61] Montesquieu, de l'esprit, bk. XI, ch. 27, pp. 478–9.

movement of things' forced them to work together.[62] The system served to distil the public interest out of certain disparate private ones, and to gain the advantage of the better elements in society in its enactment as law.

The judicial power remained hard to assimilate to this scheme, since it added a potential fourth department within the theory of mixed government. As we saw, Montesquieu believed this power would be especially dangerous if linked to either of the other two. He thought its independence was best achieved through the jury system and lay magistrates so that it did not become attached to any estate or profession.[63] This lack of a social base or permanent *cadre* rendered it the weakest power. It became 'invisible' having 'in a sense, no force', at least in the political sense.[64]

Although Montesquieu did not discuss it, a further weakness of this branch derived from the absence of a written constitution or bill of rights. There were, of course, the rights stemming from ordinary legislation. But their protection lay, as Burke famously was to point out, in the whole scheme of the mixed constitution.[65] Rights evolved along with the rest of the system as part of an institutional adaptation to particular social circumstances. To this extent, and the influence of Locke notwithstanding, Montequieu's view of the constitution remained essentially organic rather than contractual.[66] He emphasized mixed government and the balancing of the various parts of the body politic. He did not treat the constitution as a compact between the people that established government. As Paine insisted in his critique of Burke,[67] this was the distinguishing mark of eighteenth century constitutionalism. Nevertheless, as the next section reveals, this new perspective did not produce a complete break with the past and a concentration on a normative framework of rights at the expense of questions of balance and the form of government. It merely shifted the emphasis away from achieving a 'natural' balance and functional division, towards the use of artificial mechanisms for separating powers and mediating between and coordinating disparate social interests so as to obtain the on-going consent of the governed.

Montesquieu recognized all three of the benefits of the doctrine we identified earlier. He placed particular emphasis on the rule of law, but perceived that the legislature might be a greater danger to it than the executive. As a result, he made a number of modifications to the pure doctrine, which underline and develop the element of accountability. First, Montesquieu clearly identified the

[62] Montesquieu, *de l'esprit*, bk. XI, ch. 6, p. 302.

[63] Montesquieu appears to have been misled as to the importance of professional judges in England. See M. Richter, *The Political Theory of Montesquieu* (Cambridge, Cambridge University Press, 1977), p. 336 n. 15.

[64] Montesquieu, *de l'esprit*, bk. XI, ch. 6, pp. 296, 298.

[65] E.g. E. Burke, *Reflections on the Revolution in France* (Oxford, Oxford University Press, 1993), p. 60 (on rights); and 'An appeal from the old to the new Whigs', excerpted in I. Hampshire-Monk, (ed.), *The Political Philosophy of Edmund Burke* (Harlow, Longman, 1987), p. 257 (on Britain's mixed constitution).

[66] The importance of the distinction between organic and contractual metaphors of the state for understanding the history of political concepts has been stressed by T. Ball, e.g. his article on 'Party', in T. Ball, J. Farr and R. L. Hanson (eds), *Political Innovation and Conceptual Change* (Cambridge, Cambridge University Press, 1989), especially pp. 164–7. I am grateful to him for underlining its relevance for the present subject in written comments on an earlier version of this chapter.

[67] T. Paine, *Rights of Man, Part I* in B. Kuklick (ed.), *Political Writings* (Cambridge, Cambridge University Press, 1989), pp. 78–92.

judiciary as a separate power. However, he insisted that the independence essential to its role depended crucially on its not being a political power. Second, he noted that for a power to be able to check another may require that they each have some share in the others, as in the executive's veto over legislation. Third, he observed that formal functional separation serves no purpose if all are staffed by individuals of the same class or interests. Mixed government partly meets this last problem. However, it will only work in a society of ranks. In addition, it had been dismissed by proponents of the absolute sovereignty of monarchs, such as Bodin, Filmer and Hobbes,[68] as leading to either deadlock or anarchy, and as such incoherent. The same difficulty reappears with a vengeance when popular sovereignty is at issue. As James Mill made clear, all limitations are liable to appear anti-democratic and hence illegitimate.[69] Within a democracy a separation of powers will prove both practically and normatively harder to sustain, as the transformation of the British doctrine of parliamentary sovereignty from King-in-Parliament to the power of the executive to do what it wants dramatically illustrates. Montesquieu's discussion of representation and the social bases of party proved highly prescient in this respect. As we shall see, they are the crucial components of the modern republican reworking of the doctrine.

The Separation of Powers and the Modern Republic

Bernard Manin has recently remarked how the debates surrounding the ratification of the American Constitution frequently took on the character of an exegesis of Montesquieu.[70] The separation of powers played a pivotal role in this discussion. For the Antifederalists the absence of a strict demarcation of functions between distinct agencies was the chief defect of the new arrangements. This criticism was linked in its turn to a general concern that the lines of accountability between the people and the different branches of government were insufficiently clear and that the respective spheres of the state and federal legislatures inadequately demarcated. In all cases, the fear was a concentration of power at the centre, and the attendant danger of its abuse.[71]

In responding to these objections, Madison and Hamilton had once again creatively to rework the older discourses employed by Montesquieu in order to apply them to the context of a modern republic.[72] In particular, this rethinking entailed a modification of the tendency, inherent in the organicist model of

---

[68] J. Bodin, *The Six Books of a Commonweale*, R. Knolles (trans.), K. D. McRae (ed.) (Cambridge, MA, Harvard University Press, 1962), bk. II, ch. 1; Filmer, 'The anarchy of a limited or mixed monarchy'; and Hobbes, *Leviathan*, p. 225.

[69] For Mill senior's trenchant critique of the doctrine of mixed government and constitutional balance, see J. Mill, *Essay on Government*, ch. V in J. Mill (T. Ball, ed.), *Political Writings* (Cambridge, Cambridge University Press, 1992), pp. 17–20.

[70] B. Manin, 'Checks, balances and boundaries: the separation of powers in the constitutional debate of 1787', in Fontana, *The Invention of the Modern Republic*, p. 27.

[71] The Antifederalist position is neatly summarized in Manin, 'Checks, balances and boundaries', pp. 34–47.

[72] See in particular the essays collected in T. Ball and J. G. A. Pocock (eds), *Conceptual Change and the Constitution* (Lawrence, KS, University Press of Kansas, 1988). It is true to say, however, that a certain exasperation is sometimes discernable in the remarks of Hamilton and Madison on the Antifederalists' 'oracle', the 'celebrated Montesquieu'. See A. Hamilton, J. Madison and J. Jay, *The Federalist* (London, Dent, 1992), no. 9, p. 38; no. 47, p. 247; no. 78, p. 388.

mixed government, to associate functions with the different parts of the social body. Instead, there was a move towards mechanical imagery stressing the checking and balancing of forces and a corresponding down playing of the need for functional differentiation. Most important of all, the constitution was viewed as a construct that the people shape for themselves, rather than as a reflection of the nature of the polity or of human beings. As a result, it became democratic through and through – a circumstance that raised new problems calling for innovative solutions.

The Federalists' first move was to moderate the importance of a complete functional separation. They pointed out that Montesquieu himself had advocated a partial participation of each power in the activity of others as the best means of ensuring that they exercised a mutual check on possible encroachments by one agency on the functions of the others. The danger only came 'where the *whole* power of one department is exercised by the same hands which possess the *whole* power of another department'.[73] In fact, total separation was both conceptually and practically an impossibility.[74] As Locke, and following him Montesquieu, had pointed out, an efficient executive required certain prerogative powers in order to respond quickly to unforeseen circumstances, particularly with regard to foreign affairs. This frequently involved making laws if no appropriate general rule existed.[75] Similarly, as Locke and Montesquieu had also noted,[76] the legislative function had an inherent tendency to encroach on the others. In Madison's words, the legislature's powers were 'at once more extensive, and less susceptible of precise limits' than the other two, which to some degree were necessarily guided by its decisions.[77] But Madison saw that these conceptual problems with framing legislation in ways that did not entail executive and judicial elements were exacerbated by other aspects of the republican system and the nature of modern societies more generally. These features meant that the main issue confronting modern constitutions was not absolute monarchs but tyrannous legislative majorities.[78]

Madison remarked how the division of labour and the greater disparities of property ownership, which were the twin elements of a free market economy and the key to its success as a motor of prosperity, had also fragmented society into so many interest groups and factions. Modern legislation was increasingly taken up with regulating 'these various and interfering interests'. Of necessity, legislatures were no longer simply promulgating general rules but settling disputes, so that 'most important acts of legislation [were] but so many judicial determinations'.[79] However, representative democracy meant that these cases were decided by the disputants themselves, thereby undermining the main tenet of the separation of powers – that no one should be a judge in his own case.[80] As a result, there was a clear risk 'that the public good is disregarded in the conflicts of rival parties, and that measures are too often decided, not according

[73] *Federalist*, no. 47, p. 248.
[74] *Federalist*, no. 37, p. 180.
[75] Locke, *Two Treatises*, II, paras 159–60; Montesquieu, *de l'esprit*, bk. XI, ch. 6, pp. 299-300.
[76] Locke, *Two Treatises*, II, paras 149–50; Montesquieu, *de l'esprit*, bk. XI, ch. 6, p. 300.
[77] *Federalist*, no. 48, p. 255.
[78] *Federalist*, no. 10, p. 41.
[79] *Federalist*, no. 10, p. 43.
[80] *Federalist*, no. 10, p. 44.

to the rules of justice and the rights of the minor party, but by the superior force of an interested and overbearing majority'.[81]

All these problems had been amply illustrated by the constitutions of the various states. In spite of their resounding declarations pledging commitment to the doctrine of the separation of powers, other articles often breached it.[82] Moreover, state legislatures had invariably acted in a partial manner that favoured the interests of certain well-represented groups and which the judiciary and executives had been powerless to control. Power of the purse strings, in particular, had often made the latter two departments totally dependent on the legislatures, allowing them to act in a 'despotic' way.[83]

To give meaning to the separation of powers, 'parchment barriers' had to be replaced by more efficient mechanisms.[84] This approach meant dropping a fetishistic concern with delineating precise boundaries and concentrating on the realities of power politics. Giving each agency a mutual check, such as the power to veto in the case of the executive and to impeach in the case of the legislature, offered a partial answer. However, such controls would be ineffective unless a social basis for them could be found so that 'each department should have a will of its own'.[85] Mixed government appeared not to be an option in a country that had abolished both monarchy and aristocracy – all authority came ultimately from the people. In that case, though, the separation of powers seemed doomed. It was impossible to give each department an equal power of self-defence – 'legislative authority necessarily predominates'. A paradox thereby emerged: 'in framing a government which is to be administered by men over men, ... you must first enable the government to control the governed; and in the next place oblige it to control itself'.[86] In effect, the Demos must check itself.

In order to respond to this dilemma, the Federalists had to challenge the view that popular sovereignty issued in a monopoly of authority in which law meant no more than the commands of the majority. There were two sides to this problem. On the one hand, there was the need to prevent democracy degenerating into an elective despotism. On the other, there was the desire to motivate support for the common good.[87] Their solution involved showing how the idea of mixed government based on different estates of the realm might be replaced by democratic forms of power sharing that could provide the separation of powers with a material foundation.

The Federalist authors turned for inspiration to the republican tradition of Machiavelli and Harrington, updated via Montesquieu and Hume.[88] They endorsed three key elements of the republican tradition. Namely, that politics was to be analysed in terms of selfish interests and power blocks; that the task was therefore to promote civic virtue by connecting private interest to that of the public; and that government had to be accountable to the people. But, as

---

[81] *Federalist*, no. 10, pp. 41–2.

[82] *Federalist*, no. 47, pp. 249–53.

[83] *Federalist*, no. 48, pp. 255-7.

[84] *Federalist*, no. 48, pp. 254, 257; no. 51.

[85] *Federalist*, no. 51, p. 265.

[86] *Federalist*, no. 51, p. 266

[87] *Federalist*, no. 57, p. 293.

[88] See D. G. Adair, ' "That politics may be reduced to a science": David Hume, James Madison and the Tenth Federalist', *Huntingdon Library Quarterly*, XX (1957), 343–60, and Pocock, *Machiavellian Moment*, ch. XV.

Terrence Ball has shown,[89] they put these notions to work in a context that endowed the term republican with a quite new meaning. Size and social differentiation – especially differences of property ownership, far from placing a limit on the practice of republican government, as Montesquieu and certain of the Antifederalists maintained, were now recruited as positive aids. Crucially, they endorsed Montesquieu's criticism of the unworkability and undesirability of direct democracy. Highly controversially, however, they associated republicanism exclusively with the representative form. Inspired perhaps by Harrington, they saw how electoral devices might be employed to encourage adherence to the public good, select high calibre politicians, and encourage, through deliberation, the aggregation and transformation of preferences.[90] Indeed, these mechanisms allowed a move from the balancing of social interests back to the Aristotelian concern with 'mingling' them to encourage moderation and deliberation.[91] In these ways, the 'great principle of representation' made possible 'unmixed and extensive republics'.[92]

As we saw, they believed the main threat of elective despotism emanated from the existence of factions. Avoiding the development of factions, though, was only possible by suppressing liberty – a remedy worse than the disease it was supposed to cure.[93] Madison's brilliant solution was to harness factional conflict in Machiavellian manner so that the different groupings checked and balanced each other and were forced to cooperate in promoting justice and the general good. This programme involved taking advantage of the multiplicity of interests within society to ensure that no consistent majority was liable to hold absolute sway. The trick lay in introducing this diversity into the political system and 'by so contriving the interior structure of the government as that its several constituent parts may, by their mutual relations, be the means of keeping each other in their proper places'.[94] By these means, 'the private interest of every individual may be sentinel over the public rights',[95] supplementing the separation of powers with effective checks and balances. Within this set up, all authority might come from the people, but they were fragmented into 'so many parts, interests, and classes of citizens, that the rights of individuals, or of the minority, will be in little danger from the interested combinations of the majority'.[96]

This purpose is largely achieved through dividing the legislature against itself.[97] Territorial extent and the federal union of states combined with the system of representation actively to aid this scheme. The larger the political

[89] T. Ball, ' "A Republic – if you can keep it" ', in Ball and Pocock, *Conceptual Change and the Constitution*, pp. 137–64.

[90] As G. Brennan and A. Hamlin show in their chapter in this volume, these three benefits are associated with an economical approach to constitutionalism and follow from employing what they call the sanctioning, screening and summative mechanisms respectively.

[91] The Aristotelian dimension of the Federalists' thought has been stressed in a number of recent commentaries. See D. Epstein, *The Political Theory of The Federalist* (Chicago, Chicago University Press, 1984), pp. 124f; and J. Zvesper, 'Interpreting *The Federalist*' in R.C. Simmons (ed.), *The United States Constitution: the First 200 Years* (Manchester, Manchester University Press, 1989), pp. 62–4.

[92] *Federalist*, no. 14, pp. 62–3.

[93] *Federalist*, no. 10, p. 42.

[94] *Federalist*, no. 51, p. 265.

[95] *Federalist*, no. 51, p. 266.

[96] *Federalist*, no. 51, p. 268.

[97] *Federalist*, no. 51, pp. 266–7.

society, the more diverse the interests and views it was likely to contain, so that constructing a coherent and consistent majority would be much harder than in a small community. Representatives would have to gain the support of a coalition of interests within large, territorially arranged constituencies, and as members of a national assembly would tend to take a wider view. However, a federal system would also contain a number of state legislatures capable of ensuring that local interests were not neglected. In particular, they would have control over further modifications of the constitutional framework itself. Likewise, national government offered a check to local power. This balance between local and national interests would also be carried into the national legislature, which was to be divided into two chambers, with Congress elected directly and the Senate by the state legislatures. The latter also had the role of placing a patrician break on the 'irregular passions' that might occasionally animate the former, more popular, body.[98]

Robert Dahl famously argued that Madison greatly exaggerated the importance of constitutional mechanisms in controlling majority tyranny and underestimated 'the inherent social checks and balances existing in every pluralistic society'.[99] This criticism overlooks the positive role of his proposals. A prime effect of a well-designed system of representation, for example, was 'to refine and enlarge the public views' by delegating decision making to 'a chosen body of citizens, whose wisdom may best discern the true interest of their country, and whose patriotism and love of justice will be least likely to sacrifice it to temporary or partial considerations'.[100] Similarly, the benefit of a fairly 'numerous' national legislature, containing a variety of different interests and opinions, was not simply to have them check each other but to 'promote deliberation and circumspection' through the 'jarrings of parties'.[101] Bicameral-ism and federalism were further devices for encouraging dialogue between different perspectives. These positive elements complemented the negative and provided a necessary incentive for the legislators to switch from the assertion of narrow preferences to the giving of reasons capable of attaining general assent and so come to an appreciation of the public good.[102] They prevented social pluralism degenerating into stalemate, pork-barrel politics, or the rule of the strongest.

The two major innovations of the United States Constitution also form part of this democratization of the separation of powers: the elected Presidency and the Supreme Court. In the absence of an hereditary monarchy it was necessary to elect the Chief Executive. Indirect election was supposed to prevent direct appeals to the people over the heads of the legislature, thereby guarding against populist demagogues.[103] Indeed, election acted as much as a check as a method of popular legitimation, since it allowed the removal of unsatisfactory incumbents.[104] The electoral college system was also aimed more positively at

[98] *Federalist*, no. 63, p. 324.

[99] R. Dahl, *A Preface to Democratic Theory* (Chicago, University of Chicago Press, 1956), p. 22.

[100] *Federalist*, no. 10, p. 46.

[101] *Federalist*, no. 70, pp. 360, 363.

[102] For a critique of the Dahlian thesis in this respect, see R. J. Morgan, 'Madison's Theory of Representation in the Tenth Federalist', *Journal of Politics*, 36 (1974), 852–85. Vile's *Constitutionalism* is largely motivated by an attack on Dahl's behaviourial approach, see ch. XI.

[103] *Federalist*, no. 68, pp. 349–52.

[104] *Federalist*, no. 69, p. 353.

ensuring that such an important choice was made by 'the most capable' and 'under circumstances favourable to deliberation'.[105] The main rationale for a President was provided by the efficiency argument, especially with regard to foreign affairs, and the need for a qualified counter to sectional interests in the legislature.[106] The executive's discretionary powers were themselves contained, however, by the possibility of impeachment and by the Senate's participation in functions such as treaty making – a device that also served to strengthen further that arm of the legislature.[107]

The Supreme Court does not fit so obviously into this project. Unlike Montesquieu, the Federalists thought that the judiciary ought to be a professional body, so that election was not appropriate. However, the permanent tenure, so necessary to their independence, also destroyed their sense of dependence on the people.[108] Nevertheless, the Court was not totally immune from the influence of other government agencies. Not only were the judges appointed by the President and Senate, Congress had the power, under Article III section 2 clause 2, to make exceptions to and to regulate the Court's appellate jurisdiction.[109] In the face of Antifederalist criticism,[110] Hamilton also underlined Montesquieu's point that the judiciary 'is beyond comparison the weakest of the three departments of power'. With 'no influence over either the sword or the purse', it possessed 'neither FORCE nor WILL, but merely judgement; and must ultimately depend upon the aid of the executive arm for even the efficacy of its judgements'.[111]

All these devices served to place the judiciary within the general scheme of mutual checks and balances. However, the crucial limitation came from its link with the democratic will of the people. The Court protected the Constitution against the possible encroachments of the other agencies, particularly the legislature. But in performing this function, the judges were not exercising a discretionary authority of their own, stemming from the superiority of their deliberations or understanding of justice to that of the people. They were acting as defenders of, rather than proxies for, the 'will of the people', as declared in the Constitution, against the possible presumption of representatives within the legislature 'to substitute their *will* for that of their constituents'.[112]

Bruce Ackerman has argued that a dualist conception of democracy is at work here.[113] The Constitution resulted from the deliberations of delegates representing the people as a whole during an extraordinary moment of constitutional politics, when factional divisions had been temporarily put to

---

[105] *Federalist*, no. 68, p. 349.
[106] *Federalist*, no. 70, pp. 359–66.
[107] *Federalist*, no. 69, pp. 355–7.
[108] *Federalist*, no. 51, pp. 265–6.
[109] Manin, 'Checks, balances and boundaries', p. 56. Manin observes that this provision was to fall into virtually complete disuse but illuminates the Federalist plan of allowing all branches of government a share in each other's functions.
[110] Brutus had argued that 'The judicial power will operate to effect, in the most certain, yet silent and perceptible manner, what is evidently the tendency of the constitution: I mean, the entire subversion of the legislative, executive and judicial powers of the individual states'. H. J. Storing (ed.), *The Antifederalist: Writing by Opponents of the Constitution* (Chicago, University of Chicago Press, 1981), p. 165.
[111] *Federalist*, no. 78, pp. 398–9.
[112] *Federalist*, no. 78, pp. 400–1.
[113] Ackerman, *We the People: Foundations*, pp. 191–5.

one side because of the experience of the common struggle for independence and the need to consolidate the resulting polity. It had also been 'submitted to the people themselves' for their approval through irregular but popularly elected conventions.[114] Such higher law-making was to be distinguished from the day to day legislation that emerged from normal politics, when self-interest once more prevailed over a concern for the public good. Ordinary legislators were not preoccupied with defining the fundamental rules and general principles that were to govern society as a whole. Instead, they acted for certain sections of the community and sought to promote or protect their particular interests. Defending the rule of law, therefore, required that their decisions should be subordinated to the higher law of the people enshrined in the Constitution. This thesis makes the Judges of the Supreme Court the servants of the popular will rather than its interpreter. Indeed, Hamilton insisted that they had no power 'to construe the laws according to the spirit of the Constitution' or to assume themselves the role of the legislature.[115]

Ackerman's argument prompts the question of why the people might not have performed this protective function themselves, rather than delegating it to the Court. Such a proposal had been raised by Jefferson, who suggested that conventions might be specially called to correct constitutional breaches.[116] However, Madison objected that too regular a recurrence to the people had a tendency to subvert faith in the political system.[117] It would appear in need of constant adjustment, and would not acquire the prestige that comes once practices have endured a certain time and become established. Moreover, the people could only be expected to put aside their normal interests on exceptional occasions. 'The *passions*, therefore, not the reason of the public would sit in judgment', whereas it should be the latter that through government controlled the former.[118] Consequently, the Jeffersonian expedient would provide no check on the legislature since the usual motivations would operate and the public would naturally side with them. Even worse, it might tempt a populist executive similarly to manipulate their passional drives. In effect, it provided a means for subverting all the various checks and balances that prevented majority tyranny. In this sense, the Constitution offered a self-binding strategy which allowed public reason to control public passions. Nevertheless, Madison believed 'a constitutional road to the decision of the people ought to be marked out and kept open, for certain great and extraordinary occasions'.[119] Conventions did have a useful service to play when it came to amending the Constitution. It was this possibility that made good the Constitution's claim to speak in the name of 'We the people' and, as Tocqueville shrewdly noted, undermined the pretensions of others to do so – not least the judges.[120]

[114] *Federalist*, no. 49, p. 260.

[115] *Federalist*, no. 81, pp. 414–5.

[116] In letters to J. Madison of 6 September 1789 and to S. Kercheval of 12 July 1816, in M. Peterson (ed.), *The Portable Thomas Jefferson* (New York, Viking, 1975), pp. 444–51, 552–61.

[117] It is worth noting that initially Madison himself had preferred legislative to judicial review of the constitution on the grounds that it 'can never be proper' for the judicial branch to be paramount to the legislative. R. A. Rutland *et al.* (eds), *Papers of James Madison*, vol. 11 (Chalottesville, University of Virginia Press, 1977), p. 293.

[118] *Federalist*, no. 49, p. 261.

[119] *Federalist*, no. 49, p. 259.

[120] Alex de Tocqueville, *De la democratie en Amerique* (Paris, Garnier-Flammarion, 1981) vol. I, ch. VI, pp. 170–1.

In many respects, however, Ackerman's distinction between 'normal' and 'constitutional' politics is overdrawn.[121] The Federalists desired to render 'normal' law making as principled as possible through the encouragement of deliberation. They saw that this would not only mobilize greater support for the resulting decisions. It would also be far more likely to ensure that they were responsive to the diverse needs and values of different citizens and were fashioned in as concrete and practical manner as possible. Famously, they rejected the necessity of a bill of rights. It would be but one more 'paper parchment'. Indeed, it was quite superfluous since, as Hamilton put it, 'the Constitution is itself, in every rational sense, and to every useful purpose, A BILL OF RIGHTS'.[122] The privileges and liberties of citizens were integral to and protected by the political structure of the proposed federal state with its incentives to cooperate for the common good and to guard against arbitrary majority rule. Those rights that were intrinsic to the democratic process were already enshrined in the Constitution. Setting out others was inappropriate and might suggest that governments had the power to do whatever was not expressly forbidden. In any case, no formulation of rights could be so watertight that they were not capable of evasion. As Hamilton remarked, their security ultimately depended not on 'fine declarations' but 'on public opinion, and on the general spirit of the people and of the government'.[123]

The Federalists did not accept the contrast some recent theorists have drawn between the Supreme Court as a 'forum of principle' and the horse-trading of democratic politics.[124] On this view, interpretation of the Bill of Rights belongs to the former body and provides the means whereby it can oversee the decisions of the ordinary legislature. The Federalists saw matters quite differently. In a republic, they argued, rights were not privileges wrested from a monarch, they are constraints that the people place on themselves.[125] It followed that democratic politics could not be seen as inevitably factional and antagonistic to rights, since otherwise they could never have been instituted in the first place and would be unlikely to command lasting respect. For Madison a Bill of Rights was not addressed to the judiciary but the people as a whole. He hoped that by declaring these fundamental principles in a solemn manner they 'would become incorporated with the National sentiment' and 'counteract the impulses of interest and passion'.[126] They provided the people rather than judges with 'ground for an appeal to the sense of community' against the partial views of governments or majorities.[127] Subsequent history largely confirms the Federalists' position. Arguably, most major social reforms in the United States have been effected, not by judicial decisions, but by popular movements of

---

[121] For a critique, see Bellamy and Castiglione, 'Constitutionalism and democracy', section IV.

[122] *Federalist*, no. 84, p. 444.

[123] *Federalist*, no. 84, p. 443.

[124] E.g. Dworkin, 'Constitutionalism and democracy', p. 11.

[125] *Federalist*, no. 84, p. 442.

[126] J. Madison, Letter to T. Jefferson 17 October 1788, in M. Meyers (ed.), *The Mind of the Founder: Sources of the Political Thought of James Madison* (Hanover and London, University Press of New England, 1981), p. 158.

[127] Madison, Letter to T. Jefferson, p. 156; Speech in the House of Representatives, 8 June 1789, in *Mind of the Founder*, p. 169.

principle, such as the New Deal and the civil rights campaign, that have mounted just such appeals.[128]

The Federalist Papers rework the doctrine of the separation of powers in terms suited to a democratic society. In particular, they show how the added features of mixed government and checks and balances, which we saw to be vital elements even in the classic conception of the doctrine found in Montesquieu, could be employed within a democratic context. This redefinition involved adding a territorial and a representative dimension to the social and functional separation found in Montesquieu's mixed government version of the doctrine. In the process, they were able to overcome some of the problems we noted earlier. First, although the authority of each agency stems ultimately from the people, different forms of representation mean that they are not treated as a homogeneous entity with a singular, all commanding will. Recognition is given to different interests, both in the negative sense of allowing them to mutually control each other, and in the positive sense of promoting self-government and an identification with the norms underlying the political system.

Second, the difficulty of clearly distinguishing the different functions and assigning them to distinct agencies is turned into a virtue rather than a fatal flaw. What enables each branch of government to check the others is the fact that it participates to some degree in their operations. This approach also gets around some of the absurdities of making the rule of law the sole virtue of a legal system.[129] For it allows the formality of this notion to be modified to take into account the need for special rules to meet particular contexts or salient cultural or ethical differences amongst certain classes of people. Most important in this respect is the linking of considerations of power with the formulation of principles of justice. The system ensures no individuals or groups can determine the rules affecting others without reciprocation. In this way, oppression is guarded against not by virtue of abstract principles, such as rights, that might covertly embody the values and interests of the hegemonic groups administering them, but through a political process which allows the people to voice their concerns for themselves.

Conclusion

This chapter has presented an account of constitutionalism as rooted in political and social structures rather than pre-political legal norms. Although of ancient origin, this approach is well suited to the modern conception of constitutionalism as a political response to the disenchantment of the world.[130] Once societies are no longer viewed as naturally constituted according to some moral order, then the norms that animate and regulate human affairs have to be politically constructed and legitimated by those who are to submit to them. An

---

[128] For further evidence to this effect, see V. Hart's account of the minimum wage campaign, 'Righting wrongs: the normality of constitutional politics' in R. Bellamy (ed.), *Constitutionalism, Democracy and Sovereignty: American and European Perspectives* (Aldershot, Avebury, 1996), pp. 45–60.

[129] For these problems, see J. Raz, 'The rule of law and its virtue' in his *The Authority of Law: Essays on Law and Morality* (Oxford, Clarendon, 1979), ch. 11.

[130] For this thesis, see U. Preuβ's 1995 Austin Lecture, 'The political meaning of constitutionalism' in Bellamy, *Constitutionalism, Democracy and Sovereignty*, ch. 2.

internal relation is thereby established between constitutional norms and the form of government which embodies them. The two stand or fall together and are vital to the whole process of what German jurists have called the 'positivization' of natural rights.

On this view, constitutional government consists of a form of politics that strives to motivate law-making in the public interest and render it accountable to citizens. Consequently, its goals are broader than upholding the rule of law and rights against the arbitrary exercise of power, although it includes these concerns. It also brings the various groups and interests within society into dialogue with each other and ensures that the making of law reflects mutual concern and respect and a desire to promote the common welfare. These positive elements supplement and support the negative and protective purposes of constitutionalism, and increase not only popular respect for rights but also their willingness to undertake often onerous obligations to promote them. As such, it offers a political approach to constitutionalism that is of more than historical importance.[131]

---

[131] For attempts to develop this kind of approach, see Stephen Elkin's chapter in this volume; S. Elkin and K. E. Soltan (eds), *A New Constitutionalism: Designing Political Institutions for a Good Society* (Chicago, University of Chicago Press, 1993); and R. Bellamy and D. Castiglione, 'The communitarian ghost in the cosmopolitan machine: constitutionalism, democracy and the reconfiguration of politics in the new Europe' in Bellamy, *Constitutionalism, Democracy and Sovereignty*, ch. 8.

Democracy and the Constitution in Italy

LUIGI FERRAJOLI

A New Italian Case

The transition from the first to the second Republic is occurring in disquieting and unexpected ways, once again raising the question of 'an Italian case'. For better or worse, this century has seen many 'Italian cases'. One such case was at the forefront of political debate in the 1970s, centring around the prolonged epoch of struggle for social reform that arose after 1968. However the Italian flair for engendering a 'case' has more often manifested itself in the worst possible ways: one need only think of Fascism in 1922, the experience of 'blocked' democracy from 1945 to the present, or the bribery and corruption scandals associated with *Tangentopoli* (Bribesville) in the 1980s and 1990s. The novel elements in the current Italian case relate to three subtle shifts in the 'material constitution' of the state.[1] These changes followed hard on the heels of the advent of the Berlusconi government, set up in the wake of the electoral success of the right on 27 March 1994.

The first element – by far the most obvious and striking – was the return, fifty years on, of the Fascists to government. There has been a tendency in Italy to underestimate and trivialize this event. Yet it is a fact of enormous symbolic value, that strikes at the antifascist foundations of the Italian republic. Along with the United Nations Charter, the 1948 Universal Declaration of Rights, the Fundamental Law of the Federal Republic of Germany, and the European Convention on Human Rights, the Italian constitution ranks among the key documents that shaped the democratic identity of the West, effectively redefining it through the negation of Nazism and Fascism. Consequently, the fact that Italy, the very country that gave birth to Fascism seventy years ago, brought the Fascists back to power in 1994 was greeted with consternation in other countries. This general concern was by no means alleviated – quite the contrary – by the lack of understanding and displeasure that marked the

---

[1] The expression 'material constitution' was introduced into Italian legal discourse by C. Mortati, *La costituzione in senso materiale* (Milano, Giuffré, 1940). In contrast to the 'formal constitution', it denotes both the 'political values' and 'institutional aims', which are at the basis of a particular legal order, and the prevailing 'political order'. Cf. also, C. Mortati, *Istituzioni di diritto pubblico* (Padova, Cedam, VI ed., 1962); and 'Costituzione (Dottrine generali)' in *Enciclopedia del diritto* (Milano, Giuffré, 1962), vol. XI, pp. 169–78. This somewhat confused sociological notion has now become part of ordinary political language and refers to the actual organization of public powers, that is the way in which the 'formal' constitution is interpreted and applied (or not applied). The opposition between the 'formal' and the 'material' constitution has therefore been used to point out the gap between the two, either to highlight the violation and non-fulfilment of the constitutional design, or to legitimate 'realistic' reform proposals intended to bring the constitution into line with what actually happens.

Italian response, above all that of President Scalfaro, to the European Parliament's exhortation to Italy to defend the Republic's antifascist roots.

The other two elements of novelty in the current Italian case relate to changes in the nature of political representation. The new 'majoritarian' electoral system has not only distorted the representative relationship based on the classical principle of one person/one vote, but has also favoured two converging phenomena: the grouping together of the old electoral base of the former governing parties with that of the Northern League and the Fascists, and the success of an improvised political grouping in the form of 'Forza Italia' led by Silvio Berlusconi.[2] With the old governing class shattered by the *Tangentopoli* investigations, the entrenched strongholds of power, together with the vested interest groups and the mighty patronage systems on which these rested, came out into the open and opted for the post-fascist lists. They set up their own organizational machine and ran for office in their own right rather than employing a political intermediary. As a result, the rise of 'Forza Italia' has transformed the forms and subjects of political communication, and therewith of representation and democracy as well, enriching political science with two new categories: that of the company-cum-party and the firm-cum-government. These comprise respectively the second and third most significant changes in Italy's material constitution.

It is commonly said that elections, as Schumpeter pointed out, are a competition between parties for the popular vote, not altogether unlike the kind of free competition that takes place between firms in the market. However, the 1994 elections saw a radical transformation of the electoral race. An unprecedented concentration of broadcasting media was mobilized in the electoral campaign behind not a party faction or a powerful lobby or pressure group, but the media owner himself. Within the space of a few weeks a political force was constructed in the company's advertising department, which proceeded to promote it using the same techniques as those adopted for launching a commercial product, thereby endowing political communication and consensus-making with the same characteristics as marketing and advertising. What is more, this operation was carried out in a near-monopoly regime. It marked the culmination of a process started in the 1980s which has turned politics into glitzy show-business and commodified it. The judicial hearings on graft and bribery laid bare the close link that had come to exist between wealth and politics – money as a means to finance political power, and political power as the key to amass wealth. This relationship, hitherto shrouded in secrecy, was now made explicit: money had openly been transformed into a resource for acquiring political power, and politics into a tool to reinforce economic power.

---

[2] By December 1994 the improvised coalition between Forza Italia, the post-fascists of Alleanza Nazionale, and the Lega Nord had collapsed, due to the sudden withdrawal of the latter from the government. This was hardly surprising, since – contrary to the general opinion that the right had won the elections of March 1994 – the coalition was the result of two separate electoral alliances, one between Forza Italia and the Lega in Northern Italy, and the other between Forza Italia and the Alleanza Nazionale in the rest of the country. The electoral pact had no common programme, it was only conceived in order to take advantage of the majoritarian electoral system introduced the previous year. The coalition scored 42% of the popular vote, gaining the majority of seats in only one of the two chambers, but collapsed as soon as disagreements emerged over economic policy and the regulation of the broadcasting system.

Today there is a tendency to play down or even dispute the role of television in the rise of Forza Italia. It cannot be denied that its success was also due to many other factors: the political void that had come to exist within the traditional governing powers after the earth shattering revelations of *Tangentopoli*; the weakness of the left and its inability to assert itself over its opponent; the craving for renewal and the general frustration with all the old parties; and the prospect of re-legitimization that a 'new' but decidedly conservative force seemed to offer the old electorate of the centre and the traditional interests that clustered around the centre ground. Nevertheless, it would be impossible to explain Silvio Berlusconi's electoral achievement without taking into account the role played by his television channels in supporting his programme, concocted as it was on the basis of market research into which kind of promises were most alluring to the electorate. Nobody, no matter how politically talented they were, could achieve such success without the support of the media.

The demise of political accommodation and compromise and the assumption of power by a party-cum-firm and its entrepreneur, who had been suddenly shorn of the representation and protection assured by the old governing powers, represents an even more profound distortion of representative democracy. This direct take-over of government violated elementary juridical principles, breaching the fundamental rules prevailing in all civilized countries – including Italy – whereby any conflict of interest is prohibited on the grounds of incompatibility. As a result of this infringement, tremendous economic power and the immense power of government came to be concentrated in the hands of one and the same person, thereby acting as mutually reinforcing factors. The outcome was that the covert amalgam of kickbacks and graft which formed the mainstay of *Tangentopoli* deals were in effect transmuted into overtly institutionalized deals.

This illegitimate confusion of interests has attracted the wildest comments, even from the opposition. The elections were hardly over when Achille Occhetto, the then leader of the PDS, who might have been expected to argue that Berlusconi was not a suitable head of the government and that the reins of power would have to be entrusted to any other candidate among the new majority, declared the exact opposite. 'Clearly', he said, Berlusconi had a 'duty' to form a government. After such a pronouncement by the leader of the opposition, the legitimation of Berlusconi as Prime Minister was a foregone conclusion. Numerous political commentators both on the right and left went so far as to speak of his 'right' to form the government. Furthermore, President Scalfaro even asserted – amid general agreement – that were he not to appoint Berlusconi, he could be held responsible for an 'attack on the constitution'.

A similar misunderstanding lay behind arguments to the effect that the Italian constitution does not contain rulings expressly precluding an owner of sizeable private interests – and the vast business empire in question is known to span a huge range of concerns, all the way from the media to advertising, publishing, show business, insurance and commercial distribution as well – from being appointed Prime Minister. But the existence of general principles of law, embodied in the Italian legal system as in all such systems, is thereby overlooked. This is particularly true of the principle excluding from public office those who have a private interest in matters falling under its purview. This principle is derivable from a long series of rules, the most important of which

are as follows: the constitutional duty of 'impartiality' of the public administration, which is subject to the 'unity of political and administrative governance of the Prime Minister'; the obligation, entered into by virtue of the oath of
allegiance to the constitution, requiring Prime Ministers to 'exercise the
functions of public office in the *exclusive* interests of the nation'; the code of
behaviour for state employees regulating conflicts of interest, abstention and
incompatibility approved by legislative decree N. 29/1992, which cannot
conceivably fail to hold for Prime Ministers as well; the principle of equality,
which does not countenance privileges or discrimination stemming from
particular interests; the annullability of acts, the obligation to abstain and the
responsibility for damages that apply to any administrator, even in the private
sector, on the basis of Arts. 1394 and 2391 of the Civil Code, and which come
into play whenever there arises a conflict of interest with the division or body of
which the administrator is a member, and more generally in any case where the
interests of a representative happen to conflict with the organization or people
he or she represents. Finally, there is the provision that 'abuse of office'
constitutes a criminal offence, punishable by Art. 323 of the penal code 'with a
sentence varying between two and five years'. Note that this offence is deemed
to occur whenever a state official draws private profit from the exercise of his
public functions. It need hardly be underlined that Berlusconi is doomed to
commit this offence whenever he fails to abstain from decisions that could in
some way favour his private interests, including collective decisions made in
conjunction with the Council of Ministers. No country in the world may have a
law forbidding the head of government to own three national television
networks: yet in all civilized countries, as indeed has universally been acknowledged, the Berlusconi phenomenon would be totally unthinkable, for in the
civilized world the principles of law are genuinely in effect and the rules are
taken seriously.

It is this direct occupation of government by a firm above all that testifies to a
break with the fundamental principle of the modern representative state:
namely, the separation of state and society, of the public and the private sphere,
of economic and political power. This separation, which is far more important
and fundamental than the intra-institutional separation of the three functions
of government, is not written into any constitution, since it forms part, as it
were, of the deeper constitutional beliefs of every democracy. Yet it represents
nothing short of the basic premise of the political-representative state. This
form of government was made possible by overcoming the confusion between
sovereignty and property that was the hallmark of the pre-modern state based
on private estates. With the ensuing growing independence of the public from
the private sphere came the concept of political and representative mediation
between the two separate spheres.

The occupation of government by a firm is arguably the most significant and
innovative transformation of the Italian material constitution, heralding a new
form of state that has no precedent in the history of democracy. A government-
cum-firm based on the confidence of a company-cum-party provides an
extraordinary reproduction of the pre-modern pre-democratic confusion
between public and private, with a consequent distortion of both the state
and the market. This development was bound to lead, first and foremost, to a
major upset in the whole system of institutional balance, if for no other reason
than that the ruling group of the company-cum-party occupying the benches in

Parliament in their capacity as the majority party was composed of the self-same individuals as the top executives of the company-cum-party owned by the head of the government-cum-firm. Secondly, Parliament's role as a controller and watchdog has been undermined and contaminated by the private salaried employee relation that ties many of the present Members of Parliament to their leader-manager. Finally, the authoritarian model of the firm and the inegalitarian logic of the market has been imposed onto the institutions of the state, according to a neocorporative paradigm of which the Fascists form an organic and far from coincidental component.

This view is confirmed by the fact that the majority has acted without any sense of there being limits on its power. The desire of the businessman to achieve a monopoly was transferred lock, stock and barrel to the political sphere, resulting in an interpretation of the majority principle according to the logic of the stock company, as absolute dominion. The attack on the national broadcasting corporation, the RAI, launched with the aim of wiping out or controlling the state television networks and reinforcing the Fininvest[3] channels, is extremely instructive in this respect. It expresses at one and the same time a whole host of related phenomena: the major role given to television within politics, the dramatic and potentially criminal conflict between the public and private interest, and the spirit of appropriation and domination that seeks to neutralize all traces of pluralism in the name of the majority principle.

What is a Democratic Constitution?

This transformation of the material constitution of the state and the conception of democracy as the omnipotence of the majority formed the basis for the project for reform of the 1948 constitution put forward by the victorious coalition shortly after the elections. This proposal was immediately championed by numerous politicians in the governing parties, who argued that a new constitution could be framed by a majority without consulting the minority.

This thesis was formulated – with his accustomed clarity and bluntness – by Gianfranco Miglio.[4] He stated in an interview:

> It is wrong to say that a constitution must embody the wishes of the entire people. A constitution is a pact that the victorious powers impose on the defeated side. It can be changed, and in fact this possibility is provided for

---

[3] Fininvest is the holding company of Berlusconi's commercial empire.

[4] Cf. G. Miglio, *Una Repubblica migliore per gli italiani* (Milano, Giuffrè, 1983); and *La regolarità della politica* (Milano, Giuffrè, 1988). Gianfranco Miglio was professor of constitutional law at the Catholic University (Milan) and was elected to the Italian Senate in the lists of the Northern League, acting for a while as their main constitutional adviser and ideologue on the federalist issue. After the League's withdrawal from the Berlusconi government, Miglio resigned from the party and became closer to Forza Italia. Miglio's conception of the constitution as the expression of the will of the majority, and his preference for a presidential republic in opposition to the current parliamentary system, is largely indebted to Carl Schmitt, whose thought Miglio was one of the first to disseminate in Italy: cf. Miglio's 'Presentazione' in C. Schmitt (P. Schiera, trans.), *Le categorie del politico* (Bologna, Il Mulino, 1972). However, Miglio is only the most authoritarian exponent of a more general movement for the reform of the constitution, which has generated a confused debate in Italy over the past fifteen years. Although this movement contains a variety of positions, all share the idea that the crisis of the Italian political system results not from the unrepresentative nature of the political class and from mounting corruption, but from certain unspecified inadequacies of the Constitution of 1948.

within the constitution itself, as part of Article 138, which deals expressly with the question of constitutional change. All that is required is half the votes in Parliament plus one. What is my dream? That the Northern League and Forza Italia obtain half plus one. Half of the Italians frame the constitution for the other half as well. After that, it's just a question of maintaining law and order on the streets.[5]

Are there any grounds for this view? Is the amendment procedure laid down by Art. 138 – two consecutive deliberations by the two Houses, the second of which requires an absolute majority, and the possibility of a referendum at the request of the minority[6] – sufficient to modify not just a particular clause but rather the entire constitution? Should one not enquire whether there exist certain core principles not subject to amendment and an overall constitutional set-up not accessible to normal amendment procedures? In other words, can a majority impose a new constitution on a minority? Underlying this question, I would argue, there lies the deeper issue of the concept and nature of a *democratic constitution* and, more particularly, the significance of the 1948 constitution for Italian democracy. This issue in its turn is but another facet of the debate on the nature of democracy, which is generally associated both on the right and the left with the concept of the absolute power of the majority – a misconception somewhat confusedly reinforced by the lengthy campaign in favour of the majoritarian or 'first past the post' electoral system.

Against this partisan interpretation, the analysis of democratic constitutions – not only the Italian, but in general – allows us to identify two dimensions that lie at the heart of every modern democracy: the political dimension, by virtue of which democracy is the power of the majority, and the judicial dimension of the rule of law, by virtue of which even the power of the majority is subject to legal regulations and limits established to guarantee the fundamental rights of all. Both of these dimensions are embodied in their respective classes of constitutional rules: on the one hand, the formal rules determining *who* takes decisions and *how*, which, thanks to the equality of political rights, guarantee the representativeness of parliamentary institutions and government by the majority, and on the other hand, the substantive rules determining *what* must or must not be decided. These substantive rules are identified with the rights to freedom, which the state must not violate, and social rights, which it must satisfy. While the first set of rules relates to the *form* of decisions and makes up the formal dimension of democracy and of the rule of law in the broad or weak sense, the second set of rules relates to the *substance* or content of decisions and provides the substantive dimension of democracy and the rule of law in the narrow or strong sense. Thanks to this second class of norms, the

---

[5] *Indipendente*, 25 March 1994.

[6] Art. 138 of the Italian Constitution says: 'The laws for amendment of the Constitution, and the other constitutional laws, shall be adopted by each Chamber with two successive deliberations spaced not less than three months apart, and shall be approved by an absolute majority of the components of each Chamber in the second ballot.

The laws themselves shall be submitted to a people's referendum if this is requested within three months of their publication by one fifth of the members of one Chamber or by five hundred thousand electors or by five Regional Councils. The law submitted to the referendum shall not be promulgated if it is not approved by a majority of the valid votes.

No referendum shall take place if the law has been approved in the second ballot by each of the Chambers with a two-thirds majority of its components.'

principle of legality, that hallmark of the modern constitutional state based on the rule of law, has been enriched by a substantive rationality, which supplements the formal rationality of the older legal positivism founded on the absolute primacy of the legislator and the Rousseauian paradigm of political democracy as the omnipotence of the majority.[7]

These two classes of rules are to be found in all constitutions. In the Italian constitution, for instance, the substantive norms are those contained in the first part, and the formal norms those in the second. The former lay down the *ends* of the legal system, the latter establish the organs of the state as the *means* for their satisfaction. A constitutional state based on the rule of law is none other than an instrument composed of these norms. It is by virtue of these norms that no absolute powers exist within the state. All powers are subject to the law in the twofold sense that all powers, including the power of majority rule, can be exercised only in the manner established by the formal norms, and all powers are furthermore subject to substantive norms that impose limits and constraints on the content of their decisions.

What is termed a *constitution* consists precisely of such a system of rules, both substantive and formal, that bind those who hold the reins of power. This description corresponds to the definition of a constitution proclaimed two centuries ago in Art. 16 of the 1789 Declaration of Rights: 'A society where rights are not secured or the separation of powers established has no constitution at all'. Constitutions are thus characterized by a set of meta-rules concerning public powers, including powers attributed to the majority, that ensure both their reciprocal separation and their respect for the fundamental rights of all subjects. It follows that since fundamental rights form the basis of equality *en droits*, constitutions always directly or indirectly stand as a guarantee of equality: political equality through the bestowal of political rights, civil equality through the guarantee of civil rights, and at least minimum levels of social equality through the satisfaction of social rights. Seen from this perspective, a constitution represents much more than the mere fulfilment of the rule of law achieved by extending the principle of legality to all powers, including legislative power. A constitution also constitutes a political programme for the future: namely, the enunciation of negative and positive imperatives addressed to the public powers that act not only as a source of their legitimacy but also, signally, of their potential delegitimacy. They shape utopias of positive law, which may well never be perfectly achievable, yet inasmuch as they express the law concerning the law, embody prospectuses for the transformation of the law itself in the direction of the equality of fundamental rights.

This function of imposing a limit and constraint on the majority in order to safeguard the rights of all subjects would in itself suffice to preclude the risk that a constitution could become a pliant tool in the hands of the majority. It would likewise ensure that due recognition is given to the role of the constitution as a founding pact designed to keep the peace and secure the coexistence of extremes.

---

[7] I have suggested a re-definition of democracy along such lines, that establishes connections between its various dimensions and particular types of fundamental rights (political, civil, and social), in *Diritto e ragione. Teoria del garantismo penale* (Roma-Bari, Laterza, 1989), pp. 895–909. For a further elaboration of this thesis, see also my 'Il diritto come sistema di garanzia', *Ragion Pratica*, 1 (1993), 143–61, and 'Note critiche and autocritiche intorno alla discussione su *Diritto e ragione*' in L. Gianformaggio (ed.), *Le ragioni del garantismo. Discutendo con Luigi Ferrajoli* (Torino, Giappichelli, 1993), pp. 505–20.

If this pact is to guarantee civil co-existence between virtually hostile subjects, it must necessarily involve, first and foremost, an agreement among contrasting and extreme political forces. And if it provides the rules of the game that guarantee the correctness of the procedures adopted in reaching agreements, clearly the rules themselves must necessarily be established by all the players. By the same token, if the rules are intended to be binding on the constituted authorities, i.e. on the established powers that form part of the law of the land, then they cannot be modified or derogated from by these authorities, but only by a constituent assembly that will renegotiate the forms and constraints pertaining to a constituted authority. Finally, if the substantive constitutional norms are none other than the fundamental rights, then they belong to us all, since we are all holders of fundamental rights. It is this common entitlement that lies behind democracy and popular sovereignty correctly understood.

It should be clear from the foregoing arguments that its contractual nature is intrinsic to the very notion of a constitution. This is true both philosophically and historically. On the philosophical plane, it is the fruit of the contractualistic idea, formulated by Hobbes and later developed by juridical thinkers of the Enlightenment period, according to which the state, contrary to the classical and premodern conception, is not a natural phenomenon but is instead an artificial and conventional construct, built by people for the protection of their needs or natural rights. The latter, in Hobbes' view, are represented by the right to life, while Locke places emphasis on the right to freedom and property. In modern constitutionalism these categories have been extended to include political and social rights. This basic conception of modern juridical civilization entails a striking inversion of the Aristotelian conception of law and the political community: what is natural is neither law nor the state, but non-law and the state of nature, i.e. human beings made of flesh and bones with all their needs and natural rights. By contrast, the state is an artifact justifiable only as a means for the safeguarding of natural persons. In this sense the idea of the social contract is a great metaphor for democracy in both its dimensions – a metaphor for political or formal democracy, in that the legitimation of public power is founded on the consent of the contracting parties, but at the same time a metaphor for the rule of law and substantive democracy, inasmuch as this consent is conditional on respect for those natural rights that have been agreed upon and recognized as necessary for the protection of all persons.

Constitutional charters and declarations of rights are no more than a written expression of social contracts, whose clauses are composed of the fundamental principles and rights which are 'natural' in origin but become 'positive' and 'constitutional' by virtue of the very fact of being written down. Such clauses are equivalent to the democratic convention regarding those matters that are not discretionary either because they cannot be made the subject of a decision, such as denials or limitations of the rights to freedom, or because they must be decided, such as the satisfaction of social rights. In this regard the rule of law precedes political democracy, and not only historically – in the sense that it arose side by side with constitutional monarchy long before representative democracy – but also axiologically, in that it forms a set of limits and constraints on political democracy itself. That which cannot be compromised by political democracy, even when the latter is sustained by unanimous consent, is precisely this set of fundamental rights. These rights actually work against majority rule, for the very reason that they have been pre-ordained as inalienable and inviolable rights against any absolute power and for the protection of all subjects.

The historical genesis of constitutions, as written charters imposed on the sovereign in order to limit the monarch's otherwise absolute power, also confirms their contractual nature. All constitutions worthy of the name originated as breaks with the past that were also programmatic conventions on the future. The idea of a social contract is not merely a philosophical category. Rather, it coincides with the very idea of liberation through revolution and the refounding of civil coexistence on a contractual basis, accomplished through the constitutional conventions that enabled the founding fathers of the modern rule-of-law-based state to set their seal on the end of royal absolutism. On this interpretation, it is not only the American and French constitutions that can be viewed as revolutionary Charters, but also the overwhelming majority of European constitutions which emerged during the first half of the last century. None of these constitutions were granted spontaneously from on high, nor were they worked out by jurists sitting at the drawing board. All of them represented the victorious outcome of bloody popular revolts in which the people gave voice to their constitutive will. This origin is what differentiates such constitutions from those simply worked out on paper, variously *octroyé* or straightforwardly copied from European models, as was the case with many of the Latin American ones.

The Italian constitution is the product of just such a revolutionary break with the past. It represents the culmination of the Resistance and the war of liberation that rid Italy- of the Fascist dictatorship. Furthermore, it is indissolubly connected with antifascism, both theoretically and historically. It is antifascist by definition, i.e by its very nature as a democratic constitution, inasmuch as it is composed of the fundamental rights and democratic rules that were denied by Fascism and indeed represent the negation of Fascism. It is antifascist also because it originated, historically, from the Resistance. Antifascism is thus its genetic and constitutive element, mirroring the way antifascism represents the bedrock of contemporary democracy. From its antifascist roots democracy has gained self-awareness, which has allowed its substantive elements to come to the fore. In this sense 1945, no less than 1789, represents one of the crowning achievements in the history of refounded democracy, endowing the democratic concept with deeper significance: for the horrors of Nazism and Fascism, from whose ruins the constitution arose, have made it painfully clear that majority consensus, or even unanimous consensus, can no longer be considered the sole *source* of legitimate power. Fascism, in fact, was not the despotic power of a minority, but the suppression of fundamental rights, and therefore the negation of any constitution and any democracy. And this is a phenomenon no majority consensus is sufficient to legitimize.

The Limits to the Power of Amendment

If it is accepted that the meaning of a democratic constitution is that outlined above, it can readily be understood that in the current debate on constitutional reform the overwhelming concern is not the actual content of the proposals for change – federalism, presidentialism, elimination of the progressive nature of taxation, reform of the Supreme Council of the Judiciary,[8] suppression of the independence of the public prosecutor,[9] and so forth – but rather the proposed method of approval for such changes, namely the proposal to establish a 'majoritarian constitution'.

This is the most pernicious aspect of the project. It signals a willingness to call into question the constitutional contract on which Italian democracy has so far been grounded and to modify the basis of political legitimacy. Some such desire, which in the intentions of its proponents was to be brought into effect independently of the contents of the new constitution, would appear to have been backed by all the components of the Berlusconi majority coalition, each of them being interested, for reasons of their own, in creating a disjuncture in the history of the Republic. They aimed at the formal legitimation of the three changes in the material constitution mentioned at the beginning of this chapter: the end of the antifascist basis, the establishment of media power as the instrument for organizing consent, and the confusion of public and private powers inherent in the new governing coalition. These three elements, together with the affirmation of the omnipotence of the majority as a result of the transformation of the constituent pact into a pact imposed by the winners onto the losers, are tantamount to a negation of the democratic constitution in the sense defended here. Its dual function of limiting and regulating public bodies, and of guaranteeing fundamental rights and ensuring the separation of powers would have gone. The contractual nature of constitutional principles would be swept away, and with it the nature of these principles as the common heritage of all people, not merely of the majority.

What we must therefore now turn to is the juridical scope of Art. 138, i.e. that article on the basis of which it is claimed that a majority constitution can in fact be set up. A brief preliminary word on the meaning and role of this Article is in order. Art. 138 is a guarantee provided by the constitution against the enactment of rash or inconsiderate changes by ordinary law-makers.[10] Such a norm does not exist in legal systems grounded on ancient traditions of democracy and constitutionalism, such as the British. A norm of the type embodied in Art. 138 is an invention of modern constitutionalism, which in no way affects the guarantees enshrined in the constitution, nor does it impair the constitution's sacral and contractual nature. Rather, it serves to highlight and preserve such features. Consequently, it is absurd for such a rule to be interpreted as authorizing the majority to introduce whatsoever change they may desire.

The provision laid down in Art. 138, requiring a more complex procedure for constitutional reform than for the modification of ordinary legislation, should not be confused with the 'rigidity' of the constitution.[11] Constitutional law is

---

[8] The *Consiglio superiore della magistratura*, roughly translated here as the 'Supreme Council of the Judiciary', is presided over by the President of the Republic and is the supreme governing body of the judiciary.

[9] The *pubblico ministero*, roughly translated here as the 'public prosecutor', is the representative of the public interest before the judicial authorities. As soon as a civil or criminal offence becomes known to a *pubblico ministero*, the latter has an obligation to initiate the relevant penal action.

[10] The *legislatore ordinario*, roughly translated here as 'ordinary law-makers', refers to the organs empowered to enact legislation that is not protected by the special procedures laid down for constitutional laws; 'ordinary legislation' can be modified or repealed by a subsequent law.

[11] Rigidity is a term employed by jurists in order to denote the strict formality and importance of certain constitutional norms: namely, those which ought not to be violated or changed.

not uniquely characterized by rigidity, even though this quality provides it with a formal guarantee. Rather, rigidity is a structural feature of the constitution, generated, to be sure, partly by the diversified and more complex procedures laid down for its amendment, but primarily ascribable to the fact that the constitution is ranked at the apex of the hierarchy of the sources of law. It occupies this position by virtue of other constitutional norms that define its role and its nature as a series of constraints imposed on any other power. One such norm is Art. 2, which proclaims the 'inviolable' character of fundamental rights; other cases in point are Arts. 134 and 136, which establish, respectively, the invalidity of ordinary legislation held to be in conflict with the constitution, and the limit imposed on the various different powers through the constitutionally established allocation of institutional functions. Compared to the rigidity of the constitution, which is intrinsic to the hierarchical character of a constitutional state grounded in the rule of law and an inherent feature of the power to adjudicate on the constitutionality of laws and to mediate any conflict of powers, the amendment procedure laid down by Art. 138 is a simple guarantee. Its weakness certainly provides no justification for the indiscriminate subversion of the constitution.

This framework gives rise to a series of limitations on the power of amendment enshrined in Art. 138, which, it should be borne in mind, is a constituted power and not a constitutive power. These limitations are all linked to the concept of a rigid constitution, although some are explicit and absolute, while others are implicit and relative. The explicit and absolute limitations are embodied in the fundamental rights, defined in Art. 2 of the constitution as 'inviolable' and identified by Art. 16 of the 1789 Declaration with the very notion of a constitution. These rights, as incontrovertibly emerges from doctrinal writings on public law and as is plainly stated in numerous sentences handed down by the Constitutional Court (N. 1146/1988, N. 88 and 366/1991), make up a nucleus of core principles that cannot be suppressed, limited or weakened by any majority.

The implicit and relative limitations, in contrast, arise from those articles pertaining to changes in the form of the state or government. In part they follow on from the link between the first and second part of the constitution with regard to guarantees, particularly the jurisdictional ones, safeguarding the independence of the judiciary and the controlling role exercised by the Constitutional Court. Equally important in this respect, however, is the very nature of a constitution, understood as a system of rules designed to regulate the exercise of public power. If it had no special status every change in the parliamentary majority or the ruling class would potentially act as a prelude to a *coup d'état*. For example, if the Berlusconi government had enjoyed the same majority in the Senate as it did in the Chamber of Deputies, one might have envisioned the granting of full powers to the Prime Minister, or the suppression of the independence of the judiciary or of the institutional functions of the Constitutional Court, followed, say, by a referendum-plebiscite to confirm the changes enacted by the Government.

Naturally, all this does not imply that Art. 138 precludes revising the constitution in anything other than a purely marginal manner with regard to specific clauses, as has been the case to date, and as was exemplified in the recent modification of Art. 68 on parliamentary immunity. Rather, what it means is that in addition to the formal constraints laid down by Art. 138 there also exist substantive limits on constitutional amendment. Certain limits of this kind admit of no exceptions, such as the inviolability of fundamental rights, while others can be overcome but only on condition that there be no sabotaging of the contractual nature of the constitution and its role as a fundamental law safeguarding the rights of all subjects. Now in the intentions of the makers of the constitution, Art. 138 was designed precisely in order to ensure that this condition would be satisfied. But today this guarantee, which was intrinsically weak even under the old proportional electoral system, has been further weakened by the introduction of the majoritarian system, by virtue of which the absolute majority of members of parliament required for amendment can effectively be reached by a relative majority of the electorate. Nevertheless, this circumstance in no way reduces the substantive limits imposed on the power of amendment by the concept of a democratic constitution.

Thus, while it would be wrong to talk of a constitution as unchangeable, it is equally clear that what is envisioned is a possibility of reform that is almost always partial. In such cases, reform cannot be made to work merely to the advantage of the contingent majorities championing this or that proposal, since they are usually excluded from the final approval procedures. Instead, any modification must seek to evoke the participation of extremely broad and disinterested majorities, accommodate prolonged reflection and debate, and thereby necessarily lead to an outcome of improvement and reinforcement of constitutional guarantees that will be to the advantage of all.

Clearly, a constitution conceived as a founding contract for the regulation of public powers to guarantee the rights of all subjects contains within itself the space for internal amendment and sets limits on this power. These provisions allow one to identify a rigorous and highly precise meta-juridical criterion that distinguishes between those areas of the constitution that may be modified on the basis of Art. 138 from those that may not.

Art. 138 is intended to prevent any modification of the constitution that works to the advantage of one political grouping at the expense of another, or that effectively amounts to an infringement of the principle of equality. Thus it would be inadmissible for a political force that had achieved a majority in Parliament to seek to draw advantage from the situation and change the form of government from Parliamentary to Presidential, for instance by granting full powers to the Prime Minister and divesting Parliament of its functions. If there were no such restriction, any party leader who had won an election giving an absolute majority in both Chambers of Parliament – as is perfectly possible under a majoritarian system – could usher in a dictatorship within the brief space of three months. This would be absurd, since it would conflict with the very nature of constitutional democracy, or, for that matter, with the general principles of any type of constitutional law.

In contrast, Art. 138 and the contractual nature of constitutions, allow any constitutional modification which leads to the overall benefit of all subjects and reinforces constitutional guarantees. For any change in these directions will be inspired by the principle of equality, which in the last analysis, as pointed out earlier, is the guiding principle of all democratic constitutions. The contractual nature of a constitution does not entail the defence and preservation of the literal text of the constitution: rather, it invites modification and even re-foundation in order to keep abreast with the constant flow of new aspirations and techniques for the safeguarding of rights and equality. Thus Art. 138

allows any extension or reinforcement of fundamental rights and their associated guarantees in such matters as pertain to the environment, peace, newscasting and the press, criminal court proceedings, political and social rights. Similarly, it would be not only possible but right and proper in the wake of the reform of the electoral system in a majoritarian direction to raise the quorum required for election to all organs empowered with safeguarding constitutional guarantees, in particular the Presidency of the Republic, the judges of the Constitutional Court, and the members of the Supreme Council of the Judiciary. Nor would it be impossible to follow the example of Germany in extending to citizens whose fundamental rights have been violated the legitimate right to call for a review of the offending measure's constitutionality, or at least to grant such a right to substantial parliamentary minorities. Finally, a further possibility, which would be even more opportune given the circumstances, would be to strengthen the actual amendment procedures enshrined in Art. 138, in line with the kind of safeguards in force in other more advanced democracies.

It is precisely this last possibility that is proving the most fertile source of inspiration in tackling current proposals for constitutional reforms affecting changes either in the form of government, for example from a Parliamentary to a Presidential system, or in the form of the state, for example from a centralized to a federal type. It should be borne in mind that Art. 138 was conceived in the framework of a proportional electoral system, and was designed to be interpreted within this context. As a consequence, the recent electoral reform law, ushering in a majoritarian system – together with the role played by the mass media in forging consensus, and their present concentration in the hands of the majority – would imply that recourse to Art. 138 should be limited to the extension of fundamental rights and guarantees. Moreover, this new situation calls for greater weight and complexity in the procedures laid down for any constitutional reform affecting either the form of the state or that of the government. Among possible models to emulate, the type of constitutional amendment procedures offering the most meaningful guarantees are undoubtedly those in force in the United States, Belgium, Denmark and Greece, where total revision of the constitution is excluded and definitive approval of amendments is entrusted to different organs from those which proposed the amendment. However, even adoption of the model introduced in Spain, Switzerland, Germany and Japan would represent a substantial step forward, since in these countries amendments always require a two-thirds majority and total revision, where provided for, as in Spain and Switzerland, gives rise to procedures that are so intricate and burdensome as to make any hot-headed improvization or self-seeking moves by interested parties well-nigh impossible.

To disguise the wholesale rewriting of the constitution – or even of its second part, or of heterogenous parts of it – as an amendment based on Art. 138 would be illegitimate, therefore. Quite apart from any other considerations, such 'amendments' would make a mockery of the institution of the referendum enshrined in this article, since sentences 16/1978, 22, 28 and 29/1981, 27/1982 and 47/1991 issued by the Constitutional Court on the subject of abrogative referenda, which are equally valid, if not more so, when applied to constitutional referenda, specify that propositions to be decided by a referendum must deal with 'homogeneous' issues, in order to ensure free elections and the true expression of the popular will. If the object of 'amendment' were either the entire constitution or heterogeneous institutions (for instance, federalism and presidentialism), then the referendum would be nothing more than a confirming plebiscite, i.e. the exact opposite of a 'control referendum' (*referendum di controllo*), whose promotion belongs to the opposition, as intended by Art. 138. Even less legitimate would be the approval of an entirely new constitution, passed by a constituent assembly summoned for the purpose. Such a step, contemplated in some quarters, would be in flagrant conflict with Art. 138. This quandary could only be circumvented by introducing the assembly on the basis of a reform of Art. 138, for instance on the model of Art. 168 of the Spanish constitution, which provides for the convocation of such an assembly after the dissolution of the *Cortes*. In the Spanish framework dissolution is proclaimed once a two-thirds majority of the *Cortes* have proposed the new text, and the procedure is made watertight by the additional requirements that the text be approved by both the new *Cortes* and a referendum by the same majority.

The Crisis of Constitutionalism and its Roots

Unfortunately the idea that the constitution can be revised or even rewritten by a majority is widespread, not only amongst the former governing coalition but also amongst the opposition. It signals a sense of disorientation as to the meaning of the constitution, and represents the outcome of a prolonged crisis of constitutional legality.

This crisis has undermined the constitution in at least two different ways. Of particular importance is the way in which, in recent years, fundamental rules of the 1948 constitution have often been disregarded: one need only think of the Italian participation in the Gulf War in violation of Art. 11, the tendency of presidential powers to stray and trespass into other sectors during the last two years of Cossiga's presidency; the severe blow dealt to Art. 138 by the setting-up of the Bicameral Commission, not to mention the restrictions on health care, social security and fair wages brought in by the last few governments. But there have also been other deeper and more destructive pressures, which have undermined not so much the specifics of the Italian constitution but constitutionalism in general – not this particular contract, but the very idea of a binding contract, not these specific rules but the existence of rules as such. What is being called into question is the very value of rules, starting from the elementary meta-principle of the rule of law that requires all powers to be subject to a higher system of rules whose function is to safeguard fundamental rights which neither the market nor politics can encroach upon.

This is the most serious damage done by those, including the entire political class, not least the left, who, in recent years have denigrated the constitution as outmoded and outdated. Over and above any individual constitutional violations, what has been breached is the sense and value of the constitution as a rigid system of limits and constraints on politics. At one point it seemed as if all the ills of the country – 'blocked democracy', the inefficiency of the state, corruption itself – were to be blamed on the 'rules', and that the overwhelming problem was how to change them and enact constitutional reform. Throughout the past decade, the political system has endeavoured to veil its own crisis of representation and its growing alienation from society at large by making institutional reform, first in the form of a debate over the relative merits of parliamentarism and presidentialism, and then in discussions of the electoral question, the central issue of politics.

A second factor has also contributed, albeit paradoxically, to the crisis of constitutional legality: namely the discovery of *Tangentopoli* and the attendant system of illegality that has characterized political life in Italy over the last decade. The feeling of revulsion kindled by this discovery has not only led to an irreversible revolt against the old parties, but also to a profound delegitimation of the state and the public sphere. This loathing even taints the republican constitution, held to be hand in glove with government-by-the-parties (*partito-crazia*) and unscrupulous wheeler-dealing. Consequently, disgust with the old political system has resolved itself into out and out – albeit contradictory – delegitimation not only of its mode of functioning but also of its normative dimension. Rejection of the system thus extends beyond the illegal activities of politicians to include the constitutional framework in which politics should be carried out. It is in this attitude that one must seek an account of the distrust of institutions, the anti-statalist polemics and the success of slogans such as the primacy of the market and unlimited liberalism which in 1994 culminated in the electoral victory of the right.

It is hardly surprising that a delegitimizing crisis of such dimensions, which threatens to uproot the state and jeopardize its social functions, triggered a stampede towards a 'new era', sweeping away rational comprehension of the constitution and obliterating it from the political horizon. There can be no other explanation for the brash attempts to tamper with the constitution manifested by those who won the elections, and their approach to the welfare state, so eloquently revealed in their blueprint for change: for example, state funding of private education, in conflict with Art. 33 of the constitution which lays down that private schools are set up 'without financial aid from the state', or the flat taxation rate – 30% or 33% – in contrast with Art. 53 of the constitution which states that the Italian 'fiscal system is based on the criterion of progressive taxation', or again, the running down of the national health service, thereby degrading health care from 'a fundamental right of the individual', as it is described in Art. 32 of the constitution, to a commodity to be negotiated with insurance companies.

What these proposals ultimately amount to is a *de facto* break-down of the constitutional contract on which Italian democracy was founded: a contract that was grounded on the principle of equality and on a commitment to remove inequality through the guarantee of social rights. The spectre of a twofold disintegration thus rears its head: on the one hand the ominous risk of secession and fiscal federalism threatened by the Northern League, compounded by the conflict the League has opted to foment between the rich North and the poor South. On the other, the rampant animosity between the affluent sectors of the population and the working classes, between rich and poor, strong and weak. Thus a horizontal (territorial) break-down is paralleled by a vertical (social) collapse, both striking at the roots of the unity of the nation whose constitu-tional ground rules stipulate equality of fundamental social rights throughout the nation. The wording of Art. 2 is explicit on this matter, when it defines the rights to health care, education, social security and national insurance as connected to the 'inviolable rights of political, economic and social solidarity'.

Faced with a crisis of such dimensions, it is obviously purely illusory to endorse the face-saving idea – still circulating among the opposition groups – of taking part in the current re-foundation process by contributing 'constructive' proposals for change in the hope of dispelling the notion that the left is in some sense conservative. Given the current weakness of the left and the avowed intention of the Berlusconi coalition to rebuff any support from the minority, the only effect of such a decision would be to legitimize the method adopted by the majority, and therewith any constitutional changes they might see fit to introduce. Instead, if there is any chance of salvaging the constitution from subversive attacks, it consists in a principled challenge to such moves by reinforcing the sacral and contractual nature of the constitution in the popular social imagination, in order to defend the one and only truly democratic form of national identity: what Habermas calls 'constitutional patriotism'.[12]

Constitutions, and the law in general, are but a set of meanings. They stand and function as long as their values are shared by the wider community. Otherwise, they vanish, together with the principles they guarantee, without any need for a *coup d'état* or institutional change. If it is true that the present crisis of constitutional constraints derives above all from a weakening of their hold on the popular consciousness, then any proposal for a democratic alternative must start out from a re-foundation of the sense of a constitutional contract and the conception of the rule of law that flows from it. The defence of this contract will only succeed to the extent that each individual regards it as a defence of his or her own rights and identity as a citizen.[13]

---

[12] J. Habermas (L. Ceppa, Italian trans.), *Morale, diritto, politica* (Torino, Einaudi, 1992), p. 116.

[13] This essay was written before the 1996 Italian General Elections. Its focus is therefore on the constitutional fall-out of the previous elections, which resulted in the short-lived Berlusconi Government. Recent political changes, however, do not affect the arguments developed in this essay, since constitutional reform is still high on the political agenda in Italy and proposals for a 'majoritarian constitution' – which the author criticizes – find support in both political and academic discussion. [*Eds*]

Understanding the British Constitution

Tony Prosser[1]

Introduction

A familiar theme within discussions of the British constitution is that it has a peculiarly 'pragmatic' or 'common sense' character, and that this means that it is difficult to debate the constitution in specifically constitutional terms. Of course there is a lively debate about constitutional reform and constitutional politics.[2] However, it is a debate conducted in what are essentially political terms. Partly because of the lack of an authoritative source of constitutional principle in the form of a Supreme Court or Constitutional Council, we have difficulty in finding the necessary concepts for a debate which would deal in principles which are foundational in the sense of providing a framework within which key political concepts, such as the meaning of democracy and its relationship to concepts of rights, could be built up.[3] Whilst it is correct as a matter of theory to suggest that constitutions are both outside and within politics,[4] in the UK constitutional debate is particularly within politics.

In this chapter I will offer one explanation for the lack of debate over fundamental constitutional principles that is rarely explicitly acknowledged but which historically has had a fundamental effect; namely, a peculiarly anthropomorphic view of public power and of government which conceives of the state in a personalized form. I shall then contrast this conception with the developing European constitution and argue that whereas parliamentary sovereignty and a strong system of rights appear incompatible from a traditional British perspective, within the context of the more developed concept of democracy associated with European constitutionalism the two prove mutually reinforcing.[5]

---

[1] I am grateful for comments on the draft of this essay to my colleagues John Tasiolas, Elspeth Attwooll, Hilary Hiram and Jim Murdoch, and also to the editors of this volume and other participants at the Workshop on 'The Constitution in Transformation' held at the University of East Anglia in September 1995.
[2] See e.g. A. Barnett, C. Ellis and P. Hirst, *Debating the Constitution* (Oxford, Polity, 1992) and Institute for Public Policy Research, *A Constitution for the United Kingdom* (London, Institute for Public Policy Research, 1991).
[3] See, e.g., T. Daintith, 'Political programmes and the content of the constitution' in W. Finnie, C. Himsworth and N. Walker (eds), *Edinburgh Essays in Public Law* (Edinburgh, Edinburgh University Press, 1991), pp. 41–55 and I. Harden, 'The constitution and its discontents', *British Journal of Political Science*, 21 (1991), 489–510.
[4] J. Dearlove, 'Bringing the constitution back in: political science and the state', *Political Studies*, 37 (1989), 521–39.
[5] Compare R. Bellamy, 'The constitution of Europe: rights or democracy?' in R. Bellamy, V. Bufacchi and D. Castiglione (eds), *Democracy and Constitutional Culture in the Union of Europe* (London, Lothian Foundation, 1995), pp. 153–75 and J. Waldron, 'A right-based critique of constitutional rights' *Oxford Journal of Legal Studies*, 13 (1993), 18–51.

The Personalization of Government: its Origins

In the UK we lack a developed concept of the state; we have a 'stateless' society where instead of debate centring around an abstract concept of public power it has been more concerned with the exercise of that power in concrete instances.[6] As Dyson puts it:

> From the seventeenth century onwards England departed from general European development. The political and legal concept of the state was not developed and the term little used. ... Reference was made to kingdom, country, people, nation and government. The term state was occasionally used as a synonym for the nation or community as a whole, for example by Blackstone and Edmund Burke, but not as an expression for the legal personality of the executive or as a collective term for the whole or part of the machinery of government.[7]

A major influence in this was the fact that '[f]rom the seventeenth century onwards England's political development displayed a remarkable continuity from its medieval roots. One reason for this divergence from the European norm was the character of the medieval heritage from which it sprang'.[8] One important result was that, even after the end of the personal role of the monarch in government, the concept of the Crown, or of the Crown-in-Parliament, remained the main legal articulation of central public power. This is of course a highly personalized conception of government; it has 'no notion of a distinct "public power" which had been established by the people and which required its own public law'.[9] Instead, '[a] further consequence was an anthropomorphic conception of government. The hitching of monarchical prerogatives on to parliamentarianism, combined with ministerial responsibility, meant that governments became personified in the "over-life-size" role of ministers. Powers were conferred by statute on a named person, not on the impersonal state as a corporation, and were exercised in his, not the ministry's, name.'[10]

It is important to stress that this argument is distinct from what one might term sociological arguments about the actual location of power within government, for example the degree to which power has been centralized under the Prime Minister's personal control. Nor does it suggest that a Parliamentary system such as the UK is necessarily more centralized than Presidential systems elsewhere. Rather, it points to the lack of a distinctive system of public law; as J. D. B. Mitchell pointed out in a pioneering and brilliant critique, 'public law is often regarded as a series of unfortunate exceptions to the desirable generality or universality of the rules of private law, and is not seen as a rational system with its own justifications, and perhaps its own philosophy'.[11] Again the cause is historical, in particular the circumstances around the last overt revolution in 1688. This also serves to distinguish the UK from the United States where both constitutional and administrative law are far more fully

---

[6] See generally K. Dyson, *The State Tradition in Western Europe* (Oxford, Martin Robertson, 1980) and Dearlove, 'Bringing the constitution back in', pp. 522–3.

[7] Dyson, *The State Tradition in Western Europe*, p. 37.

[8] Dyson, *The State Tradition in Western Europe*, p. 38.

[9] Dyson, *The State Tradition in Western Europe*, p. 40.

[10] Dyson, *The State Tradition in Western Europe*, pp. 40–1.

[11] J. D. B. Mitchell, 'The causes and effects of the absence of a system of public law in the United Kingdom', *Public Law*, (1965), 95–118, p. 96.

developed and attain a much more distinctive character than has been the case in Britain.

My point, then, is that public law in the UK has not been able to conceive of public power in terms other than those in which it conceives of private individuals. This anthropomorphic conception of government was given theoretical support in the leading work of constitutional theory, that of Dicey. Whilst his work has come under unremitting and justified criticism,[12] and whilst other theorists such as Bagehot may have presented a more sociologically convincing account of the constitution, that of Dicey has both reflected and reinforced the peculiarities of the legal conception of public power and its control in the UK.[13]

Most critiques of Dicey have concentrated on the difficulties of applying his concept of the rule of law to modern Britain. It is only more recently that his concept of the sovereignty of Parliament has been subject to the same sort of critique in England.[14] It is worth reminding ourselves of how he characterized this sovereignty:

> The sovereignty of Parliament is (from a legal point of view) the dominant characteristic of our political institutions. ... The principle of Parliamentary sovereignty means neither more nor less than this, namely, that Parliament ... has, under the English constitution, the right to make or unmake any law whatever; and, further, that no person or body is recognized by the law of England as having a right to override or set aside the legislation of Parliament.[15]

The view of power is of course an essentially anthropomorphic one; rather than Parliament forming part of a network of institutions within which power is divided according to some more or less rational system of constitutional checks and balances, power is by its essence to be located in an individual institution which must wield it in an ultimately unlimited form. The evolution from the jurisprudence of Austin is explicit in Dicey's work, and even the terminology of sovereignty has a clearly anthropomorphic character. One implication of the theory is, of course, that, as no institution is capable of imposing restrictions on Parliamentary capacities, no other institution is capable of laying down authoritative and fundamental constitutional principles. Yet Parliament itself is unlikely to do so; nor could it do so in a way which restricted its future action.

It is well known that Dicey's conception of the rule of law is explicitly hostile to generalized statements of constitutional principles or declarations of rights; to quote a famous passage, '[w]e may say that the constitution is pervaded by the rule of law on the ground that the general principles of the constitution (as for example the right to personal liberty, or the right of public meeting) are

---

[12] Classic examples of fundamental critique of Dicey are Sir W. Ivor Jennings, *The Law and the Constitution* (1933) and I. Harden and N. Lewis, *The Noble Lie: the British Constitution and the Rule of Law* (London, Hutchinson, 1986).

[13] For a fuller discussion of this issue see C. Graham and T. Prosser, 'Introduction: the constitution and the new Conservatives' in C. Graham and T. Prosser (eds), *Waiving the Rules: the Constitution Under Thatcherism* (Buckingham, Open University Press, 1988), pp. 1–21.

[14] The position in Scotland has been different; as Lord President Cooper noted in a leading case, '[t]he principle of the unlimited sovereignty of Parliament is a distinctively English principle which has no counterpart in Scottish constitutional law'. *MacCormick* v. *Lord Advocate* 1953 S.C. 396, at 411.

[15] A. Dicey, *The Law of the Constitution* (London, Macmillan, 8th ed., 1915), pp. 3–4.

with us the result of judicial decisions determining the rights of private persons in particular cases brought before the Courts; whereas under many foreign constitutions the security (such as it is) given to the rights of individuals results, or appears to result, from the general principles of the constitution.'[16] A less remarked implication of Dicey's view of the rule of law relates to another theme within it; that government was subject to the ordinary law of the land. As he put it:

> In England the idea of legal equality, or of the universal subjection of all classes to one law administered by the ordinary Courts, has been pushed to its utmost limit. With us every official, from the Prime Minister down to a constable or a collector of taxes, is under the same responsibility for every act done without legal justification as any other citizen.[17]

Criticism of this aspect of Dicey's proposition has concentrated on the unreality of the statement; even in 1885 innumerable privileges attached to public officials and a number of important special administrative jurisdictions existed. A further implication has been less remarked however; if government is subject to the same legal responsibilities as the private citizen, it is also able to avail itself of the same legal rights and privileges as the private citizen, and this leaves no room for constraints on power based explicitly on responsibilities to the broader public interest or of rights owed by the state through its status as an institution transcending the chaos of particular interests. Again the anthropomorphic conception of government rears its head; the implications of this will be most fully shown by an examination of a couple of concrete areas of modern constitutional controversy.

Some Implications of Personalized Government: Protection of Official Information

A convenient example with which to start our discussion concerns the availability of official information, as this raises not only questions of rights but also of the meaning of democracy. It has been argued convincingly that the concept of democracy (including a Parliamentary conception) cannot make sense without openness in the provision of such information.[18] I shall not deal here with the protection of official information by the criminal law through the successive Official Secrets Acts as that has been done effectively elsewhere.[19] Instead I shall discuss the use of the civil law of confidence to protect official information, an area of law of considerable importance in recent years which illustrates vividly the ability of government to use law as if it were a private actor without the protections which could be afforded by a more institutionalized concept of constraints on public power.

The law on breach of confidence had its origins in private relations, for example, the case of *Prince Albert* v. *Strange* (1849) 1 Mac. and G. 25 concerned an attempt to prevent publication by a private publisher of a catalogue of

---

[16] Dicey, *The Law of the Constitution*, p. 115 (footnote omitted).

[17] Dicey *The Law of the Constitution*, p. 114.

[18] Harden and Lewis, *The Noble Lie*, ch. 9.

[19] See N. MacCormick, 'The interests of the state and the rule of law' in P. Wallington and R. Merkin (eds), *Essays in Memory of Professor F. H. Lawson* (London, Butterworth, 1986), pp. 169–87.

etchings by Queen Victoria, and the more recent case of *Argyll* v. *Argyll* [1967] Ch 302 was a case of domestic secrets passing between husband and wife; related doctrines are also of considerable importance in the protection of commercial secrecy. The law was applied to governmental information in *Attorney-General* v. *Jonathan Cape* [1976] QB 752, in which an attempt was made to prevent publication of the first volume of the Crossman diaries. This failed, but the court accepted that, although Cabinet secrecy was not a legal requirement but a constitutional convention, it could be enforced in principle through the law of confidentiality. This principle became of crucial importance in the 'Spycatcher' litigation in which the Government attempted to suppress publication of the book of that name by Peter Wright, a former senior member of the security services. Criminal proceedings could not be brought as Wright was outside the jurisdiction. However, interim injunctions were sought against newspapers to prevent publication of extracts from the book on the ground that Wright owed a perpetual duty of confidence in view of his position as a former member of the security services, and that this applied also to third parties such as newspapers, despite the fact that the information was already publicly available through the book's publication in the United States and its free import into the UK. The injunctions were granted, and the Court of Appeal and the House of Lords refused to lift them after the US publication. According to the majority of the House, the combination of the possible success of the Attorney General when the case came to trial and the need to protect information held in confidence by the security services prevailed over any right of the public to be informed, although this was weakened by a strong dissent from Lord Bridge accusing the Government of taking the first steps towards censorship worthy of a totalitarian regime and predicting inevitable defeat for it before the European Court of Human Rights.[20] At the full trial injunctions were not granted, and this was upheld by the House of Lords as, whilst members and ex-members of the security services did have a perpetual duty of confidence, this did not apply to third parties such as newspapers which would only be restrained from publication where it would be damaging; the previous publication in the United States meant that this could no longer be the case.[21] However, the extent to which a 'public interest defence' was available justifying otherwise unlawful publication to expose wrongdoing in government remained uncertain. Although the judge at first instance had refused to accept the Government's claim of an absolute duty of confidence applying to members of the security services, one member of the House cast considerable doubt on the existence of such a defence.[22]

The legal details of these cases are of much less importance than the obvious difficulty that the courts had in developing any approach which showed an ability to think in terms of constitutional requirements which are based on some set of principles peculiarly applicable to government's role. The law is derived from that applying to purely private relations. Clearly the members of the various courts involved were unhappy with the implications of this thorough acknowledging in various degrees the public interest elements involved; for

---

[20] *Attorney-General* v. *Guardian Newspapers Ltd* [1987] 1 W.L.R. 1248 at 1286–7.

[21] *Attorney-General* v. *Guardian Newspapers Ltd* (No. 2) [1990] 1 A.C. 109.

[22] Lord Griffiths at p. 269. See also on these issues *Lord Advocate* v. *Scotsman Publications* [1990] 1 A.C. 612.

example, the requirement that third party disclosures be damaging to the public interest and the hints at some form of public interest defence. However, to summon up the public interest is simply too vague to offer useful guidance as to the constitutional position as it can justify quite contradictory results; compare in the first of the *Guardian* cases discussed above Lord Bridge's claim that 'Freedom of speech is always the first casualty under a totalitarian regime. ... Censorship is the indispensable tool to regulate what the public may and what it may not know. The present attempt to insulate the public in this country from information which is freely available elsewhere is a very significant step down that very dangerous road' with Lord Ackner's argument that, should the injunctions be lifted, 'English law would have surrendered to the American Constitution. There the courts, by virtue of the First Amendment, are, I understand, powerless to control the press. Fortunately the press in this country is, as yet, not above the law, although like some other powerful organizations they would like that to be so, that is until they require the law's protection.'[23]

This statement raises two points; firstly that the personalized version of the state in the UK gives government some peculiar legal advantages through its ability to use law derived from private relations, and secondly the peculiar difficulties facing the courts in developing or applying anything resembling constitutional principles. I shall assess later the possible effect of European developments in providing a way of resolving the problems. For the moment, however, I will now mention another effect of the peculiarly personalized view of government we have in the UK; its effect on the modernization of governmental structures.

Some Implications of Personalized Government: 'Next Steps'

In constitutional terms, the creation of executive agencies under the 'Next Steps' programme has been of revolutionary importance as it undermines the traditional doctrine of government as embodied in the 'over-life-size' role of ministers, to use Dyson's phrase.[24] The problem has been how to create some form of accountability other than that (at the level of traditional theory rather than modern practice) through the minister directly to Parliament, and also how to create a field of operational autonomy with a degree of effective independence from the minister. To take the latter point first, the history of attempts to develop operational autonomy for institutions in other areas has not been a happy one, especially in the case of the nationalized industries.[25] Problems have arisen both from the reluctance of ministers to give up intervention and the lack of any effective legal means of preventing it. In the case of the 'Next Steps' agencies, the solution adopted has been to develop framework documents which are intended to clarify the aims and objectives of the agency and the division of tasks between agency and Department; one Agency Chief Executive likened the Document to a 'bill of rights' for the

---

[23] At 1286 and 1306.

[24] There is now a considerable literature on the 'Next Steps' programme; see for example P. Greer, *Transforming Central Government: the Next Steps Initiative* (Buckingham, Open University Press, 1994) and N. Lewis, 'Reviewing change in government; new public management and Next Steps', *Public Law*, (1994) 105-13.

[25] See T. Prosser, *Nationalised Industries and Public Control* (Oxford, Blackwell, 1986), chs 2–4.

Agency.[26] A report by the Treasury and Civil Service Select Committee noted that a recent study had found that most agencies were much more constrained than the framework document would imply and that in practice the annual process of target setting and agreeing business plans had become the main focus for relations rather than the longer-term Framework Document. Part of the problem is that the Document cannot have contractual force because of the legal doctrine that contracts of central government are made by the Secretary of State on behalf of the Crown and, as the agencies are also part of the Crown, to recognize the documents as having contractual status would amount to accepting the legal impossibility of the Crown contracting with itself.[27] An earlier report of the Committee had recommended that the framework document 'should be regarded as a contract' and that a Minister should only be entitled to overrule an agency Chief Executive by means of a formal note; however, the Government had rejected these recommendations.[28]

Related points have arisen on the question of agency accountability. After initial difficulties resulting from the non-publication of replies to Parliamentary questions referred to agency Chief Executives these are now available in Hansard; however, criticisms have continued, despite Government claims that the Agencies did not 'undermine the key constitutional principle that it is Ministers who are accountable to Parliament for all that their Departments do'.[29] The recent Treasury and Civil Service Select Committee Report recommended that Agency Chief Executives be directly and personally accountable to Select Committees in relation to their annual performance agreements and that all instructions to them from Ministers should be published in the Agency Annual Reports, save only for exceptions to protect personal confidentiality or anonymity of individual clients.[30] The Government rejected this recommendation, instead seeking to retain a unitary concept of accountability through the minister.[31]

There can be no doubt as to the large scale, indeed revolutionary, nature of the change represented by the 'Next Steps' programme.[32] Nevertheless, the continuing problems of autonomy and accountability illustrate vividly the force of the conception of the British Constitution as centred around the single figure of the minister. The constitutional myth of the unity of the Crown prevents the protection of autonomy through binding agreement, and the lack of a tradition of accountability other than through the minister before Parliament means that it is difficult to establish or indeed to conceive of other mechanisms for rendering relatively autonomous power accountable, for example through a more developed system of public law. The same point could be made through analysis of a number of other areas such as territorial politics or the decline of local government.

[26] HC 481, 1989–90, para. 15.
[27] See I. Harden, *The Contracting State* (Buckingham, Open University Press, 1992), p. 82.
[28] HC 494, 1987–8, paras 38, 46–7; Cm 524, p. 9.
[29] HC 27, 1993–4, paras 163–7; Cm 2627, para. 2.29.
[30] HC 27, 1993–4, para. 171.
[31] Cm 2748, para. 24.
[32] See Lewis, 'Reviewing change in government'.

The European Constitution

There have been a number of recent academic responses to the crisis in constitutional legitimacy which is widely accepted as existing in the UK.[33] The approaches adopted are highly varied not only in terms of the meaning of existing constitutional material but in the methodological approach to be adopted in identifying and interpreting the constitution and in proposing reform. For reasons of space I will not be able to enter the debates here. I will instead limit myself to suggesting that, irrespective of the academic debate, European influences have been such as to undermine already the traditional character of the British constitution. It will be recalled that the first form in which the peculiarly personalized conception of the constitution was expressed above was through a particularly extreme version of sovereignty in British constitutional principle. Yet this extreme version is no longer sustainable; whatever the debates concerning the original implications of membership of what is now the European Union, any belief in the survival of parliamentary sovereignty as preventing judicial review of primary legislation was laid to rest by the *Factortame* decision.[34] As I have argued elsewhere, the economic constitution of the UK is essentially that provided by European law rather than by domestic norms or practices.[35] Something rather similar has happened with the European Convention on Human Rights. It is now largely taken for granted that the most likely effective remedy for infringement of a civil right in the UK is to be found in Strasbourg, and it is well known that the UK is subject to more successful applications to the Strasbourg jurisdictions than any other signatory of the Convention save Italy. Perhaps less well-known is the growing importance of the Convention in domestic law. Governments have always resisted incorporation of the Convention into domestic law (though this is now likely to change with a change of Government as all the opposition parties are committed to such incorporation). Nevertheless, over the last few years with some changes in judicial personnel bringing in a younger and more liberal set of judges into the superior courts a change of attitude has been apparent to the Convention without waiting for formal incorporation.

The last gasp of a judicial culture hostile to the sort of reasoning which the Convention involves was in the *Brind* decision concerning the Home Secretary's decision to ban broadcasting of direct statements by Sinn Fein and other proscribed organizations.[36] The challengers argued that the ban breached principles contained in the Convention and that, whilst not part of domestic law, the Convention should be treated as a limit on the discretion of the minister as it should be assumed that Parliament had not intended to legislate so as to

---

[33] See e.g. Harden and Lewis, *The Noble Lie*; I. Harden, 'The constitution and its discontents'; N. Walker, 'The middle ground in public law' in W. Finnie, C. Himsworth and N. Walker (eds), *Edinburgh Essays in Public Law* (Edinburgh, Edinburgh University Press, 1991), pp. 57–95; R. Brazier, 'The non-legal constitution: thoughts on convention, practice and principle', *Northern Ireland Legal Quarterly*, 43 (1992), 262–87; Daintith, 'Political programmes and the constitution'; M. Loughlin, *Public Law and Political Theory* (Oxford, Clarendon, 1992); T. R. S. Allan, *Law, Liberty and Justice: the Legal Foundations of British Constitutionalism* (Oxford, Clarendon, 1993).

[34] *R.* v. *Secretary of State for Transport, ex parte Factortame Ltd (No. 2)* [1991] 1 A.C. 603. See also N. MacCormick, 'Beyond the sovereign state', *Modern Law Review*, 56 (1993), 1–19.

[35] See M. Moran and T. Prosser (eds), *Privatization and Regulatory Change in Europe* (Buckingham, Open University Press, 1994), pp. 148–53.

[36] *R* v. *Secretary of State for the Home Department ex parte Brind* [1991] 1 A.C. 696.

permit the exercise of power in a way which breached the Convention. This was roundly rejected by the House of Lords, as was an attempt to make use of the principle of proportionality, a key principle of both European human rights law and European Community law. Even in the Spycatcher litigation, however, there had been signs of a somewhat different attitude to the Convention. Thus a number of members of the House of Lords did not claim that the Convention was irrelevant to domestic law, but rather suggested that the common law was in fact compatible with the Convention.[37] This was taken a step further in *Derbyshire County Council* v. *Times Newspapers*[38] in which the House, in holding that a local authority does not have the right to bring an action in defamation, explicitly found that there was no difference in principle between the common law and the Convention in the field of freedom of speech. The Court of Appeal in the same case had fully accepted that where English law is ambiguous the Convention should be considered, and indeed that should be so in certain cases even where domestic law is clear.[39] As a result of this we are now in a situation where traditional domestic peculiarities of common law constitutional thought are increasingly developed through a more conceptual, rights-based process of constructive interpretation which gives a role to the European material.

A similar point could be made about other changes in the traditional view of the legal position of government, notably the decision that in English law injunctive relief is available against ministers of the Crown acting in their official capacities, enforceable by contempt proceedings.[40] Previously, ministers had been protected by the immunity of the Crown from coercive remedies; the removal of this immunity would have been unlikely were it not for the prior decisions in the *Factortame* litigation requiring the availability of such relief in cases based on Community Law rights. However, to point to the growing influence of different constitutional styles in the UK is not to prove that this is desirable; indeed, a debate still continues as to whether a more rights-based constitutional jurisprudence does not limit democratic possibilities. I shall conclude this chapter by addressing this argument.

Democracy and Rights

The personalization of government and sovereignty in the UK has led to a conception of democracy which is particularly de-institutionalized. Thus, any entrenched system of rights has been seen as in sharp opposition to democracy as limiting the sovereign power of the democratic will and so as preventing the implementation of what may be desirable social change. This is one explanation for the fact that opposition to entrenched rights in the UK has come not only from political conservatives (who may be expected to oppose something so alien to the British constitutional tradition) but also from the

---

[37] See Lord Keith in *Attorney-General* v, *Guardian Newspapers (No. 2)*, [1990] 1 A.C. 109 at 256–7, Lord Griffiths at 273 and Lord Goff at 283–4.

[38] [1993] 1 A.C. 534.

[39] [1992] 1 QB 770 (CA). Scots law is currently somewhat uncertain on the matter; see *Kaur* v. *Lord Advocate* 1981 S.L.T. 322; *Moore* v. *Secretary of State for Scotland* 1985 S.L.T. 38; *Hamilton* v. *Secretary of State for Scotland*, 18 December 1990 (unreported).

[40] *re M* [1993] 3 W.L.R. 433. Scots law has unfortunately so far failed to follow this lead: *MacDonald* v. *Secretary of State for Scotland* 1994 SLT 692.

political left on democratic grounds.[41] A further ground for the suspicion of such rights from the Left is because of their supposedly individualist nature which may both conflict with more communitarian goals and also encourage a view of society as composed of atomic individuals, a concern reinforced by some of the excesses of a strong rights-culture in the United States.[42] I shall not attempt here to defend the 'rights foundationalist' view according to which rights are trumps which defeat decisions of democratic institutions defining the collective welfare,[43] though I believe it can be defended. Rather I will make some suggestions about the relationship between democracy and rights suggesting that to regard the two as intrinsically or potentially contradictory is dependent on a particular conception of democracy which is being overtaken by events. Indeed, any sophisticated analysis of the relationship between democracy and rights is something which the British model has managed to avoid precisely because of the personalized view of government outlined earlier. This has assumed that the state should be free to implement the public interest just as individuals should be free to implement their personal interests, and that there is no fundamental distinction between the constitutional rights and duties of government and of individuals; this avoids discussion of more institutionalized aspects of rights.

My first point is that certain forms of rights are intrinsic to any conception of democracy beyond a crude view of democracy as a sovereign implementation of a unitary popular will. Quite simply, any vision of democracy as implying participation in popular debate involves the institutional establishment of the conditions for such debate, and this entails the recognition of participants as the bearers of certain rights to participate. This is clearest in relation to such established civil and political rights as freedom of expression and the right to form political parties; it can however be extended to support certain social and economic rights which are necessary to permit any meaningful participation to take place; these might include the right to a basic education and to a basic income.[44] Such rights will of course be controversial and potentially conflicting; nevertheless, argument about them takes a different form from that of normal democratic debate as rights themselves set the conditions for such rational debate.

Secondly, it is a mistake to characterize the rights versus policy distinction as opposing individualist rights to collectivist notions of the common good. In some cases this will be so, for example in using a right to due process to defeat arguments that a community has an overriding interest in defending itself against crime. This is what, for example, Dworkin referred to in stating that '[t]he existence of rights against the Government would be jeopardized if the Government were able to defeat such a right by appealing to the right of a democratic majority to work its will. ... In order to save them, we must

---

[41] See the discussion in T. Campbell, *The Left and Rights* (London, Routledge, 1982), and more recently Waldron, 'A right-based critique of constitutional rights', and Bellamy, 'The constitution of Europe: rights or democracy?'.

[42] See e.g. A. Ryan, 'The British, The Americans and rights' in M. Lacey and K. Haakonssen (eds), *A Culture of Rights* (Cambridge, Cambridge University Press, 1991), pp. 366–439, p. 436.

[43] The term 'rights foundationalist' is taken from B. Ackerman, 'Constitutional politics/ constitutional law', *Yale Law Journal* 99, (1989), 453–547, p. 465 ff.

[44] See e.g. N. MacCormick, 'Sovereignty, democracy and subsidiarity' in Bellamy *et al.*, *Democracy and Constitutional Culture in the Union of Europe*, p. 102.

recognise as competing rights only the rights of other members of the society as individuals.'[45] In other cases, however, rights or related entrenched principles (including some of those likely to emerge as part of the developing European Union) themselves have a collectivist base; indeed, Dworkin himself now grounds his constitutionalism in an explicitly communal conception of democracy.[46] The clearest example of such a principle is the right to national self-determination in international law. We can take also territorial and functional definitions of democracy, for example in definitions of local government powers. These are precisely the sorts of provisions one finds entrenched in many written constitutions, and their basis is a similar one to the rights discussed above in that answering certain definitional questions concerning participation is prior to democracy. Thus the outcomes of such definitional questions need protection through specially demanding procedures being required for change. Examples in a European context are the (in practice highly indeterminate) concept of subsidiarity and the principles laid out in the Council of Europe's European Charter of Local Self Government to which the UK Government has so far refused to adhere.[47] It may be misleading to refer to such protected collective interests as rights in the same sense as the more traditional individual rights, but their basis is similar. Historically it is of course true that such principles have resulted from democratic struggle; yet conceptually they provide a legitimating definition of the democratic process which cannot be regarded as of the same status as normal outcomes of democratic debate.

One of the implications of sovereignty in the strong sense associated with Dicey which has dominated British versions of the concept this century is that all rules are of equal constitutional status, in the sense that there are no fundamentals which can only be changed by a special procedure such as referendum or special majority. As Dicey put it, in the context of maintaining that the Act of Union was no more a supreme law than the Dentists Act of 1878, '[t]he one fundamental dogma of English constitutional law is the absolute legislative sovereignty or despotism of the King in Parliament. But this dogma is incompatible with the existence of a fundamental compact, the provisions of which control every authority existing under the Constitution'.[48] However, elsewhere a more complex version of democracy has emerged, for example in terms of what Ackerman has called 'dualist democracy' under which certain forms of 'higher law' require extremely demanding forms of procedure for their change.[49] This characterizes, for example, the American model of constitutional change as against the English model of 'monist democracy'.[50] Again this is something which has been quite frequent in nations with procedures for constitutional amendment by special procedure, for example in France where

---

[45] R. Dworkin, *Taking Rights Seriously* (London, Duckworth, 1977), p. 194.

[46] R. Dworkin, 'Constitutionalism and democracy', *European Journal of Philosophy*, 3 (1995), 2–11.

[47] See C. Crawford, 'European influence on local self-government', *Local Government Studies*, 18 (1992), 69–85.

[48] Dicey, *The Law of the Constitution*, p. 78 (footnote omitted).

[49] Ackerman, 'Constitutional politics/constitutional law', pp. 461–2; see also his *We the People* (London, Belknap, 1991) and Harden, 'The constitution and its discontents'.

[50] I use the term 'English' rather than 'British' advisedly here as there has been a much more lively debate in Scotland, and a more open judicial attitude to the possibility of 'higher law'.

constitutional amendment has been relatively common in recent years.[51] Even in Germany, where the list of constitutionally protected human rights is explicitly protected against amendment by special democratic procedure, similar amendments have been made in relation to other issues, for example to permit the privatization of constitutionally protected public services. Once one accepts the complexity of this view of democracy rather than the simplicity of the traditional monist view of sovereignty a number of interesting prospects arise in terms of the design of special procedures; indeed, we may already be seeing the development of something similar through the use of the intergovernmental conference for Treaty amendment and the role of national referendums. In order to conceptualize these procedures in terms other than mere political expediency, a much more sophisticated system of constitutional thought will have to emerge compared to that which we have had in the past in Britain; and this is likely to accept both rights requiring special protection through some form of entrenchment and democratic institutions.

Indeed, the dualist conception of democracy may also provide us with a response to the argument that, as rights are inherently conflicting, they cannot provide useful practical guidance; and therefore democratic decision-making is a more legitimate means of determining fundamental conflicts.[52] Of course, rights do conflict, and even the most fundamental human rights will sometimes need weighing against each other. The force of rights arguments is not to suggest that this cannot happen, but rather to assert that, just as more fundamental change may require more demanding procedures, claims of rights require a particularly strong form of argument normally relying on other rights to defeat them; certain forms of argument are by definition inadequate as a means of overriding a rights claim. This is the force of the distinction between principle and policy in Dworkin's work, though, as I suggested above, it is misleading to treat this as opposing rights to communitarian concerns. As he put it:

> ... once a right is recognized in clear-cut cases, then the Government should act to cut off that right only when some compelling reason is presented, some reason that is consistent with the suppositions on which the original right must be based. It cannot be an argument for curtailing a right, once granted, simply that society would pay a further price for extending it. There must be something special about that further cost, or there must be some other feature of the case, that makes it sensible to say that although great social cost is warranted to protect the original right, this particular cost is not necessary.[53]

He then suggests that there are three sorts of grounds for limiting the definition of a particular right; that the values protected by a right are not really at stake in the case in question, or that a competing right is at issue, or the cost to society is of a degree far beyond the cost paid to grant the original right (the 'clear and present danger' test).[54]

---

[51] See J. Jennings, 'The French constitutional tradition' in Bellamy *et al.*, *Democracy and Constitutional Culture in the Union of Europe*, pp. 21–36.

[52] See Bellamy, 'The constitution of Europe: rights or democracy?', p. 164.

[53] Dworkin, *Taking Rights Seriously*, p. 200.

[54] Dworkin, *Taking Rights Seriously*, p. 200.

An appeal to rights is then somewhat akin to the more complex forms of democracy noted above as it imposes more demanding tests for certain kinds of governmental action. It also requires a different form of argument in which some attempt is made to fit a pattern of rights into a consistent constitutional scheme at a higher level of generality.[55] In this context, however, my point is a more straightforward one; the fact that rights may conflict does not provide an argument that conflict can be resolved only by an undifferentiated concept of democracy, but that the claim of a right requires special procedures and modes of argumentation for its denial.

It would be possible to illustrate the special forms of argumentation used where rights are in issue from any number of decisions of the European Court of Human Rights and the European Court of Justice; however a particularly striking (albeit familiar) example of handling conflicting rights can be seen in the opinion of Advocate General Van Gerven in *Society for the Protection of Unborn Children* v. *Grogan*[56] as the most fundamental of rights, the right to life, was at stake. The Irish Society had commenced injunctive proceedings to prevent student associations distributing information on abortion facilities elsewhere in the Community in order to assist pregnant women obtain abortions, basing its claim on the right to life in Article 40.3.3 of the Irish Constitution. The defence of the student associations was that they could rely on the legal/economic right to provide information on services available in other member states. A number of questions arising out of the case were referred to the European Court of Justice. The Advocate-General accepted that the right of Community citizens to receive services in another member state encompasses the right to receive information about them in one's own member state: apart from the provisions of the Treaty relating to freedom of services, this was reinforced by Article 10 of the European Convention on Human Rights concerning the right to receive and to impart information. The right could only be abridged on the basis of an imperative public interest and the restriction on information supply was not disproportionate to the aim adopted, though the answer would have been different in the case, for example, of a ban on travel or the unsolicited examination of women on their return.[57]

In addition to reliance on the economic rights based on Treaty provisions, the Advocate-General also considered the compatibility of the restriction on information provision with the fundamental rights and freedoms on which general principles of community law are based, especially Article 10 of the European Convention on Human Rights relating to freedom of expression. The basis for this was once more the test of proportionality:

> does the prohibition on the provision of information which is at issue pursue a legitimate aim of public interest which fulfils an imperative public need? Secondly, is that aim being realized using means which are necessary (and acceptable) in a democratic society in order to achieve that aim? Thirdly, are the means employed in proportion to the aims pursued ...?[58]

---

[55] This is the point of the Hercules example used by Dworkin; see *Taking Rights Seriously*, ch. 4.
[56] [1991] 3 CMLR 849; for an excellent analysis see G. de Burca, 'Fundamental human rights and the reach of EC Law', *Oxford Journal of Legal Studies*, 13 (1993), 283–319.
[57] At p. 875.
[58] At p. 881.

According to the Advocate General, in view of the importance of the right to life, a considerable margin of discretion was left for Member States and the means adopted was once more not disproportionate to the aim. The Court of Justice side-stepped the issues by deciding that the link between the service suppliers and the students' associations was too tenuous for the restriction to fall within the protections in the Treaty relating to the freedom to supply services, and that it fell outside the scope of Community law. The European Court of Human Rights later considered the legality of a ban on non-directive pregnancy counselling involving information about abortion availability in Britain. The ban was held to breach Article 10 of the European Convention on Human Rights as it was disproportionate and so not 'necessary in a democratic society'.[59]

Despite the reluctance of the Court to analyse the issues in depth, what we see in the Advocate General's opinion is neither irresoluble conflict between two stark conflicting rights with the only means of resolution ordinary democratic politics, nor the treatment of rights as merely one interest amongst all the others in democratic policy-making. Rather, rights have a special weight which means that they can only be restricted on the basis of a limited number of special arguments, and a quite sophisticated system for weighing up the different arguments is employed to shape the decision. The stress on different modes of argumentation being applied when claims based on rights are challenged may also suggest that the distinction between procedural checks and controls and the supposed absolutism of substantive rights is less stark than is often suggested; the very power of substantive rights lies in their requiring particularly strong modes of argumentation for their qualification.[60]

Conclusion

I have argued in this chapter that in the UK we have had a very peculiar view of government and the state (and indeed it is a further peculiarity that the two terms are treated as effectively interchangeable). These characteristics have prevented any principled assessment of the role of constitutional controls, replacing this with a highly simplistic view of sovereignty and a related anthropomorphic view of government. We are now in contact with radically different traditions embodied in the legal arrangements of the European Community and the Council of Europe and this is leading to the rapid demolition of previously cherished constitutional fundamentals including parliamentary sovereignty itself. Not only is European Constitutionalism to a large degree rights-based, but it also suggests a more sophisticated concept of democracy than the simple monist one; indeed, through the building of democratic institutions and the assessment of the interests that need special protection, we may be able to have a richer understanding of the meaning and requirements of both democracy and rights. This is emphatically not an argument for complacency; the democratic structures of the European Community are rightly regarded as ramshackle, whilst the necessity of judicial determination of rights makes more urgent, not less, the problems of judicial appointment and education which are so apparent in the UK. By acknowledging that democracy

---

[59] *Open Door Counselling and Dublin Well Woman Centre* v. *Ireland* (1993) 15 E.H.R.R. 244.
[60] See Bellamy, 'The constitution of Europe: rights or democracy?', pp. 166, 171.

and rights may in principle (if not always in practice) be mutually reinforcing concepts, we can at least emphasize the need to address both sets of institutional concerns rather than collapsing them into an undifferentiated concept of sovereignty, something which the British Constitution has done so consistently in the past.

From 'Imperial State' to *'l'Etat de Droit'*: Benjamin Constant, Blandine Kriegel and the Reform of the French Constitution

JEREMY JENNINGS

Introduction

Since its creation in 1958 France's Fifth Republic has been subject to nine constitutional revisions. Of these the most important was that in October 1962 which allowed for the direct election by universal suffrage of the President. Yet the 1990s alone have seen four revisions of the constitution: in June 1992 to allow ratification of the Maastricht treaty; in July 1993 to achieve reform of the *Conseil supérieure de la magistrature*; in November 1993 to restrict the right of exile in France; and in July 1995 to extend the range of issues that could be subject to vote by referendum and the length of parliamentary sessions. Each has been either a direct or indirect response to a pressing political issue: European integration; widespread corruption amongst politicians and political parties; mounting opposition to the scale of immigration; and the desire to overcome the ever widening gap between the French state and a large section of its citizens, *'les exclus'*. Taken together these revisions are a reflection of the sense that recent economic success has been matched by growing disillusionment amongst electors. In short, former Prime Minister Edouard Balladur has not been alone in believing that a way has to be found to *'mieux associer les citoyens'*.[1]

The 1995 Revision of the Constitution

Yet the question has to be asked if any of the recent revisions of the Constitution will serve to lessen the feeling of alienation felt by the people towards their elected representatives and the institutions of the state. I have already argued that the 1993 revisions will only serve to heighten the sense of exclusion felt by members of France's immigrant communities[2] but what of the most recent changes, described by *Le Monde* as 'the most important reform since 1962'?[3]

The political considerations that lay behind President Chirac's reform proposals were of various kinds. A promise had been made to hold a referendum on the educational system, and this could only be done if the range of the

---

[1] E. Balladur, 'Mieux associer les citoyens', *Le Monde*, 17 November 1994.
[2] J. Jennings, 'The French constitutional tradition' in R. Bellamy, V. Bufacchi and D. Castiglione (eds), *Democracy and Constitutional Culture in the Union of Europe* (London, Lothian Foundation, 1995), pp. 21–36.
[3] C. Chambraud and G. Courtois, 'La constitution connait sa plus importante réforme depuis 1962', *Le Monde*, 1 August 1995.

referendum was extended beyond the prevailing limitation to institutional and constitutional matters. It also served to give an air of dynamism to an administration that had quickly revealed that little of substance existed behind its rhetoric of tackling the problems of homelessness and unemployment. By apparently strengthening the workings of parliament Chirac also paid a debt to one of his staunchest supporters, Philippe Séguin, president of the *Assemblée nationale*.

The broader aspirations that informed the measures were placed firmly in the context of a 'democratic deficit' lurking at the heart of the French political system. Writing in *Le Monde*[4] Jacques Toubon, the Minister of Justice, commented that 'obviously in the present situation the will of the citizens is not sufficiently taken into account'. To rectify this the intention was 'to give back the final word to the people' and to ensure 'greater participation of citizens in the most important of decisions'. This view was confirmed by Prime Minister Alain Juppé when the revisions were debated by the members of both parliamentary chambers at their joint meeting in Versailles on 31 July. 'Our country', he proclaimed, 'has need of a strengthening of democracy'. The reforms were therefore designed to give its 'exercise a new vigour'.[5]

All of these assertions were greeted with near total indifference amongst the general public and with growing scepticism amongst members of parliament and the press, the editor of *Le Monde* going so far as to argue that by further strengthening the power of the President the reforms were 'potentially dangerous'.[6] For his part Juppé found himself having to deny that the revisions 'upset the institutional equilibrium' of the Fifth Republic, the old republican fear of Bonapartism having re-surfaced amongst opponents of the changes.[7]

Initially, however, the proposals had received considerable favourable comment. Pierre Avril and Jean Gicquel, both professors of constitutional law at Paris, judged the revision 'necessary, if not sufficient',[8] whilst Georges Vedel, former member of the *Conseil constitutionnel*, thought the proposals 'wise and to be welcomed'.[9] The doubts initially focused on the extent of the changes envisaged. Jean-Louis Quermonne, for example, questioned the wisdom of retaining the right to call a referendum in the hands of the President alone and argued that extending parliamentary sessions would serve no purpose if further curbs were not put on the proliferation of electoral mandates by parliamentary deputies and ministers.[10]

Put under closer scrutiny the criticisms became more searching. The most obvious was that the lengthening of parliamentary sessions alone [11] would not strengthen the position of parliament and that this goal was contradicted by a

[4] J. Toubon, 'Deux nouveaux espaces pour la démocratie', *Le Monde*, 8 July 1995.

[5] 'Un nouvel élan à l'exercice de notre démocratie', *Le Monde*, 2 August 1995.

[6] J.-M. Colombani, 'Danger', *Le Monde*, 1 August 1995.

[7] See 'Jacques Toubon accepte le principe d'un débat parlementaire avant tout référendum', *Le Monde*, 26 July 1995.

[8] P. Avril and J. Gicquel, 'La révision de la Constitution: nécessaire, pas suffisante', *Le Monde*, 1 July 1995.

[9] G. Vedel, 'Une réforme constitutionnelle sage et bienvenue', *Le Monde*, 6 July 1995.

[10] J.-L. Quermonne, 'La révision annoncée', *Etudes*, 383 (1995), 15–22.

[11] In the course of debate the government agreed to minor changes in the procedures of parliament which increased the possibility of cross-examination of government policy, thus necessitating modification of Article 48 of the Constitution.

proposal which would enhance the opportunities of the President to appeal directly to the people whilst by-passing their parliamentary representatives. In other words, the proposed revision was a not too well camouflaged step towards the further presidentialization of the regime. By re-writing Article 11 of the Constitution to extend the range of the referendum to cover 'reforms relative to social and economic matters' the position of both the government and parliament was potentially diminished to the advantage of the President.

Critics also observed that parliament was being weakened in a less obvious manner. The original proposal was that a measure would be put before the people by way of referendum without prior discussion by parliament. In response to fears expressed by its own supporters the government accepted that a debate in parliament would take place but that no vote would occur. More ominously still it was stipulated that while all laws passed by the *Assemblée nationale* and Senate are subject to control by the *Conseil constitutionnel*, measures ratified by referendum were not to be. Parliament thus finds itself constrained by principles of constitutionality that do not apply when the President chooses to make direct appeal to the people.

Thus to the reproach that these revisions would do nothing to resolve the problems of social division was added the contention that we are witnessing another exhibition of Gaullist Bonapartism. More profitably, it can also be argued that the most recent changes to the constitution are a major challenge to the principles of an *état de droit* that have come increasingly to have a role in the workings of the French state.

The Awakening of Interest in *L'Etat de Droit*

In 1789 the priority of those who challenged the *ancien régime* was to legitimize the transfer of sovereignty from the monarch to an elected assembly. When married to republicanism, sovereignty, one and indivisible, was located in the will of its citizens as expressed in law. In addition the framers of the new political order deliberately set out to weaken the capacity of the judiciary to curtail the legislative and executive branches of government on the grounds that the courts of the *ancien régime* – the *parlements* – had restrained the monarchy in a reactionary manner. This essentially Rousseauian perspective was given a national and imperial twist as first the Revolution and then the Bonapartist experience saw the doctrine of rights buried beneath a universalist vision of democracy and the power of the French state. As republicanism evolved, it came to be seen that it was Parliament alone that embodied the national will and the sovereignty of the people. Henceforth the judiciary's role was to resolve private disputes, with the actions of the State only being subject to review by special administrative courts after 1872. As Laurent Cohen-Tanugi comments: 'Legislation was the supreme source of law; judges could only apply it, not review it'.[12]

This did not mean that the Rousseauian mythology that informed French politics went completely unquestioned. Benjamin Constant, as we shall shortly see, quickly challenged the premises of the republican *état légal*, as did the *doctrinaires* led by Royer-Collard and defenders of the July Monarchy such as

---

[12] L. Cohen-Tanugi, 'From one revolution to the next: the late rise of constitutionalism in France', *The Tocqueville Review*, 12 (1990–1991), 55–60.

François Guizot.[13] Just as significantly, the doctrine of *Rechtsstaat* made its entry into France at the beginning of this century.[14] According to Carré de Malberg, France's Third Republic was not an *état de droit*, where the rights of individual citizens were beyond challenge, but rather an *état légal* characterized by the supremacy of its legislative body. Thus transposed this French version of the doctrine of *Rechtsstaat* was used to challenge the supremacy of parliamentary sovereignty by calling for guarantees of the constitutionality of all laws.[15]

However, as the acrimonious debate between George Jellinek and Emile Boutmy on the origins of the doctrine of the rights of man illustrated, discussion of the 'self-limitation' of the state's activities became embroiled in rival nationalistic claims with numerous French writers only too eager to deny that our modern conception of liberty had its source in the German reformation.[16] Kelsen's legal positivism met similar criticisms from an array of eminent French philosophers and jurists,[17] all seeking to give law a reality and foundation distinct from that of the state. Thus the hostility to the idea that law, the unerring expression of the general will, could be subject to superior principles continued until after the Second World War.

This subsequently changed. Conscious of the abuse of power associated with Nazism (and the ease with which the Vichy regime was able to establish its dictatorial existence) the Constitutions of the Fourth and Fifth Republics contained preambles detailing a commitment to a range of individual and social rights, most notably those detailed in the *Déclaration des droits de l'homme et du citoyen*. In 1971 the *Conseil constitutionnel*, in one of its most important rulings, gave these rights constitutional status.[18]

The manner in which the *Conseil constitutionnel* has extended its role during the Fifth Republic is of utmost importance but for the moment it is useful to concentrate upon the broader intellectual and political context that from the 1970s onwards has provided such a favourable environment for discussion of an *état de droit*. As François Furet has frequently repeated, the revolution is over, and with this has come a wholesale assault upon the Jacobin model.[19] An appreciation of the full horrors of the totalitarian experience combined with a dramatic rejection of a once hegemonic Marxism opened up the way for a re-invigoration of interest in the rights of man that pre-figured the bi-centennial celebrations. It can be found for example in the writings of the so-called '*nouveaux philosophes*'.[20] So too the near-total jettisoning of the deadweight of structuralism removed the presuppositions of humanism from discredit and

---

[13] See my 'Rousseau, social contract and the modern Leviathan', in D. Boucher and P. Kelly (eds), *The Social Contract from Hobbes to Rawls* (London, Routledge, 1994), pp. 115–31.

[14] R. Carré de Malberg, *Contribution à la théorie générale de l'Etat* (Paris, Sirey, 1920–1922), 2 vols.

[15] See J. Chevallier, *L'Etat de droit* (Paris, Montchrestien, 1992).

[16] See *Revue française d'histoire des idées politiques*, 1 (1995), 79–178.

[17] See D. Salas, 'Droit et institution: Léon Duguit et Maurice Hauriou' in P. Bouretz (ed.), *La Force du droit: Panorama des débats contemporaines* (Paris, Esprit, 1991), pp. 193–214.

[18] Since then 'the Preamble has been treated as giving legally binding constitutional force to all the values it mentions': J. Bell, *French Constitutional Law* (Oxford, Clarendon, 1992), p. 66.

[19] See S.L. Kaplan, *Farewell, Revolution: the Historian's Feud, 1789–1989* (Ithaca NY, Cornell University Press, 1995).

[20] See for example B.-H. Lévy, *Le Testament de Dieu* (Paris, Grasset, 1979) and Lévy's *La Barbarie à visage humaine* (Paris, Grasset, 1977).

freed talk of rights-bearing subjects from ridicule.[21] This in turn opened up the way for the emergence of a consensus built around the values of liberal democracy. If at times this took on a radical complexion – in, for example, Cohen-Tanugi's *Le Droit sans l'état*[22] where, with Stanley Hoffman's blessing, the advantages for France of the American model of a self-regulated and contractual society are advocated – it usually rested upon an endorsement of the benefits of pluralism and the market.[23] From the mid-1980s onwards a new urgency was added to this theme as writers began the analysis of what came to be accepted as '*la crise de l'Etat-providence*'. This, as Pierre Rosanvallon has argued,[24] was not merely a financial but also philosophical crisis that called not only for a radical re-thinking of the mechanisms of welfare provision but also for a re-definition of rights and 'a new political culture'.

New thinking about the state also came from the political forces of the Left. In part this was driven by a political imperative. As the socialists and communists together prepared for power in the 1970s a commitment to 'democratize' the state was an electoral necessity. When, by the mid-1980s, the socialist economic experiment had been abandoned there was need for a more serious re-consideration of both means and ends.

The best way of illustrating this change is to refer to the report commissioned by President Mitterrand and presented at his request by Blandine Kriegel, *L'Etat et la démocratie*.[25] Quoting Minister of Justice Robert Badinter to the effect that 'I dream of France becoming an *état de droit*',[26] Kriegel defined the principal concerns of such a type of state for Mitterrand as: 'the rights of man, with in first place personal security; the rights of the citizen and the extension of individual liberties; the regulation of society by law'.[27] Judged by these criteria, Kriegel argued, the achievements of the socialist-led government had been substantial: the abolition of the death penalty; a strengthening of the judicial guarantees and rights of the accused; measures designed to enhance freedom of information and pluralism in the media; the extension of civil rights to the workplace; and laws prohibiting racial and sexual discrimination. Kriegel had her own ideas about how these positive steps could be improved – for example with regard to such groups as the mentally ill, minors, and immigrants – but for the moment it is sufficient to emphasize the extent to which a document of such importance illustrates that reference to an *état de droit* had ceased to be a topic of interest for legal specialists alone and had entered a broader political discourse.

---

[21] See M. Lilla (ed.), *New French Thought: Political Philosophy* (Princeton NJ, Princeton University Press, 1994).

[22] L. Cohen-Tanugi, *Le Droit sans l'état* (Paris, PUF, 1985). For a recent variant on this position see A. Minc, *L'Ivresse démocratique* (Paris, Grasset, 1995).

[23] See M. Mialle, 'Le retour de l'Etat de droit', in D. Colas (ed.), *L'Etat de droit: Travaux de la mission sur la modernisation de l'Etat* (Paris, PUF, 1987), pp. 215–51.

[24] P. Rosanvallon, *La Nouvelle Question Sociale: repenser l'Etat-Providence* (Paris, Seuil, 1995).

[25] B. Barret-Kriegel, *L'Etat et la démocratie: Rapport à François Mitterrand, président de la République française* (Paris, La Documentation française, 1985).

[26] Kriegel, *L'Etat et la démocratie*, pp. 60–1. The quotation is taken from *Le Monde*, 28 August 1981.

[27] Kriegel, *L'Etat et la démocratie*, p. 53.

The Conseil Constitutionnel

In institutional terms it has been in the gradual emergence of the *Conseil constitutionnel* as a 'specialized, third chamber of government' that the most decisive shift has occurred.[28] The literature on the *Conseil constitutionnel* is extensive and I therefore limit myself to endorsing the argument presented by John Bell in his study of *French Constitutional Law*.[29] The *Conseil constitutionnel* formally fulfils five main functions of which the most important was intended to be that of policing the boundaries of the legislative competence of Parliament. As such the *Conseil constitutionnel* was designed to offer a strong executive further protection from an over-powerful and unruly legislative assembly. This intention has now been substantially overturned, principally because 'reference of enacted *lois* to the *Conseil* has become a procedure for challenging them on wider, substantive grounds, particularly for breach of fundamental rights'.[30] Far from being a mechanism that has assured the workings of a 'rationalized parliamentarism', the *Conseil constitutionnel* has secured a dramatic extension of the process of judicial review and in so doing has redressed the imbalance within the political institutions of the Fifth Republic.

How this development fits into the argument about an *état de droit* is demonstrated in the report of the *Comité consultatif pour la révision de la Constitution*, a committee established by President Mitterrand which reported in February 1993.[31] '*L'Etat de droit! L'Etat de droit!* This incantation figures on every page of the report', writes Michel Ameller.[32] The document begins by announcing that its 'philosophy' has been that any

> revision of the Constitution would proceed from a system of values
> recognizing the rule of law not as the ultimate goal of value in and for itself
> but as the indispensable means of promoting the rights of man and of
> giving life to the Republic and its ideas.

This 'reference to *l'Etat de droit*', it goes on, was ever-present in the committee's deliberations and informed many of its recommendations, especially those relating to the 'protection of persons'. Even more emphatically, the report proclaims that 'the citizen wishes to live in an *Etat de droit*'. In terms of practical recommendations this translated itself into calls for a strengthening of the independence of the magistracy, the introduction of what is described as *le référendum d'initiative minoritaire* (with the important proviso that the conformity of any such referendum with the Constitution must be approved

---

[28] See A. Stone, 'Where judicial politics are legislative politics: the French constitutional council', *West European Politics*, 15 (1992), 29–49 and *The Birth of Judicial Politics in France* (Oxford, Oxford University Press, 1992). See also the articles by M. Shapiro, Y. Mény, O. Duhamel and R. Cicchillo on judicial review in the *Tocqueville Review*, 12 (1990–91), 3–82.

[29] Bell, *French Constitutional Law*.

[30] Bell, *French Constitutional Law*, p. 32.

[31] 'Rapport remis au Président de la République le 15 février 1993 par le Comité consultatif pour la révision de la Constitution', *Journal Officiel de la République Française*, 16 February 1993, 2537–54.

[32] M. Ameller, 'Le Comité consultatif pour la révision de la Constitution et le Parlement', *Revue française de droit constitutionnel*, 14 (1993), 259–70. See also O.Passelecq, 'La philosophie du rapport Vedel: une certaine idée de la République', pp. 227–48. The whole of this issue of the *Revue française de droit constitutionnel* is devoted to a discussion of *La Révision de la Constitution de 1958*.

by the *Conseil constitutionnel*),[33] the incorporation of new rights (especially those relating to 'liberty and pluralism' in audio-visual communication) into the Constitution; and access for individual citizens to the *Conseil constitutionnel*. Moreover, the *Conseil constitutionnel* was recognized as the sole institution capable 'of guaranteeing the authority of law'.

Criticism of the Idea of an *Etat de Droit*

Given the break with the dominant French conception of democracy and popular sovereignty that these developments represent, it is not surprising that they have received sustained criticism. At its centre is the charge that an *état de droit* produces a government of judges. It is they, and not the elected representatives of the people, who become the key to the political system and who control its norms and procedures. But, it is asked, 'who is in fact the best interpreter of the Constitution, the legislator or the judge?'[34] What is the 'magic potion' that gives these 'sages' the gift of infallibility and makes their secret deliberations more wise than the public discussions of parliament?[35] How, moreover, can this legalistic version of politics be reconciled with democracy? Is it, as Michel Troper asks, 'a complement to, an alternative to, or a break upon democracy?'[36] As such will it not accentuate the already existing crisis of representation in French society? Does it not assume that a consensus exists and is this not an illusion? To that extent is the doctrine of an *état de droit* not prejudicial to a pluralistic conception of democracy? Are we not left with what Claude Emeri has termed an '*Etat Zorro*', a form of state which even the Left will accept because it best serves their interests?[37] And what will be left of the activity of politics itself? Emptied of content will the end result be the 'demoralization of politics'?[38] Likewise, by endorsing the idea of an *état de droit*, are we not endorsing a minimalist state and a negative conception of liberty with primacy given over to the individual?[39] As one of the most eminent of French jurists, the Durkheimian Léo Hamon, commented: 'The *Etat de droit* tends, even in its very vocabulary, to reduce the function of the state to enforcing the law; that is, to forget the fundamental community to the advantage of the legitimate rights of the individual'. The guarantee of these rights, he contended, should not be to the detriment of 'the identity, the unity and the existence of the collectivity'.[40]

Other critics have pointed to equally fundamental problems. If, for example, the term *état de droit* has achieved widespread currency what exactly does it

---

[33] The idea was that fifty parliamentary deputies supported by one tenth of the electors could call a referendum. See R. Darnoux, 'Les techniques de démocratie semi-directe sous le Ve République', *Revue de droit public*, 2 (1995), 413–47.

[34] Y. Aguila, 'Cinq questions sur l'interprétation constitutionnelle', *Revue française de droit constitutionnel*, 21 (1995), 9–46.

[35] Ameller, 'Le Comité consultatif', p. 262.

[36] M. Troper, 'Le concept d'Etat de droit', *Droits*, 15 (1992), 51–63.

[37] C. Emeri, 'L'Etat de droit dans les systèmes polyarchiques européens', *Revue française de droit constitutionnel*, 9 (1992), 27–41.

[38] 'Le droit contre la politique', *Le Débat*, 64 (1991), p. 148.

[39] See F. Tinland, 'L'Etat de droit: héritage du XVIIe siècle', *Philosophie politique*, 1 (1992), 55–65.

[40] L. Hamon, 'Une Lettre sur la théorie de la constitution de Carl Schmitt', *Droits*, 19 (1994), 153–9.

mean? Is it simply a French version of the doctrines of *Rechtsstaat, stato di diritto* and the rule of law? If so, which one? But this raises a more serious ambiguity. As Michel Troper has argued:

> the expression *Etat de droit* ... designates two types of relationship between the state and the law: an *Etat de droit* could be a state subjected to a law which is exterior to itself or it could simply be a state which acts according to the law.[41]

In both cases there are difficulties. With regard to the first option, from Machiavelli onwards the very meaning of modernity has entailed 'the rupture of law from all forms of transcendence'.[42] The positivist variant of a hierarchy of norms arguably fares no better, as this would make every judicial order an *état de droit*. As for the second definition, there is absolutely no guarantee that law will not be oppressive and a threat to the liberty of the individual. Faced with these challenges critics of the idea of an *état de droit* in France (as with critics of liberalism in this country) have found merit in the decisionism of Carl Schmitt.

The Liberalism of Benjamin Constant

Are these criticisms justified and do they dispel the attractions of arguments in support of an *état de droit*? In the remainder of this article I shall consider what has been the most sustained and coherent defence of an *état de droit* in France, that provided by Blandine Kriegel. I intend to begin, however, by discussing the writings of Benjamin Constant. The justification for doing so is twofold. Firstly I accept the force, if not the legitimacy, of Schmitt's criticisms of liberal constitutionalism and to that extent, like Schmitt, take Constant to be 'the initiator of the whole liberal spirit of the nineteenth century'.[43] Secondly, Kriegel shares many of Constant's preoccupations, even if she is determined to avoid what she describes as his 'arrogant conclusion' that citizenship should be tied to the competence and not the dignity and conscience of the individual.[44] Moreover it is in developing their shared opposition to the 'imperial state' that Kriegel reveals that an advocacy of an *état de droit* need not be (as it was with Constant) antithetical to an inclusive conception of democracy. This in turn allows us to dispense with Schmitt's reduction of the concept of the political to the distinction between friend and enemy.[45]

Summarising his work in 1829 Constant wrote:

> For forty years I have defended the same principle: liberty in everything; in religion; in philosophy; in literature; in industry; in politics. And by liberty I mean the triumph of individuality as much over an authority which wishes to govern by despotism as over the masses who demand the right to enslave the minority to the majority.[46]

---

[41] Troper, 'Le concept de l'Etat de droit', p. 55.

[42] P. Bouretz, 'La force du droit' in Bouretz, *La force du droit*, p. 19.

[43] C. Schmitt, *Political Sovereignty: Four Chapters on the Concept of Sovereignty* (Cambridge MA, MIT Press, 1988), p. 74.

[44] Kriegel, *L'Etat de la démocratie*, p. 14. See also B. Kriegel, 'La crise de la citoyenneté' in P. Herzog (ed.), *Quelle démocratie? Quelle citoyenneté* (Paris, Ouvrières, 1995), pp. 45–50.

[45] C. Schmitt, *The Concept of the Political* (New Brunswick, Rutgers UP, 1976).

[46] B. Constant, *Mélanges de littérature et de politique* (Paris, Pichon et Didier, 1829), p. vi.

Underpinning this statement was Constant's distinction between the liberty of the ancients and that of the moderns, the politics of the modern age having gone terribly wrong because its practitioners had imposed the ancient vision of active participation in civic life and war upon a people that now sought 'the peaceful enjoyment of individual independence' through trade and commerce.[47] It had been in the name of liberty that France had been subject to 'prisons, scaffolds, countless persecutions' and, of course, the Terror.[48] But if for Constant the figure of Robespierre denoted despotism so too did Napoleon and his system of imperial government.

The charge was that it embodied a system of usurpation and arbitrary government, with arbitrary power cast as 'the great enemy of all liberty, the corrupting vice of every institution, the seed of death that one cannot modify or mitigate only destroy'.[49] As such, power was 'necessarily stamped with the individuality of the usurper', with corruption, injustice, violence, treachery and perjury the inevitable consequence. All are turned into slaves and, worse still, must voice their public approval, the oppressed being deprived of their last remaining consolation – silence. There is, Constant comments, 'one kind of interest which is not crushed under arbitrary power ... it is that which leads [man] to beg, to pillage, to enrich himself through the favours of power and the spoils of weakness'.[50] The entire edifice, he concludes, rests upon the utterly implausible assumption of the 'universality of disinterestedness'.

Constant's responses to this new form of despotism varied over time, often for strategic reasons; but he presents at least three arguments that position him close to later defenders of an *état de droit*. The first was a rejection of all forms of sovereignty that claimed to be unlimited and indivisible, and therefore of any attempt 'to confer upon the legislator an almost boundless empire over human existence'.[51] This rebuke to 'the terrible consequences and incalculable dangers' of Rousseau's ideas was accompanied not only by a plea for the recognition that there was a part of human life that was legitimately beyond social and legislative control but also by calls for the decentralization of governmental functions, an independent judiciary, the separation of powers and the institutionalization of what he termed 'a neutral power' at the heart of the state capable of guaranteeing political liberties.

Constant argued secondly for constitutional government and the rule of law. As he observed in his *Commentaire sur l'ouvrage de Filangieri*:

> When governments offer peoples legislative improvements they should reply by demanding constitutional institutions. Without a constitution a people can have no certainty that the laws will be observed. It is in constitutions, in the punishments that they pronounce against the unfaithful possessors of authority, in the rights that they ensure for citizens, in the publicity that they afford, that resides the coercive force necessary to compel government to respect the law.[52]

---

[47] See B. Fontana (ed.), *Benjamin Constant: Political Writings* (Cambridge, Cambridge University Press, 1988).

[48] See his 1797 text: *Des Effets de la Terreur* (Lausanne, Terreaux, 1947).

[49] B. Constant, *Des Réactions politiques* (Paris, 1797), p. 94.

[50] Constant, *Political Writings*, pp. 122–3.

[51] B. Constant, *Commentaire sur l'ouvrage de Filangieri* (Paris, Didot, 1822), p. 37.

[52] Constant, *Commentaire*, p. 34.

Political institutions thus properly exist only as an 'assemblage of rules' upon which the citizen must be able to count.

But, Constant asked, 'was the name of the law always sufficient to oblige a man to obey?'[53] Herein lies Constant's third important argument. If sovereignty was not unlimited, then nor was the authority of the law. What it could not challenge were 'the individual rights' of the citizen, rights possessed 'independently of all social and political authority'. Constant defined those rights as individual and religious liberty, freedom of opinion, guarantees against arbitrary power and the enjoyment of property.[54] Stephen Holmes has argued that Constant gives us a 'contextual theory of individual rights', the ideal of rights only making sense in the cultural and institutional setting of modern society where they serve to 'counter the threat posed by the expansionistic tendency of the modern political sphere'.[55] This is undoubtedly the case with the right to property, which Constant describes as 'merely a social convention', and he was certainly no admirer of abstract formulations of rights. But in rejecting Bentham's utilitarian critique of rights Constant also seemed to want to give them greater substance, seeing them as both timeless and inherent to the human personality. 'No duty', Constant writes, 'binds us to those pretended laws [which] demand from us actions contrary to those eternal principles of justice and mercy that man cannot cease to observe without debasing and betraying his nature'.[56]

Where Constant runs into trouble is in his rejection of universal suffrage and a fully representative democracy. Required for 'the exercise of the rights of citizenship', he writes, 'is the leisure indispensable for the acquisition of understanding and soundness of judgement. Property alone makes men capable of exercising political rights.'[57] This is a view that can be found with relative ease in French liberal constitutionalism in the first half of the nineteenth century. It has since been used to discredit liberalism as a whole and still serves (as is revealed by Blandine Kriegel's eagerness to deny the claims of an 'expert élite') to give an anti-democratic air to defences of an *état de droit*.

If this challenge can be met it is through a recognition that a contemporary advocacy of an *état de droit* entails a reformulation and renovation of our concept of democracy. It too would ironically share Constant's doubts about the indivisibility of sovereignty and about representative democracy, refusing to accept that good government was synonymous with the limitless power of the elected and believing that an enlarged pluralistic democracy would rest upon other forms of legitimation than universal suffrage. However, as Constant recognized, this would still leave a place for participation and civic involvement. Falsely accused of an exclusive concern with the merits of negative liberty, Constant's position was rather that 'the danger of modern liberty is that, absorbed in the enjoyment of our private independence, and in the pursuit of our particular interests, we should surrender our right to share in political

[53] B. Constant, 'De l'obéissance à la loi' in M. Harpaz (ed.), *Constant: Recueil d'articles* (Geneva, Droz, 1972), p. 318.

[54] Constant, *Political Writings*, pp. 180–2.

[55] S. Holmes, *Benjamin Constant and the Making of Modern Liberalism* (New Haven, Yale UP, 1984), pp. 53–4.

[56] Constant, *Political Writings*, p. 181.

[57] Constant, *Political Writings*, p. 214.

power too easily'. Our goal, he wrote, must not be to renounce one or other of the forms of liberty but 'to learn to combine the two together'.[58]

The Illiberalism of French Political Culture

Yet the views of Constant have been foreign to a 'French political imagination' that until recently continued to be wedded strongly to 'illiberalism'.[59] The 'central question' remained that of who held power rather than what form should that power take, 'the dynamic of sovereignty' pushing France between the opposites of absolute monarchy and a radical republic with no thought to sovereignty's limitation. It has been, Pierre Rosanvallon writes, 'the kings of war and the kings of glory that [the French] admire'. Their ideal has been only 'to democratize absolutism', a secret aspiration given flesh in the 'republican monarchism' of de Gaulle's Fifth Republic.

Of late this liberal heritage has been re-appraised, the emphasis falling not merely on past mistakes but upon lessons to be learnt. And this itself has invited a more fundamental re-reading of France's past and, specifically, the history and meaning of the Republic. One of the people most seriously involved in this massive enterprise combining historical scholarship and political philosophy is Blandine Barret Kriegel.

Blandine Kriegel and the History of the State

Kriegel's first book, *L'Etat et les esclaves*,[60] was published in 1979 although prior to this she had begun work on a *doctorat d'Etat*, supervised by Michel Foucault,[61] entitled *Constitution de l'histoire savante aux XVII–XVIII siècles*. This was subsequently published in four volumes in 1988 and had as its overall theme 'the entropy which restricted, distorted and finally wrecked the policy of historical research pursued by the monarchy'.[62] Despite its esoteric sound this project has underpinned all Kriegel's other work, its major conclusion being that the substance of that historical research was intended to free the French state from the influence of Roman law and thus from the clutches of the Holy Roman Empire.[63] It was the failure of this policy that prevented France from becoming a fully-fledged *état de droit* and which later led to the establishment of what she terms '*la République incertaine*'.

At the intellectual heart of this analysis is a rejection of the influential thesis advanced by Ernst Kantorowicz in *The King's Two Bodies*[64] and which Kriegel

---

[58] B. Constant, 'The liberty of the ancients combined with that of the moderns' in Constant, *Political Writings*, pp. 326–7.

[59] P. Rosanvallon, *La Monarchie impossible: Les Chartes de 1814 et de 1830* (Paris, Fayard, 1994), pp. 149–81.

[60] B. Barret-Kriegel, *L'Etat et les esclaves* (Paris, Calmann-Lévy, 1979). Subsequent references will be to the 1989 Payot edition. An English language version of this text under the title *The State and the Rule of Law* was published by Princeton University Press in 1995.

[61] For Kriegel's views on the significance of Foucault see 'De l'Etat de police à l'Etat de droit', *Le Monde*, 13 October 1989.

[62] B. Kriegel, *Les Historiens et la monarchie: I Jean Mabillon; II La Défaite de l'érudition; III Les Académies de l'Histoire; IV La République incertaine* (Paris, PUF, 1988).

[63] See B. Kriegel, *Les Chemins de l'Etat* (Paris, Calmann-Lévy, 1986), pp. 1–120.

[64] E. H. Kantorowicz, *The King's Two Bodies: a Study in Medieval Political Theology* (Princeton NJ, Princeton University Press, 1957).

does not hesitate from equating with the political positions endorsed by Schmitt and Heidigger.[65] Kriegel's interpretation of Kantorowicz's argument is that the modern state is the direct descendent of the Holy Roman Empire, which itself had been successful in transposing and secularizing from papal theocracy the doctrine of the two natures and bodies of Christ. In its political form this produces a 'theologico-political system' that roots politics in 'the mystery of the sacred body of the sovereign', with power divinely embodied in the person of the emperor, the latter now cast as 'the Caesar-Christ'. 'Stripped to its essentials', Kriegel writes, 'the political system of Kantorowicz can be reduced to the equation: State = Empire'.[66] Kriegel's objections to this thesis are not only that it is inaccurate – at least with regard to certain states, most notably France and Britain – but also politically dangerous. It gives priority to power over rights. Moreover, by giving credence to those who believe that all states are the same it supports the view that even the liberal state is a 'despotic state'.

By way of refutation Kriegel offers her own account of the emergence of the modern state, an emergence which, she believes, in France had provided the foundations of an *état de droit* by the time of the death of Henri IV. This type of state is described as one where 'power is made subject to right and is controlled by law'.[67] Its appearance ran parallel to the advent of a new concept of sovereignty that has since been incorrectly equated with absolutism. It was new in that it divorced sovereignty from seignorial power, being neither a form of *imperium* (because it was not established upon military power) nor *dominium* (because it was not based upon a master-slave relationship). 'Feudal authority', Kriegel writes, 'was servitude; the sovereign state heralds emancipation'. And this was so because endorsement of the legitimacy of the supremacy of the state did not entail the establishment of 'a power without limits' but one limited 'by the law and above all by individual rights'.[68]

This was made possible by the anti-imperial nature of the new state which was fashioned to secure internal peace and which no longer saw its subjects as property. It sought as its 'first concern' to dispense justice and to guarantee the safety and personal liberty of its people. 'To be safe, to be free, to live in security', Kriegel comments, 'means that each person has the right to life and the right to possess his own body'.[69] This innovation she in part attributes to Bodin and Loyseau but Kriegel also contends that its development owes much to Hobbes, Spinoza[70] and Locke in particular. 'From each of them', she argues, 'we owe the fundamental idea of the equality of persons which itself rests upon the idea of the unity of humanity'.

This latter point is of immense importance to Kriegel's argument and goes right to the heart of her understanding of the rights of man.[71] For all three thinkers, she argues, the philosophical foundation of the rights of man was natural law. Each believed that 'man had a nature' and that it was only through 'madness or stupidity' that this was denied. Each too believed that this nature,

---

[65] See especially B. Kriegel, *La politique de la raison* (Paris, Payot, 1994).

[66] Kriegel, *La politique de la raison*, p. XXII.

[67] Kriegel, *L'Etat et les esclaves*, p. 33.

[68] Kriegel, *L'Etat et les esclaves*, pp. 63–4.

[69] Kriegel, *L'Etat et la démocratie*, p. 28.

[70] Spinoza has an important place throughout Kriegel's writings but see especially 'Spinoza et la doctrine de la liberté politique' in Kriegel, *Les Chemins de l'Etat*, pp. 267–88.

[71] See B. Kriegel, *Les Droits de l'homme et le droit naturel* (Paris, PUF, 1986).

and the laws that sprang from it, could be discovered by reason. Thus if men wished to live together in society these rights had to be respected. It was Kant, Kriegel argues, who first fully acknowledged the implication of this argument. If the law of nature exists then the rights of man were valid for all men since they shared the same nature. Therefore, Kriegel writes, 'they are susceptible of being properly realized only in the context of a humanity that has finally been unified through the co-existence of *Etats de droit*, that is, a universal republic'.[72]

This 'anticipation' of a possible future for 'the development of nations' has clearly not yet been realized. 'In place of the state', Kriegel comments, we have 'the nation; in place of justice, education; in place of internal peace, external war; in place of law, faith; in place of the rights of man, the imperatives of society'. This she regards as an especially German phenomenon but placed there is also the object of Constant's displeasure: Napoleon Bonaparte.[73] What Kriegel sees is a return to the traditions of Roman law and therefore the continuation of the imperial state based upon domination and slavery. 'The prince is not he who enforces the law', she writes, 'but he who displays his strength'. In the twentieth century this has meant totalitarianism.

But why was France in particular unable to build upon its earlier efforts to break from medieval and imperial notions of power? Kriegel's argument is that the initial moves towards the establishment of an '*Etat de justice*', where 'the application of the law constituted the core of the state's functions', were subverted when financial and administrative considerations turned the application of the law into the prerogative of a private, self-interested corporation. France was turned into an '*Etat de finance*', only for it later to become an '*Etat de police*', a process brought to fruition under Napoloeon's regime of 'police surveillance' and 'military-political dictatorship'.[74]

The French Revolution and its Consequences

How did the French Revolution affect this slide away from the principles of an *état de droit*? There are three important points that Kriegel emphasizes. The first is that the Revolution was characterized by a return to the 'model of Roman antiquity' and therefore the tradition of Roman law.[75] Here she makes much of the significance of David's painting *The Oath of the Horatii*. The point of reference is the citizen-soldier with power residing in the sword (a vision of society where both women and children are ostracized).[76] With the Revolution therefore we return to a pre-modern notion of *imperium*, and the fateful equation of liberty with death, the salvation of the nation with the right to conquest. The consequences unfolded with the Terror: 'No more private affection, no more family bonds, no more individual rights: all are effaced before the sacred love of the homeland'.

[72] Kriegel, *La politique de la raison*, p. 95. See also the chapter in this volume entitled 'Kant et l'idée de république universelle', pp. 25–40.

[73] On Napoleon see 'Le Code civil et le droit naturel', in Kriegel, *La politique de la raison*, pp. 215–9.

[74] See Kriegel, *La République incertaine*.

[75] Kriegel, *Les chemins de l'Etat*, pp. 231–42.

[76] Kriegel, *La politique de la raison*, pp. 250–60.

The second point is that sovereign power continued to be defined in terms of a will, and therefore in terms of decision. Here for once the source of the original error (an error that ultimately produces the theories of Schmitt) is located in Bodin. In all essentials the character of sovereignty remained the same, the 'royal will' being replaced only by 'the national will'. In consequence the sovereign republic always ran the risk of becoming imperial government.

It is Kriegel's third point that is arguably the most portentous. Again there is reference to David's painting, this time to indicate that society is judged to have its origin in a pact voluntarily entered into by its male citizens. In 1789 this is reflected in a declaration of rights that puts the emphasis upon the rights of the citizen rather than upon the rights of man. This 'subjectivist' reading of rights, Kriegel argues, has its philosophical source in Descartes[77] but she most extensively explores its significance in a discussion of article X of the *Déclaration des droits de l'homme et du citoyen* and the arguments of the Protestant pastor Rabaut Saint-Etienne in defence of the right to liberty of conscience.[78] The rejection of Rabaut Saint-Etienne's proposal, Kriegel argues, reveals that for the revolutionaries of 1789 the rights of man were not thought to derive from man's nature, were not natural rights, but had their origin in a civil convention; hence freedom of opinion would be allowed 'provided that it did not disturb the public order established by law'.

By refusing to acknowledge the right to religious toleration, Kriegel argues, the revolutionaries were debarred from recognizing individual conscience as the source of citizenship and thus were obliged to establish its foundation upon ideas not drawn from Spinoza and Locke but from the French Enlightenment. It was understanding and culture that defined the 'civilized citizen'. In effect, citizenship was equated not with conscience but competence, first defined in terms of property and then knowledge. Such a conception of citizenship, Kriegel states, was necessarily 'exclusionary'. Obviously excluded were women and children, but so too are the poor, the ignorant, and 'those peoples thought to be barbarian'. It is this emphasis upon competence, Kriegel contends, which explains the republican enthusiasm for public education and instruction that itself was a reflection of an elitist and exclusive conception of citizenship.

It was this perspective that determined the development of the French state in the nineteenth century. Judged incompetent the workers turned their back on politics, believing its promises to be illusory, the result being a 'compromise' designed to secure 'civil peace': *l'Etat-providence*. In inspiration this had nothing to do with an extension of democracy or of rights but was rather a form of 'public and social hygiene'.[79]

The Crisis of Citizenship

In Kriegel's opinion, therefore, the roots of France's present crisis of citizenship lie deep in her history. It is a crisis that derives from the republican tradition itself and from the fact that the republican state remains a direct descendent of the imperial state. The Fifth Republic she regards as a renewed form of *imperium* and a 'regime of public power'. To financial and administrative

[77] Kriegel, *La politique de la raison*, pp. 3–24.
[78] Kriegel, *La politique de la raison*, pp. 191–214.
[79] Kriegel, *Les chemins de l'Etat*, pp. 243–66.

tutelage has been added a 'corporatism of élites' and the emergence of a new 'techo-structure' with power (and therefore effective citizenship) confined to the 'caste' system of the *grands corps* (and specifically the *énarques*). 'The tradition of our country', she writes, 'has been to balance the *imperium* of administration with the sovereignty of the law'.[80]

To remedy these defects and the civic malaise they engender Kriegel's recommendation is that a break must be made with the doctrine of sovereign power and specifically with the language of its indivisibility. In their place should be 'the separation of powers and the institutionalization of the rights of man'.[81] In addition therefore to an enhanced role for the *Conseil constitutionnel*, in her 1985 Report to Mitterrand she called for the creation of an *Haute Autorité de protection des libertés publiques* designed to safeguard civil rights as well as to bring France in line with the European Convention on Human Rights. She likewise spoke of the need to formulate a 'code of citizenship' in order that everyone had a proper sense of their rights in society. Conscious of the charge that she could be accused of advocating a 'government of judges' (here referred to as the 'American solution')[82] Kriegel is also of the view that the enhanced judicial power should be 'independent, but controlled, in line with the requirements of a democratic society'.[83] In a way that is unclear it is to remain linked to the sovereignty of the people.

Also lacking in clarity are Kriegel's views on representation. She acknowledges that few people would wish to make a return to the practices of the Fourth Republic and she herself disputes the claims of direct and non-parliamentary forms of representation. She is clearly not happy with the idea of a 'democracy of opinion' articulated via the media nor with handing power to interest groups masquerading in the form of 'civil society'. Rather, her line is that if there is a crisis of democracy it is less a problem of representation than a 'problem of the state'. What is required, Kriegel has recently written, 'is a surgical operation on the French state' in order that less decisions are taken automatically by the state's administrative apparatus.[84] 'This means', she argues, 'leaving an area of greater initiative to bodies elected by democracy whilst at the same time putting them under the control of the judiciary'.

One clear example of this would be reform of the procedures of welfare provision and of *l'Etat-providence* in general, where 'dialogue' must replace the practices of *imperium*. 'Tutelary power', Kriegel comments, 'must now be replaced by a set of services from which the citizen has a right to expect benefits responding to his needs'.[85] There should likewise be less state administrative interference in industry although this should be accompanied by an extension of workers' rights. 'We are invited too hastily,' Kriegel comments, 'to abandon social rights when we should civilize the social and individualize citizenship'.

---

[80] Kriegel, *L'Etat et la démocratie*, p. 79. It is interesting to note that these criticisms of the French state received vigorous expression in the wave of popular protest that engulfed France in the final two months of 1995.

[81] B. Kriegel, *Propos sur la démocratie* (Paris, Descartes et Cie, 1994), p. 42.

[82] Kriegel, *L'Etat et la démocratie*, p. 85.

[83] Kriegel, *Propos sur la démocratie*, p. 70.

[84] B. Kriegel, 'La démocratie' in Herzog, *Quelle démocratie? Quelle citoyenneté*, p. 135.

[85] Kriegel, *L'Etat et la démocratie*, p. 127.

One area where Kriegel is adamant that representation must be increased is in the representation of women.[86] But this itself figures as part of a wider argument against the elitist conception of citizenship characteristic of republicanism in France. What has to be abandoned, Kriegel writes, is a 'republican anthropology' that itself rests upon 'an ontological deficiency'.[87] It is this 'subjectivist' and 'conventionalist' account of a citizen's rights that underpins the exclusionary character of the present system. What is required 'is a doctrine of the rights of man ... based upon an anthropology of human nature, the equality of human beings and the necessary relationship that unites them when this conforms to their reason'.[88] It is only this alternative anthropology that will enable the creation of a truly democratic republic.

Here above all lies Kriegel's reply to those who believe that modern politics cannot but be reduced to will and decision, and therefore to the division between friend and enemy. The plea is for a return to what she consistently (and perhaps unconvincingly) describes as the natural law tradition of Hobbes, Spinoza and Locke, deriving the rights of man from the state of nature and therefore emphasizing man's natural sociability.[89] 'The sole foundation of society and the only legitimation of the political order,' Kriegel argues,

> does not lie in an act of free choice made by the individual consciousness. They lie in delegating the executive power of the natural law that founds sovereignty and justice, so as to guarantee the conservation of life and to assure human rights to security, freedom and equality. Human rights determine civil rights, but natural law remains an abiding principle.[90]

We are far removed from the Cartesian philosophy of the subject and are in the realm of rights that are valid for all men and for all women regardless of their situation and position. All states that disregard them are by definition despotic states. Moreover Kriegel is clear that this 'juridical foundation of the *Etats de droit* comes not from Roman law but from the Bible'.[91]

Conclusion

The argument of this article, therefore, is that no reform of the Constitution of France's Fifth Republic will begin to address the problems of exclusion, social division and citizenship as long as the proposed changes remain wedded to the traditions and practices of the imperial state. This is precisely the case with the most recent revisions and specifically that of 1995. The preoccupation remains that of sovereignty over rights, centralization rather than the separation of power, and the direct relationship of the state with the individual. Faced with the need to extend and re-define rights, as well as to affirm the opportunities of citizens to be involved, such a strategy is doomed to failure. Most pressingly 'republican elitism', with its emphasis on assimilation through education, cannot respond to the ever-growing multicultural nature of French society. As

[86] See 'La crise de la citoyenneté' in Herzog, *Quelle démocratie, Quelle citoyenneté*, p. 57.

[87] Kriegel, *Propos sur la démocratie*, p. 27.

[88] Kriegel, *Propos sur la démocratie*, p. 30.

[89] See, for example, 'Un entretien avec Marcel Gauchet et Blandine Kriegel', *Le Monde*, 12 July 1994.

[90] Kriegel, *Les Droits de l'homme et le droit naturel*, p. 98.

[91] Kriegel, *L'Etat et les esclaves*, p. 12.

Joël Roman has commented: 'What threatens [French society] is its refusal to accord a place to its differences, its forced homogenization'.[92] Armed with this conceptual weaponry it is small wonder that Le Pen and the *Front national* prove such difficult opponents.[93]

By contrast there is a tradition of thinking in France – for long buried beneath a dominant anti-liberalism – which is better able to accommodate the parallel demands for individual autonomy and involvement in the decisions of public life. It breaks with both the absolutist heritage of French politics and the Rousseauian image of the general will, placing the emphasis upon the rights of the individual and the superiority of the Constitution over the law. It does not wish to subordinate politics to a regime of judicial dominance and activism, believing that many of France's contemporary ills derive from a lack of participation and deliberation, but it does entail an endorsement of a new, emerging conception of republican democracy freed of Jacobin and imperial impedimenta. Moreover, it is in line not just with recent constitutional thinking on the nature of an *état de droit* but with a gradual evolution of the French judicial system (as the handling of the recent *affaire Juppé* illustrates).[94] It is manifestly not without its difficulties (nor its opponents) but in writers such as Constant and Kriegel we get a vision of a different type of politics where priority is given to rights, where the state is subject to law, sovereignty is divided and all of society fully represented. In the words of Blandine Kriegel, it presages the 'humanization' rather than the 'divinization' of the state.

---

[92] J. Roman, 'Un multiculturalisme à la française?', *Esprit* 212 (1995), 157–8.

[93] See the views of Henri Leclerc, President of the *Ligue des droits de l'homme*, in *Le Monde*, 25 August 1995. Leclerc comments that 'the present climate' represents 'a victory for the ideas of Le Pen'.

[94] A. Garapon, 'Le Droit et l'affaire Juppé', *Esprit* 216 (1995), 166–70.

The Basic Law versus the Basic Norm?
The Case of the Bavarian
Crucifix Order

HOWARD CAYGILL AND ALAN SCOTT

The German Constitutional Court's ruling published in August 1995 that the so-called 'Bavarian crucifix order' (*Kreuzesbefehl*) was unconstitutional stimulated widespread public debate. Subsequent events, which included threats by the Bavarian Prime Minster to ignore the ruling and a large religious demonstration led by both Catholic and Protestant bishops, suggested that the implications of the case are wider than a conflict between federal and state constitutional courts. Indeed, the judgement was thought to have ramifications not just for 'Catholic Bavaria' but for the very idea of a Christian-occidental identity within an increasingly culturally and religiously heterogeneous Germany and Europe.

The ruling raises in a particularly stark fashion questions concerning the relationship of constitutions and constitutional courts to normal politics, on the one hand, and to the specific culture within which they are embedded and whose values they may be said to embody and protect, on the other. The reunification of Germany had already produced a sharpening of cultural and value conflicts, some of which were mediated through constitutional debate. Examples include abortion, where the incompatibility between the law in (West) Germany and that in the ex-GDR had led to considerable controversy; the constitutional status of 'ethnic Germans', and asylum rights.

Under such conditions of cultural and value pluralism, appealing to the values and 'traditions' of any one community is clearly problematic. This makes an implicit or explicit appeal to the seemingly more neutral and abstract values embodied in the constitution itself an attractive alternative. The hope here would be that a minimum consensus might be reached on the basis of which less easily reconcilable differences might be bridged, the constitution acting as bridgehead. In this way pluralism seems to lend support to the Habermasian notion of 'constitutional patriotism'.[1] However, here we shall argue that the ruling on the crucifix order suggests that problems of cultural diversity and the reconciliation of conflicting beliefs are not necessarily resolved via the constitution or through an appeal to constitutional patriotism. Indeed, we suggest that such conflicts may even be exacerbated where they become the object of constitutional scrutiny. If cultural conflicts are not made more amenable to resolution through constitutional means, this prompts the

---

[1] For a recent discussion in the light of German reunification and the developments within Europe – particularly the political development of the EU – see J. Habermas, 'Citizenship and national identity: some reflections on the future of Europe', *Praxis International*, 12, 1 (1992), 1–19.

further question as to how far claims to universality embedded in a particular constitutional order may work to deconstitute the very cultural values which it should protect.

What makes the case of the crucifix order such an interesting demonstration of these broader problems of constitutional politics is the fact that the conflict involved is not the familiar one of the confrontation between a 'minority' and a new constitutional order or political tradition, but a conflict *within* a single national political culture. This raises the further possibility that a constitutional culture stands in as problematic relationship to 'its' own national culture as it does to those that do not share 'its' political-cultural 'traditions'.

In this chapter we discuss these wider issues through an examination of the two conflicting rulings – that of the Bavarian Constitutional Court and that of the German Federal Constitutional Court (colloquially, the 'Karlsruher Gerichtshof') – which lie at the legal centre of this controversy and the debate which surrounds these judgements.

The Crucifix Affair

The *Kreuzesbefehl* which reads '*In jedem Klassenzimmer ist ein Kreuz anzubringen*' [A cross is to be hung in every classroom] is contained in §13 I3 of the *Schulordnung für die Volksschulen in Bayern* [School Ordinance for Primary Schools in Bavaria], 1983. It had legal force in all Bavarian primary schools. A case was brought against the order by a family who adhered to the anthroposophic teachings of Rudolf Steiner. Their objections to the mandatory presence of crucifixes in school classrooms were broadly twofold. First, as non-Christians the enforced learning under a Christian symbol – '*unterm Kreuz lernen*' – injured their right to religious freedom and to bring up their children in accordance with their beliefs. Secondly, the symbol itself, that of a 'dying male body' [*sterbenden männlichen Körpers*], was held by the family to have detrimental effects upon their children. To accommodate these objections the original large crucifix (80 × 60 cm) over the blackboard in their eldest daughter's classroom was exchanged for a more discrete cross placed over the door. But this compromise on the part of the school authorities in 1986 was not in the long run thought by the family to meet their objections. Lacking the means to avoid the dilemma by keeping their three children in Waldorf Schools, they took their case to the Bavarian Constitutional Court. This ruled against them in 1991. They then appealed to the Federal Constitutional Court and this body found in their favour in 1995.

That such an explicit order concerning religious practice should have been passed is consistent with the intentions of the authors of the Bavarian Constitution of 1946 which, like those of other predominantly Catholic *Länder* (e.g. Baden-Württemberg), attempted to give Christian culture constitutional form. For example, Article 131, which specifically addresses education reads:

> (1) Schools should not only transmit knowledge and skills, but also build heart and character.
> (2) The foremost aims of education are: reverence before God, respect for religious conviction and for the dignity of persons, self-control, a sense of and joy in responsibility, readiness to help, receptivity for all that is true,

good, and beautiful, and awareness of responsibility for nature and the environment.[2]

(3) Pupils are to be educated into the spirit of democracy, the love of their Bavarian homeland and of the German people and in accordance with reconciliation between peoples.

(4) In addition girls in particular are to be instructed in the care of infants, education of children and home economy.[3]

At the same time, like other liberal constitutions, the Bavarian Constitution recognizes rights to freedom of religious confession and practice, for example Article 107, I guarantees religious freedom (see also 107, VI: 'No-one may be forced into religious act or participation in religious practice or services or into the use of a religious oath'). Thus anyone objecting to the *Kreuzesbefehl* could point to the Bavarian Constitution itself as well as to those Articles of the Basic Law concerning religious freedom (Article 4, I), the rights of parents in determining their children's upbringing (Article 6, II), and the protection of basic rights (Article 19, IV). The tension between the cultural content of the Bavarian Constitution and its liberal universalizing form, and between the attempt to reconcile constitutionally a catholic and still (at least in 1946) predominantly rural society with the Basic Law as the embodiment of a liberal modernity was at the heart of the legal dispute over the *Kreuzesbefehl*. The rulings of the two constitutional courts lay bare these tensions, and it is to these that we now turn.

The Bavarian Constitutional Court's Ruling

The Bavarian Constitutional Courts' ruling of June 1991 against the family reads as follows:

> The placing of a crucifix or other representation of the cross in classrooms of state schools does not injure the basic right to negative religious freedom of pupils and parents who on religious or philosophical [*weltanschaulich*] grounds reject such representation.[4]

We shall abstract somewhat the grounds for this judgement from the context of their legal precedents. The Court argued that the plaintiffs could not enjoy unrestricted rights to negative religious freedom because such rights were bounded, for example by rights and duties of the *Länder* and schools to determine the pedagogic aims which were to direct children's education. In this spirit the judges noted that '... it is in fact impossible for the school to

---

[2] This rather contemporary final environmental thought was added as part of a fifth amendment to the Bavarian constitution in 1981. Similar amendments were added to other *Länder* constitutions around this time under the influence of the growing environmental movement.

[3] Current German *Länder* constitutions plus the Basic Law are published in C. Pestalozza (ed.), *Verfassungen der deutschen Bundesländer* (Munich, DTV, 1991). Historic constitutions (plus again the Basic Law) are published in H. Hildebrandt (ed.), *Die deutschen Verfassungen des 19. und 20. Jahrhunderts* (Padernorn, Schöningh, 1971). A translation of the Basic Law can be found in S. E. Finer (ed.), *Five Constitutions* (London, Penguin, 1979).

[4] The full ruling is contained in *Neue Zeitschrift für Verwaltungsrecht*, (hereafter, *NZfV*), 11 (1991), 1099–1101, p. 1099.

represent all religious/philosophical wishes and educational desires. The recognition of this must not lead the school to restrict itself to teaching in a completely value-neutral fashion or to forgo any educational aim or style of teaching where there exist differences of opinion among parents' (*NZfV*, p. 1100). Indeed they go further by arguing that such a restriction would damage the positive religious freedoms of the majority and they posit a tension between negative and positive religious freedom ('*Spannungsverhältnis zwischen negativer und positiver Religionsfreiheit*') as a further limitation on the former's sphere of validity.

However, the most remarked upon and controversial aspect of the Bavarian ruling was the judges' argument that the parents did not have the right to demand the removal of the cross because that symbol did not in and of itself carry any specific confessional baggage:

> With the representation of the cross as the icon of the suffering and Lord-ship of Jesus Christ ... the plaintiffs who reject such a representation are confronted with a religious worldview in which the formative power of Christian belief is affirmed. However, they are not thereby brought into a constitutionally unacceptable religious-philosophical conflict. Representa-tions of the cross confronted in this fashion are – like the cross-confessional school prayer – not the expression of a conviction of a belief bound to a specific confession. They are an essential object of the general Christian-occidental tradition and common property of the Christian-occidental cultural circle. (*NZfV*, p. 1101)

From this they concluded that 'the mere presence of the representation of a cross demands neither an identification with the ideas or beliefs thereby embodied nor any other form of active behaviour oriented thereto'. For the sake of our later argument, the irony here is that the Bavarian Constitutional Court is ascribing a neutrality and universality to Christianity which is at least analogous to that more usually ascribed to the constitution itself. Christianity is cast as an (almost) culture-neutral backdrop against which only the other minority religions stand out:

> The problematic presented [here] is distinct from cases in which the teacher through especially determined behaviour – in particular through the wearing of attention-drawing [*auffällig*] clothing (Baghwan) – which unambiguously indicates a specific religious or philosophical conviction impermissibly impairs the basic right to negative religious freedom of pupil and parent. (*NZfV*, p. 1101)

This last quotation probably makes clear why the Bavarian Constitutional Court's ruling should have occasioned considerable amusement and disdain in Germany's liberal press. In fact the ruling rests to a considerable degree upon the putative neutrality of Christian symbolism. It is upon this basis that the judges were able to conclude that the *Kreuzesbefehl* did not entail missionary activity on the part of the school and therefore did not injure the right of negative religious freedom. It was this claim of neutrality which also attracted the attention of the German Constitutional Court in overturning the initial ruling.

The Federal Constitutional Court's Ruling

By majority verdict the Federal Constitutional Court ruled against the Bavarian Court as follows:

> (i) The placement of a cross or crucifix in classrooms of a state compulsory school, which is not a confessional school, violates Article 4, I of the Basic Law.
>
> (ii) 13 I3 of the School Ordnance for Primary Schools in Bavaria is irreconcilable with Article 4, I of the Basic Law and is void.[5]

The grounds for the judgement constituted a comprehensive rebuttal of the arguments made by the Bavarian Constitutional Court and took issue with its ruling on practically every point. After criticizing the Bavarian school authorities and courts for procrastination and failing to seek with sufficient vigour an acceptable provisional solution to the conflict, the judges launched a direct attack on the legal and theological arguments used by the Bavarian Constitutional Court in supporting its decision. The core disagreements turn on (i) the interpretation of Article 4, I; (ii) the issues of the imputed neutrality of the cross as a mere symbol of occidental culture; (iii) the constitutional implications of cultural pluralism.

Regarding Article 4, I, the Karlsruher Gerichtshof judges argued that the guarantee of religious freedom means that 'the decision for or against a faith is a matter for the individual, not the state. The state must neither prescribe nor forbid a faith to the individual' (*NJW*, p. 2478). Furthermore, such a right also entails the 'freedom to avoid the cultural activities of a faith which one does not share'. But where the two rulings depart most abruptly is in the claim of the Federal Constitutional Court that Article 4, I entails a positive duty on the part of the state to guarantee this freedom of religious conviction: 'It accords to the state the duty to secure a sphere of action in which the personality within the philosophical/religious domain can develop, and to protect that sphere of activity from attack or hindrance by adherents to other religious faiths or competing religious groups' (*NJW*, p. 2478). It was this duty of the state which the judges ruled to be irreconcilable with the *Kreuzesbefehl*. Because the pupil was legally bound to attend school and therefore involuntarily exposed for extended periods to the cross, the *Kreuzesbefehl* was deemed to violate the child's right to a self-determined development of religious or philosophical conviction. This fact was thought to 'unambiguously distinguish the placement of a cross in the classroom from frequent daily encounters with religious symbols of diverse religious conviction' (*NJW*, p. 2478).[6]

The 'theological' dispute between the two constitutional courts focused upon the claim that the cross was a common object and property of Christian-occidental culture. The Federal Constitutional Court insisted against this view that 'the cross is a symbol of a particular religious conviction and not somehow merely an expression of an occidental culture partially formed by Christendom'.

---

[5] The full ruling can be found in *Neue Juristische Wochenschrift*, (hereafter, *NJW*), 38 (1995), 2477–83, p. 2477.

[6] One populist reaction to the judgement was to claim that every religious symbol from '*Wegkreuze*' (crosses and small chapels at road forks – very common in Bavaria) to the ringing of church bells would be affected by the judgement. But it is clear that the ruling is confined to cases where there is this particular combination of legal obligation, unavoidability of contact and length of exposure.

More precisely, the Court agreed that:

> The cross belongs, as it always has, to the specific symbols of the faith of Christendom. It is all but its symbol of faith *per se*. It iconographizes the redemption of mankind from original sin through the sacrifice of Christ's death, and at the same time Christ's victory over Satan and death, and His Lordship over the world; his suffering and triumph in one ... To render the cross profane would be to contradict the self-understanding of Christendom and the Church [it would] as the decision criticized here does, see it merely as an expression of an occidental tradition or a cult sign without specific implications of faith. (*NJW*, p. 2479)

In what looks like intended irony, the judgement goes on to note that 'the religious significance of the cross is clear from the context of the School Ordinance for Primary Schools in Bavaria 13 I3'.

The third area of disagreement between the Bavarian and the Federal constitutional courts concerns minority rights under conditions of increasing cultural pluralism. Whereas the Federal Constitutional Court argued for a maximalist interpretation of Article 4, I, it went for a minimalist interpretation of legal duties of the *Länder* in the setting of pedagogic aims for schools. While the Bavarian Constitutional Court had argued that cultural pluralism should not inhibit the school and school authorities from inculcating children with the religious and philosophical values of the majority (in the name of the latter's positive religious freedom), the Federal Constitutional Court argued (in the name of the negative religious freedom of the minority) that such pluralism placed a duty on the school to minimize the specificity of the substantive moral/religious values into which children were to be educated. The Federal Court thus drew precisely the opposite conclusions from the 'tension between positive and negative religious freedom' to those drawn by the Bavarian Court. In so doing, it came close to arguing that precisely the thin content of Christianity which it had maintained was not the whole content of the Christian symbol of the cross might nevertheless legitimately provide the basis of a minimal consensus for educational purposes:

> The affirmation of Christendom refers [here] to the formative cultural and educational element, not to the specific validity of faith. To Christianity as a cultural element belongs precisely also the idea of tolerance towards those who think differently. The latter's confrontation with a worldview formed by Christianity does not lead in such a case to a discriminatory rejection of non-Christian worldviews, because we are dealing here not with the transmission of faith but with the striving for the realization of an autonomous personality in the religious philosophical sphere in accordance with the fundamental principle of Article 4 of the Basic Law. (*NJW*, p. 2480)

This claim, apart from its arguably over-optimistic reading of the history of Christianity, suggests the possibility – to which we shall return – that what we have in these two judgements is a dispute over and within Christianity between its broadly Catholic and its secularizing and broadly Protestant wings. Earlier we noted the irony that the Bavarian judgement imputed to Christianity that neutrality normally accorded to the constitution. Here we have exactly the mirror argument with the Federal Constitutional Court ascribing to

Christianity the fundamental principles and values embodied in the constitution. What the cross symbolized for the Bavarians, the constitution now appears to represent for the Constitutional Court! It is the constitution which now emerges as 'an essential object of the general Christian-occidental tradition and the common property of the Christian-occidental cultural circle'.

Enough has now been said to enable us to move on to the wider implications of these judgements for our understanding of constitutions and of the notions of constitutional culture and constitutional patriotism.

The Perplexities of Constitutional Culture

The case of the Bavarian Crucifix Order illustrates the problematic relationship of a constitution both to normal politics and to the community in which it is embedded. In the following discussion we examine some aspects of this relationship, and make critical observations on some lacunae in 'actually existing constitutionalism'.

What Kant described as the fallacy of 'paralogism' – taking something which could only exist within given spatio-temporal conditions, and then speaking of it as if it were free of those conditions – can be found in what may be described as vaguely 'Kelsenite' constitutionalism which identifies, proposes, or even assumes, universal basic norms to inform a constitutional order. Whatever their source – 'nature', 'human reason', the 'supreme being' or 'the ideas of scientific communism' – such *Grundnormen* profess to be universal and immune to the effects of time. If they fail to be instantiated in or sustained over time it is because of external factors. But what if the failure of a constitution is intrinsic to it, and the language of *Grundnormen* is a rhetorical means to defer this moment, and perhaps even to conceal other, political interests at play in constitutionalism?

In an essay on the *Verfassungsentwurf* – the draft constitution drawn up by the Round Table shortly before the collapse of the GDR[7] – we cited Rousseau's characteristically paradoxical and insightful statement in the *Social Contract* concerning the conditions of a successful constitutionalism: 'the social spirit, which should be created by these institutions, would have to preside over their foundation; and men should be before law what they should become by means of law'.[8] We then understood this to mean that successful constitutional politics required not only the promulgation of a constitution but also the creation of a 'constitutional culture', if we may so translate Rousseau's 'social spirit'. Thus we adjusted Rousseau's paradox to the demands of a normative constitutionalism, in which 'constitutional culture' passes for Platonic participation in bringing the universal and eternal ideas or basic norms into historical time. Indeed, many modern constitutions resolve Rousseau's paradox by building into themselves the conditions for creating a 'social spirit' or 'constitutional culture'. The 'social spirit' presiding over the 'Declaration of the Rights of Man and the Citizen' precisely looks to create itself, in others, by means of the constitution: beginning with the claim that 'ignorance, forgetfulness, or contempt of the rights of man are the sole causes of public misfortune and governmental depravity', the

[7] H. Caygill and A. Scott, 'The subject of the constitution: the debate in Germany, 1989 and after' in R. Bellamy, V. Bufacchi and D. Castiglione (eds), *Democracy and Constitutional Culture in the Union of Europe* (London, Lothian Foundation, 1995), pp. 3–20.

[8] Cf. J.-J. Rousseau (G. D. H. Cole, trans.), *Social Contract and Discourses* (London, Dent, 1973), II, vii: 'The Legislator'.

declaration resolved to be 'perpetually present to all members of the body social . . . a constant reminder to them of their rights and duties'. Thus the body social will be educated in, and perpetually reminded of, their duty to respect the 'social spirit' informing the Declaration of the Rights of Man and the Citizen. Similarly, the preamble to the 1977 Soviet Constitution seeks, in the social spirit of scientific communism, to create a communist culture in which 'to mould the citizen of communist society'.

Before returning to the case of the crucifix order in the conclusion, we wish to raise two questions to emerge from the attempt to create a constitutional culture: (i) what implications for the stability of the constitution itself might the political act of cultural de- and reconstitution have? (ii) with what exactly does a constitution replace a pre-constitutional culture?

The Politics of Constitutional Culture

Constitutions fail when they are unable to recreate the 'social spirit' which presided over their foundations, to create a constitutional culture or produce an affect of what Habermas, again modernizing Rousseau's 'social spirit' has called 'constitutional patriotism'. This all important constitutional culture is not, strictly speaking, justiciable; it is not something within the letter of the constitution, but is its essential supplement. What is more, the character of such a culture is neither unequivocal nor uncontested; indeed the very promulgation of a formal constitution may be said to destroy the social spirit which presided over it, and which it seeks to recreate in its constitutional culture. It is in these issues that we encounter the 'political' side of 'constitutional politics', where the *Grundnorm* encounters the cases of power and violence. For 'constitutional politics' does not stop with the implementation of a constitution, but continues with the incessant effort of creating and recreating a constitutional culture, one which, in the eyes of some, is intrinsically self-defeating.

The phrase 'constitutional culture' rather like the word 'constitutionalism' is a rather neutral and innocuous term, but informing it is the ambition, in the candid words of the Soviet Constitution, to 'mould the citizen'. Rousseau was very clear about what this meant earlier in the passage on the legislator, where he says, in effect, that the 'constitutional moment' involves a de- and a re-constitution of society. The projection of a pre-constitutional state of nature makes the thought that pre-constitutional 'natural' forces have to be 'annihil-ated' in order to ensure that those acquired are 'the greater and more lasting'. An important aspect of constitutional politics is, as we all know but perhaps do not say, the deconstitution of existing social relations and their reconstitution under the new constitutional order. Yet perhaps the work of deconstitution is more permanent and irreversible than the hoped for reconstitution; the 'constitutional moment' may irreversibly break the mould for the new citizen.

The 'constitutional moment' then is intrinsically political, regardless of the constitutionalist normative rhetoric of inalienability and universality, and the causes of its success or failure are political. In order to succeed in creating a new constitutional culture, the advocates of the new constitutional order have to be prepared to wield force when other political tactics, such as appeals to reason and persuasion fail. But there is an understandable tendency among advocates of constitutional reform to pass over this aspect of constitutional politics – namely, that constitutions are politics by other means. It is far less troubling to regard them as concatenations of legal norms than as instruments for the deconstitution of existing patterns of government and social relations. In a sense, constitutionalism offers the luxury of engaging in normative politics without the responsibility of gaining and wielding political power.

Yet, as Carl Schmitt showed in his *Verfassungslehre* [constitutional studies],[9] if this refusal of political responsibility is consistently pursued by constitutionalists, then the constitution will fail. It will fail not because of external forces, but because it was not prepared politically to create and defend a constitutional culture. He diagnoses the malaise of the Weimar Republic in precisely these terms – showing that the advocates of the Weimar constitution were not prepared to exercise political power in creating a democratic constitutional culture. An even more striking example of such failure is posed by the failure of the GDR Round Table's *Verfassungsentwurf* [draft constitution]. The Citizens Movements such as New Forum which played a pivotal role in the 1989 Revolution were not prepared to assume the political responsibility which would have been necessary in order to implement their constitutional draft and defend the 'social spirit' of grassroots direct democracy which presided over its drafting.

Constitutional Abstraction

If the first problematic element of constitutions resides in their relationship to normal politics and to the deconstitution of pre-constitutional culture, the second resides in the no less problematic nature of the communities which they constitute, or attempt to constitute, in the process.

Recent criticism of the language or discourse of rights has accustomed us to the argument that the subject of such rights is not liberalism's abstract universal individual but rather a disguised form of a particular – male, white or European – empirical subject.[10] But there is another tradition of the critique of rights discourse which makes what appears to be the opposite claim; namely, that there is no real subject of rights whom those putative rights can or do protect. The most dramatic formulation of this argument we owe to Hannah Arendt's discussion of the 'perplexities of the Rights of Man' in *The Origins of Totalitarianism*, in which she asserts that 'the world found nothing sacred in the abstract nakedness of being human'.[11] Arendt's argument here is that the abstraction of such notions as the 'Rights of Man', 'human rights' the 'rights of the individual' etc. do not so much disguise the identity of some empirical subject as rob all empirical subjects of any social identity whatsoever. Those who are not members of any political community can make no claims, not even the claim to physical protection or to life.

Provocatively, she points out that it is the stateless who come closest to embodying the abstraction of rights subjects, but it is precisely they who are the victims of violence and arbitrary (in)justice within the modern world of nation states and whom rights are least effective in protecting:

> The Rights of Man, supposedly inalienable, proved to be unenforceable –
> even in countries whose constitutions were based upon them – whenever
> people appeared who were no longer citizens of any sovereign state.

[9] C. Schmitt, *Verfassungslehre* (Berlin, Duncker and Humboldt, 1928).
[10] C. Pateman, *The Disorder of Women* (Cambridge, Polity, 1989).
[11] H. Arendt, *The Origins of Totalitarianism* (London, Allen and Unwin, 1951), p. 299.

And she goes on to note:

> The first loss which the rightless suffered was the loss of their homes, and
> this meant the loss of the entire social texture into which they were born
> and in which they established for themselves a distinct place in the world ...
> The second loss which the rightless suffered was the loss of government
> protection, and this did not imply just loss of legal status in their own, but
> in all countries.[12]

Underlying this criticism of liberalism is a philosophical anthropology in
which that which is 'specifically human' is held to be precisely our nature as
social beings; as members of particular human communities rather than a
'human race'. We have on such a view, no human qualities other than those we
possess by dint of the fact that we are members of particular human communities which have 'established for themselves a distinct place in the world'.
The subject of universal rights is as conceptually denuded of their cultural
heritage or 'social texture' – and hence their specifically human qualities – as
are politically the stateless victims of twentieth century totalitarianism. It is the
deprivation of their social identity which, for Arendt, is the primary and prior
tragedy of the rightless:

> The calamity of the rightless is not that they are deprived of life, liberty,
> and the pursuit of happiness, or of equality before the law and freedom of
> opinion – formulas which were designed to solve problems *within* given
> communities – but that they no longer belonged to any community what-
> soever.[13]

For these reasons Arendt sides with Edmund Burke who preferred to speak of
the 'Rights of Englishmen' rather than the 'Rights of Man', the language of
the French Revolution. By stripping subjects of a 'local habitation and a name'
the abstraction of right discourse, Arendt argues, rendered real subjects
vulnerable.

The relevance of Arendt's argument to the case in question is that it suggests
that the culture which is de-constituted may – or can – never fully be recon-
stituted through constitutional means with their universalizing principles and
abstracted constitutional subjects.

Conclusion

The above discussion raises the possibility that constitutions may stand in an
antagonistic relationship to the context in which they are embedded for two
reasons: first, because of the necessity of an act of cultural deconstruction in
order to create a constitutional culture; secondly, because that constitutional
culture may itself be too abstract to accommodate or sustain a substantive
normative system.

There may be two possible readings of this state of affairs: a strong reading to
the effect that constitutions are in constant danger of failure due to the strains
to which they give rise, or a weaker reading to the effect that there is a
permanent tension between the constitution and constitutional culture which

---

[12] Arendt, *The Origins of Totalitarianism*, pp. 293–4.
[13] Arendt, *The Origins of Totalitarianism*, p. 295.

can only be addressed imperfectly by constitutional means. We shall not adjudicate between these two readings but rather point out that on either of them: (i) the universalizing language of constitutions is problematic, and (ii) the distinction between constitutional and normal politics blurred. These points can both be made with reference to the crucifix case.

The Bavarian Constitutional Court tried to resolve the tensions between the universalizing culture of the constitution and the local culture – rather naively – by ascribing universalism to Christian values. Any such claim can be trumped by the higher universalism of constitutional culture itself. This is precisely what the Federal Constitutional Court did. But, and this is the problem which occupies those who in the words of the Bavarian Prime Minister 'would not understand' the Constitutional Court's judgement, just what substantial values can a constitution defend against the right of any real or hypothetical individual to the 'free formation of opinion'? If no such values can be constitutionally grounded, then in what is the constitution itself based? Here the problem is not merely that constitutional culture may be 'too thin' to be the basis of either public or private virtue, but that it may be incompatible with the values and virtues of any given community. This is a form of Arendt's worry about the effects of rights discourse. What we earlier described as the constitution's 'essential supplement' may not merely be incapable of incorporation into a constitution, but may be hollowed out or even deconstituted by the abstract logic of the constitution's legal formalism.

In the case we have discussed we see an attempt by a particular State constitution to mould its citizens in the spirit of Catholic Christian virtues. It then responds to a complaint against a symbolic aspect of this culture by trying to universalize it. The Federal Constitutional Court, in its turn, restores the particularity of the symbol, but in the name of provisions informed by a secular/ Protestant 'social spirit' which it seeks to impose on both the Bavarian State and civil society. Is this an example of successful constitutional politics, or rather the source of new conflicts which may not easily be contained within the framework of constitutionalism? As was widely observed, behind this conflict lies the changed religious/political composition of the new Federal Republic, which with the accession of the ex-GDR has exchanged a Catholic for a Protestant religious majority. Is this decision an imposition of an allegedly universal secular, but actually Protestant 'social spirit' on Catholic citizens, and if so what implications will it have for citizens who subscribe to either or neither religious persuasion? Should they make a tactical alliance with the Protestant universalism, or with a Catholic defence of particular religious communities against that universalism, even if that defence is itself couched in universalistic terms? These are political decisions whose stakes are not clarified by the confusing rhetoric of constitutional universalism.

With this we return to Rousseau's paradox, because a democratic constitution which has to mould its citizens – forcing them to be free – is an extremely precarious one, vulnerable to the fate of the constitutionally hypocritical cultures of the socialist democracies. In other words, the 'social spirit' produced by the constitution cannot be the same as that which presided over its foundation. The constitution deconstructs the very culture necessary for its survival, or in the words of an earlier German Constitutional Court Judge, Ernst-Wolfgang Böckenförde, already in the early 1960s 'The free secular state lives according to presuppositions that it cannot itself guarantee without putting its freedom into question'.[14] This has been made glaringly clear in the Constitutional Court decision which exposes the tensions which exist between a Federal and a State constitution as well as those between both and civil society. In this case the State constitution's attempt to constitute a particular constitutional culture began to deconstitute civil society, proving a source of potential civil conflict, which the Federal Constitutional Court attempted to resolve according to the Basic Law, but which in turn has generated fresh conflict.

A related aspect of the decision which was widely noted was the way in which it succeeded in politicizing the classroom wall. The absence of a symbol has become replete with significance, provoking memories of other classroom decorations which might better have been forgotten. In the GDR, it was required to adorn classroom walls with the photograph of Erich Honecker. His removal from the classroom wall was obviously political, but the space now occupied or not by a crucifix has become similarly charged. The constitution by deconstituting an existing culture has become a source of conflict, and in this case politics has invaded civil society by virtue of the constitutions very universalism that was meant to put it above the competing partial political interests.

One of the issues raised in the *Kreuzesbefehl* decision concerns the resort to conflicting arguments for the universality of particular constitutional provisions. Of course *Bundesrecht bricht Landesrecht* [Federal law overrides State – *Land* – law], and the Federal Constitutional Court's definition of what is universal will prevail, even though it is seen by some to be partial. Perhaps this points to a problem with constitutionalism in general, which is that it translates particular political disputes into a language of universal and eternally valid norms, which, precisely by universalizing a particular conflict risks extending it to other, previously unconcerned parties. This can be considered from two standpoints: for the constitutional believer, the constitution is successful in reconstituting social relations according to a universal and eternally valid norm; for the constitutional sceptic, this may happen on occasion, but on the whole constitutions deconstitute social relations, potentially escalating conflict by enforcing universal norms where they may be inappropriate.

We would like to end by questioning the constitutionalists' monopoly of virtue. While not rejecting constitutional politics, we would underline the intrinsically violent and destructive side of constitutionalism, its capacity to generate, escalate and proliferate social conflict through its universalizing rhetoric. This rhetoric may have been necessary in the context of the absolutist societies in which modern constitutionalism was born, but is perhaps obsolete in a pluralistic democracy. What we have in mind is a fallible constitution which does not need to resort to universal claims in order to protect particular rights, but whether such a constitutionalism is conceivable and what institutional shape it would assume or require, we remain unsure. In any case, constitutional patriotism may not be enough.

[14] Quoted in *Die Zeit*, nr. 34, 18 August 1995.

European Neo-constitutionalism: in Search of Foundations for the European Constitutional Order

J. H. H. Weiler

Introduction

The core Articles of Faith in the orthodox version of European Constitutionalism find their expression in some key legal doctrines which determine the relationship between the Community and Member States. So much has been written about these as to obviate any need for recapitulation. Simple codes will suffice: Direct Effect, Supremacy, Implied Powers and European *judicial Kompetenz-Kompetenz* define the hierarchy of norms between the two orders. The combination of these legal doctrines positions European law, in its self-defined sphere of competences, as the 'supreme law of the land' – a position of practical as well as symbolic significance given the extraordinary system of judicial enforcement and compliance. From this legal perspective, Europe has a place in the Premier League of constitutional orders akin to that of the USA, Germany and Italy as defined by the most formalist definitions of constitutionalism, which require the presence of a 'higher law', judicial review as well as some material elements such as the protection of fundamental human rights.[1] These doctrines, it is said, are what differentiate the Community and Union from 'normal' international organizations and from the classical framework of international law.

These articles of faith, catholic in their reach and all encompassing in their scope, are accepted as defining the system even by its critics. As we shall see, the typical complaints of 'loss of sovereignty' or 'democratic deficit' are implicitly premised and only make sense on a formalist constitutional depiction of the Community and Union.[2] Also by the yardsticks of altogether more sophisticated understandings of constitutionalism,[3] the institutional political discourse of and within the European Polity would qualify as having a strong constitutional 'accent', indeed constitute an important constitutional conversation.

And yet, in the current 'Constitutional Moment', a process of Reformation is at hand which can be encapsulated in a metaphor from Antiquity. When Moses came down from Mount Sinai with His Constitutional Covenant and offered it to 'the audience of the people ... they said, All that the Eternal hath spoken we

---

[1] F. Mancini, 'The making of a constitution for Europe', *Common Market Law Review*, 26 (1989), 595–614.

[2] K. Neunreither, 'The democracy deficit of the European Union', *Government and Opposition*, 29 (1994), 299–314.

[3] Cf. D. Castiglione 'The political theory of the constitution', in this volume; and A. S. Stone, 'Constitutional dialogue in the European Community', *EUI Working Paper RSC* (1995).

will do, and hearken' (Ex. XXIV: 7). Very imprudent, we might think, to accept to *do* before you *hearken*. To accept a constitution without a constitutional debate. Over the last three decades or so, European public authorities – governments, legislatures, courts – have, similarly, accepted to do (what comes out of the Union and its Institutions as the supreme law of the land) with remarkably little hearkening.

If one explores beyond the repetitive description of those formal doctrines and searches for a theoretical and prescriptive (normative) underpinning of European constitutionalism – a justification for, say, the supremacy of Community law – one comes up with little, usually a barely concealed variant of the internationalist *Pacta Sund Servanda* and the functionalist need to ensure the uniformity of Treaty obligations and rights among and within the various High Contracting Parties. Ironically, for this justification one does not have to go beyond the Vienna Convention on the Law of Treaties – a centrepiece of classical international law. This is somewhat embarrassing given that the claim to constitute a new legal order which had cut its umbilical cord from international law forms a centrepiece of the very orthodoxies of European constitutionalism.

The condition of Europe on this reading is not, as is often implied, that of constitutionalism without a constitution, but of a constitution without constitutionalism. What Europe needs, therefore, is not a constitution but an ethos and *telos* to justify, if they can, the constitutional order it has already embraced.

The 'doing' without 'hearkening' has characterized academia as well. Law, as an academic discipline, has for the most part, with only a few notable recent brilliant exceptions,[4] been content to focus on the *manifestations* of constitutionalism in its discrete legal doctrines without supplying any justificatory apparatus other than the formal validity of legal norms. The social sciences, waking rather slowly to the European constitutional revolution, have attempted to give an explanation and an assessment of the reception of constitutionalism by political and social actors in the Member States – with some remarkable and illuminating results.[5] There has, however, been little in the way of political theory concerning the claims for authority which are at the basis of constitutional rules such as Supremacy. There has been, to be sure, a rich and impressive literature on Community governance, including an avalanche of writing on the democratic deficiencies of the Community and Union. Interestingly, this literature has tended to focus on the institutional mechanics and political processes of governance and has taken for granted – very often unconsciously – its constitutional architecture. In other words, the Democratic Deficit literature has accepted *as a given* Direct Effect and Supremacy and the other constitutional hallmarks. Absent Direct Effect and Supremacy, and the

---

[4] Cf., for example, B. De Witte, 'Droit communautaire et valeurs constitutionelles nationales', *Droits* 14 (1991), 87–96; N. MacCormick, 'Beyond the sovereign state', *Modern Law Review*, 56, 1 (1990), 1–19; N. MacCormick, 'Sovereignty, democracy and subsidiarity' in R. Bellamy, V. Bufacchi, D. Castiglione (eds), *Democracy and Constitutional Culture in the Union of Europe* (London, Lothian Foundation, 1995), pp. 95–104; C. Joerges, 'Das Recht im Prozess der europaeischen Integration' *EUI Working Paper LAW*, 95/1 (1995); and A. von Bogdandy, *Die europäische Option* (Baden-Baden, 1993).

[5] A. M. Burley and W. Mattli, 'Europe before the court: A political theory of legal integration', *International Organization*, 47 (1993), 41–76; Stone 'Constitutional dialogue'; and K. Alter, 'Explaining national court acceptance of the European Court of Jurisprudence: a critical evaluation of theories of legal integration', *EUI Working Paper RSC*, (1995).

Democracy Deficit critique would lose much of its bite. No one speaks of the Democracy Deficit of the Council of Europe or the United Nations General Assembly and Security Council whose processes are no more transparent or accountable than the Council of Ministers. This is so mainly because they do not operate within a binding constitutional order.

It was, perhaps, the negative public reaction to Maastricht – highlighting visibly, albeit at a different if more immediate manner – the problems of legitimacy, which may explain the emergence of a new critical enquiry into European constitutionalism.[6] It is not only the search for new normative foundations which characterizes the new discourse. Another aspect of the New Constitutionalism is its challenges to the dualist prism of the traditional constitutional image. The dualist approach places the relationship between Community/Union and the Member States at the centre of the discourse and puts a huge premium on a Hierarchy of Norms – centrist and uniform – as a representation and resolution of constitutional conflict. It is not by accident that Article 177, with its centralizing, uniformizing ethos and function, has been placed at the centre of traditional constitutional description.[7] The new constitutional discussion recognizes and at times suggests a different, 'horizontal', 'polycentred', 'infranational' image of the European Polity[8] and makes conversation a metaphor for constitutional ethos.

Picking up on these strands, in this essay I hope to make a small contribution to two aspects of the New Constitutionalism debate which is taking place: the issue of citizenship and Demos and the issue of Union competences.

The Two Paradoxes of European Constitutionalism

Let us return to the issue of Direct Effect and Supremacy. By what authority, then, if any – *understood in the vocabulary of normative political theory* – can the claim of European law to be both constitutionally superior and with immediate effect in the polity be sustained? Who is the constituent power? Why should the subjects of European law in the Union, individuals, courts, governments etc. feel bound to observe the law of the Union as higher law, in the same way that their counterparts in, say, the USA are bound, to and by, American federal law?[9] It is a dramatic question since constitutionalization has formally taken place and to give a negative answer – as has been recently given by some[10] – would be tantalizingly subversive. The failure to address this question is partly why the critique of European Union constitutional democracy often involves conflicting arguments. One can, it seems, proclaim a profound democracy deficit and yet insist at the same time on the importance of

[6] Cf. Bellamy *et al.*, *Democracy and Constitutional Culture*; especially the essay by U. K. Preuß, 'Citizenship and identity: aspects of a political theory of citizenship', pp. 107–20.

[7] J. H. H. Weiler, 'The transformation of Europe', *Yale Law Journal*, 100 (1991), 2403–83.

[8] D. Curtain, 'The constitutional structure of the Union: a Europe of bits and pieces', *Common Market Law Review*, 30 (1993), 17–69; R. Dehousse, 'Integration ou disintegration: cinq theses sur l'incidence de l'integration europeenne sur les structures étatiques', *EUI Working Paper RSC*, 96/4 (1996); G. Majone, 'The European Community: an "Independent Fourth Branch of Government"?', *EUI Working Paper SPS*, 93/9 (1993); J. H. H. Weiler, U. R. Haltern and F. C. Mayer, 'European democracy and its critique', *West European Politics*, 18 (1995), 4–39.

[9] U. K. Preuß, 'Constitutional powermaking for the new polity: some deliberations on the relation between constituent power and the constitution', *Cardozo Law Review*, 14 (1993), 639–60.

[10] F. Vibert, *Europe: a constitution for the Millenium* (Brookfield VT, Dartmouth, 1995).

accepting the supremacy of Union law. It is a dramatic question too, since it goes back to membership, to citizenship and nationality and seems to bring European constitutionalism into direct conflict with the constitutionalism of its Member States. To whom is primary allegiance owed? By whom is it owed?

As already mentioned, one place to look for the answer to the issue of normative authority would be international law. The High Contracting Powers – the Member States of the European Union – entered into an international Treaty based on international law which created an Organization with these wide capacities and established Institutions empowered to exercise the various powers. What, then, of authority? On this view the transnational authority of the Union writ, so long as *Jus Cogens* was not violated (and it clearly was not), derives from international law: *Pacta Sunt Servanda*. The internal authority of the Union writ, so long as internal constitutional norms were not violated (and apparently they were not) derives from the constitutional authority which governments enjoy to engage their respective States, including the authority to undertake international obligations with internal ramifications in national law. The nature of the European polity on this reading is an international organization belonging to the States which created it.

The international view has been out of vogue for a long time. Despite its terse elegance it runs against one of the great orthodoxies of the system: if we look to the rhetoric of the European Court in the celebrated *Van Gend en Loos* case – the embodiment of constitutional orthodoxy – the Community is not an 'old' order of international law; it is more than

> an agreement which merely creates mutual obligations between the contracting states ... the Community constitutes a new legal order of international law for the benefit of which the states have limited their sovereign rights ...[11]

In subsequent cases the Court dropped the reference to International Law altogether and in the 1980s, in cases such as *Les Verts*, it referred to the Treaties as the Constitutional Charter of the Union.[12]

The internationalist view does not simply contradict rhetoric. Given the massive transfer of competences to the Union, the unprecedented empowerment of Community Institutions (and through them, indirectly, of the executive branch of the Member States at the expense of, say, national parliaments), and the consequent creation of considerable democratic deficiencies in central aspects of European public life, the internationalists' construct provides a poor legitimation to this new architecture of power. But if we reject the internationalist view as grounding Direct Effect and Supremacy what comes in its place? Answering this question is exactly where, at least in the first place, political theory has to replace social science.

In Western, liberal democracies, under one guise or another, public authority requires legitimation through one principal source: the citizens constituting the political subjects of the polity.[13] The principal hallmark of citizenship is not

---

[11] Case 26/62, *N.V. Algemene Transportäen Expeditie Oderneming Van Gend & Loos* v. *Nederlandse administratie der belastingen*, 1963 E.C.R. 1
[12] Case 294/83, *Parti ecologiste, 'Les Verts'* v. *European Parliament*, 1986 E.C.R. 1339
[13] G. Andrews (ed.), *Citizenship* (London, Lawrence and Wishart, 1991); D. Heather, *Citizenship: the Civic Ideal in World History, Politics and Education* (London, Longman, 1990); A. Oldfield, *Citizenship and Community* (London, Routledge, 1990).

simply the enjoyment of human rights characterized by their extension to all in their quality as humans rather than citizens.[14] The deepest, most clearly engraved hallmark of citizenship in our democracies is that in citizens vests the power, by majority, to create binding norms, to shape the political, social and economic direction of the polity. More realistically, in citizens vests the power to enable and habilitate representative institutions which will exercise governance on behalf of, and for, citizens. Note too, that this huge privilege and power of citizenship has, traditionally, come with duties – not simply a duty to obey the norms (that falls on non-citizens too) but a duty of loyalty to the polity with well-known classical manifestations. Citizenship is so basic that, for the most part, it is simply assumed in democratic political theory which engages mostly in the conditions and practice of its exercise.

One might think that this issue has been addressed in the Community constitutional architecture. In the same *Van Gend en Loos* we read:

> Independently of the legislation of Member States, Community law ... not only imposes obligations on individuals but is also intended to confer upon them rights which become part of their legal heritage.[15]

This phrase wonderfully sharpens the issue, for here are obligations imposed on individuals *independently of the legislation of Member States*. Member State legislation derives its authority and legitimacy to impose obligations on individuals because it is made by, or in the name of, its subjects – the citizens of the Member States. If Community law imposes obligations independently of the legislation of Member States, who are its subjects?

Surely this is where the legal doctrine of Direct Effect is so significant. For Direct Effect purports not simply to address the issue of the status of norms (so essential to individuals qua litigants – and thus to their lawyers) but also the political status and identity of the subjects of those norms.

Lawyers recite dutifully that the:

> Community constitutes a new legal order ... for the benefit of which the states have limited their sovereign rights, albeit within limited fields, and the subjects of which comprise not only Member States but also their nationals.[16]

Individuals, not only states, are thus subjects. Semantically, in English, 'subjects' is often synonymous with citizenship. The Queen's subjects of old are the present citizens of the Realm. It could seem, therefore, that in the very articulation of one of the principal 'constitutionalizing' doctrines – Direct effect – the condition for its authority was provided by elevating individuals to the status of full subjects alongside Member States.

But this would be a highly problematic construction. Direct Effect means that obligations among States created by a Treaty confer rights on individuals which courts must protect, even against their own statal public authorities. It is in this sense that calling individuals subjects of the Treaty alongside Member States may be justified. But note, individuals are 'subjects' only as a consequence of the (direct) *effect* of the law. In this sense alone is Europe a new legal order.

[14] Preuß, 'Citizenship and identity'.
[15] *Van Gend & Loos* v. *Nederlandse administratie.*
[16] *Van Gend & Loos* v. *Nederlandse administratie.*

Consider the following *reductio ad absurdum*: imagine three states which still allow slavery. There is trade among these states, including trade in slaves. Imagine further that the three get together and conclude a Treaty which creates mutual obligations among them such as prohibiting a workday for slaves of more than 20 hours. They also create institutions which are henceforth empowered to regulate all matters concerning slavery. Imagine now that they do not wait for a judicial decision but include explicitly in their Treaty what the ECJ 'found' in *Van Gend en Loos*: that these obligations are, independently of national legislation, intended to create rights for the slaves themselves, and that national courts would have to protect those rights. Another new legal order will have come into being. Does the fact that the obligations *created by the States, the High Contracting Parties* which bestow rights on our poor slaves make them subjects of the Treaty? Yes, in the limited sense of deriving rights created by others. No, in the sense that they have no say in the making of those rights. Enjoying rights created by others does not make you a full subject of the law. Thus, in *Van Gend en Loos*, to the extent that the High Contracting Parties retained the prerogatives to make the obligations bestowing rights on individuals, there was, in this sense, little new in the legal order, except that it *accentuated* the problem of legitimacy. For if the Community and Union have the capacity to exercise law making power over individuals *independently of national legislation*, by whose authority does it enjoy that power?

One could object to my absurd example and claim that in the Union context the Member States are composed of citizens, not slaves; citizens who enabled their States to create institutions which create obligations. It is the act of authorization of the Treaties that bestows these powers on the Community, but national parliaments provide the authority. That is true, but note, first, how that argument re-introduces legitimation through the mediation of the State and authority through public international law, thus waving good-bye to the 'new legal order' and constitutionalism. Note, too, that in a strange, paradoxical balance of what is gained and lost, there is one respect where the citizens' relative position has worsened compared to the slaves. Whereas before all obligations were created in a national forum over which they exercised citizen control, the European situation as described/created by *Van Gend en Loos* is that now they will be subject to obligations 'independently of the legislation of Member States', i.e. without that direct legitimation.

To use our current vocabulary, though the Community seen through the eyes of *Van Gend* recognized nationals as subjects in one sense (effect of law), it stripped them of citizenship in another. One paradox, then, has been that the very doctrine which is foundational to European Constitutionalism is, at the same time, its denial.[17]

Supremacy and Demos

Citizens constitute the Demos of the polity. This is the other, collective side, of the citizenship coin. Demos provides another way of expressing the link

---

[17] It is not that one has to exclude all norm-making authority and legitimating power to States as such. After all, in all federations, States or their equivalent, form part of the legitimation at the federal level. But one expects, likewise, direct legitimation by citizens – *de jure* or *de facto* – at the Union level.

between citizenship and democracy. Democracy does not exist in a vacuum. It is premised on the existence of a polity with members – the Demos – by whom and for whom democratic discourse with its many variants takes place. The authority and legitimacy of a majority to compel a minority exists only within political boundaries defined by a Demos. Simply put, if there is no Demos, there can be no operating democracy.

Is there, can there be a European Demos which would legitimate the authority of European constitutionalism? As part of the Neo-Constitutional debate there has emerged an articulate and powerful No Demos Thesis. One implication of this thesis, espoused, among others, by the German Constitutional Court, is to deny any meaningful democratization of the Union at the European level, to reassert the implicit underpinning of the Community legal order in international law, and if one is to be intellectually consistent, to negate likewise any meaningful content to European Citizenship. Space does not permit full elaboration,[18] but a few hints will suffice.

Under this view, the nation or the people, which is the modern expression of Demos, constitutes the basis for the modern democratic State: the nation and its members – which may be defined in many different ways – constitutes the polity for the purposes of accepting the discipline of democratic, majoritarian governance. Both descriptively and prescriptively (how it is and how it ought to be) a minority will/should accept the legitimacy of a majority decision because both majority and minority are part of the same Demos, the same people. That is an integral part of what rule-by-the-people, democracy, means on this reading. Typically (though not necessarily) the State constitutes the arena, and defines the political boundaries within which the nation/people exercise their democratic power. The significance of the political boundary is not only to the older notion of political independence and territorial integrity, but also to the very democratic nature of the polity. A parliament is, on this view, an institution of democracy not only because it provides a mechanism for representation and majority voting, but because it represents the Demos, often the nation, from which the authority and legitimacy of its decisions derive. To drive this point home, imagine an *Anschluss* between Germany and Denmark. Try and tell the Danes that they should not worry, since they will have full representation in the Bundestag. Their screams of grief will be shrill not simply because they will be condemned, as Danes, to permanent minorityship (that may be true for the German Greens too), but because the way nationality, in this way of thinking, enmeshes with democracy is that even majority rule is only legitimate within a Demos, when Danes rule Danes.

Turning to Europe, it is argued as a matter of empirical observation that there is no European Demos – not a people not a nation. Neither the subjective elements (the sense of shared collective identity and loyalty) nor the objective conditions which could produce them (the kind of homogeneity of the organic national-cultural conditions on which peoplehood in the European tradition depend such as shared culture, a shared sense of history, a shared means of communication) exist. Long term peaceful relations with thickening economic

---

[18] For a fully annotated analysis and critique, see J. H. H. Weiler, 'The state *Über Alles* – Demos, telos and the German Maastricht decision', *Harvard Jean Monnet Working Paper*, 6/95 (1995).

and social intercourse should not be confused with the bonds of peoplehood and nationality forged by language, history, ethnicity and all the rest.

The consequences of the No-Demos thesis for the European construct are interesting. The rigorous implication of this view would be that, absent a Demos, by definition there cannot be a democracy or democratization at the European level. This is not a semantic proposition. On this reading, European democracy (meaning a minimum of binding majoritarian decision-making at the European level) without a Demos is no different from the previously mentioned German-Danish *Anschluss* except on a larger scale. Giving the Danes a vote in the Bundestag is, as argued, ice-cold comfort. Giving them a vote in the European Parliament or Council is, conceptually, no different. This would be true for each and every nation-state. European integration may have involved a certain transfer of state functions to the Union but this has not been accompanied by a redrawing of political boundaries which can occur only if, and can be ascertained only when, a European people can be said to exist. Since this, it is claimed, has not occurred, the Union and its institutions can have neither the authority nor the legitimacy of a Demos-cratic State. Empowering the European Parliament is no solution and could – to the extent that it weakens the Council (the voice of the Member States) – actually exacerbate the legitimacy problem of the Community. On this view, a parliament without a Demos is conceptually impossible, practically despotic. If the European Parliament is not the representative of *a* people, if the territorial boundaries of the EU do not correspond to its political boundaries, then the writ of such a parliament has only slightly more legitimacy than the writ of an emperor.

But the problem goes even deeper. The No-Demos thesis in its strongest version is not descriptive. It is not simply an empirical observation that *as yet* the conditions for European peoplehood do not exist. At its most serious the thesis is normative. The *telos* of European Integration is ' ... an ever closer union among the *peoples* of Europe'. Europe is not meant to be about nation building, or a Melting Pot – quite the contrary. There is no European Demos and there should not be one.

Here, then, is the second paradox. The Constitutional architecture is a feature of the Union which defines its uniqueness and, functionally, emerged as necessary for attaining the objective of an ever closer union among the peoples of Europe. The normative legitimation of this constitutionalism requires a Demos, the emergence of which would however negate that very basic *telos*. Put differently: to realize the objectives of the Union in a democratic way, the only way which enjoys political legitimacy, a European Demos would seem necessary. But a European Demos would seem to negate those very objectives.

European citizenship and peoplehood are problematic in another sense. The 'Union among Peoples' *telos* does not represent a second best option chosen out of political pragmatism. It is not simply the most that would be acceptable politically in Europe, but something falling short of the ideal-type – a European people. The 'Union among Peoples' *telos* is, instead, a reflection of a deep moral ethos. The alternative *telos*, creating one people out of the many, would contradict one of the most basic European ideals: inventing new ways and contexts which would enable distinct nations and states to thrive, interact and resolve their conflicts without the disastrous apocalyptic results witnessed in Europe this century. The Union among Peoples is, in part, about creating a political culture which learns new ways to deal with the Other.[19] A European citizenship could be seen as part of a statal *telos* and an exclusionary ethos – according to which Europe is about redefining a polity in which the Us may no longer be Germans or French or Italians and the Them no longer British, or Dutch or Irish. The Us would become European and the Them non-European. Of course the question could then be asked: if Europe – part of whose roots were an attempt to tame the nationalist excesses typical of the classic nation-state – embraces, even if 'only' at the symbolic level, European citizenship by simply defining a new Other – on what moral ground can one turn against French National Fronts, German Republicans and their brethren elsewhere who embrace Member State nationalism. On the ground that they chose to embrace the wrong nationalism?

Is one faced, then, with a 'tragic choice' in which absent citizenship the normative authority of European constitutionalism would become untenable but in which the introduction of citizenship would not only mean a redefinition of the 'peoples' *telos*, but introduce an exclusionary ethos of dubious moral credentials?

Decoupling State, Nation and Citizenship – towards a Different European Demos

The choice would, indeed, be tragic if the understanding of European citizenship and European Demos were to embrace that strand in European political thought and praxis which: (a) understands nationality in the organic terms of culture and/or language and/or religion and/or ethnicity; and (b) conflates nationality and citizenship so that nationality is a condition for citizenship and citizenship means nationality.

Is it mandated, we should ask, that Demos in general and the European Demos in particular be understood exclusively in organic cultural homogeneous terms? Can we not break away from that tradition and define membership of a polity in civic, non-organic-cultural terms? Can we not imagine a Demos understood in non-organic terms, a coming together on the basis not of shared ethnos and/or organic culture, but a coming together on the basis of shared values, a shared understanding of rights and societal duties and a shared rational, intellectual culture which transcend organic-national differences? Article 8 TEU offers a strange promise in this regard:

> Citizenship of the Union is hereby established. Every person holding the nationality of a Member State shall be a citizen of the Union [...]

The introduction of citizenship to the conceptual world of the Union could be seen as just another step in the drive towards a statal vision of Europe, especially if citizenship is understood as being premised on statehood. But there is another more tantalizing and radical way of understanding the provision, namely as the very conceptual decoupling of nationality from citizenship and as the conception of a polity the Demos of which, its membership, is understood in the first place in civic and political rather than ethno-cultural terms. On this view, the Union belongs to, is composed of, citizens who *by definition* do not

---

[19] J. H. H. Weiler, 'Idéaux et construction européenne' in M. Telò (ed.), *Democratie et Construction Europeenne* (Bruxelles, Editions de l'Université de Bruxelles, 1995).

share the same nationality. The substance of membership (and thus of the Demos) is in a commitment to the shared values of the Union as expressed in its constituent documents, a commitment, *inter alia*, to the duties and rights of a civic society covering discrete areas of public life, a commitment to membership in a polity which privileges exactly the opposites of nationalism – those human features which transcend the differences of organic ethno-culturalism. On this reading, the conceptualization of a European Demos should not be based on real or imaginary trans-European cultural affinities or shared histories nor on the construction of a European 'national' myth of the type which constitutes the identity of the organic nation. The decoupling of nationality and citizenship opens the possibility, instead, of thinking of co-existing multiple Demoi.

One objection to this concept of Demos and citizenship would be that it all happens in the space between the ears, that it is cerebral, rational and does not have the necessary emotional charge and psycho-sociological attraction which are indispensable for the kind of cohesion, identification and collective identity which are part of the hall-mark of nationality. This is absolutely true, but the question is whether Demos, even if understood as citizenship rather than nation, has to be always associated with the emotional, romantic notion of its classical manifestations in modern European thought. Is not this critique also wedded to the notion that when it comes to Demos we are dealing with a monolithic concept?

What I am suggesting is to conceptualize European Demos and citizenship as part of a polity with multiple political Demoi to which its members would belong simultaneously. One common view of multiple Demoi consists in what may be called the 'concentric circles' approach. On this approach one feels simultaneously as belonging to, and being part of, say, Germany and Europe; or, even, Scotland, Britain and Europe. What characterizes this view is that the sense of identity and identification derives from the same sources of human attachment albeit at different levels of intensity. Presumably the most intense (which the nation, and State, always claims to be) would and should trump in any normative conflict.

The view of multiple Demoi which I am suggesting, one of truly variable geometry, invites individuals to see themselves as belonging simultaneously to two Demoi, based, critically, on different subjective factors of identification. I may be a German national, or French or Italian in the in-reaching strong sense of organic-cultural identification and sense of belongingness with all the attendant emotional charge which may (at least to many) seem necessary and positive. I am simultaneously a European citizen in terms of my European transnational affinities to shared values which transcend the organic-national diversity and which are the subject not of emotional identification but of reflective, deliberative rational choice. So much so, that in a range of areas of public life, I am willing to accept the legitimacy and authority of decisions adopted by my fellow European citizens in the realization that in these areas I have given preference to choices made by my outreaching Demos, rather than by my in-reaching Demos.

So understood, the Union Demos turns away from its antecedents in the European nation-state. But equally, it should be noted that I am suggesting here something that is different to transferring to Europe either simple American Republicanism or Habermassian Constitutional Patriotism. Americanism was too, after all, about nation building albeit on different premises. Its end state, its myth, as expressed in the famous Pledge of Allegiance to the America Flag – One Nation, Indivisible, Under God – is not what Europe is about at all: Europe is precisely not about One Nation, not about a Melting Pot and all the rest, for despite the unfortunate rhetoric of Unity, Europe remains (or ought to remain) committed to ' ... an ever closer union among the peoples of Europe'. Likewise, it is not about indivisibility nor, blessedly, about God. And the Habermas concept was to provide a new basis for traditional German nationalism. What is more, both concepts continue to conflate citizenship and nationality even if making the latter conditional on, even synonymous with, the former.

According to the multiple Demos concept I am suggesting there is a recognition of the potential value in the survival of the traditional European Nation-State imbued with the force of national identification, cultural differentiation, a vision in which the Tower of Babel dispersal was not a punishment but a blessing. The Eros of nationalism is, thus, recognized and approved. But there is also, or should be – especially in the European tradition, an acknowledgment of the huge destructive potential, moral and physical, of nationhood unchecked. Nationalism, of all types, German, French, American evokes fate and destiny in constructing its mobilizing myths. Indeed, it is by evoking fate and destiny that nationalism can respond to the deepest existential yearning in a secular age, that of giving meaning and purpose to life which extends beyond mere existence or selfish fulfilment. Who am I? A member of 'a great' nation, is the national answer. What am I here for and why? To serve national destiny. That is the pull and the claim of nationality and its embodiment in the State. Religion, with greater legitimacy, occupies itself with these deeper recesses of the human spirit and it is not surprising that in its iconography the Nation State appropriates religious imagery, often latently. The mixing of State loyalty and religion risks, of course, idolatry from a religious perspective and can be highly dangerous from a political one. Historically, it seems as if, in one notable case, *Volk* and *Staat*, Blood and Soil, did indeed come to occupy these deepest parts of the human spirit to the point of being accepted '*Über Alles*' with terrifying consequences. My view of the matter is not that the very idea of nation and State was murderous nor even evil. It is the primordial position which Nation mixed with State occupied, instilling uncritical citizenship which allowed evil, even murderous designs to be executed by dulling critical personal faculties, legitimating extreme positions, subduing transcendent human values and debasing one of the common strands of the three monotheistic religions: namely that human beings, all of them, were created in the image of God.

How does one tame this tantalizing but terrifying Eros? Not by replacing the national with the European. Instead, supranational citizenship, deliberative, rational, transcendent – is the civilizing force which helps keep this Eros at bay. The European construct I have put forward, which allows for a European civic, value-driven Demos co-existing side by side with a national organic-cultural one (for those nation-states which want it), could be seen as a deeply conservative construct. Designed to re-establish a new framework for a new epoch in the life of the European Nation State, and, at the same time, give legitimacy to the normative claims of European constitutionalism. For on this reading, the Treaties would have to be seen not only as an agreement among States (a Union of States) but as a 'social contract' among the nationals of those States that they will in the areas covered by the Treaty regard themselves as associating as citizens in this civic society. We can go even further. In this polity, and to this Demos, one cardinal value is precisely that there will not be a drive towards, or an acceptance of, an over-arching organic-cultural national identity displacing those of the Member States. Nationals of the Member States are European Citizens, not the other way around. Europe is 'not yet' a Demos in the organic national-cultural sense and should never become one.

Maybe in the realm of the political, the special virtue of contemporaneous membership in an organic national-cultural Demos and in a supranational civic, value-driven Demos is in the effect which such double membership may have on taming the great appeal, even craving, for belonging and destiny in this world which nationalism continues to offer but which can so easily degenerate into intolerance and xenophobia. Maybe the in-reaching national-cultural Demos and the outreaching supranational civic Demos, by continuously keeping each other in check, offer a structured model of critical citizenship.

One should not get carried away. Even this construct of the European Demos, like the national-organic construct, depends on a shift of consciousness. Individuals must think of themselves in this way before such a Demos could have full legitimate democratic authority. The key to a shift in political boundaries is the sense of feeling that the boundaries surround one's own polity. I am not making the claim that this shift has already occurred. I am simply saying that it is in this sense we should understand European citizenship and Demos and seek to realize it. This understanding of Demos makes the need for the democratization of Europe even more pressing. A Demos which coheres around values must live those values.

Competences – Fundamental Boundaries?

I turn now to another issue which has become the subject of re-evaluation in the new constitutional debate – the jurisdictional limits of the Union. Let me first repeat a truism of formal constitutionalism. Although the principles of universal suffrage and majoritarianism inform all modern systems of democratic governance, they are not absolute principles. Modern democracies, taking their cue generally from the American rather than the British democratic tradition, increasingly acknowledge a higher law – typically a constitution – which binds even the legislature. In a growing number of modern democracies the higher law is backed up by courts and a system of judicial review which give it, so to speak, teeth. Within this constitutional ethos judicial protection of fundamental human rights has a central place. Constitutionalism, despite its counter-majoritarian effect, is regarded as a complimentary principle to majoritarianism rather than its negation. One formulation which describes the complex relationship between the two is the notion of protection against a tyranny of the majority – seemingly an oxymoron. I will not enter into the complex theoretical discussion of rights and their relationship to democracy. The appeal of rights, whatever their theoretical justification, has to do with two roots. The first of these two roots regards fundamental rights as an expression of a vision of humanity which vests the deepest values in the individual and which may not be compromised by anyone. Probably one of the oldest and most influential sources of this vision is to be found in the Pentateuch: 'And God created man in His own image, in the image of God created He him'.

(Gen. I: 27). With this trademark, what legislator has the authority to transgress the essential humanity of the species? Naturally, there are secular, humanist parallels a plenty. The second root for the great appeal of rights, and part of the justification of their countermajoritarian semblance, looks to them as an instrument for the *per se* value of putting constraints on power. Modern democracy emerges, after all, also as a rejection of absolutism and absolutism is not the prerogative of kings and emperors.

Similar sentiments inform the great appeal of fundamental boundaries in non-unitary systems – federal states and the European Union. I use the term fundamental boundaries as a way of conceptualizing in a normative sense the principle of enumerated powers or limited competences of the central authorities in these systems. The appeal of fundamental boundaries stems from two parallel roots. First as an expression of a vision of humanity which vests the deepest values in individual communities existing within larger polities which, thus, may not be transgressed. The vision of humanity derives from an acknowledgment of the social nature of humankind, as a counterbalance to the potential atomism of fundamental rights – 'And the Lord God said: It is not good that man should be alone' (Gen. II: 18) – and from the realization that smaller social units can suffer parallel oppression to that inflicted on individuals by stronger societal forces. That enumeration is also said to work as a bulwark against aggregation of power is its second appeal.

I am unaware of any federal system which does not claim to give expression to these notions. But there are as many variants as there are systems. Comparative analysis can be particularly alluring here. In Europe there has been a practical eruption of the hitherto dormant question of Community 'competences and powers', a question and debate which has found its code in the deliciously vague concept of Subsidiarity. This is inevitably connected to the continued pre-occupation with governance structures and processes, the balance between Community and Member State, and the democracy and legitimacy of the Community.[20]

What accounts for this eruption? First a bit of history. The student of comparative federalism discovers a constant feature in practically all federative experiences: a tendency, which differs only in degree, towards controversial concentration of legislative and executive power in the centre/general power at the expense of constituent units. This is apparently so independently of the mechanism for allocation of jurisdiction/competences/powers between centre and 'periphery'. Differences, where they occur, are dependent more on the ethos and political culture of polities than on mechanical devices.

The Community has both shared and differed from this general experience. It has *shared* it in that the Community, especially in the 1970s, has seen a weakening of any workable and enforceable mechanism for allocation of jurisdiction/competences/powers between the Community and its Member States. How has this occurred? It has occurred through a combination of two factors: (a) profligate legislative practices especially in, for example, the usage of Article 235; (b) a bifurcated jurisprudence of the Court which, on the one hand, has extensively interpreted the reach of the jurisdiction/competences/powers granted to the Community and, on the other hand, has taken a self-limiting

---

[20] J. P. Jacqué and J. H. H. Weiler, 'On the road to European Union – a new judicial architecture', *Common Market Law Review*, 27 (1990), 185–208.

approach towards the expansion of Community jurisdiction/competence/ powers when exercised by the political organs.[21]

To make the above statement is not tantamount to criticizing the Community, its political organs and the Court. This is a question of values. It is a sustainable thesis that this process was overall beneficial, in its historical context, to the evolution and well-being of Community, Member States and its citizens and residents. But this process was also a ticking constitutional time bomb which one day could threaten the evolution and stability of the Community. Sooner or later, 'Supreme' courts in the Member States would realize that the 'Socio-legal Contract' announced by the Court in its major constitutionalizing decisions, namely that 'the Community constitutes a new legal order ... for the benefit of which the states have limited their sovereign rights, albeit within limited fields' had been shattered, that although they (the 'Supreme' courts) had accepted the principles of the new legal order – Supremacy and Direct Effect – the fields no longer seemed to be limited, and that in the absence of Community legislative or legal checks it would fall on them to draw the jurisdictional lines of the Community and its Member States.

The interesting thing about the Community experience, and this is where it does not share the experience of other federative polities, is that despite the massive legislative expansion of Community jurisdiction/competences/powers there has not been any political challenge or crisis on this issue from the Member States. How so? The answer is simple and obvious and resides in the pre-Single European Act decision-making process. Unlike federal states, the governments of the Member States themselves (jointly and severally) could control absolutely the legislative expansion of jurisdiction-competences-powers. Nothing that was done could be done without the assent of all national capitals. This fact diffused any sense of threat and crisis on the part of governments.

This era passed with the shift to majority voting after the entry into force of the SEA and the seeds – indeed the buds – of crisis became visible. It became simply a matter of time before one of the national courts would defy the European Court on this issue and the Member States would become aware that in a process that does not give them a *de jure* or *de facto* veto, the question of jurisdictional lines has become crucial.

To be sure, the European Court already has jurisdiction to resolve this kind of issue under Article 173 and 177(b) (lack of competences), but since to date no Commission or Council measure has been struck down for pure and simple lack of competences, our assessment is that this existing provision in itself will not satisfy the fears of the Member States. And indeed, somewhat later than predicted,[22] the German Constitutional Court, in its Maastricht decision, rejected the ECJ's claim to exclusive *Kompetenz-Kompetenz* and claimed that the limits to Community legislative powers was as much a matter of German constitutional law as it was a matter of Community law. As such, the German Constitutional Court regards itself as competent, indeed as mandated by the German constitution, to monitor the jurisdictional limits of the Community legislative process.[23]

---

[21] Weiler, 'The transformation of Europe'.
[22] Jacqué and Weiler, 'On the road to European Union'.
[23] I. Winkelmann (ed.), *Das Maastricht-Urteil des Bundesverfassungsgerichts vom 12. Oktober 1993. Dokumentation des Verfahrens mit Einführung* (Berlin, Duncker and Humblot, 1994).

Formally, the decision constitutes a flagrant act of defiance vis-à-vis the European Court of Justice in direct contradiction with its jurisprudence on the power of national courts to declare Community law invalid. It flies in the face of, *inter alia*, the third paragraph of Article 177. It is also untenable in a legal functionalist sense. There would be as many fundamental boundaries to the Community as there are Member States. And how can the same Community measure be considered *intra vires* in one Member State and *ultra vires* in another?

But this view is grounded in the classical, hierarchical, centrist view of European constitutionalism. How should one evaluate this development given the questions concerning the normative authority of European constitutionalism and a more horizontal, conversation based view of that very same constitutionalism? Somewhat inappropriately – given the conversation metaphor – I want to use some of the dynamics of the Cold War as a device for evaluating the *Kompetenz-Kompetenz* aspect of the Maastricht Decision of the German Constitutional Court.

On this reading, it is not a declaration of war but the commencement of a Cold War with its paradoxical guarantee of co-existence following the infamous MAD logic: Mutual Assured Destruction. For the German Court actually to declare a Community norm unconstitutional rather than simply threaten to do so, would be an extremely hazardous move, so hazardous as to make its usage unlikely. The use of tactical nuclear weapons always was considered to carry the risk of creating a nuclear domino effect. If other Member State courts followed the German lead, or if other Member States legislatures or governments were to suspend implementation of the norm on some reciprocity rationale, a veritable constitutional crisis in the Community could become a reality – the legal equivalent of the Empty Chair political stand-off in the 1960s. It would be hard for the German government to remedy the situation especially if the German Court decision enjoyed general public popularity. Would the German Constitutional Court be willing to face the responsibility of dealing such a blow (rather than a threat of a blow) to European integration?

But the logic of the Cold War is that one has to assume the worst and to arm as if the other side would contemplate a first strike. The European Court of Justice would have to be watching over its shoulder the whole time, trying to anticipate any potential move by the German Constitutional Court.

If we now abandon the belligerent metaphors, it could be argued that this situation is not unhealthy. That the German move is an insistence on a more polycentred view of constitutional adjudication and will eventually force a more even conversation between the European Court and its national constitutional counterparts. I would suggest that in some ways the German move of the 1990s in relation to competences resembles their prior move in relation to human rights and that it was only that move which forced the European Court to take human rights seriously.[24] Thus, the current move will force the Court to take competences seriously. This view is not without its functional problems.

(i) There is no 'non-proliferation treaty' in the Community structure. MAD works well, perhaps, in a situation of two superpowers. But there must

---

[24] J. H. H. Weiler, 'Fundamental rights and fundamental boundaries: on standards and values in the protection of human rights' in N. Neuwahl and A. Rosas (eds), *The European Union and Human Rights* (1996, forthcoming).

be a real fear that other Member State Courts will follow the German lead in rejecting the exclusive *Kompetenz-Kompetenz* of the ECJ. The more courts adopt the weapon, the greater the chances that it will be used. Once that happens, it will become difficult to turn back the clock.

(ii) Courts are not the principal Community players. But this square-off will have negative effects on the decision-making process of the Community. The German Government and Governments whose courts will follow the German lead, will surely be tempted to play that card in negotiation. ('We really cannot compromise on this point, since our court will strike it down ...').

Here, too, there is an interesting paradox. The consistent position of the European Court, as part of its constitutional architecture, has been that it alone has judicial *Kompetenz-Kompetenz*, since those limits are a matter of interpretation of the Treaty. The German Court, as part of its reassertion of national sovereignty and insistence on legitimation of the European construct through statal instrumentalities and the logic of public international law, has defied this position. It seems to me that the internationalist logic claimed by the German Court negates its own conclusions. Surely the reach of an international treaty is a matter of international law and depends on the proper interpretation of that Treaty. Since the EU Treaties give the ECJ jurisdiction over all disputes concerning their proper interpretation, from an internationalist perspective there can be little foundation for the position of the German Court.

If, however, the European polity constitutes a constitutional order as claimed by the European Court of Justice, then this issue is far more nuanced. There has been no Constitutional Convention in Europe. European constitutionalism must depend on a common-law type rationale, one which draws on and integrates the national constitutional orders, and the constitutional discourse in Europe must be conceived of as a conversation of many actors in a constitutional interpretative community rather than a hierarchical structure with the ECJ at the top. It is the constitutional perspective, then, which paradoxically, gives credibility to the claim of the German Court. A feature of neo-constitutionalism in this case would be that the jurisdictional line (or lines) should be a matter of constitutional conversation, not a constitutional *diktat*.

And yet, the solution offered by the German Court is no conversation either. Although the German Court mentions that these decision have to be taken in cooperation with the European Court of Justice, it reserves the last word to itself. A European *diktat* is simply replaced by a national one. And the national one is far more destructive, if one contemplates the possibility of fifteen different ones.

How, then, can one square this circle? One possible solution is institutional, and I would like to outline its bare bones. What is proposed is the creation of a Constitutional Council for the Community, modeled in some ways on its French namesake. The Constitutional Council would have jurisdiction only over issues of competences (including subsidiarity) and would decide cases submitted to it after a law was adopted but before coming into force. It could be seized by any Community institution, any Member State or by the European Parliament acting on a majority of its Members. Its President would be the President of the European Court of Justice and its Members would be sitting members of the constitutional courts or their equivalents in the Member States.

Within the Constitutional Council no single Member State would have a veto power. The composition would also underscore that the question of competences is fundamentally also one of national constitutional norms but still subject to a Union solution by a Union institution.

I will not elaborate in this essay on some of the technical aspects of the proposal. Its principal merit, if it has any, is that it gives expression to the fundamental boundary concern without however compromising the constitutional integrity of the Community as did the German Maastricht decision. Since, from a material point of view, the question of boundaries has an inbuilt indeterminacy, the critical issue becomes not what are the boundaries but who gets to decide. The composition of the proposed Constitutional Council removes the issue, on the one hand, from the purely political arena and, on the other, creates a body which, on this issue, would, we expect, enjoy a far greater measure of public confidence than the ECJ itself.

Conclusions

There are, of course, no conclusions. Neo-Constitutionalism is, at best, a conceited label for two interrelated phenomena. First, a series of attitudinal changes among the principal institutional actors of the European polity who are challenging some of the core Articles of Faith of classical constitutionalism. The *Kompetenz-Kompetenz* decision of the German Constitutional Court is an egregious example of this. Second, a new academic discourse that is not simply trying to track these developments and explain them but to rethink, in the language of political and normative theory, the implications of classic European constitutionalism and to offer new or alternative constructs. The rich academic debate on European identity and citizenship is a striking example of this development.

Depending on one's measure of ontological scepticism, the line between these two faces will be more or less blurred. Be that as it may, whether a truly new constitutionalism will emerge, unbound by the conceptual shackles of the nation state, has yet to be seen.

Two Challenges to European Citizenship

ULRICH K. PREUß

Introduction

One of the major steps in the transformation of the European Community into the European Union by means of the Maastricht Treaty, has been the establishment of the citizenship of the Union in Articles 8 to 8e of the EC Treaty. Although the rights which have been added to those which EC nationals already enjoyed are not nearly as extensive as their respective national rights, the governments of the Member States regard the creation of European citizenship as a successful attempt to further the goal of 'creating an ever closer union among the peoples of Europe' (Article A of the Treaty). Yet, academic assessments of the importance of the institution of Union citizenship are vague and cautious at best. For example, Corbett speaks of a 'notable achievement' without explaining what this achievement might consist of,[1] Curtin considers the insertion of Part Two of the EC Treaty a 'real progress', while stating at the same time that what, *inter alia*, constitutes the 'unique *sui generis* nature of the European Community, its true world-historical significance', namely the character of the Union as a 'cohesive legal unit which confers rights on *individuals*', is endangered by the serious shortfalls of the Maastricht Treaty.[2] For Meehan, Union citizenship is part of a complex development from 'national citizenship to European civil society',[3] while according to the seemingly more practical and realistic statement of a lawyer (written before the conclusion of the Maastricht Treaty, but anticipating the idea of Union citizenship), it will, at least over the medium term, be hardly more than the subsumption of the single rights and duties of the individual under the label 'Union citizenship', without challenging either the intermediary role of national citizenship or its salience in the lives of Europeans.[4] Finally, an even more critical assessment denounces European citizenship as a betrayal of the 'deepest symbols of statehood' and 'the rhetoric of a superstate'.[5]

Whatever the real importance of Union citizenship for the future development of the EU may be, the concept seems to embody a symbolic meaning which the authors of the Treaty obviously considered significant for understanding the Union's political character. After all, given the intrinsic connection between the concept of citizenship and the nation state during the last two

[1] R. Corbett, *The Treaty of Maastricht. From Conception to Ratification: a Comprehensive Reference Guide* (Essex, Longman, 1993), p. 52.
[2] D. Curtin, 'The constitutional structure of the Union: a Europe of bits and pieces', *Common Market Law Review*, 30, (1993), 17–69, p. 67.
[3] E. Meehan, *Citizenship and the European Community* (London, Sage, 1993), pp. 16ff.
[4] T. Oppermann, *Europarecht* (München, Beck, 1982), pp. 563ff.
[5] J. H. H. Weiler, 'Fin-de-siècle Europe' in R. Dehousse (ed.), *Europe after Maastricht. An ever closer Union?* (München, Beck, 1994), pp. 203–16, at p. 213.

hundred years, the idea of supra-national citizenship requires theoretical explanation and a new political legitimation.

In the rest of this chapter I shall briefly sketch the inherent rationale of citizenship, relating it to the idea of modern statehood, and to the emergence of both democracy and the nation state. I shall then discuss two challenges to the concept of citizenship traditionally associated with the idea of the nation state, returning to the concept of citizenship within the European Union in the conclusion.

The Rationale of Citizenship

The modern notion of citizenship gained universal prominence with the idea of equal national citizenship developed and established by the French Revolution. Yet, its connotations and semantics refer to traditions that date back to premodern times. The etymological roots of the term refer to the dwellers of a city. The significance of the ancient Greek 'city' (*polis*) consisted less in its quality as a physical location than in its character as a symbolic space. Citizenship replaced the familial and tribal bonds of individuals and entailed a new city-like, i.e. civic, ethics of cooperation. Its essence lay in the new idea of a commonness of individuals based on the abstract ties of common religion[6] and, above all, of common laws.[7] From its origins in ancient Greece, citizenship has included a distinct status which draws symbolic boundaries not only against those who live physically outside the community, but, what is even more important, also against those who live within the physical space of the community but who do not belong to it socially. In other words, in its original meaning citizenship was a social construction which was not only constitutive of the identity of a particular political community, but which, at the same time, defined the social identity of the individuals who, in their quality as members, replaced their family, clan, or tribal affiliations with their status in a more abstract community, the polity. Thus, citizenship not only sharply distinguished between the physical and the social boundaries of a society, it also transcended the boundaries of the 'natural' groups of the family, the clan, and the tribe by establishing a *political* organization of a social group. Citizenship was the central element of the Greeks' invention of the political, i.e. of an autonomous sphere of social life dealing with the aspirations of the community as such.[8]

In fact, a common feature of the concept of citizenship throughout different historical contexts has been its polemical usage as a counter-term to other social roles: a citizen is not only different but is, in a way, the positive counter-image of a person whose defining social characteristics are his or her qualities as a consumer, a producer, a client, a subject, a family member, or simply a private person. This is perhaps the consequence of a more fundamental historical property of citizenship: namely, its inherent bent towards a universalist perception of the individual and the ensuing refusal to tie him or her to narrow, parochial, and particularistic social roles.

[6] M. Weber, *Economy and Society: an Outline of Interpretive Sociology* (Berkeley/Los Angeles/London, University of California Press, 1964), pp. 1226ff.

[7] P. Riesenberg, *Citizenship in the Western Tradition. Plato to Rousseau* (Chapel Hill/London, University of North Carolina Press, 1992), pp. 20ff.

[8] D. Schnapper, *La Communauté des Citoyens. L'idée moderne de nation* (Paris, Gallimard, 1994), pp. 83–8.

As Max Weber remarked in his sociology of the city,[9] citizenship is a genuinely Western institution. Unlike oriental cities, the occidental medieval city, and with some qualifications the ancient Greek *polis* as well, was not the place of settlement of clans, families, tribes, or other primordial communities (i.e., of communities which existed *prior* to this locus). Rather, it consisted of individuals who were alien to each other and who were bound together through oaths of fraternization which affirmed a secular community.[10] The corporate unity of the city was based on acts of association between individuals, it was the corporation of the 'burghers as such' who were subject to a law to which only they had access and which was only shared by them.[11] Membership of the corporation of the city was an original state of social embeddedness; it was neither derived from membership of a prior social community, nor did it imply a purely physical association to a particular place of settlement. It was an exclusive social-political status which had a distinct symbolic meaning and relevance. Hence the conditions of access were highly selective because this status was of great importance both for the would-be member and for the host community.

This conception of an abstract 'civic' community is embodied in the idea of the republic. Essentially, citizenship means membership of the republic. Republicanism incarnates the Aristotelian idea of a body politic whose public authority is rooted in the association of free men possessing a shared understanding of the common good and who govern themselves through law. The city is a symbolic space in which individuals, who are strangers to each other, are linked together through the visibility of the institutions to which they adhere: the agora, the court house, the palace of the head of the republic, etc.

Citizenship is a status of equality, but only among equals. Hence, in its premodern meaning it was fully compatible with social hierarchy. Citizenship was a status of eminence by which a distinguished class of individuals were recognized as having a particular stake (i.e., particular rights, duties and burdens, frequently coupled with a particular status of honour) in the polity. In the republican polity citizenship denoted the legitimate and permissible status of aristocracy. Thus, the centuries-old idea that those who are subject to the laws must be their authors does not apply to the premodern republic. Both in the ancient and in the medieval city republics, the rulers – the citizens – were a small minority which ruled over the majority of non-citizens.[12] Still, the idea of a political community based on the commitment of its members to their common affairs and the creation of institutions which symbolize this separate *res publica* has not been destroyed or devalued through its social exclusivity. Admittedly, at the beginning of political modernity, i.e. in the era of the emergence of the modern state, republicanism was outdated and rejected by the theorists of statehood.[13] But ultimately these two seemingly incompatible ideas were connected and assimilated within the ideal of national citizenship – based on the modern nation's statehood.

---

[9] Weber, *Economy and Society*, part 2, ch. XVI, pp. 1212–372.

[10] Weber, *Economy and Society*, pp. 1244–8.

[11] Weber, *Economy and Society*, pp. 1228–9.

[12] Riesenberg, *Citizenship in the Western Tradition*, pp. 203–34.

[13] Cf. the historical account of the concept of republic from antiquity to the present by W. Mager, 'Republik' in O. Brunner, W. Conze and R. Koselleck (eds), *Geschichtliche Grundbegriffe. Historisches Lexikon zur politisch-sozialen Sprache in Deutschland* (Stuttgart, Klett, 1994), vol. 5, pp. 549–651.

Citizenship and Modern Statehood

Whilst the republic symbolized the idea of political freedom through the association of citizens, statehood reflects the emergence of an individualistic society which becomes the object of a centralized sovereign power within a demarcated territory.[14] Modern states are anxious to define sharply the physical boundaries of the territorial and the personal substrate of their authority and responsibility in the international system of states. Hence territoriality and nationality are essentials of modern statehood.

Ideally, the boundaries of the state define at the same time its territory and its subjects: all individuals residing within the confines of a given state are subject to its rule and hence by virtue of their physical affiliation are its nationals. Permanent residence within the territory of a state may be regarded as providing the most visible evidence for the less tangible 'genuine link' and 'true bond of attachment' and 'reciprocity of rights and duties' between an individual and a state which the International Court of Justice has stated are requirements of international law for the acknowledgement of the status of 'nationality', i.e. an individual's membership of a given state.[15] However, on an ideal understanding of the principle of territoriality, the mere physical attachment of an individual to the territory of a particular state would already be a sufficient condition for belonging to it. Note, that I avoid the term 'membership' because this is clearly an inappropriate understanding of the relation between the state and those who are subject to its authority.

Of course, political rule has always had a spatial dimension. Geographical boundaries have been drawn in Europe since the fourteenth century. But the sharp territorial demarcation characteristic of the modern state and its specific kind of rule is entirely recent; it did not exist prior to the end of the eighteenth century.[16] The European medieval system was structured by 'a nonexclusive form of territoriality' in which different political units like cities 'viewed themselves as municipal embodiments of a universal moral community'.[17]

In contrast, the modern state delimits its authority and sovereignty along physical boundaries, and its claim to obedience is (with a few exceptions) based on physical control over its territory. Thus, the well-known *ius soli* appears to be the appropriate and congenial principle for the determination of state membership which consequently is acquired by everybody born within its territorial boundaries. In early times, the *ius soli* was the obvious institution of settled agricultural societies and served to define the community. Conversely, the *ius sanguinis* primarily maintained the symbolic boundaries and the coherence of migrating nomadic societies. Wherever there is no physical locus, the symbolic bonds of common blood, descent, history, fate, culture, religion or language evolve into the primary source of commonness and of communal life. The *ius sanguinis* is the most important legal expression of this claim. When Marx, analysing pre-capitalist economic formations, compared the Greek and

[14] For a more detailed analysis of modern statehood cf. D. Held, *Democracy and the Global Order. From Modern State to Cosmopolitan Governance* (Cambridge, Polity, 1995), pp. 48–72.

[15] See the opinion of the International Court of Justice in the famous Nottebohm Case, ICJ Reports 1955, pp. 4ff. [23].

[16] W. Conze, 'Staat und Souveränität I – II' in *Geschichtliche Grundbegriffe. Historisches Lexikon zur politisch-sozialen Sprache in Deutschland* (Stuttgart, Klett-Cotta, 1990), vol. 6, pp. 1–25.

[17] J. G. Ruggie, 'Territoriality and beyond: problematizing modernity in international relations', *International Organization*, 47 (1993), 139–74, at p. 150.

Roman ancient cities (*poleis*) with the ancient Germanic communities he discovered a significant difference: the city, although a symbolic community, was represented in the physical demarcation of the urban space; it was the materialization of the permanence of the citizens' permanent community. By contrast, the Germanics lived separated in the forests and existed as a community only by virtue of 'every act of reunion of its members'.[18] In order to exist as a community beyond those reunions the Germanics constituted themselves as a community based on their common descent, language etc., i.e. as a '*Volk*'.[19]

Modern statehood did not entirely abolish the difference between the two approaches to linking individuals to the community, even if territoriality seems to have made the *ius sanguinis* dispensable. At first glance this fact is somewhat surprising. On closer scrutiny, however, it becomes clear that the territorial character of the modern state does not eliminate the need for criteria of membership which are more demanding than the mere *ius soli*. A patent expression of this need is the obvious distinction between nationality and citizenship. Nationality denotes an individual's legal belonging to a particular state.[20] In the pluriversum of contending sovereign states each of them is interested in a sharp and unequivocal demarcation of the territorial and personal reach of their authority in order to avoid an overlap with the similar claims of other sovereign states. This interest is satisfied, among other things, by the concept of nationality. 'Nationality' defines the category of persons who sovereign states mutually recognize as the legitimate objects of their respective sovereign power; consequently, it is a term and a concept which is of primary importance in the realm of international law.

In the sphere of domestic law the corresponding concept is subjecthood. Subjects are the individuals whom the sovereign state power defines as the personal substrate of its rule.[21] Hence, nationality and subjecthood define an identical multitude of individuals, viewed from different legal perspectives – the former from the international, the latter from the domestic point of view. By contrast, citizenship and nationality do not necessarily coincide: even today in some states, not all nationals are citizens, and not all citizens are necessarily nationals.[22]

Statehood established, claimed and enforced public authority solely on account of effective and sovereign power over a physically demarcated territory, irrespective of the capacity or willingness of its residents to understand, to accept or even to participate in the exercise of that authority. This is why subjecthood is the appropriate concept for this kind of rule. Subjecthood and

[18] K. Marx, *Pre-Capitalistic Economic Formations*, E. J. Hobsbawm (ed.) (London, Lawrence and Wishart, 1964), p. 78.
[19] C. Gamberale, 'National Identities and Citizenship in the European Union and in the US', unpublished paper (Florence, EUI, 1995), p. 11.
[20] D. Gosewinkel, 'Die Staatsangehörigkeit als Institution des Nationalstaats' in R. Grawert (ed.), *Offene Staatlichkeit. Festschrift für Ernst-Wolfgang Böckenförde* (Berlin, Duncker und Humblot, 1995), pp. 359–78.
[21] D. Gosewinkel, 'Citizenship, Subjecthood, Nationality. Concepts of Belonging in the Age of Modern Nation-states: Notes on the History of Concepts', unpublished paper, European Forum 1995–96 Project on Citizenship (Florence, EUI, 1995).
[22] However, empirically this is a rare case. The most eminent case is Article 4 of the French constitution of 1793 according to which the legislature could bestow the rights of a French citizen on an alien who 'had done humanity great service'. Yet, this constitution was never put into force.

citizenship – or, to refer to the basic structures of political rule to which they are attached, statehood and republicanism – are different, even opposed to each other. They embody different principles of political rule: citizenship and republicanism include activity, social exclusivity and public mindedness; subjecthood and statehood require and presuppose passivity and submissiveness, they are socially inclusive because they encompass all individuals within certain territorial boundaries, and they restrict individuals to their private spheres like the family, business, leisure etc. This does not mean that statehood and republicanism, subjecthood and citizenship cannot occur at the same time in the same polity. Unlike democracy, republicanism does not require political equality, and consequently equal subjecthood – the requirement of statehood – and unequal citizenship – the requirement of republicanism – could coexist and in fact did coexist in the French republican constitutions of 1791, 1795, 1799 and 1848. Even Kant, the 'German Rousseau', did not argue for universal equal citizenship. Similarly, the 'Declaration of the Rights of Man and Citizen' celebrates the distinction between those who, in spite of their capacity as bearers of universal human rights, are merely subjects of the laws of the republic and those who are simultaneously the law-makers, i.e. its citizens.

Bridging the Gap between Statehood and Republicanism: Democracy

The principle which attempts to bridge the gap between citizenship and subjecthood or, more generally, between republicanism and statehood, and to reconcile the social exclusivity of the former with the physical inclusiveness of the latter is of course democracy. Democracy stands for the Rousseauian ideal that all subjects of the laws should be their authors by virtue of their subjecthood alone, not by virtue of some particular personal aptitude which qualifies them for the noble task of law-making. The ideal result of this universalization of an exclusive political status is the democratic republic.

However, even in this ideal institutional framework the reconciliation of republicanism and statehood via the bridge of democratic egalitarianism can only be achieved approximately; a tension between the original concept of citizenship based on republicanism and the new concept based on the idea of democratic equality remains. Note that the republican citizen is entitled to participate in the act of law-making because he – indeed, only he – is personally qualified to do so; he must have a stake in the polity and hence be committed to the public good in order to be competent to make laws. In the republican framework *citizenship entails law-making*. This is why it was a matter of course even for the most committed and radical republicans that only male property owners qualified for citizenship.

By contrast, the democratic citizen is a citizen by virtue of the fact that he (and some decades later also she) is granted the right to take part in the process of law-making. In the democratic framework the equal right to participate in *law-making entails citizenship*. No prior social qualification is required, and hence a person who is only committed to his (or her) private business and affairs is also a citizen. In other words, democratic citizens are the passive and submissive subjects who have been collectively emancipated by the democratic revolution and whose commitment to the common good has still to be brought about. Rousseau's distinction between the *volonté générale* and the *volonté de tous* is as much a reflection of the split between the republican and the democratic character of a collective will as the distinction between *citoyen* and *homme* in the 'Declaration of the Rights of Man and Citizen' of 26 August 1789. While the *volonté générale* represents the social, public and common good orientation of the citizen who exercises his political freedom, the *volonté de tous* embodies the will of the private and isolated, pre-social man, who is primarily the subject of state power and is defended by no more than mere *droits de l'homme*.[23] Thus, the social diffusion of the status of citizenship has undermined its republican spirit.[24] To draw an obvious analogy to the economic sphere: the inflation of the republican status of citizenship caused by democracy has entailed its devaluation. Yet, this is the price which democrats have been ready to pay for the principle of self-government: everyone who is subject to political authority shall be its co-author.

So far I have discussed the structural tensions between the republican concept of citizenship and both statehood and democracy. In contrast, statehood and democracy seem to be thoroughly compatible and even mutually reinforcing. The physical inclusivity of statehood (arising from the principle of territoriality) and the symbolic inclusivity of democracy (arising from its egalitarian-universalist character) formed an efficient coalition which was able to reform the social exclusivity of the republican principle and to create the congruity of subjecthood and citizenship, i.e. the identity of rulers and ruled. Every resident of the state is, by virtue of the very fact of his or her residence, subject to its public authority, and the democratic principle requires that the subject of public authority must be its author. Ideally the physical boundaries of statehood and the symbolic boundaries of belonging to the category of persons who matter in the democracy coincide.

As a matter of fact, experience tells us that this is not the case. Despite its close connection with modern statehood, the democratic principle does not simply overlap with the latter's territorial boundaries. It draws symbolic boundaries of personal relevance which are narrower than the physical ones. Given the universalist tenets of democratic theory – every person has the same stakes in the democratic polity, enjoys the same rights and benefits and has to bear the same duties and burdens – this is somewhat surprising. Instead, a different concept provides the criteria for an individual's belonging to the democratic community: the concept of the nation.[25]

Statehood, Nationhood and the Nation State

Membership of a society, be it based on the *ius soli* or on the *ius sanguinis*, presupposes some kind of community among the individuals who form it. We cannot conceive of a purely physical belonging of an individual to a group, much less of course of a merely physically defined group; a group is a social, not a physical entity. For that reason the modern state's territoriality as such is not

[23] The reasons for downplaying the practical value of *droits de l'homme* as opposed to the *droits du citoyen* have been impressively analysed by H. Arendt, *The Origins of Totalitarian Rule* (New York/London, Harcourt Brace Jovanovich, 1973 [1951]), pp. 290–302.

[24] This is a challenge to the idea of citizenship which has been analysed by D. Schnapper, *La Communauté des Citoyens. L'idée moderne de nation*, pp. 185–202.

[25] Of course nationhood plays this selecting role also in the framework of non-democratic regimes as in ethnicist or racist political systems. But this is unsurprising and requires no theoretical explanation.

able to create a social entity out of the multitude of individuals who form the personal substrate of its sovereign power. In its incipient manifestation statehood produced the commonness of subjection of individuals under its power, but it was unable (and unwilling) to create the two main institutions which later became the indispensable preconditions for the success story of West European states: markets and an active community amongst their subjects.[26] The latter idea is embodied in the concept of the nation, which did not emerge before the end of the eighteenth century.[27] In many European nation states it was inherently linked with the idea of the constitutional state.[28]

Since the end of the eighteenth century, in Europe statehood and nationhood have engaged in a close relationship whose complexity is mostly due to the ambiguity of the concept of the nation.[29] The modern state is a nation state, but this statement embraces two extremely different meanings. Their ideal types are best represented by France and Germany. According to the French concept, the nation is a purely political community, 'la communauté des citoyens' who form an association under common laws. Their unity and coherence as a political community is incarnated in the state. Statehood is an essential element of this concept of nationhood. The nation consists of the active citizenry, and since the only political community of modernity is the state, French nationhood is inconceivable without statehood. Consequently, no individual can be a member of the nation, i.e. nobody can be a citizen without being by the same token simultaneously a subject of the state. Ideally, the reverse should apply as well: every subject of the state should be a member of the nation, i.e. a citizen. However, physical and social inclusion in the society are necessary, but not sufficient preconditions for becoming a full member, i.e. a citizen of the polity. To form an association under common laws requires the will and the capacity to participate in a common undertaking, i.e. to cooperate and to communicate with the other members, to recognize them as equals, and to be recognized by them as an equal. The droits de l'homme protect the individual against the violation of his or her basic rights as isolated persons; they do not include a person's right to be recognized as a fellow-citizen by the others. Conversely, the droits de citoyen protect the rights of individuals in their capacity as active members of the nation, but they do not include the right of every individual living within the boundaries of the state to be and to become a citizen. Subjecthood per se does not qualify one for citizenship. Yet, once the subjects are recognized as free and equal persons their demand to become active members of the nation could only be delayed for a limited time; it could not be rejected permanently, because the political definition of the nation state coupled

---

[26] C. Tilly (ed.), *The Formation of National States in Western Europe* (Princeton NJ, Princeton University Press, 1975).

[27] Cf. S.N. Eisenstadt and S. Rokkan (eds), *Building States and Nations* (Beverly Hills/London, Sage, 1973); P. Flora et al., *State, Economy, and Society in Western Europe 1815–1975*, vol. I, *The Growth of Mass Democracies and Welfare States* (Frankfurt, Campus, 1983).

[28] Schnapper, *La Communauté des Citoyens*, pp. 83–101; U. K. Preuß 'Problems of a concept of European citizenship', *European Law Journal*, 1 (1995), 263–277; Held, *Democracy and the Global Order*, pp. 50–2.

[29] Cf. the most recent accounts of D. Schnapper, *La France de l'integration. Sociologie de la nation en 1990* (Paris, Gallimard, 1991); D. Schnapper, *La Communauté des Citoyens* (Paris, Gallimard, 1994); R. Brubaker, *Citizenship and Nationhood in France and Germany* (Cambridge MA, Harvard University Press, 1992); H. Schulze, *Staat und Nation in der Europäischen Geschichte* (München, Beck, 1995).

with the idea of human rights was incompatible with the exclusion of major parts of the population from citizenship. Still, it is undeniable that even in the most inclusive French concept of nationhood, subjecthood in the state and citizenship in the nation do not fully coincide. The ideal of the identity of rulers and ruled is doomed to remain an ideal.

In the German (and, following its tradition, the East European) model, this ideal does not exist at all. This conception conceives the nation as a prepolitical community of individuals who are bound to each other by the commonness of either their 'nature' (their blood) or their culture (their language, literature, religion, and history). Perhaps this is still the heritage of the Germanic dispersion in the forests, which made them form a community according to non-physical criteria like common blood, language etc. The nation exists prior to the state, and occasionally without the state, like the Polish nation between 1795 and 1918, or Germany before 1871. It is the nation which creates the state, not vice versa. However, statehood is still important, even though in a different sense to the French model. The state does not generate the nation. Rather, it provides the nation with the power necessary for the satisfaction of its quest for glory and recognition. Members of the nation belong to the community because they share its 'natural' or cultural particularities. Membership in the community is not a matter of choice but of 'fate'. The *ius sanguinis* is the most appropriate criterion for the definition of the symbolic and social boundaries dividing the community from non-members. In this model neither residence within the boundaries of the state, nor the capacity and the willingness to participate as an equal in the association of equals under common laws, are sufficient conditions for citizenship. Obviously the gap between subjecthood and citizenship within this conceptual framework of the nation state is wider than in the French model.

Why do statehood and nationhood encompass both quantitatively and qualitatively different categories of individuals? Essentially, the modern state is a political organization, and so is the nation.[30] Territoriality is essential for the state; it defines its boundaries and the object of its power. We can assume that the sharp physical demarcation of political power and its historically unprecedented efficiency are mutually reinforcing, and this in turn explains the superiority of the modern state over all preceding political orders. Statehood includes, as Max Weber put it, 'coercion through jeopardy and destruction of life and freedom of movement applying to outsiders as to the members themselves. The individual is expected ultimately to face death in the group interest [which] gives to the political community its particular pathos and raises its enduring emotional foundations.'[31] Only political, not economic or other merely instrumentally rational (in the Weberian sense of *Zweckrational*) communities can legitimately ask their members to lay down their own lives.

From this it follows that membership of the political community requires a deeper, more existential and emotional kind of commonness than common residence within the boundaries of a given territory; common subjecthood under the sovereign power of the state does not constitute the kind of community capable of demanding individuals to sacrifice their lives for it. A society able to procure its members' willingness to assume duties of human

---

[30] Weber, *Economy and Society*, pp. 901–40.
[31] Weber, *Economy and Society*, p. 903.

solidarity vis-à-vis their fellow creatures, even of a less dramatic kind, requires bonds of commonness among them which are more specific and tighter than the commonness of subjection under a centralized sovereign power. This community is the nation. However broadly this is defined – whether in the political sense of the French model or in the ethno-cultural terms of the German tradition – it is not identical with the multitude of individuals who reside within the territorial boundaries of the state. The principles of territoriality and personality do not produce the same degree of individual belonging. That is why, despite recognition of the universal rights of man, not only the republican, but also the democratic polity establishes criteria of personal qualification which individuals have to meet in order to obtain its more moderate, though still eminent, status of citizenship. The boundaries of the state tend to be broader than those of the nation, and citizenship is associated with the latter, not with the former.

If, even in French political doctrine, the nation is the political concept which ultimately defines the individual's relationship with his or her fellows – what is the role of statehood in the democratic polity? Why not realize the identity of rulers and ruled, i.e. the identity of citizens and subjects, by defining the state and the nation by the very same boundaries? The answer is that the state's claim to sovereign power over a territory and the claim of a multitude of individuals to rule themselves have different subjects. The state's claim to the monopoly of the means of violence is based on the claim to comprehensive control over the whole social life in that *territory*. By contrast, democracy aims at the self-rule of a collectivity of *persons*. The democratic claim to collective self-determination aspires to the ideal situation which Rousseau proclaimed for the first time, namely the identity of rulers and ruled. He or she who does not rule cannot and must not be the object of the commands of the ruler. This condition places an inherent limitation on the rulers' sovereignty which prevents it from becoming despotic,[32] while the sovereign power of the state is inherently unlimited and for that reason susceptible to perversion into oppression and tyranny. The democratic nation state links the two claims in that the people become the heir of the unlimited, pervasive and comprehensive state power. When democracy goes statist and adopts the power structure of statehood it is no longer a device of self-determination for a multitude of individuals who associate themselves under common laws. It also embraces the territorial dimension of sovereignty and oversteps the intrinsic boundaries set by the self-rule of the association of citizens. Hence the discrepancy between citizenship and subjecthood is the result of the combination of statehood with democracy, or, in the conceptual framework of modern statehood, of the principles of territoriality and personality.

This combination is embodied in the idea of the nation state. Irrespective of the conception of the nation – be it the prepolitical ethno-cultural German or the universalist political French conception – the idea of the nation state contains a tension between national principles of group solidarity and the claims to sovereign power of the modern state. This tension is expressed in the duality of the physical boundaries of the state and the symbolic boundaries of the political community, the nation. While the state boundaries impose merely

---

[32] J. J. Rousseau (M. Cranston, trans. and introduced), *The Social Contract* (London, Penguin, 1968), book 2, ch. 4, pp. 74–8.

external restrictions on the sovereign power, community boundaries guarantee, by virtue of the identity of rulers and ruled, inherent limitations on the sovereign power of the nation. As Rousseau argued, no associate is interested in imposing more severe limitations on the freedoms of his or her fellow citizens than he or she would be ready to accept.[33] Only in an ideal hypothetical case do the physical and the symbolic boundaries come together. This may occur in a country where a pure and unqualified *ius soli* applies and where the political community is exclusively based on universalist principles, i.e. is accessible to everybody. Yet, even in this ideal case the analytical distinction between the physical and the symbolic character of a boundary would remain necessary in order to understand their different functions. Thus, the complementarity and the incongruity of physical and symbolic boundaries is the defining feature of citizenship in the democratic nation state. The physical boundaries of an individual's belonging to the state take shape in the *ius soli* or the *ius sanguinis*; they define the multitude of individuals who are merely subjects in the first place and who have still to be transformed into a political community, i.e. into the nation. The symbolic boundaries are embodied in the rights and duties of the members of the political community which are simultaneously the source and the result of their mutual solidarity. Like every boundary, this one is exclusive in that it defines the Demos, i.e. the persons who matter in the democracy and who constitute the nation. Yet democratic principles require that this symbolic boundary be fixed according to universalist principles. This means that the criteria of exclusion of the non-members must not discriminate according to criteria which ultimately deny a person's human dignity as an equal, like race or ethnicity.[34]

Challenges to the Nation State Centred Concept of Citizenship

In the last decade we have been faced with two serious challenges to this ideal-typical inner balance of the nation state. The first refers to the occurrence of a new wave of international migration which is about to reach Western Europe. The second is the emergence of the European Union.

The Challenge of International Migration

Although today nomadic societies exist at best marginally, migration has never ceased to be a major element in human history.[35] Therefore the modern state's principle of territoriality may not be sufficient. In a situation where there is no migration, the *ius soli* and the *ius sanguinis* yield the same outcome with respect to the acquisition of citizenship. Of course, this ideal situation has hardly ever existed in human history and does not exist in the contemporary world.

---

[33] Rousseau, *The Social Contract*, book 1, ch. 7, pp. 75–7; see also pp. 62–4.

[34] Cf. M. Walzer, *Spheres of Justice* (New York, Basic, 1983), pp. 61–3; B. Ackerman, *Social Justice in the Liberal State* (New Haven and London, Yale University Press, 1980), pp. 69–103.

[35] Cf. W. H. McNeil and R. S. Adams (eds), *Human Migration. Patterns and Policies* (Bloomington, Indiana University Press, 1978); M. Kritz, C. Keely and S. Tomasi (eds), *Global Trends in Migration* (Staten Island, Center for Migration Studies, 1981); S. Castles and M. J. Miller (eds), *The Age of Migration. International Population Movements in the Modern World* (London, MacMillan, 1993); D. S. Massey *et al.*, 'An evaluation of international migration theory: the North American case', *Population and Development Review*, 19 (1993), 431–66.

Migration is a basic fact of human life which reflects the quest of individuals and collectivities to improve their life conditions. Individuals and groups are either pushed to leave their homeland by war, civil war, famine, exhaustion of resources and the like, or they are pulled by the prospects of a better life in other parts of the world. Very frequently the push and the pull effect occur simultaneously.

The relation between migration and statehood is ambivalent.[36] On the one hand, statehood encourages migration in that it liberates the individual from the bonds of belonging to feudal estates and parochial communities based on inborn and ascriptive qualities which tie the individual to a particular place and to particular forms of working and living. In the earliest ages of modern statehood, the state's principle of founding affiliation on mere physical residence was a strong incentive for free movement because it lowered the barriers to the access to new life conditions and life chances. The principle of territoriality gave rise to the expectation and the hope of many oppressed individuals that the demarcation of the state was not just physical but also symbolic, in that it served as a constitutive force for the creation of a genuinely statist society based on the exchange of obedience for protection.

On the other hand, statehood and migration do not go well with each other. Statehood requires a sharp demarcation both of the territory and the people that are subject to the state's control. Moreover, the state claims to be the only and exclusive embodiment of the political community of the individuals settling within its physical territory. Only in the second half of the twentieth century was the state able to overcome its inherent individualism and to integrate political, economic, social and cultural communities into the structure of its constitutions. Yet its social coherence and political stability is fragile. There is a widespread awareness that the modern state depends upon economic, social, and cultural preconditions which provide the indispensable forces of social cohesion. While at the dawn of modern statehood religious homogeneity was considered to embody this essential condition, the relevant candidates have changed several times, including alternatively or cumulatively national, ethnic, racial, economic, social and cultural homogeneity.[37] However convincing and exhaustive this list may be, it reflects the modern state's demand for nonphysical qualities of sameness amongst its subjects. They are regarded as imperative for the maintainance of a peaceful and cooperative society within its territorial boundaries since collective subjecthood *per se* does not constitute the scheme of social cooperation which produces the resources necessary for the state's operation. As argued above, the modern state's principle of physical affiliation is incomplete and needs a complementary principle of belonging which delivers the symbolic forces for the creation and maintainance of a community which generates the resources of social solidarity necessary for social cohesion.

The inherent complementarity of the physical and the symbolic criteria of belonging to the modern state makes migration a particularly difficult

---

[36] R. Bauböck, *Transnational Citizenship. Membership and Rights in International Migration* (Brookfield, Edward Elgar, 1994).

[37] For the most recent discussion about the integrating or disintegrating role of social conflict see A. O. Hirschman, 'Social conflicts as pillars of democratic market societies', in A. O. Hirschman, *A Propensity to Self-subversion* (Cambridge MA and London, Harvard University Press, 1995), pp. 231–48.

problem.[38] Migration involves the loosening of the two ties which link individuals to the state, since they leave the territory and evade the control of the power of their home state. Obviously, there cannot be a smooth transition from one political community to another, because the host state may be prepared to accept the physical presence of the newcomers, but normally it is either unwilling or unable to accept them immediately as full members and to integrate them into its social, economic, and cultural life, and to make them full members of the nation. Thus, the modern state's promise that the enjoyment of its protection, as well as other benefits following from one's affiliation to it, are not dependent upon inborn and unchangeable qualities of a person but solely upon a physical affiliation to its territory, is reneged by its character as a nation and hence remains unfulfilled.

This experience gives rise to two parallel developments. On the one hand, the distinction between subjecthood and citizenship is established in order to make sure that the newcomers are subject to the host state's power without having the same claims as its citizens to those benefits and assets to whose production they did not contribute. On the other hand, the newcomers have good reason to form communities within the host society in order to improve the chances of survival and advancement of their members, and to provide them with the moral and psychic support which they need in order to cope with the difficulties of their new environment. Not surprisingly, they draw the symbolic boundaries which delineate them from 'the others' in terms of commonness, which is independent of the state's criteria of belonging: ethnicity.[39]

When physical affiliation to a territory does not provide a sufficient criterion of an individual's belonging to a particular community, non-physical boundaries are created. Individuals who are exposed to the common fate of exclusion from basic benefits of the society, and at the same time share the commonness of descent, history, language and the like, will form sub-political communities within the physical realm of the modern state. Thus, the modern state's conceptual structure is self-contradictory: whereas its principle of territorial rule offers an incentive to physical and social mobility in that it neglects the individuals' particular ascriptive qualities, community affiliations and loyalties, it discourages migration in that the principle of physical affiliation needs the underpinning of a coherent, perhaps even homogeneous society, which cannot be provided by mere physical belonging. Since the symbolic boundaries of the modern nation state are much narrower than the physical boundaries of its territory, migration actuates the duality of the principles and the potential tension between them in that it spurs both the natives and the immigrant newcomers to mobilize their respective prepolitical properties in order to draw sharp symbolic boundaries between each other. Mass migration has rendered the physical boundaries of statehood almost completely insignificant as a means of demarcating the distinctiveness of societies.[40] Consequently, the importance

---

[38] See also S. Spencer (ed.), *Strangers & Citizens. A Positive Approach to Migrants and Refugees* (London, Rivers Oram, 1994); P. Close, *Citizenship, Europe and Change* (Houndmills and London, MacMillan, 1995), pp. 55–137.

[39] W. Kymlicka, *Multicultural Citizenship* (Oxford, Oxford University Press, 1995), pp. 10–33; D. Schnapper, *La France de l'intégration. Sociologie de la nation en 1990* (Paris, Gallimard, 1991), pp. 33–51.

[40] J. G. Ruggie, 'Territoriality and beyond: problematizing modernity in international relations', *International Organization*, 47 (1993), 139–74.

of symbolic boundaries and their exclusionary potential has enormously increased. This may give rise to a separation of citizenship from its modern affiliation to statehood and even entail a return to the ethos of the pre-democratic age, when it was the privilege of a minority. This is one potential path of development which may finally destroy the inherent rationale of the concept of citizenship as the incarnation of the idea of the republic. Once democracy has been established, the republic can no longer be conceived in an aristocratic sense.

However, the separation of citizenship from statehood does not necessarily mean the disappearance of the universalist-egalitarian qualities which it had acquired through its affiliation with modern statehood. This alternative leads to the second challenge to citizenship: the emergence of a supranational political community, the European Union.[41]

The Challenge of Supranationality: the European Union

The gradual evolution of the European Union indicates a profound change in the role and the significance of the nation state. It may affect not only the criteria of membership in the nation state itself but also create new forms of supra-national belonging. Although the idea of European citizenship is not entirely novel,[42] it was not until the Treaty on European Union that 'citizenship of the union' was formally established in a legal text of the Community.

For the time being these articles embody the last step of a development of the European Economic Community which started with the purely economic aspiration of the Treaty of Rome of 1957 to mobilize the 'factors of production' in the Member States. The (political-pathetic) term 'citizen' was not in the wording of the original Treaty and probably thoroughly alien to its spirit. When the treaty dealt with persons, they were addressed in their roles as economic actors, i.e. as employers, employees, or self-employed persons. The main goal of the Community was the integration of the economies of the Member States, and consequently the rights of individuals – primarily the right to equal treatment of all participants in the market irrespective of their nationality – were tailored according to the functional requirements of economic integration. In the meantime, the development of the Community has clearly gone beyond the 'functional integration' of the economies of the Member States. The narrow conception of individuals as workers or self-employed persons has been

---

[41] From a legal point of view we must distinguish between 'European Community' and 'European Union'. In fact, the 'European Union' is a strange and legally opaque combination of the European Communities proper (European Community, formerly: European Economic Community, the European Coal and Steel Community, and the European Atomic Energy Community) and certain modes of intergovernmental cooperation (see Articles A para. 3, J and K of the Treaty on European Union, signed in Maastricht on 7 February 1992). Hence, the European Union is not a legal entity which could be the subject of rights and duties in the framework of international law.

[42] See, e.g., E. Grabitz, *Europäisches Bürgerrecht zwischen Marktbürgerschaft und Staatsbürger-schaft* (Köln, Europa Union, 1970); R. Plender, 'An incipient form of European citizenship' in F. G. Jacobs (ed.), *European Law and the Individual* (Amsterdam, New York, Oxford, 1976), pp. 39–53; A. Durand 'European citizenship', *European Law Review*, 4 (1979), 3–14; G. v. d. Berghe, *Political Rights for European Citizens* (Aldershot, Gower, 1982); A. Evans, 'European citizenship: a novel concept in EEC law', *American Journal of Comparative Law*, 1984, 679–715.

loosened. In particular, the basic freedoms of movement and residence are no longer restricted to economic actors.[43]

The list of rights which Articles 8 to 8e associate with the status of Union citizenship is not very impressive; it includes, beyond the already existing rights to free movement and residence within the territory of the Member States, the right to vote and to stand as a candidate in elections to the European Parliament and in municipal elections at the place of one's residence on the same terms as nationals of that state, the rights to diplomatic and consular protection by any Member State, and the right to petition to the European Parliament and to an Ombudsman. Yet, the creation of an immediate legal bond between the nationals of the Member States and the European Community, and the continual dissociation of their legal protection 'from their functional status as workers'[44] signify a major step towards European citizenship. Nonetheless, because Union citizenship presupposes national citizenship of one of the Member States, supra-national citizenship seems to be no challenge or even threat to the entrenched status of national citizenship. Thus, depending on one's political values, neither hopes nor fears appear justified that national citizenship might disappear in the course of European integration.

However, in the long run European citizenship may become more important and eclipse national citizenship. Two sorts of development are conceivable. We may imagine the emergence of a *common European criterion* which defines a class of persons who enjoy some consequential rights or privileges.[45] A common European criterion which would render an individual a 'citizen of the Community' could be, for instance, her legal residence for at least five years within the territorial boundaries of the Community. For the sake of analytical clarity, we may even make the unrealistic assumption that residence within the physical boundaries of the Community is entirely independent of the – existent or non-existent – quality of a person being a national of a Member State. Thus, it would be possible to be a Union citizen without being the national of any of the Member States because the Member States do not serve as an intermediary between the individuals and the Community. The possession of this status would be the indispensable link to the enjoyment of rights and benefits granted by the Community. This path to European citizenship may be called the *status path*, because the acquisition of the status of citizenship takes logical precedence over the consequential rights attached to it. Rights are derived from the status.

An alternative developmental path could pursue an approach according to which the Community would confer rights on the citizens of all Member States. Individuals would enjoy these rights irrespective of their particular nationality. Three different classes of Community rights have to be distinguished:[46] (1) rights against institutions and agents of the Community – e.g. against the

---

[43] See Council directives No. 364/90 of June 28, 1990, in *OJ* 1990, L 180, p. 26 (right of residence); No. 365/90 of June 28, 1990, in *OJ* 1990, L 180, p. 28 (right of residence for employees and self-employed persons who have ceased their occupational activity); No. 366/90 of June 28, 1990, in *OJ* 1990, L 180, p. 30 (right of residence for students).

[44] G. F. Mancini 'The making of a constitution for Europe' in R. O. Keohane and S. Hoffmann (eds), *The New European Community. Decisionmaking and Institutional Change* (Boulder CO and Oxford, Westview, 1991), p. 185.

[45] Plender, 'An incipient form of European citizenship', p. 40.

[46] Cf. A. Clapham, *Human Rights and the European Community: A Critical Overview. European Union – The Human Rights Challenge* (Baden-Baden, Nomos, 1991), vol. 1, pp. 31 ff.

Commission or the Council; (2) rights against institutions of the individual's own nation state applying Community law; (3) rights against the institutions of a Member State other than the individual's own nation state applying Community law. All three classes of Community rights drop the otherwise important criterion of Member State nationality. If the number of this 'supranational' class of rights gradually increases, then the resulting bundle of Community rights would (or at least could) eventually create a bond of commonness among individuals who enjoy the same rights and who are protected by the same law, and this common bond of mutual loyalty may finally constitute the status of Community citizenship.[47]

The Treaty on European Union has pursued the latter path, if only reluctantly. A further development in this direction, and even more so a development according to the *status path*, may weaken the bonds of Europeans to their respective nation states provided that a European constitution furnishes them with the appropriate institutional means for an active participation in the supranational polity. Yet, Union citizenship should not be misunderstood as a mere expansion of the traditional concept of citizenship of nation states. There is a broad consensus among experts that there are obvious dissimilarities between supranational citizenship and the traditional notion.[48] European citizenship is a particular kind of membership in the Community which is only partially comparable with citizenship based on nationality. Neither the *ius soli* nor the *ius sanguinis* are appropriate criteria for the acquisition of Union citizenship. They are related to modern statehood and its comprehensive, homogeneous, penetrating and exclusive sovereign authority, which claims to maintain a coherent social and political order within the very physical boundaries of the state territory. Although there is a territorial element in the structure of the European Union – its space consists of the territories of its Member States – its public authority is not defined in spatial terms, nor does it claim to be as monolithic, homogeneous, hierarchical, and effective as the traditional state power. Thus, clear-cut demarcations in terms of territory and persons do not fit into the conceptual framework of the European Union. Citizenship of the European Union is as novel, unprecedented, imperfect, and evolving as the European Union itself. This is why it can be defined only tentatively and in rather vague and speculative terms.

The Potential Meaning of European Citizenship

While it is easy to give a negative definition of the European Union – it is *not* a state, not even a federal state, it is *not* a traditional alliance of states, it is *not* a confederacy – it is impossible, at least up until now, to define it positively. Several characteristics can be enumerated:

  (i) The EU is a dynamic polity.[49] In contrast to the modern state's objective to maintain and reproduce the given order, the Community is

---

[47] T. H. Marshall, *Citizenship and Social Class – and other Essays* (Cambridge, Cambridge University Press, 1992); R. E. Goodin, *Reasons for Welfare. The Political Theory of the Welfare State* (Princeton NJ, Princeton University Press, 1988), pp. 83ff.
[48] v.d. Berghe, *Political Rights for European Citizens*, p. 3; T. Oppermann, *Europarecht* (München, Beck, 1982), pp. 565ff.
[49] J. H. H. Weiler, 'The transformation of Europe', *Yale Law Journal*, 100 (1991), 2403–83.

directed at change, namely an ever further integration of the Member States. This is an open-ended process of the Community's continual self-transformation which requires institutional devices of permanent learning, self-observation and self-adaptation. This inherently changing character of the Community is in striking contrast to the structural characteristics of modern statehood.

(ii) The constitution of the Union – its basic politico-institutional structure – is meant to be complementary to the constitutions of the Member States. It is parasitic upon the political orders of the Member States not on the ground of its imperfection, but intentionally and on conceptual grounds. In contrast to federal states, the dualism of constitutions which is characteristic of the European Community does not presuppose a basic homogeneity and hierarchical relationship between the central and the federal units and a clear-cut fixed demarcation of competencies between them. Rather, the interactions between the several units are determined by the dynamics of an open process of different kinds of cooperation in which various institutional and policy solutions for a concrete problem can be generated.

(iii) Finally, unlike traditional states the European Community is characterized by its polycentric character. Although the Community is vested with power for the realization of its policy goals, there is no single political centre in which the political substance of the Community is incarnated. Rather, the processes of policy generation and implementation take place within a web of a plurality of actors and interactions which leaves the impression of a quite diffuse concept of politics.

In sum, dynamism, openness and polycentricity are basic properties of the European Community, and they are likely to shape the future concept of a no longer mono-statist polity. Consequently, citizenship of that polity will differ considerably from our traditional, state-centred notion. Borrowing a phrase from a quite different historical and political context, we may understand European citizenship as an instrument which serves to remove 'from the citizens of each state the disabilities of alienage in the other States'.[50] This judgement was made with reference to Article 4 section 2 of the US Constitution, which stipulates that 'the citizens of each State shall be entitled to all privileges and immunities of citizens in the several States'. In another opinion, issued almost a century later, the Supreme Court made the assessment[51] that 'the primary purpose of this clause ... was to help fuse into one nation a collection of independent sovereign states'.[52]

In the American case the establishment of national citizenship served to render the Union the protector of individual rights which were jeopardized by the Member States. The Federal State had to protect freedmen against the likely infringement of their rights – particularly by the former slaveholder states. National citizenship became a safe harbour against interferences by the states. Obviously this interpretation does not apply to the establishment of Union citizenship in Part Two of the EC Treaty, because individual rights are well protected within the constitutional systems of the Member States. Rather, the

---

[50] US Supreme Court Case *Paul* v. *Virginia*, 75 U.S. 168, 180 (1869).
[51] L. Tribe, *American Constitutional Law* (Mineola, NY, Foundation, 1988), pp. 548–53.
[52] US Supreme Court Case *Toomer* v. *Witsell*, 334 U.S. 385, 395 (1948).

structural significance of the rights of the citizens of the Union consists in the creation of a socio-legal sphere of the Union which embodies the goal of the Union to diminish, perhaps even to abolish, the 'disabilities of alienage in the other States'. This includes not only those who settle in a Member State other than their own, but those who live in their own Member State as well. They have to cope with the fact that persons who used to be aliens have become their fellow-citizens in one respect – in their quality of citizens of the Union – without becoming full members, i.e. citizens in all respects of the daily life of their own Member State. What seems paradoxical at first glance, expresses the very specificity of the European Union. Union citizenship is not so much a relation of the individual vis-à-vis Community institutions but rather a particular socio-legal status vis-à-vis national Member States which have to learn how to cope with the fact that persons, who are physically and socially their citizens, are acquiring a kind of legal citizenship by means of European citizenship without being their nationals.

'Alienage' will probably be the hallmark of Union citizenship, a kind of permanent and structural cognitive and emotional dissonance which, in contrast to the American case, is not likely to disappear in a unitary national culture in the forseeable future. In contrast to most federal states, Union citizenship is not likely to supersede national citizenship or to make it a status of minor importance frequently verging on mere irrelevance; rather, both statuses will co-exist, representing two different principles of political organization. National citizenship uses territoriality as the basic means for integrating individuals within society. Union citizenship presupposes a more abstract polity, whose membership serves mainly to integrate individuals who, by all traditional standards, are aliens, or, as the 'Proposals Towards a European Citizenship' submitted by the Spanish Government in September 1990 put it, 'privileged foreigners'. The Spanish Government expected that making the step towards Union Citizenship 'will eliminate the negative effects presently accompanying the condition of foreigner for a citizen of a Member State in another Member State'.[53] It remains to be seen whether the 'abolition of the disabilities of alienage', which sometimes amounts to the attempt to avoid a 'clash of political cultures', can be understood in terms of the distinction between *territorial federalism* and *personal federalism*.[54] In any case, it seems safe to assume that the meaning of Union citizenship will be shaped to a considerable extent by the prevailing concepts and traditions of the Member States, because it is the emerging dualism of national and Union citizenship which will finally determine the legal status of European citizens.

It is possible that out of the dissonances resulting from the dualism between the more concrete national citizenship and the more abstract Union citizenship serious conflicts may arise which ultimately may thwart the goal of integration. The removal of 'the disabilities of alienage' requires the removal of 'alienage', and this in turn requires the mutual understanding of what the involved parties – migrating individuals originating in the several Member States, and the hosting Member States and their citizens themselves –understand when

---

[53] See the document in the book of R. Corbett, *The Treaty of Maastricht. From Conception to Ratification: a Comprehensive Reference Guide* (Essex, Longman, 1993), pp. 156–8.

[54] T. Fleiner-Gerster and L. R. Basta-Posavec, 'Federalism, Federal States and Decentralization', unpublished paper (Institute of Federalism, Fribourg, 1993).

they claim or have to accept, respectively, the institution of Union citizenship. Therefore, the future of a concept of European citizenship depends very much on the learning capacities of the would-be citizens of Europe itself, namely on their capability and willingness to accept and cope with alienage in their daily lives.

Liberalism, Nationalism and the Post-sovereign State

NEIL MACCORMICK

Introduction

Any discussion of constitutions and constitutionalism in contemporary Europe, whether Europe in its entirety or the narrower Europe of the European Union, has to handle the issue of nationalism. The violent clashes of ethnic (or putatively ethnic) nationalities in the former Yugoslavia and on the island of Ireland, the smouldering issues of ethnicity and of national minorities in the countries of the former Soviet Union and in other post-communist states are one area of obvious concern. Within the European Union, its internal 'pillar' the European Community has been declared by its Court of Justice a 'new legal order' to which member states have irrevocably transferred certain of their sovereign rights, thereby subordinating their own domestic legal systems to Community law. Yet here nationalistic pretensions and concerns of member states have posed, and continue to pose, challenges to the further evolution of Community institutions and powers. These challenges are fuelled by serious concerns and sometimes stridently expressed Euroscepticisms among substantial bodies of opinion in the political classes and political parties of the member states.

The very legitimacy of the project for European Union, and with it the claim that the Community is a duly constituted and self-standing legal order, can be held to presuppose or to require the constructing of a new European identity, or even, as Joseph Weiler puts it in this volume, the actualization of a European Demos. Such an identity, such a Demos would play somehow the same role that national identity, or the identity of the people as a self-aware Demos, plays in the legitimation of the institutions of a state. Within the states themselves, however, constitutions are challenged or amended in the light of the claims of internal nations or countries, as in the case of Flanders and Wallonia, or of Catalunya and Euskadi and other autonomous regions within Spain, or the Länder in Germany who secured a significant constitutional amendment as part of the enabling legislation for the Maastricht Treaty, or Scotland and Wales in the United Kingdom.

Perhaps what is now needed is a new take on this set of issues: bracket off the nation for a moment, and reflect on the state. The post-revolutionary world, the world of modernity, was the world of the states. These states were in their essence sovereign states, thus states in a state of nature towards each other, bound *inter se* only by the law of nature and nations. They were nation states asserting the inalienable sovereignty of a sovereign nation or people. Maybe most truly of all, as Jeremy Jennings's present chapter revealingly suggests, they were imperial states extending their imperium out over the peoples of other continents whose forms of social order were in the main substantially different from those of the European monarchies that were transforming themselves into centralizing states in this imperial phase of their development, and moulding to more-or-less uniform membership of the metropolitan nation their own internally diverse parts.

The view of world order to which we have fallen heir is dominated by that conception of statehood. The world we know, or have until recently known, is a world of mutually independent states. In its most recent phase, completed with the dissolution of the former Russian Empire by the collapse of the Soviet Union, the process of decolonization involved a notable numerical multiplication of states, all with a legally equal sovereignty to assert. And yet again, the more states there are, the harder it must be to deny the claims to full statehood of such obvious nations as Kurdistan, Slovakia, Catalunya, Euskadi, Wales, or Scotland, if their members choose so to exercise self-determination.

Federal unions within this vision of world order may have started out as, or at times aspired to become, sites for the taming of sovereign power, by disseminating it both vertically and horizontally, and hence in a way dissolving it. But the logical and geopolitical necessities of the ruling conception of world order forced them into the mould of sovereign statehood in the form of sovereign federal unions, however decentralized internally. With the exception, arguably the sole exception, of Switzerland, to which the history of Europe bequeathed a special status, federations exhibited in any event a long-term tendency to centralization of power in the general government, to the detriment of local self-government. Even Canada, which for long protected its federal structure by leaving final constitutional authority with the 'Imperial Parliament' in London, resorted in 1982 to a patriation of its final sovereignty at the unilateral instance of the Federal Government and Parliament, adjusting proceedings only at the eleventh hour to allow for the ruling by its own highest court, obtained at the instance of certain provinces, that the unilateral way of proceeding was 'unconstitutional' by the ruling standards of Canadian constitutional convention, even though it was not contrary to strict law. Recent developments – and non-developments – in Quebec have to be read in part as later reverberations of this episode.

A growing body of thought proposes a new approach to nationalism, one more sympathetic to nationalism than is nowadays common among enlightened folk. This is both a qualified and non-absolutist view of nationalism, perhaps even a revisionist one. Here, I shall argue the case for such a new look at nationalism. I shall suggest that the problems ascribed to nationalism are perhaps at least as much problems about the state. The idea that states must be sovereign entities and that they should coincide with or contrive to become nations, the whole rhetoric of the 'nation-state' as the essential building block of world order, may be at least as much a source of current concerns as the idea that nations and their members have significant rights of self-determination. The attempt to match up nations with states, and then to accord sovereignty to each state may be the true source of the evils we perceive.

There are arguments of principle for this new line on nationalism.[1] I have contributed to these in other places, and shall attempt in the third section of this

---

[1] I have particularly in mind Y. Tamir, *Liberal Nationalism* (Princeton NJ, Princeton University Press, 1993); J. Bengoetxea, 'L'Etat, c'est fini?', *Rechtstheorie*, Beiheft 15 (Berlin, Duncker und Humbolt, 1993), 93–108; N. MacCormick, 'What place for nationalism in the modern world', *Hume Papers on Public Policy*, 2 (1994), 79–95; 'Nation and nationalism' in N. MacCormick, *Legal Right and Social Democracy* (Oxford, Clarendon, 1982), ch. 13.

chapter to offer some further backing for the idea of a liberal nationalism cut adrift from the absolutism of the sovereign state. But there is an obvious and urgent prior question, namely one of practicality.[2] Can we in fact do without the sovereign state? If our very idea of world order is shackled to this concept, what point would there be in some abstract political theory that pretends to wish it away?

To answer this question, the next section of the chapter offers a fresh look at the constitution of Europe and the openings for a new constitutionalism in the setting of European Union. It is not inevitable, but it is possible, that what we are now embarked on in Western Europe is a thoroughgoing transcendence of the sovereign state as the essential model for legal security and political order. If it is possible to discern in Europe a new order beyond the sovereign state, then the whole question of the place and meaning of nationhood in our political ideas will genuinely be up for revision. Premature as it would be to announce a new world order on the foundation of an experiment in one corner of one continent, it just might be that if the sovereign state goes out of fashion among the polities that invented it, others will be ready to reconsider it too.

Europe without Sovereignty

In Western Europe, the European Union has brought about a new form of legal and political order among states. It is worth considering first the legal aspect, so far the more fully and articulately developed. The European Community (to use the post-1992 name to refer compendiously to the prior communities) was originally constituted by foundational treaties, and still finds its constitutional definition, and achieves constitutional revision, through treaties among its member states. To the extent that the transference of powers to Community organs has potentially infringed domestic constitutions, the states have amended their constitutions, by some combination of legislative act and referendum, in order to secure legitimacy of the transfer. The German Constitutional Court (*Bundesverfassungsgericht*) has lately, however, given notice that there are limits on the extent to which the German Constitution can be amended so as to transfer further powers to European organs, absent any fully democratic constitutional order at the European level.[3]

The European Court of Justice, from a time shortly after the Rome Treaty, asserted that the legal order constituted by it and related treaties, is not to be interpreted simply as a framework of norms binding in international law under the principle that agreements freely entered are binding on the parties – *pacta sunt servanda*. On the contrary, this has to be construed as a new legal order, comprising both treaty norms and norms made under the treaties or recognized by community organs as valid under the treaties for the Community. This is a legal order of a new and unique kind to which the member states have freely transferred certain of their sovereign rights.[4]

---

[2] Compare G. Gottlieb, *Nation against State* (New York, Council on Foreign Relations, 1993); E. Gellner, *Nations and Nationalism* (Oxford, Basil Blackwell, 1983).

[3] This is the case raised by Manfred Brunner and others, often called the 'Maastricht-Urteil', BvR 2134/92; for a discussion, see N. MacCormick, 'The Maastricht-Urteil: sovereignty now', *European Law Journal*, 1 (1995), 259–66.

[4] Case 6/64, *Costa* v. *ENEL* [1964] ECR 585.

Certainly, so far as states which subsequently joined the Community are concerned, it can scarcely be disputed that they did so well aware (through their governing authorities at least) that this was the juridical character already ascribed to the Community by its authoritative judicial organ. Acts of accession consented to by newly-joining member states, with the reciprocal agreement of existing ones, might reasonably be deemed to have confirmed the existence of the Community as indeed a 'new legal order'. That neither new nor old member states saw fit to cast doubt on the principles established by the Court of Justice seems to entail at the very least tacit assent to the thesis that the Community has truly the character of a legal order existing in its own right, albeit having its origin in international treaties and thus binding in the first instance as a matter of international law.[5]

How is it possible to account for the emergence in this way of something that can claim to be a new legal order, something whose claim to be a new legal order wins at least tacit consent among all participating states? The question forces us to scrutinize closely the resources of legal theory, particularly those parts of it directed to explaining the nature and existence of legal systems. In turn, however, the claims of the Community pose a challenge to legal theory, which has hitherto restricted itself to accounting mainly for the legal systems of states, and the legal system, or at any rate the loose congeries of legal norms, that goes by the name of international law.

Within broad limits, one can assert the following with reasonable confidence as a commonplace among legal thinkers: international law fundamentally depends upon international custom; but since international custom includes the norm that treaties are to be kept, those norms that are laid down in binding international treaties are also norms of international law, binding on the states parties to the treaty. In the case of multilateral treaties, it is possible for treaty norms to acquire the status of generally binding international norms. Other subordinate sources of international law, including general principles of law recognized in civilized societies, norms elaborated in the writings of jurists, and norms laid down by tribunals with authority to decide international disputes, may also be added.[6]

The legal orders of sovereign states are more complex. They depend in some form on a systematic interrelationship of norms belonging to at least three levels: the first is the constitutional level, laying down the competences of organs of state, regulating their interactions and the way in which one may set limits on another, or may not, and setting whatever limits there are to be by way of charter-entrenched rights protecting citizens from inordinate state action. The second is the general-legislative level, comprising norms laid down either through legislation authorized by constitutional norms or by other recognized means such as judicial precedent; norms at this level regulate the conduct and affairs of persons subject to the legal system, and empower them in their capacity as private citizens to carry out various forms of legally-recognized activity. The third level is that of individual norms imposed through judicial or other official action, implementing and enforcing remedies or penalties for breaches of legislative-level norms.

---

[5] See the speech by Lord Bridge of Harwich in the House of Lords case *R* v. *Secretary of State for Transport ex p. Factortame* [1991] A.C. 603 at p. 658; [1991] All E.R. 769.

[6] Compare Article 38 of the Statute of the International Court of Justice.

Law of that sort, with its establishment of interlocking agencies empowered respectively to legislate, to adjudicate, and to pursue public policies within the spheres of action legally ascribed to the competence of the state and its organs, is a prime example of institutional normative order. It is, of course, not properly to be understood as comprising exclusively a fabric of explicitly articulated and enacted norms. Such normative orders work only within a framework of institutional morality and background legal principle, and depend on a wide-spread, though not universal, practice or custom of recognition or acceptance of the normative character of the order as a whole.[7] An order that is effective on that basis can, according to Hans Kelsen, be conceptualized as a coherent legal system through the hypothesis of a 'basic norm', or *Grundnorm*.[8] H. L. A. Hart, in rejecting the idea of the basic norm as pure juristic presupposition or hypothesis, grounds legal order in the very custom of acknowledging common criteria of validity, criteria which he presents as the content of the fundamental 'rule of recognition', the final and unifying 'secondary rule' for any legal system.[9]

There is also, of course, a political context. Law and politics always overlap without ever becoming identical. Politics is about power, as law is about normative order. Neither can endure without the other. In any event, legal thought is never without some political presuppositions. In particular, there must be some background thought concerning the political order to which a putative legal order belongs. Law as we presently conceive it achieves its primary manifestation in the political context of the state. States exist where there is a territorially defined and in some measure effective structure of government, grounded not in any personal bond of fealty or loyalty but in some ideological claim to legitimacy, exercising power over persons, things and natural resources available in the territory. Law as such is normally taken to be the law of some territorial state, except to the extent that it may also cover the normative order recognized by states as governing their international inter-actions. The practices and usages that constitute normative unity and order are self-consciously practices carried on relative to some particular state or federal union. Law is German law, or French law, not legal order *in vacuo* or *in abstracto*. Hence the prime example of institutional normative order for contemporary humanity is state law. Conversely, to the extent that the exercise of political power in a discretionary, potentially arbitrary, way is here or there effectively constrained by legal norms, the state has the character of a *Rechtsstaat*, or 'law-state' – it is a state under the rule of law.[10]

As already noted, states themselves share an over-arching legal order, that of international law. One recognized and binding norm of prevailing international

---

[7] For a fuller argument to this effect see 'Institutional morality and the constitution' in N. MacCormick and O. Weinberger, *An Institutional Theory of Law* (Dordrecht, Reidel, 1986), ch. 8.

[8] H. Kelsen (M. Knight, trans.), *The Pure Theory of Law* (Berkeley and Los Angeles, University of California Press, 1967), chs 1 and 5.

[9] H. L. A. Hart, *The Concept of Law* (Oxford, Clarendon, 1961), ch. 6.

[10] The 'law-state' is the admirably suggestive translation of *Rechtsstaat* proposed by Professor Åke Frändberg of Uppsala University in an unpublished manuscript with that title; for discussion of the idea, essentially of a 'state under the rule of law', see T. O'Hagan, *The End of Law?* (Oxford, Basil Blackwell, 1984), esp. ch. 6; compare MacCormick, 'Constitutionalism and democracy' in R. Bellamy (ed.), *Theories and Concepts of Politics* (Manchester, Manchester University Press, 1993), ch. 6.

law concerns the independence of states – there is not to be intervention by any one in the affairs of any other. This presupposes that states can be identified, but international law in turn has a norm that provides for this, namely the principle of governmental efficacity. A government actually in power over a proclaimed state-territory must *prima facie* be treated as legitimate by other state governments. Kelsen took this proposition to imply that there is in effect an overall legal unity that embraces both state law and international law. Each state with a constituted government in *de facto* control of territory is in effect authorized by international law to carry on government in that territory in terms of its own constitution, and any intervention by any other state is wrongful in international law.[11]

This made possible a simplification of the problem of normative order from Kelsen's point of view. He advanced the thesis of 'legal monism', according to which the only necessarily presupposed basic norm is a *Grundnorm* for international law, prescribing that states ought to behave in accordance with the customs established among them. Given this presupposition, and the above-mentioned international legal principle of efficacity, one can construct a single conception of normative order embracing every state's law within the underlying normative framework of international law.

To this thesis, Hart replied that it ignores the 'internal attitude', of those working in official and unofficial roles within actual states and legal systems.[12] French judges, for example, regard themselves as sufficiently empowered by and under the French constitution, and do not regard their empowerment as in any way contingent upon authorization via international law, and French citizens accept and act upon the judgments of French courts as arbiters of French law; British citizens respond to enactments of the UK Parliament, whose members do not impute its constitutional sovereignty to international law, but to domestic constitutional principle, and so on.

These reflections suffice to let us return to the question of the European Community and its law. There can be no reasonable doubt but that the Community has law at least on the constitutional-empowerment and general-legislative level; as for the issuance through judges of individual norms, the jurisdiction of the ECJ under Article 177 is restricted to an interpretative one, advising member-state courts how to interpret and apply community law; but then, the remedies for breach of community law are in turn implemented through state courts. And other jurisdictional provisions give more direct remedial power to the ECJ. The use of the legislative powers of community organs in the way of issuing regulations and directives has in fact given rise to a dense body of law at general-legislative level, and the interpretation and application of this dense body of law involves much time and expertise.

In this context, even the Kelsenian monist might pause in the project of simply envisaging a unity of international and state law; there is, at least, a thicker and more substantial, more internally-institutionalized, body of norms at Community level than anything else to be found in general international law. The existence of norms which have an acknowledged direct effect both to confer

---

[11] Kelsen, *The Pure Theory of Law*, ch. 9.

[12] The argument was most clearly stated by Hart in his (unpublished) lectures on Kelsen, given in Oxford in the early 1960s (I heard the course in 1964); but it is prefigured somewhat in ch. 10 of Hart, *The Concept of Law*.

rights and to impose obligations on citizens of member states, and well-entrenched practices of upholding these rights and obligations in ways involving a collaboration of ECJ with member-state courts, further marks out the law of the community from general international law.[13]

The monistic theory does not, however, have to retire baffled before all this. It can offer one or other of three models for explaining the phenomena:

Model A: We can postulate a *Grundnorm* that validates the foundational treaties as a *sui generis* legal order interposed between the legal orders of the states and the legal order of general international law. The chain of validation will then be such that international law validates the basic norm of Community law, and now delegates to Community law the validation of member-state law. If this view is adopted, each member state becomes a legal dependency of the Community, with international legal validity now transmitted to member-state law through the norms of Community law.

Model B: We can postulate an independent *Grundnorm* for Community law, validated by international law under its principle that *pacta sunt servanda*, such that Community law and member-state law enjoy co-ordinate validity. Neither validates the other, but both are validated independently by international law. They are then engaged in legal interactions as co-ordinately valid systems of law – respectively Community law and member-state law – both validated by international law.

Model C: We can postulate that the validity of Community law is in fact subordinate to the validity of member-state law. International law validates state law, and in effect enables states, if they wish, to create organs of shared government that remain subordinate to the constitutional and other norms of the member states' legal systems, except to the extent that they have bound themselves *inter se* under international law to accept and implement in a unilaterally irrevocable way norms constituted in or under the Community Treaties. Under this model, the chain of validity runs from international law through the law of each member state to Community law. Shared organs such as the ECJ ensure a community of interpretation and application of Community law in each member state, but it is strictly the case that it has a different root of validity in each locus of its uniform implementation; Community law functions in France as a valid but special part of French law, in Belgium as a valid but special part of Belgian law, in Portugal as a valid but special part of Portuguese law, and so on.

Those who reject the monistic approach do so on the ground that it neglects the 'internal point of view'. It fails to ask whether or not agents within a system whose norms are valid in terms of another system do or do not accept the norms of the local system on account of their validation by a more extensively authoritative system, or simply for their own sake, without regard to the more extensive system. This point of difference should not be overstated, for, as can now be seen, a monist's choice between Models A, B, and C could quite properly be justified, and indeed guided, by suppositions concerning the 'internal point of view'.

---

[13] This point is rather disappointingly handled by F. Dowrick in his pathbreaking work on the application of analytical jurisprudence to Community law; see F. E. Dowrick, 'A Model of the European Communities' legal system', *Yearbook of European Law*, 3 (1983), 169–237; compare J. H. H. Weiler's contribution to the present volume.

On that ground, indeed, though subject to one caveat, Model A must seem implausible; the member states have not yet, notwithstanding the Union Treaty of Maastricht, committed themselves to the project of an all-embracing Federal Union such that the validity of any local law would be regarded not merely as requiring compatibility with, but also some derivability from, foundational Community norms. The German Constitutional Court's judgement in the case of Manfred Brunner and others, the so-called 'Maastricht-Urteil', is a weighty statement of this point.[14]

The caveat that has to be added concerns the principle of the supremacy of Community law (supremacy, at least, within the spheres of competence of Community organs). How can it be that there is a body of law, Community law, that is 'supreme' in respect of every member state, without its being the case that the validity of Community law is now prior to and presupposed as a condition for the validity of every legal norm in any member state? There is an obvious reading of this principle that would imply that, at least from the point of view of judges in the Court of Justice, and lawyers practising mainly in Community law, the Community *Grundnorm* has become a necessary presupposition for the validity of member-state law *holus-bolus*.

This is not, however, a necessary or inevitable reading of the supremacy principle. In the context either of Model B or of Model C, one can postulate that, in order to maintain co-ordinate validity, or (under Model C) common subordinate validity, for Community law in fulfilment of the mutual obligations of the member states, it is necessary that they incorporate Community law into domestic law either as independently valid (B) or as subordinately valid (C) on terms that give this law the same effect and priority in each member state as in every other. The concept of 'supremacy' therefore serves to qualify the standing of this source of law, this criterion of validity of law, in relation to other sources, other criteria, operating within the state system. Looking at the matter from the state system point of view, it is a question of state law on the constitutional plane to settle what priority in relation to other sources of valid norm-creation community norms shall have. Only if all systems accord the same level of priority, overriding local contrary legislation, will the project of achieving a common market with common rules be possible.

The case for Model C is that hitherto any alteration or reform of the framework or constitution of Community law has required the adoption of enabling legislation, where necessary including express constitutional amendment (and hence subject to any limitations on the power of constitutional amendment, as the *Bundesverfassungsgericht* sharply points out), in each of the member states; this suggests a continuing subordination of the grounds of validity of Community law to the processes of validation, and thus the ultimate grounds of validity, that prevail in the member states severally.

Model C is, however, very sharply exposed to critique from the 'internal point of view' as evinced by judges of the Community Courts. Their perspective on the law they administer is, and perhaps is necessarily, that of a single legal system with a single and common ground of validity. They do not conceptualize Community law as a set of commonly agreed norms that belong strictly to as many legal systems as there are member states, validated by each state in view of

[14] Compare footnote 3 above.

its international-legal obligations to all the others, but having no special systemic validity of their own.

All in all, if forced to choose among models from the monistic point of view, Model B, whereby member-state law and Community law enjoy co-ordinate validity under international law, seems the most credible. For this model can allow for the facts that both Community judges and member-state judges from their distinct viewpoints accord primacy to norms of the system in which they work, but recognize as also valid within it the norms of the other system. The 'otherness' of the other system, in either perspective, is to do with the fact that changes in norms are brought about by implementation of norms of competence extraneous to the norm-recognizing system.

An alternative, and arguably more satisfactory, approach involves rejecting the monistic conception of relations among legal systems, and accepting instead a pluralistic one. From the internal point of view of each legal system, its ultimate grounds of validity are in principle distinct from those of every other; but there can in fact be intimate interaction between systems. Such interaction is exhibited by those state legal systems which accept the norms of international law as enjoying internal validity *ipso vigore*. It is also exhibited in the case of Community law, which is both a legal order constituted by the common actions of member states under the foundation treaties and also from the point of view of member-state legal orders, a source of norms that are valid internally within the state legal order, and that override otherwise valid norms emanating from domestic sources, with the exception of specially entrenched elements of constitutional law. This version of pluralism, for which I have argued in greater detail elsewhere,[15] shares strengths with the Model B version of monism. Yet, whereas monism might be said to elevate the logic of norm-derivations above the social realities of actually-held grounds for acceptance and implementation of legal norms, pluralism is grounded explicitly on acknowledgement of these very grounds. In any event, the most credible monistic view is that which has most in common with the pluralistic one, so each to an extent supports the other in competition with the Model A and Model C versions of monism.

Without here finally deciding between the pluralistic and the Model B view, we can safely accept the thesis they jointly support: the best way to conceptualize Community law and member-state law at present requires us to acknowledge these as co-ordinately valid legal systems. Each can be described as a system with the three-level structure that was described above. Each for certain purposes presupposes the validity of the other. Legislation in the Community depends on the joint action of office-holders validly appointed under member-state law. Valid norms of Community law have to be recognized as prima facie overriding norms for application by organs of member states performing executive or judicial functions, and they have direct effect in favour of, or over, citizens of the member states, now also citizens of the Union. Neither exists in a vacuum, and a presupposition of the validity of international law and of respect for treaty obligations is present in respect of both; but only the monistic theory makes it a condition of their validity.

This conclusion has far-reaching consequences for the notion of national sovereignty. In the traditional legal sense of 'sovereignty', member states of the

---

[15] See N. MacCormick, 'Beyond the sovereign state', *Modern Law Review*, 56 (1993), 1–23; compare also my above cited 'Maastricht-Urteil' essay.

European Union no longer constitute legally sovereign entities. Nor does the Union, nor its internal pillar the Community, constitute a sovereign entity. The distribution of sovereign rights at various levels of course leaves a compendious 'external sovereignty' of all the member states intact and even in a sense strengthened.

Politically, the same goes. Political sovereignty cannot be ascribed to the Union as a political association of member states, nor to that part of it, the Community, which does constitute a distinct legal order. But the constraints of economic co-operation, even short of economic and monetary union, of maintaining a common market, and of observing even to an imperfect extent the obligations of a common body of law, also deprive member states of that full freedom of action which was traditionally taken to be the hallmark of politically sovereign states.

Liberal Nationalism beyond Sovereignty

On this view, we confront in Western Europe now a politics 'beyond the sovereign state'. Old conceptions of state sovereignty and of the absolutism of the nation state are now radically challengeable. This does not abolish either states or nations as politico-cultural communities. Nor therefore does it necessarily abolish nationalism. Opposition to the new order can arise from certain forms of nationalism, as we have already noted. But the new politics may also create space for a new nationalism, an acceptable and even perhaps mandatory nationalism that is intrinsically liberal in character.

The case to be made here, as in some other recent writing, is in favour of a liberal version of nationalism.[16] To show how nationalism, in one variant, can be compatible with liberalism, it is helpful to differentiate various conceptions of nationalism, and to explore how we should characterize liberal nationalism in this context. First, let us note the differentiation between 'civic' and 'ethnic' forms of nationalism.[17] We shall treat the former as identifying the nation in terms of its members' shared allegiance to certain civic institutions, understood in broad terms to include, for example legal norms and institutions, political representative organs, branches of public and local administration, the organization of education, churches and religious communities in their secular aspect, and other like institutions having an understood territorial location with which they are connected. Territorially located civic institutions can be objects of allegiance, understood as 'ours' by the people over whom they purport to have jurisdiction. As civic institutions, they are necessarily of great political significance to the community which, to an extent, they define.

Naturally, it is possible, and perhaps desirable, for such civic institutions to go the length of including a constitution and the full panoply of statehood. Perhaps without that the civic quality of civic institutions is too precarious. But I shall not require this by definition (though some do), for to do so is simply to endorse the plainly challengeable assumption that the states that currently exist comprise also the totality of nations, at any rate, the totality of nations

---

[16] Tamir, *Liberal Nationalism*; MacCormick, 'What place for nationalism in the modern world?'.

[17] Discussed in, though not invented by, Gellner, *Nations and Nationalism*. I ought freely to concede that I somewhat extend the notion of civic institutions beyond some usages, to include the civic institutions of non-state nations (e.g., in Scotland, Scots law, the Church of Scotland, the Scottish Office, the Scottish Football Association, The National Trust for Scotland, The Scottish National Orchestra, and many other like institutions).

understood in the civic sense. Whether or not the civic nation is or has a state, or *a fortiori* an independent sovereign state, the point of the idea of a civic nation is that it is in principle open to voluntary membership. The community defined by allegiance to institutions is open to anyone who chooses to dwell in the territory and give allegiance to the institutions. Departure to a different place and different allegiances is also possible, and not traitorous. Treachery is only remaining in place and unfairly undermining its institutions.

To contrast with this is the conception of nation as racial or ethnic community, defined as the possessor of a distinctive culture, including perhaps a language thought of as the special possession of those and only those belonging to the original ethnic community, grounded ultimately in some kind of shared ancestry or genetic bond. Nationality so defined is necessarily and unavoidably given. It has no voluntary element nor opening thereto. You either are a member of this nation or not; if you are, it has a claim on your loyalty whether you like its institutional arrangements and cultural manifestations or not. Ethnic nationalism thus focusses on a shared ethno-historico-cultural identity as defining the community whose self-determination is in issue. This entails some exclusiveness of attitude towards those deemed not to possess the relevant ethnic identity.

We should avoid seeing or defining the civic and the ethnic in straightforward either/or terms. They are more ideal types than exclusive alternatives, for of course civically identified communities develop cultural practices and institutions around them, and of course there will tend to be more or less long-standing familial and historical associations with given institutions, so that the community of allegiance will easily and naturally perceive itself as also a community of culture and of historical belonging; on the other hand, the community that conceives itself primarily in terms of blood and belonging, ancestral culture and history will also develop its own institutions, and may tacitly acknowledge a kind of adoption of incomers who over time come to accept the institutions. There can, then, be a kind of 'cultural nationalism' associated with civic nationalism, and yet tending towards the ethnic to the extent that racial or ethnic difference is postulated (usually or always as a kind of fiction or myth, I suppose) as the source of culture or of its special value.

There remain all-important differences of emphasis and degree between civic and ethnic poles or ideal-types. It is plainly enough evident that a liberal commitment to individualism and autonomy is one that would restrict its endorsement to the claims of civic nationalism, with only such associated elements of the ethno-historico-cultural as are compatible with personal freedom and autonomy.

From this follows naturally some reflection on the idea of 'personal nationalism' put forward by the social anthropologist Anthony Cohen in a recent lecture.[18] Cohen's idea is that nations are not entities wholly independent

---

[18] A. P. Cohen, 'Personal nationalism: a Scottish view of some rites, rights, and wrongs', the 1994 Distinguished Lecture to the Society for the Anthropology of Europe, American Anthropological Association; forthcoming in *American Ethnologist* (1996). I am much indebted to Professor Cohen for sight of his revised text, and for searching criticisms of the present chapter, including an expressed doubt about the use of the term 'ethnic' in so-called 'ethnic nationalism', and about the absence of a (more credible, in his view) 'cultural nationalism' as a distinct type. I fear that my adaptation of Cohen's concept of 'personal nationalism' departs somewhat from the original, in ways its author does not wholly endorse. See also A. P. Cohen, *Self-Consciousness: an Alternative Anthropology of Identity* (London, Routledge, 1994).

of consciousness; rather they are socially given, but essentially interpretive, elements of the possibility of a certain kind of consciousness and self-consciousness experienced by individuals as persons who know where they are and where they belong and do not belong. For any country or nation, each of us has her or his own conception of it, and our sense of identification is not with some objective 'out-there' entity, but rather with our idea or interpretation of the nation developed out of reflection on civic institutions, social institutions, culture and history. Thus there must be as many Englands as there are English people, and though there is a certain communality of thought, they are not all identically the same. Rather, there is at best a partially overlapping consensus of England-ideas from the point of view of those who self-identify as English, and then also, perhaps, from the point of view of self-defined outsiders. England as a nation is not something that externally guarantees the overlapping consensus, but an idea that emerges from it, to the extent that a broad consensus does in fact emerge.

This is in many ways an attractive idea that liberates nationalism from anti-individualism. But it does so at the expense, as I see it, of tending to displace an essentially political idea from the domain of politics, or at any rate from the armoury of normative political theory. For present purposes, I would prefer to adapt the theory of personal nationalism and transform it into an account of the way in which a civic nationalism, defined around objective civic institutions, can also constitute through the self-conceptions of members an always evolving, always diversifying, always contestable, cultural community through the overlapping but also diverging ideas of those who identify with the civic nation.

So transformed, however, it is an important corollary of civic nationalism as ideal-type. The stress on individualism and autonomy is what makes this approach compatible with liberalism. Or is it? It may, after all, be doubted whether autonomous individuals would need, or have any truck with, nationalism. The decisive counter to this doubt is a vital observation by Yael Tamir, namely, the reminder that individuals are necessarily, in her words, 'contextual individuals'.[19] People acquire character and self-consciousness, and a capacity for self-command, only in a specific social setting. An axiological individualism[20] that treats individuality as a value, not as a biological, ontological, or methodological given, stipulates indeed that social contexts favourable to the developing of autonomous selves have fundamental value morally and politically.

Implicit in the understanding of liberalism deployed here is acknowledgement of the principle of respect for persons as fundamental for political as for

[19] Tamir, *Liberal Nationalism* throughout.

[20] 'Individualism' is both contested, and many-faceted. One can distinguish value-individualism (the stance which says it is good that there be autonomous individuals, and that ultimate goods are experienced only through the consciousness of individuals) from ontological or methodological individualism, some versions of which deny the real existence of society, or the dependence of individual self-consciousness upon social context (the idea that individuals are necessarily 'contextual individuals'). I repudiate such methodological individualism while embracing value-individualism, or, more grandly, 'axiological individualism'. I concede that there are more moderate versions of methodological individualism, with which my own approach may be compatible; compare Geoffrey Brennan and Alan Hamlin's essay in this volume, and A. P. Hamlin and P. Pettit 'The normative analysis of the state' in A. P. Hamlin and P. Pettit (eds), *The Good Polity* (Oxford, Basil Blackwell, 1989).

personal morality. We are to respect each human being as a distinct human individual, with all that goes to his or her constitution as such. But since all individuals are contextual individuals, in respecting individuals, we are committed to respecting what enables them to have self-understanding and self-respect as individual persons, though always under the qualification that no particular individual can be entitled to conditions of self-respect that are incompatible with the self-respect of others. Liberal universalization of the right to respect makes fundamentally unacceptable any disparagement of individuals on such grounds as nationality, ethnicity or gender.

Let us now suppose, as seems to be true, that a sense of national identity and belonging does for a very large part of the present population of the world play an important part in individuals' self-understanding. Contextual individuals may have as one among their most significant contexts some national identity. On that account, respect for national identities, and acceptance of the legitimacy of a civic-cum-personal variant of nationalism, do not conflict with liberalism. Indeed, liberalism may require this. The point is one for which I have argued more fully elsewhere,[21] so I assert it here somewhat summarily.

There have, however, been weighty objections posed to the argument as previously stated, notably that there seems no reason to select out a sense of national identity as anything particular alongside of one's family membership, of professional or religious affiliations, political convictions and loyalties, local identity (city, town, village, rural area), state citizenship, transnational identity (citizen of the European Union, for example). Given that the contextual individual finds personal identity through many contexts, it is argued that we should not merely not privilege the context of national identity; on the contrary, we should perhaps consciously down-grade this aspect of identity precisely because of its almost inevitable association with atavistic and exclusivist sentiments, and in general all those objectionable nationalist particularisms that do conflict with any recognizable version of liberal universalism.[22]

To this, the plain reply is that in the modern state, state politics have also been national politics. The state-as-nation is the primary theatre of political activity and participation. If one very crucial element of individual autonomy is the opportunity of participating as a full and equal member in fora of political self-government, then the primary such forum for the contemporary world is the state. States-as-nations, often imperial states, have, however tendentiously, characterized themselves as 'nation-states'. Moreover, the modern state, the post-revolutionary state, has inherited from feudal monarchy the claim to sovereignty. The nation state has been a sovereign state, and as such has purported to express the sovereignty of the unitary people, the nation, which is the owner of the state.

It is not then strange that national minorities within states have been centres of dissatisfaction and unrest, and also sometimes targets of repression and discrimination. The claim to self-determination for such groups seems difficult to dispute in a context in which the dominant politico-legal culture asserts the unity of state and nation, and locates the opportunity for involvement in the

[21] MacCormick, 'What place for nationalism in the modern world?' Compare also N. Mac-Cormick, 'Is nationalism philosophically credible?' in W. Twining (ed.), *Issues of Self-Determination* (Aberdeen, Aberdeen University Press, 1991), ch. 2.

[22] The point is taken in A. Vincent, 'Liberal nationalism: an impossible compound?', *Political Studies* (forthcoming).

political self-constitution of community either wholly at the level of the state, or at least only within the limits of tolerance prescribed through the politics and law of the state. It is not theoretical nationalist imaginings, but the facts of political life, that give national identity a special place in the contextual definition of the contextual individual in her/his character as political animal.

It is often said, and rightly, that on any reasonable definition of 'nation' we have too many of them, too badly distributed, to allocate a territory and a sovereign state to each of them.[23] Sometimes this is taken to justify a do-nothing policy, accepting the states that we have, with all their pretensions to sovereignty and to nation statehood. If the only alternative were bloodshed and war, I would agree. But if it is injudicious to increase excessively the number of states, it may in the alternative be possible to diminish their pretensions, and thus to adjust the position between those nationalities who have and those who have not a fully sovereign state of their own. The principle of subsidiarity springs to mind as a useful principle for liberal reflection in this context.

In the context of the present chapter, however, it is easy to see why the deconstruction of sovereignty in the context of European Union (political sovereignty) or Community (legal sovereignty) is considered so admirable a project, indeed achievement. For it is nationalism allied to sovereign statism that is incompatible with liberalism in the condition of the world as we find it. There cannot be a perfect match between the nations that exist in the world and any possible set of sovereign states that have absolute authority over exactly demarcated territories.[24] But historically, and to a degree at present, the whole point of acknowledging sovereign states is that they should have absolute authority over an exactly demarcated territory. Peace can then be secured provided there is no intervention by any state in any other. But that peace, when it is secured, is only a relative peace, and is all too compatible with violations of rights of individuals and minorities within states. For this and other reasons, such a peace has never been a stable peace.

The upshot of this line of thought is to suggest the following principle as defining an acceptable nationalism for the present day: 'the members of a nation are as such in principle entitled to effective organs of political self-government within the world order of sovereign or post-sovereign states; but these need not provide for self-government in the form of a sovereign state'. Allied to a primarily civic nationalist conception of membership in a nation, this seems to me to be perfectly compatible with one defensible version of liberalism. It is of course only a principle, not an absolute rule. This means that in any real-life situation there may be competing principles, such that it is a question of weighing and balancing to decide how far and in what ways our principle is susceptible of implementation without injury to equally important, or more important, values and principles.

Conclusion

The thesis of this chapter has been that state-absolutism and nationalist absolutism are both untenable. Liberal nationalism is a morally permissible and

---

[23] See Gellner, *Nations and Nationalism*, and cf. Gottlieb *Nation against State*, ch. 2.

[24] On this point, Gottlieb and I are in entire agreement; I read this as the central thesis of *Nation against State*.

indeed morally imperative position, but its point is that national rights must not be interpreted as moral absolutes. To delineate a practical possibility, it requires the context of a conception of statehood or polity stripped of the old assumptions about sovereignty. It requires development and elaboration of the principle of subsidiarity. Both these developments are possible within Western Europe, given the interpretation of the legal and political order of the European Union and Community offered here. They are possible, but not certain; but if the arguments of this chapter are well-founded, they are worth working for.

Constitution Making or Constitutional Transformation in Post-Communist Societies?

ISTVAN POGANY [1]

Introduction

It is commonly assumed, at least in the West, that post-Communist societies are engaged in the twin tasks of economic restructuring, leading to the creation of market economies and constitutionalization. The latter may be understood as the establishment of genuine, multi-party democracies, committed to the rule of law and the protection of individual and minority rights.[2]

Without doubt, since 1989 the former Communist states have been actively involved in the adoption of new constitutions or in the radical amendment of Communist-era texts. However, it is far from clear that this spate of constitution making will necessarily result in (let alone has resulted in) constitutional transformation. The two are by no means synonymous. While 'constitution making', as used here, denotes a largely technical exercise in which one set of constitutional norms and/or structures is replaced by another,[3] 'constitutional transformation' involves not merely changes to the formal constitutional arrangements in a state but also, and crucially, a genuine transformation of the character and habitual mode of operation of a society's political and legal institutions. In other words, constitutional transformation can be said to have occurred only where the process of constitution making results in the general and habitual application of the new constitutional norms.

This article reviews the nature of the 'revolutions' of 1989 and after, which swept Communist governments from power throughout Central and Eastern Europe. It is scarcely self-evident that *all* of these 'revolutions' were motivated by an unambiguous zeal for democracy and human rights while, in some

[1] I am grateful to all of those who participated in the Political Studies Workshop in Norwich in September 1995 for their helpful and insightful comments on an earlier draft of this article. My thanks are due, in particular, to Richard Bellamy, Dario Castiglione and Joseph Weiler. Needless to say, responsibility for any deficiencies in the final text are mine alone.
[2] This definition of 'constitutionalism' emerges clearly from a series of texts adopted by the Organisation for Security and Cooperation in Europe (formerly the CSCE). See, in particular, the Charter of Paris for a New Europe, adopted in November 1990 by the leaders of the thirty-four states then participating in the CSCE mechanism. For the text of the Charter see e.g. *International Legal Materials*, 30 (1991), 193–208.
[3] 'Constitution making', as used in the academic literature, tends not to spell out the underlying distinction between (a) the technical process of constructing new constitutions and (b) the socio-logical issue of whether these new constitutions are generally observed in practice. See e.g. A. E. Dick Howard (ed.), *Constitution Making in Eastern Europe* (Washington DC, Woodrow Wilson Center, 1993); J. Elster, 'Making sense of constitution-making', *East European Constitutional Review*, 1, 1 (1992), 15–7.

instances, a genuine aspiration for reform may have been thwarted by political and/or bureaucratic élites seizing (or clinging to) power in a rapidly changing ideological landscape. Thus, a critical assessment of the *actual* (as opposed to the merely *superficial*) character of the post-Communist 'reforms' is called for.

In addition, this article considers 'the legacy of the past' in terms of its possible impact on current efforts to promote democracy and constitutionalism. While it is widely acknowledged that the Communist experience was profoundly damaging to the societies of Central and Eastern Europe, whether in moral, political or economic terms,[4] far less attention has been paid to the pre-Communist history of these states. This omission is both surprising and worrying. An examination of pre-Communist conditions will show whether current efforts to promote democratic and constitutional government can draw on long-standing local traditions (which were merely interrupted by Communism), or whether these efforts represent a novel and altogether uncertain experiment.[5] In other words, are we truly witnessing a *'return* to Europe', as some would have us believe, or is this a journey without precedent for the peoples of Central and Eastern Europe?

Some tentative conclusions will be drawn as to the types of political, economic and constitutional *processes* (not merely *structures*) which are emerging amongst the post-Communist states. It will be argued that, rather than viewing the transformation process as unilinear, i.e. Communism→ democracy + the market, the transformation of the post-Communist societies should be understood as an inherently uncertain process with a plurality of possible outcomes, particularly in the short and medium term.

The Legacy of the Past

In seeking to understand the difficulties which beset the processes of democratization and constitutionalization in Central and Eastern Europe, it is important to reflect on the political and constitutional history of the region.[6] In doing so, one is reminded of an incontrovertible (if uncomfortable) fact − we are witnessing the *second* attempt during the course of this century to democratize and to constitutionalize Central and Eastern Europe. The first attempt, part of the general political settlement following the First World War, was almost wholly unsuccessful.[7] Despite international guarantees respecting the treatment of national minorities and the drafting of impeccably democratic constitutions, frequently modelled on that of the Third French Republic,[8] the region rapidly succumbed to nationalism, dictatorship and political extremism. Only the former Czechoslovakia established a genuine and potentially stable

---

[4] For a consideration of some of these points see e.g. G. Schöpflin, 'The rise of anti-democratic movements in post-Communist societies' in H. Miall (ed.), *Redefining Europe* (London, Pinter, 1994), pp. 129–46, esp. pp. 130–5.

[5] See, generally, I. Pogany, 'A new constitutional (dis)order for Eastern Europe?' in I. Pogany (ed.), *Human Rights in Eastern Europe* (Aldershot, Edward Elgar, 1995), pp. 217–39.

[6] See e.g. Miall, *Shaping the New Europe*, esp. pp. 63–4.

[7] See e.g. A. Polonsky, *The Little Dictators* (London, Routledge and Kegan Paul, 1975).

[8] Polonsky, *The Little Dictators*, pp. 20–3. On the international protection of minorities in the inter-war period see P. Thornberry, *International Law and the Rights of Minorities* (Oxford, Clarendon, 1991), pp. 38–52.

constitutional democracy in the inter-War period.[9] By contrast, Poland, having adopted a democratic constitution in March 1921, lapsed into quasi-constitutional authoritarianism following a military coup in May 1926.[10] Hungary, having emerged from the First World War as a defeated power, was governed in rapid succession by a revolutionary 'Soviet' headed by Béla Kun, by a socialist administration under Gyula Peidl, and by the repressive and counter-revolutionary regime led by (the land-locked) Admiral Horthy.[11] Thereafter, the democratic 'experiment' in inter-war Hungary remained notably circumscribed.[12] Under the premiership of Count Bethlen the proportion of the adult population entitled to vote was dramatically reduced while the secret ballot was removed in country areas.[13]

The fate of democracy and of constitutionalism in the other states of Central and Eastern Europe was almost equally dismal.[14] For example, in inter-war Romania, elections 'were generally rigged',[15] while the country gradually descended into dictatorship, extreme nationalism and officially-sanctioned anti-semitism.[16]

With the exception of the Czechs, therefore, the Central and East European states can be said to lack any real or extended experience of functioning as democratic societies governed by the rule of law before sovietization excluded even the possibility of democratic and constitutional development. This fact remains of critical importance to a proper understanding of the difficulties which beset efforts to constitutionalize post-Communist societies. Thus, it is not simply a matter of 'returning to Europe', as some have suggested. A 'return' to *their* pre-Communist past would, in reality, be a return not to some mythical golden age of liberal enlightenment and economic contentment, but to political authoritarianism, economic underdevelopment and an often stifling social stratification.

Western-type democratic and constitutional structures have been introduced, since 1989, in the Czech Republic, Hungary, Slovakia and Poland, enshrining the principles of constitutionalism, individual and minority rights and parliamentarianism.[17] With varying degrees of conviction, comparable structures have been installed in virtually all of the other post-Communist states. However, why should we assume that these mechanisms will prove durable throughout Central and Eastern Europe? Or, more fundamentally, that the values which they embody have actually transformed the character of political and judicial activity in these states? Social scientists have commented on the tendency to 'facade politics' in the societies of Central and Eastern Europe

[9] See, generally, J. Rothschild, *East Central Europe between the Two Worlds Wars* (Seattle, University of Washington Press, 1974), pp. 73–135.

[10] See e.g. N. Davies, *Heart of Europe* (Oxford, Oxford University Press, 1986), pp. 121–9.

[11] See, generally, Rothschild, *East Central Europe*, pp. 139–53.

[12] See, generally, on Hungary during the inter-war period, Rothschild, *East Central Europe*, pp. 137–99.

[13] Longworth, *The Making of Eastern Europe* (New York, St. Martin's Press, rev. ed., 1994), p. 77.

[14] For an overview see e.g. Polonsky, *The Little Dictators*.

[15] Longworth, *The Making of Eastern Europe*, p. 74.

[16] Polonsky, *The Little Dictators*, pp. 78–93.

[17] For details see e.g. Howard, *Constitution Making in Eastern Europe*; J. Elster, C. Offe and U. Preuß, *Constitutional and Economic Transitions in Eastern Europe* (Cambridge, Cambridge University Press, forthcoming).

during the inter-War period, when a *semblance* of democracy and constitutionalism frequently masked corrupt and/or authoritarian political cultures.[18] Much the same may be said of contemporary political and constitutional practice in a number of states in the region, including Slovakia, Romania and many of the post-Soviet states.

Appearances, especially as reflected in the statute books, should not necessarily be confused with reality. This is a simple, indeed an obvious truth. It is therefore all the more surprising that it is frequently overlooked. However, it would be extraordinarily naive to imagine that human (or social) conduct has changed simply *because* the laws and political institutions have. Or, that social patterns of behaviour can be modified as rapidly as the amendment or repeal of unsatisfactory or discredited laws. As noted by Vojtech Cepl, changing the law or political institutions is altogether easier than transforming human conduct:[19]

> The rules of human conduct are the most difficult to transform because there are not necessarily any models for it and there is the tremendous force of inertia to contend with. Political and legal changes can be modelled on the systems of Western democracies ... In contrast, *rules of human conduct are learned by observing societal conduct and are not changed by amendments to legal texts* but only by people actually modifying their behaviour.

Cepl, now a Justice of the Czech Constitutional Court, concludes that a 'dissonance' has arisen between 'the abstract principles of law and constitutional government introduced since 1989 and peoples' actual conduct', and that the former 'must be infused over time into the actual life of society, absorbed into the collective consciousness'.[20]

The difficulties involved in transforming the consciousness of entire peoples habituated to authoritarian and oppressive government are formidable. As Cepl points out, 'Eastern Europe had Communist regimes in place for two generations, so that the core of the population under fifty never experienced any other societal norms'.[21] However, even for those *over* fifty, particularly outside the Czech Republic, the individual and collective experience of government was frequently of an institution that was remote, arbitrary and dictatorial. Thus, freedom under the rule of law, political pluralism and the enjoyment of individual and collective rights was far from typical of the societies of Central and Eastern Europe before the advent of Communism.[22] Consequently, the time-lag between the adoption of new, liberal constitutions (a process which has been largely accomplished) and appropriate modifications in the behaviour of politicians, judges and ordinary citizens throughout the region is likely to be considerable, *even assuming that the latter wish to transform*. People, unlike laws, have memories and established patterns of behaviour. These can be changed only gradually, if at all.

---

[18] See e.g. Schöpflin, *Politics in Eastern Europe 1945–1992*, p. 12.
[19] V. Cepl, 'Transformation of hearts and minds in Eastern Europe', unpublished paper (1995), p. 3. My italics.
[20] Cepl, 'Transformation of hearts and minds', p. 3.
[21] Cepl, 'Transformation of hearts and minds', p. 2.
[22] See, generally, Pogany, 'A new constitutional (dis)order for Eastern Europe?', pp. 222–30.

The Prospects for Democracy and Constitutionalism in the Post-Communist States

Present-day conditions in Central and Eastern Europe are substantially differ- ent to those which existed during much of the inter-war period. In particular, the region no longer finds itself between two aggressively expansionist totali- tarian states, Nazi Germany and Stalinist Russia, and is therefore free of the destabilizing and debilitating impact (ideological, diplomatic and occasionally military) of these former neighbours.[23] However, the continuing and apparently chronic lack of political or economic stability in the Russian Federation since the dissolution of the Soviet Union, and the popularity of extremist politicians and of maverick military leaders, suggest that Central and Eastern Europe remains vulnerable to threats or pressures from the East, particularly if Russia were to pursue a more aggressively nationalistic foreign policy. This remains a particular concern so long as the Central and East European states are denied entry to NATO, a step which Russia has consistently opposed.

The 'negative externalities' which contributed to the collapse of democracy in the inter-War period have been replaced by a range of 'positive externalities' calculated to support and facilitate the transition to democracy and constitu- tionalism. This is not the place for a detailed analysis of these legal and institutional mechanisms. However, it is clear that they serve a particularly important function in the context of post-Communist societies which lack a developed culture of human rights, where democracy is frequently understood as crude majoritarianism, and where the state continues to exercise a decisive role in the economy.[24]

These 'positive externalities' include the Council of Europe and the numerous conventions concluded under its auspices, particularly the European Conven- tion on Human Rights and Fundamental Freedoms.[25] As of November 1995, Bulgaria, the Czech Republic, Hungary, Poland, Romania, Slovakia, Slovenia and Lithuania had become parties to the Human Rights Convention, while Estonia, Latvia, Moldova, Macedonia, Ukraine and Albania were signatories. All of the above states had become members of the Council of Europe, while applications for membership had also been received from Belarus, Bosnia- Herzegovina, Russia and Croatia.[26] The Council of Europe has drawn up a Framework Convention for the Protection of National Minorities although, at the time of writing, this has not yet entered into force.[27] The adoption of this Convention signifies an important stage in the progressive evolution of human rights protection at the European level, particularly in terms of the recognition

---

[23] G. Stokes, *The Wall came tumbling down* (New York, Oxford University Press, 1993), pp. 253–4.

[24] See, generally, G. Kardos, *Emberi Jogok egy új Korszak Határán* ('Human Rights on the Frontiers of a New Era') (Budapest, T-Twins Kiado, 1995), pp. 181–2.

[25] For commentaries on the European Convention see e.g. A. H. Robertson and J. G. Merrills, *Human Rights in Europe* (Manchester, Manchester University Press, 3rd ed., 1993); D. J. Harris, M. O'Boyle and C. Warbrick, *Law of the European Convention on Human Rights* (London, Butterworth, 1995).

[25] Information supplied by the Treaties Office, Directorate of Legal Affairs, Council of Europe.

[27] For the text of the Council of Europe's Framework Convention for the Protection of National Minorities see *International Legal Materials*, 34 (1995), 351–9. As of November 1995, the post- Communist states which had signed the Framework Convention comprised Estonia, Hungary, Lithuania, Poland, Romania, the Czech Republic, Slovakia, Slovenia, Albania, Latvia, Moldova and the Ukraine.

and protection of minority rights. While the European Convention on Human Rights requires states to refrain from instituting discriminatory measures against persons on account of their membership of a minority group (Art. 14), the Framework Convention entails positive measures of support, including the promotion of 'the conditions necessary for persons belonging to national minorities to maintain and develop their culture, and to preserve the essential elements of their identity' (Art. 5(1)).

The Organisation for Security and Cooperation in Europe, formerly the CSCE, should also be considered in this context. The OSCE has a variety of functions extending beyond issues of human rights and constitutionalism.[28] Nevertheless, as part of its 'human dimension' mechanism, the OSCE has introduced a range of norms and mechanisms specifically concerned with the promotion of human rights, democratization and constitutional development in the post-Communist states.[29] Thus, it complements and, in certain areas, supplements the obligations assumed by states pursuant to the treaties adopted under the auspices of the Council of Europe. Significantly, a number of post-Communist and particularly post-Soviet states participating in the OSCE, including Russia, Georgia and Belarus, are not members of the Council of Europe. Thus, the OSCE represents the principal institutional framework for these states, at the international level, concerned with questions of democracy and constitutionalism.

As part of the Human Dimension mechanism, OSCE states have assumed a range of obligations. In the Document of the Copenhagen Meeting of the Conference on the Human Dimension of the CSCE, held in June 1990, participating states expressed their 'conviction that the protection and promotion of human rights and fundamental freedoms is one of the basic purposes of government, and reaffirm[ed] that the recognition of these rights and freedoms constitutes the foundation of freedom, justice and peace'.[30] The Document goes on to list a variety of specific commitments regarding the establishment of democratic government, the rule of law and the protection of individual and minority rights. These include recognition of the principle that free elections are to be held 'at reasonable intervals by secret ballot or by equivalent free voting procedure', of 'the duty of the government and public authorities to comply with the constitution and to act in a manner consistent with law', and that 'human rights and fundamental freedoms will be guaranteed by law and in accordance with their obligations under international law'.[31]

Institutionally, the OSCE possesses a variety of organs concerned wholly or in part with the promotion of the objectives set forth in the 'Human Dimension' mechanism. These include meetings of the Heads of State or Government, the Ministerial Council, the Senior Council, the Permanent Council, the High Commissioner on National Minorities, the Office for Democratic Institutions and Human Rights and the Parliamentary Assembly.[32]

---

[28] For the functions of the OSCE see 'Strengthening the CSCE', Budapest Decisions of the Organisation for Security and Co-operation in Europe, in *International Legal Materials*, 34 (1995), 773–6, pp. 773–4.

[29] See, generally, Robertson and Merrills, *Human Rights in Europe*, pp. 352–60.

[30] For the text of the Document see *International Legal Materials*, 29 (1990), 1306–21, p. 1307.

[31] *International Legal Materials*, 29 (1990), p. 1308.

[32] On the functions of these various bodies see 'Strengthening the CSCE', Budapest Decisions of the Organisation for Security and Cooperation in Europe, p. 774.

Of the numerous other international instruments that may have a bearing on the recognition and protection of human rights and democracy in the post-Communist states, attention is drawn, in particular, to the International Covenant on Civil and Political Rights.[33] This treaty is important because of the breadth of participation in it,[34] because of the wide range of civil and political rights protected, and because of the relative sophistication of the mechanisms of supervision and enforcement.[35] All contracting states are required to submit periodic reports to the Human Rights Committee, established under the Covenant, while the Committee is empowered to make 'general comments'. In addition, there is provision for inter-state claims, while parties to the Optional Protocol accept the jurisdiction of the Committee to receive complaints from individuals.

The usefulness of the Covenant is thus not confined to standard-setting. It represents a vehicle not merely for the articulation of basic rights, but also for the rigorous assessment of the performance of contracting states. This latter function, which derives principally from the duty of participating states to submit periodic reports on their compliance with the Covenant, has permitted an increasingly vigilant Human Rights Committee to formulate detailed comments on the *actual*, as opposed to the merely *superficial*, changes in the constitutional practice of the post-Communist states.

It is too early to predict how effective the regional and international mechanisms, discussed above, will be in constraining the conduct of states and in promoting and consolidating the processes of democratization and constitutionalization. It is an unfortunate paradox of international (and national) affairs, that guarantees of human rights and constitutional safeguards work best where they are needed least. Thus, it is precisely those societies which are most heedful of international norms and which are least given to the violation of human rights, that are most likely to strive for scrupulous conformity with the international obligations arising from membership of the Council of Europe and the OSCE, or those stemming from binding international human rights conventions. Conversely, dictators and demagogues are far less likely to be swayed by largely unenforceable (albeit binding) international norms.

However, it would be simplistic to dismiss matters in this way. International norms may be persuasive and influential, even where the target governments are not inclined to automatic compliance. A post-Communist state which rejected clearly-enunciated international obligations, concerning individual or minority rights, would seriously compromise the argument that it was 'returning to Europe'. Such a state would risk not merely loss of legitimacy, but also denial of membership in, or lack of benefits from, important economic and security organizations. For example, Slovakia's Prime Minister was recently warned by the European Union that further harassment of opposition politicians or of the

---

[33] For the text of the Covenant see e.g. I. Brownlie, *Basic Documents in International Law* (Oxford, Clarendon, 4th ed., 1995), p. 276.

[34] As of 31 December 1994, there were 128 parties to the Covenant. These included the following post-Communist states: Albania, Armenia, Azerbaijan, Belarus, Bosnia Herzegovina, Bulgaria, Croatia, Czech Republic, Estonia, Georgia, Hungary, Kyrgyzstan, Latvia, Lithuania, Macedonia, Mongolia, Poland, Republic of Moldova, Romania, Russian Federation, Slovakia, Slovenia, Ukraine, and Yugoslavia (Serbia and Montenegro). See *Human Rights: International Instruments* (Chart of Ratifications as at 31 December 1994), ST/HR/4/Rev.11.

[35] See, generally, Robertson and Merrills, *Human Rights in the World*, pp. 27–69.

country's President would result in Slovakia being removed from the list of post-Communist states currently being considered for membership of the Union.[36]

Of course, this does not mean that every post-Communist society will be consistently intimidated into conformity with its international obligations. Rather, it suggests that the disincentives to non-compliance are substantially higher than in any previous historical period. For most states in Central and Eastern Europe, which are dependent on high levels of foreign direct investment and which are reliant on the good-will of the European Union and of the United States for access to lucrative markets for their exports, the potential costs of flouting human rights norms could well outweigh the political or other advantages of such unlawful action. However, instances may arise where a particular government perceives greater gains, if only to itself, in inflaming nationalist sentiment against ethnic minorities or in curbing opposition elements, notwithstanding the potential loss of economic benefits. Also, of course, the potential impact (or even likelihood) of Western sanctions may depend on the size, economic resources and political or military significance of the target state. Thus, Slovakia is more vulnerable to such pressures (and a more likely target) than the Russian Federation.

In addition to such 'positive externalities', a range of internal elements in the various post-Communist states also promote the consolidation of the new, democratic, constitutional structures. Such internal factors include elements of the political and administrative process that are genuinely committed to the success of the new constitutions, institutions or agencies, including Constitutional Courts, Ombudsmen etc. which have, by and large, a vested interest in the new constitutional structures, progressive elements within the media and the intelligensia which support the principles of democratic pluralism and the rule of law, sections of the business community concerned at the potentially harmful effects of an authoritarian or despotic political system on the flow of inward investment, on the availability of foreign credits and on access to foreign markets, as well as a variety of interest groups, such as those representing national and other minorities. However, it is important to recognize that the weight or significance of these democratic and constitutionalizing elements will vary from state to state. Thus, their importance within a particular society will depend on a range of factors including the history of the country in question, its economic circumstances, the prevailing social and political culture and the presence of potentially divisive elements, such as sizeable national, ethnic, religious or linguistic minorities.

On the basis of the factors outlined above, and having regard to developments in the post-Communist states since the commencement of the transformation process, some tentative conclusions can be offered as to the probable course of developments within particular states. Post-Communist societies may develop along four distinct and essentially divergent paths. These comprise (i) successfully transformed(ing) political democracies and market economies; (ii) authoritarian and/or populist societies in which both constitutionalization and marketization are, at best, partial and equivocal; (iii) military or fascist dictatorships, a largely self-explanatory category; and (iv) societies in which clear or stable patterns of development (whether economic or political) are

---

[36] *The Times*, 26 October 1995, p. 14.

lacking owing to chronic civil conflicts focused on ethnic, religious or political divisions. However, firm conclusions as to the appropriate categorization of particular societies is rendered problematic because of divergent tendencies within individual countries, because of the relative superficiality of many of the changes to date, and because of inherent uncertainties about the future course of developments.

(i) Successfully Transformed(ing) Societies

Since the dissolution of Czechoslovakia and the creation of independent Czech and Slovak states, on 1 January 1993, the Czech Republic has made rapid strides towards the establishment of a Western-type parliamentary democracy, committed to the rule of law and the protection of individual and minority rights.[37] The Constitutional Court has contributed to the consolidation of the democratic process and to the recognition of the new constitutional values.[38] In the economic sphere, while the process of marketization is far from complete (and has been markedly slower than in either Poland or Hungary), it is evident that further and far-reaching privatization and the creation of a genuine market economy are central to the government's strategic economic thinking. Diplomatically, the Czech Republic has sought to foster good relations with its neighbours while asserting its claims to early membership of the European Union.

Slovenia, which seceded from the Yugoslav federation in the summer of 1991, is also widely considered to be successfully transforming itself into a genuine democracy and a market economy. Despite certain problems arising from the dissolution of the Yugoslav Republic, involving the delimitation of national borders and the division of the national debt, Slovenia is believed to have benefited from the absence of large national minorities and from the fact that the process of liberalization began as far back as the mid-1980s, while the Communists were still in power. Consequently, Slovenian society did not experience a sudden and dramatic shift from rigid political and economic authoritarianism to democratic pluralism and the market. Rather, Slovenia's transformation has been 'a classic case of controlled and gradual system change instigated from below'.[39]

Both Poland and Hungary can, albeit with certain reservations, also be classified as states that belong to the category of 'successfully transformed(ing) political democracies and market economies'. In contrast to the former Czechoslovakia, the GDR, Romania or Bulgaria, the political and economic process during Communism, in both Poland and Hungary, was characterized in general by the absence of ideological rigidity, by extensive (if sometimes fitful) liberalization and by the consensual manner in which the transition from one-party rule to multi-party democracy was effected. In Poland, the bulk of the agricultural sector was never collectivized, the Church retained a significant

---

[37] See e.g. V. Cepl, 'Constitutional reform in the Czech Republic', *University of San Francisco Law Review*, 28 (1993/94), 29–35.

[38] For a discussion of the role of the Czech Constitutional Court and of its first judgment see J. Přibáň, 'The Constitutional Court of the Czech Republic and a legal-philosophical perspective on the sovereignty of the law' in Pogany, *Human Rights in Eastern Europe*, pp. 135–48.

[39] J. Seroka, 'Yugoslavia and its successor states' in S. White, J. Batt and P. Lewis (eds), *Developments in East European Politics* (Basingstoke, Macmillan, 1993), pp. 98–121, p. 106.

measure of independence and influence, and the industrial work-force became the focal point of resistance to the Communist authorities.[40] In Hungary, substantial decentralization was introduced in the economic sphere, beginning in the late '60s, while the political process was characterized by a comparatively high level of tolerance. In legal and economic terms, the basic elements of a market economy, including a modern companies law and a liberal foreign investments code, were devised and enacted *before* the transition to multi-party democracy.[41] In addition, both Poland and Hungary took significant steps towards recognizing (and implementing) the separation of powers doctrine during the last decade of Communist rule. Poland established a Constitutional Tribunal in 1986, while Hungary instituted a more modest Constitutional Law Council in 1984. Thus, Poland and Hungary prepared the ground for an eventual transition to democracy, constitutionalism and the market more thoroughly than any other ex-Communist state.

Nevertheless, certain reservations remain about the categorical inclusion of these states in this group. The political process in Poland has been characterized by considerable instability and by an underlying lack of social or political consensus since 1989.[42] This has meant, *inter alia*, that a new post-Communist constitution has not been adopted, nor laws dealing with the thorny issue of restitution, i.e. the 'reprivatization' of property expropriated during the Communist (or earlier) eras.[43] Thus, the formal, legal aspects of transformation,[44] or even of constitution making, are incomplete. In addition, the social and cultural identity of Polish society has been significantly affected by a resurgent and staunchly conservative Catholic Church. Consequently, it is not yet entirely clear whether the transformation process is likely to result in the establishment of a Western-type liberal, pluralist (and largely secular) society, or whether it is leading to the 'rechristianization' of the country, with all that implies in terms of educational, social, cultural and related issues.[45]

Significantly, the governments of both Poland and Hungary are presently coalitions in which the former Communists are the leading party. In addition, as noted above, a former minister in a Communist' government, Aleksander Kwasniewski, was recently elected President of Poland, in place of Lech Walesa.[46] While the Communist (now Left Democratic and Socialist) Parties of Poland and Hungary have abandoned their Marxist dogmas and converted themselves into Western-style social democratic movements, it is at least questionable whether constitutional transformation can be said to have

---

[40] On the Polish experience see N. Davies, *God's Playground: a History of Poland* (Oxford, Clarendon, 1981), vol. II, pp. 556–643; T. Garton Ash, *The Polish Revolution: Solidarity* (London, Granta, rev. ed., 1991).

[41] See, generally, I. Pogany, 'The regulation of foreign investment in Hungary', *ICSID Review – Foreign Investment Law Journal*, 4 (1989), 39–62, esp. pp. 56–61.

[42] This was reflected, for example, in the voting in the recent presidential elections, with 51.7% of the votes cast going to Aleksander Kwasniewski, leader of the Democratic Left Alliance (former Communists) and 48.3% for Lech Walesa.

[43] For an examination of these issues see I. Pogany, *Righting Wrongs in Eastern Europe* (Manchester, Manchester University Press, forthcoming, 1997).

[44] In the view of some, the restitution of property to the persons from whom it was expropriated during the Communist (or earlier) eras, represents a crucial dimension of the transformation process. See Cepl, 'Transformation of hearts and minds in Eastern Europe', pp. 4–5.

[45] See, generally, on this point, J. Kurczewski, *The Resurrection of Rights in Poland* (Oxford, Clarendon, 1993), pp. 433–6.

[46] *The Times*, 21 November 1995, p. 13.

occurred when the leading politicians in a society have merely, or so it seems, changed their labels. Whether they have also changed their principles remains, necessarily, uncertain. However, for Vojtech Cepl, '[a]ny fundamental change in a society is, and must be, accompanied by a replacement of the élite'.[47] Thus, Cepl, is adamant that 'lustration', in which those compromised by their association with the former, undemocratic elements are systematically purged from public life,[48] represents a necessary and integral feature of transformation:

> ... lustration, restitution and condemnation of the communist regime have their specific and practical purposes. In the case of lustration [in the Czech Republic], this was to exclude persons from exercising governmental power if they cannot be trusted to exercise it consistently with democratic principles, as they have shown no commitment to or belief in them, in the past. It also gives democracy a breathing space, a period of time during which it can lay down roots without the danger that people in high positions of power will try to undermine it (keeping in mind that these people are usually more experienced and organized in the arts of governing and using power).[49]

Whether Cepl's fears concerning the effects of failing to replace the political élite are justified cannot yet be known. However, the rapidity with which former Communists have returned to power in both Poland and Hungary (as well as in Bulgaria, Latvia and Lithuania), must be a cause for some disquiet. In part, there are genuine doubts as to whether former Communists now exercising power have really (or completely) transformed their own political and ethical values. In truth, how could they conceivably have done so, particularly in the space of a few years? At the same time, the willingness of the electorate in both Poland and Hungary to vote for ex-Communists may be seen less as an expression of confidence in the new ideological orientation of the candidates than as an indication of fear and exasperation at the social and economic costs of the transformation process, and its severely damaging effects on jobs, prices and social benefits. If the Communists cannot 'deliver' on these issues, the same voters may opt for a right wing or populist 'solution' next time. Thus, only the underlying volatility of the electorate can account for the extraordinary surge in the popularity of the Independent Smallholders' Party in Hungary. By August, 1995, the populist and backward-looking Independent Smallholders' had become the second most popular party in Hungary, after the Socialists, and were on the verge of overtaking them.[50]

Post-Communist politics in Hungary, as in most other Central and East European states, have been characterized by a resurgent and intermittently exclusivist nationalism.[51] Most notoriously, István Csurka, then a Vice-President of the ruling Hungarian Democratic Forum, published an article in 1992 containing numerous thinly-veiled antisemitic comments.[52] Although

---

[47] Cepl, 'Transformation of hearts and minds in Eastern Europe', p. 5.

[48] For a theoretical discussion of lustration and related practices see C. Offe, 'Disqualification, retribution, restitution: dilemmas of justice in post-Communist societies', *The Journal of Political Philosophy*, I (1993), 17–44, esp. pp. 27–35.

[49] Cepl, 'Transformation of hearts and minds in Eastern Europe', p. 5.

[50] See Heti Világgazdaság, 23 September 1995, pp. 113–21.

[51] See, generally, F. Fejtö, *La fin des democraties populaires* (Paris, Seuil, 1992), pp. 475–87.

[52] See *Magyar Fórum*, 20 August 1992, pp. 9–16.

Csurka's political fortunes have since declined, much of his former constituency are now coalescing around the Independent Smallholders'.

Nevertheless, the general tenor of the political and constitutional process, in both Poland and Hungary, is democratic, pluralist, rooted in respect for the rule of law. The force and weight of these tendencies owes much to the countries' respective Constitutional Courts. In Hungary, the Court has played a particularly important role in ensuring observance by both government and legislature of the country's revised, democratic Constitution.[53] It has been said that the Hungarian Court, 'has in a few years become one of the most important factors in safeguarding Hungary's transition to democracy and constitutionalism'.[54]

The process of economic transformation in Poland and Hungary is fairly advanced as compared with most other post Communist states. Poland is now in its 'fourth year of significant growth', while Hungary has made substantial progress in terms of 'privatization and restructuring, the liberalization of prices and trade and foreign exchange systems, the building of financial institutions and the implementation of legal reforms.'[55]

(ii) Authoritarian and/or Populist Societies

Many, perhaps most, post-Communist states, including Slovakia, Romania, Bulgaria, Ukraine, the Russian Federation, Belarus, Moldova and the Baltic Republics ought to be included in this category at the present time. Arguably, the ex-Yugoslav states (other than Slovenia) should also be listed here, although the future course of developments in these countries, even in the short-term, remains subject to a significant measure of uncertainty.

The states in this category are not following a common path of political, constitutional or economic development. The differences between the various states, whether in terms of constitutionalization or in the scope of their economic reforms, are profound. Nevertheless, they can be classified together, not so much because of their common features as because of what they lack in common. As yet, none of these states can be described unreservedly as having successfully transformed (or even as successfully transforming) itself into a genuine political democracy or a market economy. Too many uncertainties remain, both about the nature of the changes to date, and about the future course of developments. Both constitutionalization and marketization have been, at best, partial and equivocal. The 'shortfall', whether in political/ constitutional or economic terms, is different in each case. Some of the states listed in this category may eventually transform themselves into functioning democracies governed by the rule of law and with a genuine market economy. However, such an outcome is far from certain and, in some cases, remains

---

[53] See, generally, I. Pogany, 'Constitutional reform in Central and Eastern Europe: Hungary's transition to democracy', *International and Comparative Law Quarterly*, 42 (1993), 332–55, esp. pp. 340–55; A. Sajó, 'Reading the invisible constitution: judicial review in Hungary', *Oxford Journal of Legal Studies*, 15 (1995), 253–267; G. Halmai, 'The constitutional court' in B. Király (ed.), *A Lawful Revolution in Hungary 1989–94* (New Jersey, Atlantic Research, forthcoming, 1996).
[54] Venice Commission, *Bulletin on Constitutional Case-Law* (Strasbourg, Council of Europe, spec. ed., 1994), 35–7, p. 37.
[55] *Financial Times*, 2 November 1995, p. 2.

distinctly improbable. Moreover, at the present time, all of these states, albeit in different ways and to different degrees, have failed to furnish clear or wide-ranging evidence of their having embarked on a successful course of constitutional and economic transformation.

Slovakia. While the initial impetus for ousting the Communist regime, in 1989, was largely identical in both the Czech and Slovak parts of the former Czechoslovakia,[56] the subsequent process of political reform in Czechoslovakia was influenced by long-standing tensions over Slovak aspirations for autonomy. Thus, democratization created the conditions in which the dissolution of Czechoslovakia became possible.[57]

Since gaining independence in January 1993, Slovakia's political, constitutional and economic orientation appears increasingly to be diverging from that of its Western-looking neighbours due to a variety of cultural, historical, political and personal factors. In terms of an emerging political culture, Slovakia has been characterized by a propensity for nationalist rhetoric, by intolerance (or at the very least insensitivity) towards national minorities, interpersonal feuding amongst the political élite, and by apparently politically-sanctioned assaults on opposition figures and on the close relatives of senior politicians. This represents a partial *balkanization* of the political process in Slovakia, in marked contrast to the urbanity and Westernization of the political process in the neighbouring Czech Republic.

The antagonism between Slovakia's Prime Minister, Vladimir Meciar and the President, Michal Kovac,[58] is symptomatic of the personalization of politics in Slovakia, a trend which has clearly undermined efforts to establish sound, democratic and constitutional government. The feud between the Prime Minister and the President is also believed to have prompted the kidnapping, at gun point, of Kovac's son by members of Slovakia's security services (with or without the knowledge of the Prime Minister). The younger Kovac, who was dumped by his captors in Austria, is now under arrest and awaiting extradition to Germany where he faces possible fraud charges.[59] The operation was evidently carried out in the hope of intimidating and embarassing the President.[60] Nor can this incident be dismissed as an isolated affair. On 12 September 1995, Frantisek Miklosko, deputy leader of the opposition Christian Democratic Movement, was beaten up by three unknown assailants outside his home. Nothing was taken from him. Miklosko has maintained that the Slovak security services, which came under the control of the Prime Minister in April, were implicated in the assault. 'Everything that's going on here is intimidation', commented Miklosko.[61]

---

[56] See, generally, on the political developments which led to the removal of the Communist regime in the former Czechoslovakia, P. Lewis, *Central Europe since 1945* (London, Longman, 1994), pp. 254–8.

[57] On the factors which led to the breakup of Czechoslovakia see e.g. J. Elster, 'Consenting adults or the sorcerer's apprentice?', *East European Constitutional Review*, 4, 1 (Winter, 1995), 36–41.

[58] On the causes of this antagonism see e.g. 'Constitution watch: Slovakia', *East European Constitutional Review*, 3, 2 (Spring 1994), 23–4. See, also, S. Zifcak, 'The battle over presidential powers in Slovakia', *East European Constitutional Review*, 4, 3 (Summer 1995), 61–5.

[59] See e.g. *Independent on Sunday*, 10 September 1995, p. 16.

[60] *The Prague Post*, 20–6 September 1995, p. 1.

[61] *The Prague Post*, 20–6 September 1995, p. 4.

These examples, which are by no means exhaustive, have been chosen merely to illustrate the nature of the current political process in Slovakia. They suggest that, at least in the short and medium term, constitutionalism and thorough-going democratization may prove elusive. Indeed, it is far from clear that they are even the goals which Meciar, and his supporters in the Movement for a Democratic Slovakia, have set themselves. As the *East European Constitutional Review* comments, '[i]f this past quarter's events are any indication of the future, agents of the police will become an increasingly common tool in Slovak politics'.[62] The *Review* also emphasizes that 'the trend towards monocratic government in Slovakia continues'.[63]

Relations in Slovakia between the executive and the judicial branches of government also call for comment. As emphasized above, constitutional courts have played a decisive role in helping to consolidate the process of democratic and constitutional reform in a number of post-Communist states by safe-guarding the principles of the new or revised constitutions. This has proved necessary, in part, because governments in post-Communist societies are unaccustomed to operating within constitutional constraints and sometimes behave as though they have the right to implement their policies simply because they were elected to office. This impatience with the niceties of constitutional rule and a pronounced authoritarian tendency are scarcely surprising in view of the accumulated experience of the post-War years, as well as pervasive traditions of political authoritarianism in much of the region.[64] For government ministers who, in a previous incarnation (i.e. before 1989), were active members of traditional Communist Parties, the psychological gymnastics required to function as liberal, Western-oriented democrats, is even more striking. Thus, there is a profound need for independent, tough-minded Constitutional Courts, willing and able to uphold the norms (and values) of the new, democratic Constitutions. The necessity of such Courts is all the greater where, as is often the case, the executive branch has gained effective control over a largely quiescent legislature.

The potential importance of the region's Constitutional Courts also derives from the numerous interpretative problems thrown up by the new or revised constitutions, and by the need to vet existing laws and administrative regulations to ensure their conformity with the new Constitutional norms.[65] Constitutional Courts are thus of critical importance in securing a transition to genuinely democratic, constitutional rule.

There are a number of reasons why a dispassionate observer might be at least a shade sceptical in regard to Slovakia's Constitutional Court. In the first place, the President of the Court, Milan Cic, was Slovakia's last Minister of Justice before the 'velvet revolution' of 1989. Therefore, his credentials for presiding

---

[62] Constitution watch: Slovakia', *East European Constitutional Review*, 4, 3 (Summer 1995), 28–30, p. 28.

[63] 'Constitution watch: Slovakia', *East European Constitutional Review*, 4, 3 (Summer 1995), p. 29.

[64] See, generally, Pogany, 'A new constitutional (dis)order for Eastern Europe?', p. 217.

[65] See, generally, on the functions of the Constitutional Courts established in the region, H. Schwartz, 'The new East European Constitutional Courts' in A. E. Dick Howard (ed.), *Consti-tution-Making in Eastern Europe* (Washington DC, Woodrow Wilson Center, 1993), pp. 163–207. For an overview of the composition, procedures and powers of the post-Communist Constitutional Courts, as well as of comparable Western judicial bodies, see e.g. Venice Commission, *Bulletin on Constitutional Case-Law*.

over a Constitutional Court created to safeguard the principles of a democratic, pluralist, rights-centred Constitution are clearly suspect. Secondly, the fact that the judges were appointed to the Court by Meciar himself, apparently in breach of the Constitution, can scarcely escape comment.[66] Thirdly, the intimate links between Cic and Meciar, who collaborated closely in the establishment of an independent Slovakia, would seem to undermine the spirit (if not the letter) of the separation of powers. Finally, the behaviour of Cic himself has at times called into question his independence from the government. For example, in February 1994, when the Meciar government lost its parliamentary majority because of the defection of a deputy to the opposition, all of the deputies who supported the coalition walked out of the Chamber in protest. After opposition members, who constituted a quorum, had continued the parliamentary session, Cic appeared on Slovak television to give his personal opinion that the session had been unlawful.[67] Subsequently, the Constitutional Court ruled that it lacked jurisdiction in the matter.

Some, though by no means all, of the decisions of the Slovak Constitutional Court have confirmed the fears of observers. For example, after representatives of the substantial Hungarian minority had protested to the Council of Europe, in August 1993, that the Slovak authorities were disregarding minority rights standards laid down by the Council, the Slovak authorities petitioned the Constitutional Court. The Court ruled that Council of Europe recommendations 'do not and cannot have ... legal implications for the state organs of the Slovak Republic'.[68] The formalism of the reasoning of the Slovak Court would seem to have been a reflection of its unwillingness to interpret national laws or policies in the light of international, or even regional, norms as well as of a chauvinistic disinclination to accommodate minority (especially Hungarian) rights.

When the Court has manifested genuine independence from the government, the response of the latter has sometimes been striking. In late December 1994, the Court declared that an order issued by the Ministry of Health, requiring patients to meet the costs of some medicines and of certain medical services, was unconstitutional because only parliament could modify the provision of health care to Slovak citizens. In response, the Ministry of Health stated that it would ignore the Court's ruling. At the same time, the government pointedly withdrew the car that hitherto had been provided to the Chief Justice of the Court, along with his bodyguards.[69] For his part, the Prime Minister upbraided the Court, warning that, 'a situation where the Constitutional Court, by its interpretation of the law either broadens or changes the Constitution cannot be tolerated'.[70]

Since the establishment of an independent Slovakia, in January 1993, relations between the Slovak authorities and the country's substantial Hungarian minority, amounting to approximately 10 per cent of the population, have been

[66] 'Constitution watch: Slovakia', *East European Constitutional Review*, 2, 1 (Winter 1993), p. 10.

[67] 'Constitution watch: Slovakia', *East European Constitutional Review*, 3, 2 (Spring 1994), p. 23.

[68] 'Constitution watch: Slovakia', *East European Constitutional Review*, 2, 4 (Fall 1993) and 3, 1 (Winter 1994), 18–19, p. 18.

[69] 'Constitution watch: Slovakia', *East European Constitutional Review*, 4, 2 (Spring 1995), 28–31, pp. 28–9.

[70] Quoted at, 'Constitution watch: Slovakia', *East European Constitutional Review*, 4, 2 (Spring 1995), p. 29.

severely strained. These tensions, which are the product of the government's persistent efforts to assert Slovak national identity at the expense of minority (particularly Hungarian) cultural rights, have also worsened Hungarian-Slovak relations. The Slovak parliament, acting by an overwhelming majority, recently passed a language law which prohibits the use of minority languages in dealings with state institutions or with local authorities, and introduces significant restrictions on the exclusive use of minority languages in the media or in the course of cultural activities, *even when the target audience is composed almost entirely of minority communities.*[71] A Hungarian-Slovak treaty, signed in 1994 and recognizing the minority rights of the Hungarian community, has not yet been submitted to the Slovak legislature for ratification. The Slovak government is apparently unwilling to seek parliamentary approval for the draft treaty at this time owing to the strength of opposition. To many outside (and not a few internal) observers, it seems that the Meciar government, whose political and economic reforms have been equivocal at best, has sought refuge in nationalism and in the scapegoating of national minorities as a means of rallying mass support.

In the economic sphere, Meciar's return to power in October 1994, following a spell in opposition, has been marked by the abrupt reversal of plans for rapid and wide-ranging privatization of state-owned assets. In September 1995, the Slovak Parliament approved an economic programme that prohibits the privatization of some two-dozen enterprises designated as 'strategic'. These are mainly in the energy, public utilities, telecommunications and defence sectors.[72] There are persistent rumours that privatization in other parts of the Slovak economy is enriching circles close to the Meciar government, and that the National Property Foundation has seriously under-valued state assets in such transactions.[73] Fears concerning Slovak economic policy have had an inevitable effect on flows of foreign direct investment. It is doubted whether inward investment in 1995 will reach $200 million.

Romania. The 'transition' from Communist rule has been strikingly ambiguous in Romania. The first 'post-Communist' administration, formed in December 1989, was established by the National Salvation Front (NSF), a movement chiefly notable for the large number of (former) high-ranking Communists in senior positions.[74] It was the National Salvation Front which first declared Ion Iliescu, a former Communist Party propaganda secretary, President of Romania, although Iliescu has since been confirmed in office at elections. In the eyes of many, the Romanian 'revolution' has been 'a revolution highjacked'.[75]

Following parliamentary elections in 1992, a minority government was formed by the newly established Party of Social Democracy (PSD), which was created by former members of the National Salvation Front who merged with two smaller groupings, the Republican Party and the Co-operative Democratic

---

[71] *Heti Világgazdaság*, 25 November 1995, p. 29. A total of 108 deputies voted in favour of the legislation, 18 abstained and 17 voted against. The negative votes were cast by members of opposition parties representing the Hungarian minority.

[72] *Heti Világgazdaság*, 16 September 1995, p. 29.

[73] *Heti Világgazdaság*, 16 September 1995, p. 31.

[74] See e.g. Sword, *The Times Guide to Eastern Europe* (London, Times, rev. ed., 1991), pp. 140–1

[75] R. East, *Revolutions in Eastern Europe* (London, Pinter, 1992), p. 139.

Party.[76] With ex-members of the National Salvation Front exercising a predominant role in the PSD, the influence of former Communists in the executive branch of government in Romania remains decisive. This influence has been strengthened further by the PSD's *de facto* alliance with the Romanian Socialist Labour Party, the former Communists. Two right wing and ardently nationalistic parties, the Romanian National Unity Party and the Greater Romania Party, have also joined the coalition.[77] These latter parties are opposed to the extension of the rights of Romania's national minorities, particularly those of the substantial Hungarian population, some two million strong, concentrated in Translylvania. The Greater Romania Party is also widely regarded as antisemitic.

The political process in Romania has not demonstrated a clear or convincing transition to liberal democracy and constitutionalism. This is scarcely surprising as the governing coalition is composed, to a significant degree, of populist, nationalist, collectivist or otherwise unreconstructed elements who lack the intent to embark on Western-style democratic and constitutional transformation. In addition, of course, the underlying political culture remains decidedly authoritarian, a predisposition which the Communists inherited (and embellished), rather than implanted. Thus, it should not come as a surprise that the new, democratically-elected Romanian government has behaved in a markedly authoritarian and, sometimes, unconstitutional fashion. According to one source, since the coalition parties signed a protocol, in January 1995, consolidating their alliance, the government, 'now openly defies Parliament and the courts, and ignores pressure from international institutions'.[78]

The role of Romania's Constitutional Court in the transformation process also merits scrutiny. Attention has been drawn to the seemingly indiscriminate fashion in which the Court has struck down numerous pieces of legislation on a range of topics, including social security, education, privatization and even on parliamentary matters.[79] At the same time, the composition of the Court, following the expiry of Justice Miklós Fazekás' term of office in 1995, and his replacement by an ethnic Romanian, Justice Costica Bulai, has caused disquiet amongst Romania's Hungarian community.[80] Acceptance of the Court as an impartial arbiter of constitutional questions, particularly amongst minority groups, remains a somewhat distant prospect.

The ethnification of politics in Romania (as in other parts of Central and Eastern Europe) was probably inevitable following the collapse of Communism.[81] The demise of the socialist order both created the conditions in which national minorities could press for the recognition of their collective rights, while also permitting nationalist and right wing movements to articulate their

[76] 'Constitution watch: Romania', *East European Constitutional Review*, 2, 3 (Summer 1993), 14–5, p. 15.
[77] 'Constitution watch: Romania', *East European Constitutional Review*, 4, 2 (Spring 1995), 21–4, p. 22.
[78] 'Constitution watch: Romania', *East European Constitutional Review*, 4, 2 (Spring 1995), p. 22.
[79] For details see e.g. 'Constitution watch: Romania', *East European Constitutional Review*, 4, 3 (Summer 1995), p. 22.
[80] 'Constitution watch: Romania', *East European Constitutional Review*, 4, 3 (Summer 1995), 21–3, p. 23.
[81] See e.g. C. Offe, 'Strong causes, weak cures', *East European Constitutional Review*, 1, 1 (Spring 1992), 21–3.

emotive message. The inclusion of two overtly nationalist parties in the ruling coalition in Romania, together with the radicalization of DAHR, the Democratic Alliance of Hungarians in Romania, has served to increase the drift towards ethnification.[82] Crucially, despite considerable pressure from the Council of Europe and other international agencies, Romania has yet to conclude a bilateral treaty with Hungary providing, *inter alia*, for the reciprocal recognition of minority rights. In a society where 'education, health and cultural expenditures remain the lowest in Eastern Europe',[83] the dangers of a further ethnification of the political process remain especially strong.

Economic transformation in Romania has also been slow and faltering. By mid-1995, according to estimates drawn up by the European Bank for Reconstruction and Development, Romania's private sector accounted for only 40% of the country's GDP. This compares with 60% in Poland, Hungary and Slovakia, and 70% in the Czech Republic.[84] Privatization, which stalled in 1992 after general elections saw left-wing parties achieve considerable success, has once again become a priority. This is due, in no small measure, to pressure from the World Bank and from other international bodies.[85] However, it remains to be seen how the proposals for privatization, which are loosely based on the Czech model, will operate in practice.

Russia and certain other post-Soviet states. This is not the place for a detailed analysis of the prospects for democracy, constitutionalism or market economics in Russia, or in certain other post-Soviet states. The subject is too vast to be dealt with satisfactorily in the space of a few pages. Nevertheless, certain general observations can be made about developments in these states.

In the first place, 'the legacy of history' constitutes a much more formidable obstacle to successful transformation for Russia (and for most of the other post-Soviet states) than for many countries in Central and Eastern Europe. Whereas socialism was adopted in the latter only after 1945,[86] it had been firmly implanted some three decades earlier in Russia following the success of the Bolshevik revolution. Thus, the impact of socialist (or more properly Soviet) ideas and practices in the realms of politics, law, economics, culture, or even in inter-personal relations, has been much more profound and will, correspondingly, be much more difficult to dislodge.[87] Moreover, in contrast to Poland or Hungary, for example, Communism was not perceived by most Russians as an alien ideology, identified principally with a foreign power. It had emerged from within the Russian state itself so that potential resistance was lessened by the sense that the Soviet system, for all its imperfections, was endogenous. Crucially, even the pre-Soviet experience of Russia, and of the post-Soviet states generally, differs fundamentally from that of Central and Eastern

---

[82] A. Craiutu, 'A dilemma of dual identity: the democratic alliance of Hungarians in Romania', *East European Constitutional Review*, 4, 2 (Spring 1995), 43–9.

[83] 'Constitution watch: Romania', *East European Constitutional Review*, 4, 2 (Spring 1995), p. 22.

[84] *Financial Times*, 2 November 1995, p. 2.

[85] *Financial Times*, 10 November 1995, p. 3.

[86] A short-lived communist regime had been established in Hungary in 1919, under Béla Kun. However, it remained in office for only 133 days.

[87] The Baltic states, Latvia, Lithuania and Estonia, offer a partial exception to this rule. They gained a precarious independence after the First World War, only to lose it again, in 1940, when the Soviets annexed them. See e.g. R. Misiunas and R. Taagepera, *The Baltic States: Years of Dependence 1940–1990* (London, Hurst, rev. ed., 1993), pp. 8–20.

Europe. Whatever reservations may be felt about the degree to which democracy or constitutionalism were practised in Poland, Hungary, or Romania before the postwar process of sovietization, these pale into insignificance in comparison with the deep-rooted traditions of political absolutism that were characteristic of Czarist Russia.[88]

Secondly, while the trappings of democracy and constitutionalism (periodic elections, diverse political parties, constitutional courts, a liberalized press etc.) have been introduced in Russia and in many of the other post-Soviet states, it should not be assumed that they have come to represent ineradicable features of the political and constitutional landscape, or that they function in much the same way as in the West. There is abundant evidence of deep dissatisfaction on the part of many 'ordinary' voters with the social and economic costs of transformation in the former Soviet Union, a dissatisfaction which extends to the institutions and values of democracy itself. Indeed, 'democracy' and the socioeconomic costs of the abandonment of the Soviet model have been at least partially conflated. Thus, there is a possibility that democratic processes may be displaced by an openly authoritarian leadership.[89] Alternatively, democracy itself could furnish a constitutional basis for the election of an authoritarian and/or populist government, suspicious of market reforms, harsh in its treatment of ethnic minorities and political opponents, and fundamentally unsympathetic to the goals of genuine transformation. Russian parliamentary elections, held in December 1995, add weight to these fears. The largely unreconstructed Communists emerged as the most successful party with 189 seats in the 450-seat Duma. The ultra-nationalist Liberal Democrats, led by Vladimir Zhirinovsky, obtained 51. By contrast, Our Home is Russia, the party led by the Prime Minister Viktor Chernomyrdin, gained 54 seats and the liberal reformist Yabloko movement emerged with only 46.[90] Thus, it is clear that democratic forms, in a volatile and only partially modernized society such as Russia, may produce a largely illiberal and only nominally democratic legislature, untroubled by Western notions of constitutionalism.

Thirdly, constitutional declamations of human rights or the establishment of institutional safeguards against abuse are frequently no more than symbols of democracy and constitutionalism. They do not always (or necessarily) correspond with practice. For example, the UN Human Rights Committee has expressed its concern that, in Russia:

> ... the profound legislative changes taking place within the State ... have not been matched by the actual protection of human rights at the implementation level. Specifically, it regrets that many of the rights established under the Constitution have not been put into effect through the enactment of implementing laws and regulations and that the relationship of the various bodies entrusted with the protection of human rights has not been clearly defined.[91]

---

[88] See, generally, R. Sakwa, 'Russia, communism, democracy' in S. White, A. Pravda and Z. Gitelman (eds), *Developments in Russian & Post-Soviet Politics* (Basingstoke, Macmillan, 3rd ed., 1994), pp. 287–308, esp. pp. 287–92.

[89] Apparently up to 70% of Russians are yearning for a 'firm hand', according to a respected Russian polling institute, while a third of the population favours a military or KGB-style dictatorship. *The Observer*, 14 May 1995, p. 18.

[90] See e.g. *The Guardian*, 23 December 1995, p. 11.

[91] UN Doc. CCPR/C/79/Add. 54 (26 July 1995), para. 13.

In addition, the Committee commented adversely on 'the lack of independence and efficiency of [the] judiciary', on 'reports of growing numbers of homeless and abandoned children in need of measures of protection', and on 'the lack of familiarity of law enforcement and prison officers with the guarantees provided in the new Constitution'.[92] Similar observations were made by the Committee concerning the situation in the Ukraine.[93] Regarding Estonia with its substantial ethnic Russian minority (amounting to some 39% of the population in 1989), the Human Rights Committee recorded its concern that:

> ... a significantly large segment of the population, particularly members of the Russian-speaking minority, are unable to enjoy Estonian citizenship due to the plethora of criteria established by law, and the stringency of language criterion, and that no remedy is available against an administrative decision rejecting the request for naturalization under the Citizenship Law.[94]

The Committee also deplored the fact that, 'numerous rights and prerogatives, such as the right to participate in the process of land privatization and the right to occupy certain posts or practise some occupations, are granted solely to Estonian citizens' and that, 'permanent residents who are non-citizens are thus deprived of a number of rights'.[95]

The gap between rhetoric and reality, concerning constitutionalism in the post-Soviet states as a whole, remains profound.[96] Even the gains which have been achieved in Russia and in the other post-Soviet states, whether in terms of the formal recognition of human rights or the introduction of quasi-democratic political systems, could be lost with startling rapidity.

(iii) Military or Fascist Dictatorships

At present, none of the post-Communist states can be characterized as a military or Fascist dictatorship. However, tendencies within several post-Communist societies suggest that regimes of this type could come to power. Scepticism concerning the benefits of democracy and the market are, as noted above, particularly strong in Russia, where there is substantial support for a military or Fascist-style dictatorship, particularly if headed by a 'charismatic' leader such as General Alexander Lebed. The General is, according to polls, the most popular political figure in Russia.[97] Of course, such a regime need not come to power solely on the basis of mass electoral support. It could result from a seizure of power by military and security personnel, exasperated at the decline in the nation's international standing and by the collapse of social and economic order.

---

[92] UN Doc. CCPR/C/79/Add. 54 (26 July 1995), paras 18, 22, 24.

[93] CCPR/C/79/Add. 52 (26 July 1995).

[94] CCPR/C/79/Add. 59 (9 November 1995), para. 12.

[95] CCPR/C/79/Add. 59 (9 November 1995), para. 13.

[96] On efforts to secure democracy and respect for human rights, particularly in Russia and in the post-Soviet states see R. Müllerson, *International Law, Rights and Politics* (London, Routledge, 1994), pp. 160–94; R. Müllerson, 'Perspectives on human rights and democracy in the former Soviet Republics' in Pogany, *Human Rights in Eastern Europe*, pp. 47–86.

[97] *The Independent*, 7 December 1995, p. 17.

A similar course of events is conceivable elsewhere, including in some of the ex-Yugoslav states. The authoritarian tendencies displayed in both Serbia and Croatia, where an extreme form of ethnic nationalism has replaced the civic nationalism of the Tito era, could result in an explicitly Fascist type of government. In both states myths of cultural exclusivity have been elevated into principles of national self-determination, creating a 'moral' and political climate which is scarcely remote from Fascism. The extensive and horrific resort to violence against 'enemy' populations, by both Serbs and Croats, is both evidence of this tendency and also a contributory factor. As elsewhere in Central and Eastern Europe, Fascism also represents an essentially familiar feature of the recent past.[98]

Even the more rapidly modernizing societies, such as Hungary, may not be entirely immune from the 'appeal' of demagogic and extreme-right political elements. As noted above, the Independent Smallholders' under their populist leader, József Torgyán, are now one of the most popular political parties in Hungary. This illustrates the volatility of the electorate in even the more successfully transforming post-Communist societies, and the consequent fragility of the hastily-erected democratic and constitutional structures.

(iv) Societies lacking Clear Patterns of Development

As suggested above, certain post-Communist societies may be distinguishable by the fact that they lack clear or stable patterns of development (whether economic or political), owing to chronic civil conflicts focused on ethnic, religious or political divisions. Since the collapse of the former Yugoslavia, Bosnia has clearly been a case in point. Nor can it be taken for granted that the recent political settlement achieved with American mediation in Dayton, Ohio, will result in democratic, orderly government.[99]

Following the dissolution of the USSR a number of the newly-independent states, especially in the Caucasus, have had to contend with an array of ethnic, religious, separatist and other problems. Georgia is a particularly striking example, with separatist movements springing up in Ossetia and Abkhazia and, at least until very recently, chronically unstable central governments challenged by (or even dependent on) powerful private militias such as the Mkhedrioni or 'Horsemen'. In such circumstances, it has been impossible to pursue clear or consistent economic policies, or to introduce constitutionalism in any meaningful sense. These anarchic tendencies may finally be curbed as a result of the overwhelming victory of Eduard Shevardnadze in recent presidential elections.[100] However, reliance on a single, ageing politician of the Soviet era to reverse an entire pattern of political behaviour creates obvious problems. If Shevardnadze were removed from the political scene, whether through illness or assasination, the future course of developments in Georgia could easily revert to the chaos and disorder of the early 1990s.

Conditions in the neighbouring states of Armenia and Azerbaijan are also highly unstable, with increasingly autocratic leaderships seeking to consolidate

[98] On the notorious Fascist regime in war-time Croatia see M. Almond, *Europe's Backyard War* (London, Mandarin, rev. ed., 1994), pp. 134–7.
[99] For details of the settlement see *The Times*, 23 November 1995, p. 16.
[100] For details see e.g. *Financial Times*, 15 November 1995, p. 2.

their power.[101] Protracted civil conflict in one or both countries remains a distinct possibility.

While other post-Communist states have, to date, managed to avoid the general collapse of civil authority or the outbreak of chronic conflicts focused on ethnic, religious or political divisions, this does not mean that they are immune from such developments. Amongst many of the post-Soviet states, in particular, the absence of established national political cultures (other than Communism), the stresses and dislocation resulting from transition to a quasi-market economy (characterized by corruption and incompetence) and the general absence of ethnic, linguistic or religious homogeneity (a factor which was frequently exacerbated by the policies pursued during the Soviet era) have combined to create conditions in which many of the new state structures remain vulnerable and fragile. In such circumstances, even if a general collapse of state authority can be avoided (or recovered from), the alternative may not be liberal democracy. It is altogether more probable that authoritarian governments, drawing on ethnic, religious or other loyalties, will provide a more credible basis for the preservation and continuation of central authority in these states.

Conclusions

My central purpose in this essay has been to show that constitution making, the formal act of drafting or revising a constitution, does not lead automatically to constitutional transformation. The latter can be said to have occurred only where the new or revised constitution becomes not merely prescriptive but, in large measure, descriptive of constitutional practice. This is by no means a universal phenomenon.

Constitution making and constitutional transformation may go hand in hand. However, there is no logical reason why this should always be so. Indeed, there are numerous reasons why governments engage in spates of constitution making, apart from the wish to transform the way in which a society is governed. These include the desire for international (or national) legitimacy, a need to encourage foreign aid or investment, or even the wish to avoid genuine transformation. Constitution making may, thus, constitute a form of political deception, helping cynical and manipulative regimes to pursue policies which are the reverse, or merely a parody, of the principles enshrined in the constitution (this is at least partially the case in Slovakia, Romania and in some of the post-Soviet states).

While almost every post-Communist state has unveiled a new Constitution, or substantially modified its Communist era texts, such legislative activity does not, on its own, tell us very much. While a number of post-Communist societies are undoubtedly overcoming 'the legacy of the past' and are successfully transforming themselves into political democracies and market economies, others are developing along significantly different, less democratic lines. Neal Ascherson has referred to 'post-Communist one-party police states, where semi-free economies nourish seething corruption'.[102] There is no reason to believe that such authoritarian structures are likely to prove short-lived.

---

[101] On developments in Armenia see *The Guardian*, 19 April 1995, p. 10. On the recent and apparently fraudulent elections in Azerbaijan see *The Guardian*, 14 November 1995, p. 12.
[102] N. Ascherson, 'Post-Communism triumphs by default', *Independent on Sunday*, 26 November 1995, p. 14.

The causes of the profoundly different patterns of development found amongst post-Communist societies would seem to be rooted in the past. But it is important to recognize that the 'legacy of the past' is different for each post-Communist state. Levels of industrialization, for example, were markedly higher in inter-war Poland or Hungary, than in inter-war Romania, Bulgaria or Yugoslavia. In Czechoslovakia, they were significantly higher than in any of these states, reaching levels consistent with those of 'the typically industrialized countries of the inter-war years'.[103] Similarly, while levels of literacy were lower during the inter-war period in Czechoslovakia, Poland and Hungary than in Western Europe, they were substantially higher than in Yugoslavia, Bulgaria or Romania. For example, while 7% of Hungary's population (aged 10 and above) were illiterate in 1937, the figure was 39% in Yugoslavia, and 29% in Bulgaria.[104]

Broadly comparable differences can be observed in terms of political and constitutional structures during this period. Thus, Czechoslovakia established a functioning (albeit imperfect) constitutional democracy, while the Polish experience, although considerably less encouraging, was scarcely on a par with the dictatorships prevalent in Romania or Yugoslavia. Only in the case of Hungary does there appear to have been a major discontinuity between the political authoritarianism characteristic of the inter-war years and the genuinely democratic system introduced in 1990.[105] However, even here, it is significant that parliamentarianism survived in inter-war Hungary, providing a basis for subsequent efforts, in 1945–48 and from 1989 onwards, to introduce a multi-party democracy. In addition, although judicial review was alien to Hungary's pre-Communist constitution, the legal culture and respect for constitutional forms was highly developed. Thus, there are important elements in Hungary's pre-Communist experience which have been helpful to the post '89 efforts to create a genuine constitutional democracy.

The legacy of the Communist era was also significantly different in the various Central and Eastern European states. As explained above, there was generally greater freedom in Poland and Hungary, whether in political, cultural or economic terms, than in the other Communist states. Thus notions of pluralism, compromise and dialogue were already well-established in the political sphere (hence the 'refolutions' rather than revolutions of Poland and Hungary), while market elements had already been introduced into the economic sphere. Here, Czechoslovakia, with its ideologically inflexible post-1968 governments, was the odd one out. However, as explained above, the process of economic transformation in the Czech Republic has been able to draw on pre-war traditions of industrial dynamism.

The 'legacy of the past' has also had major demographic consequences. It surely cannot be a coincidence that the four most successfully transforming

[103] A. Teichova, 'Industry' in M. Kaser and E. Radice (eds), *The Economic History of Eastern Europe 1919–1975*, vol. I (Oxford, Clarendon,1985), pp. 222–322, p. 227.
[104] See Table 6.19 in E. Ehrlich, 'Infrastructure' in Kaser and Radice, *The Economic History of Eastern Europe 1919–1975*, vol. I, pp. 323–78, pp. 358–9.
[105] This can be explained, in part, by the elimination from Hungarian society after the War of a significant part of the traditional conservative and right wing elements, often through emigration. In addition, the comparatively liberal character of Communist rule in Hungary, from the 1960s onwards, together with high levels of education and the reduction of earlier patterns of social stratification, no doubt facilitated the introduction of democracy.

political democracies and market economies – the Czech Republic, Slovenia, Poland and Hungary – are strikingly homogeneous in ethnic, religious and linguistic terms. They are truly 'nation' states. This has been accomplished either as a result of a change of borders (Poland after World War II, Hungary after World War I and World War II), as a consequence of genocide (all of these states were occupied by, or allied to, Nazi Germany), or as a result of the forcible expulsion of minorities (the bulk of the ethnic German population was expelled from Poland, Czechoslovakia, Hungary and Yugoslavia after World War II). Apparently, national cohesion and political democracy has been easier to achieve in societies lacking sizeable minorities, whose integration (or indeed 'separateness') has posed chronic problems for a number of other post-Communist states. By contrast, in Romania, Slovakia, Bulgaria, Ukraine, the Russian Federation, the Baltic states and the former Yugoslavia, tensions over minorities have undoubtedly complicated a possible transition to democracy and constitutionalism.

This is, in many respects, a depressing conclusion. It suggests that democracy and constitutionalism will be slow to develop, or may never develop, in many of the post-Communist states. Even if these countries succeed in overcoming the legacy of the Communist era – political, social and economic infantilization,[106] economic backwardness, pollution etc., they must continue to wrestle with the ghosts of their pre-Communist pasts. For some, these may prove to be altogether more formidable adversaries. Thus, 'the more fundamental trend may be a return to indigenous political traditions'.[107]

[106] Fejtö, *La fin des democraties populaires*, p. 474.
[107] H. Miall, *Shaping the New Europe* (London, Pinter, 1993), p. 71.

Madison and After: the American Model of Political Constitution

STEPHEN L. ELKIN

The United States is different. Unlike most contemporary popular regimes, Americans have taken as central the republican task of designing political institutions that are simultaneously effective means for governing and that limit the exercise of political authority.[1] For many Americans, past and present, this effort has been the touchstone for the legitimacy of the regime. Unlimited government cannot be legitimate government, and weak and ineffective government is of little value. Much more than the citizens of other Western regimes, in their thought and practice Americans have also given private control of productive assets an honoured place. And, again, for many, this has been crucial to any positive evaluation of the regime. A regime without private property cannot be legitimate.

Americans then are committed to a great political experiment. Their founding documents, the pattern of their political speech, and their practices all proclaim that they aspire to be a regime that has its foundations in popular self-government. But, while government is to be popular, it is also to be constitutional, to carry on its business through well-understood and widely approved forms, and towards destinations that respect and foster their desire to be secure in their own persons and to be free to exercise their own powers.

The regime is also to be a commercial one in the sense that republican government is to be combined with an enterprise system which has a substantial private component and which subjects these enterprises to the test of consumer preference through the marketplace. Americans suppose that many of the decisions about how to use society's resources ought to be in the hands of private persons variously organized who will enter into a variety of co-operative and exchange relationships to deploy those resources. Such an economy is thought to facilitate republican government, not least because it will bring prosperity which, in turn, will increase attachment to republican principles.

---

[1] Since the term 'republican' will be used throughout the text, it will help to set out here what I mean by it. By republican I mean to connote that set of historical efforts to create regimes in which the people are to rule and their rule is to consist not of anything they (or more to the point, a majority of them) care to do. What the substance of these limits and the means of giving them life are to be has been the subject of much discussion and there has been much variety in the actual practices aimed at doing so. 'Republican' is to be contrasted with 'civic republican' which is an older doctrine that, whatever else it may be, is not centred on the rule of the people. On these two republicanisms, see the discussion by Thomas Pangle, *The Spirit of Modern Republicanism: the Moral Vision of the Founders and the Philosophy of Locke* (Chicago, University of Chicago Press, 1988). For a view that tends to merge the two see J. G. A. Pocock, *The Machiavellian Moment* (Princeton, University of Princeton Press, 1975).

Commerce is thought to be useful for self-government not a principal source of its subversion. Americans aspire then to be a commercial republic.[2]

What political constitution will give life to these aspirations? What theory of the political constitution of a commercial republican regime should guide Americans in their efforts to realize the regime to which they are committed? The best place to begin an answer is with James Madison's account of such a theory. Those who participate in the founding of some great undertaking are particularly valuable guides to its underlying theory since, in trying to bring about this new enterprise, they will be forced to think in depth about its foundations. What must be changed if we are to proceed, they ask. Unlike those who come after, those present at beginnings have before them the old as a living presence, and the comparison with the new helps to bring a clarity to their thinking. For those who come after such comparisons can only be imaginary.

In the case of Madison, there is a second reason to start with his account of the theory of political constitution. It is simply the most comprehensive and compelling account we have[3] – as well as being the most authoritative in the sense of the one most commonly turned to when Americans seek guidance about how their regime is to work. Madison is both the leading architect of American institutions, and their most persuasive defender.

Madison's account, however, is seriously flawed. My principal concern here is to remedy the flaws by setting out a partial account of what might be called a neo-Madisonian theory. I start with an outline of Madison's theory of political constitution, and then turn to my own neo-Madisonian theory.[4]

The Madisonian Theory and its Flaws

The design of government that Madison proposed has five principal elements: (1) institutions that are designed to prevent faction, particularly majority faction, which Madison believed was the principal disease of popular government; (2) institutions that are designed to promote deliberative ways

---

[2] For some evidence about our aspirations, see Robert Lane, 'Market justice, political justice,' *American Political Science Review*, 80 (1986), 383–402; Herbert McClosky and John Zaller, *The American Ethos: Public Attitudes toward Capitalism and Democracy* (Cambridge, Harvard University Press, 1984); Pamela Johnston Conover *et al.*, 'Duty is a Four Letter Word: Democratic Citizenship in a Liberal Polity' (University of North Carolina, n.d.); and Stephen L. Elkin, *City and Regime in the American Republic* (Chicago, University of Chicago Press, 1987), esp. ch. 6.

[3] Cf. Edmund S. Morgan's comments that 'Madison wrote not only the United States Constitution, or at least most of it, but also the most searching commentary on it that has ever appeared'. 'The Fixers,' *New York Review of Books*, 2 March (1995), 25–27, p. 25.

[4] For a longer account of Madison's theory see the chapter by Richard Bellamy, 'The political form of the constitution: the separation of powers, rights and representative democracy,' in this volume. In my understanding of Madison, I have been helped by the many excellent discussions of his thought, particularly those by Jennifer Nedelsky, *Private Property and the Limits of American Constitutionalism* (Chicago, University of Chicago Press, 1990); Garry Wills, *Explaining America: the Federalist* (Garden City, Doubleday, 1981); David F. Epstein, *The Political Theory of the Federalist* (Chicago, University of Chicago Press, 1984); Joseph Bessette, *The Mild Voice of Reason* (Chicago, University of Chicago Press, 1994); and Marc F. Plattner, 'American democracy and the acquisitive spirit' in Robert Goldwin and William A. Shambra (eds), *How Capitalistic is the Constitution?* (Washington, American Enterprise Institute, 1982). Two recent and thoughtful overviews of his thought can be found in Drew A. McCoy, *The Last of the Fathers: James Madison and the Republican Legacy* (New York, Cambridge University Press, 1989) and Richard K. Matthews, *If Men were Angels: James Madison and the Heartless Empire of Reason* (Lawrence KA, University Press of Kansas, 1995).

of law-making, which are necessary to 'refine'[5] the people's voice; (3) more specifically, institutions that are designed to encourage law-making that gives concrete meaning to a substantive conception of the public interest; (4) a citizenry capable of choosing law-makers who are disposed to deliberate over the concrete meaning of the public interest; and (5) a social basis for the regime, that would make all this possible – in particular, men of property and standing whose self-interest overlaps with the public interest, and who might be induced to take a large view of their interests, thus increasing the overlap.

There are many connections between the various elements, making it an integrated design for a whole regime. Of particular importance is that the prevention of faction is the foundation on which deliberative ways of law-making in the public interest is to rest. The prevention of factional rule opens up the possibility of serving the public interest: it is when law-makers turn away from factional schemes that they can turn to larger interests. Factional politics is understood by Madison to be the underside of a politics of the public interest.

Of the five elements, the first has received the greatest attention by students of Madison's thought. Indeed, for some it constitutes the whole of his constitutional theory. In any case, Madison's account of how to prevent majority factions from controlling governmental authority is persuasive and no more needs to be said here.[6] The last element, the social foundations of the regime is perhaps the most complex since it concerns how and whether class interest can be expanded to correspond to the public interest. I will argue below that Madison's analysis here is not convincing, but in the context of the present chapter, it will not be possible to do more than point to an alternative formulation. The bulk of my account of a neo-Madisonian theory will concern the other three elements.

The most apparent weakness of the Madisonian theory is that we are told that there is a public interest, but its essential dimensions are nowhere systematically set out. Unless one supposes that the public interest is an empty honourific – as Madison plainly does not – if republican law-making is to aim at giving concrete meaning to it, a conception of its broad outlines must be available.

Madison said surprisingly little directly about the content of the public interest, I believe, because he thought that little of a very precise nature *could* be said. The concrete meaning of the public interest at any given moment must reflect the circumstances of law-making. An attempt to spell out the public interest in detail would not only be impossible, since impossibly complex, but also unwise. It would be an effort to bind law-makers without regard to the circumstances in which law-making occurred, and circumstances should sharply influence just how the public interest is to be interpreted.

We must, however, say something about these broad dimensions since, if Madison is correct, we cannot rely on law-makers to search them out. Few law-makers will be statesmen,[7] and so we must rely on institutional design to see that the basic elements of the public interest are regularly brought to the attention of law-makers. Defining the broad dimensions of the public interest is a crucial first step in the theory of political constitution: to design the

---

[5] *The Federalist*, no. 10 in J. E. Cooke (ed.), *The Federalist* (Middletown CT, Wesleyan University Press, 1961).
[6] Again see Bellamy, 'The political form of the constitution'.
[7] *The Federalist*, no. 51.

institutions properly we must know what the elements of the public interest are so that we can engender pressures that will focus law-makers' attention on the right questions. Otherwise, law-making will be bootless or, what is worse, destructive of the public interest.

The flaws in the other three elements are best treated together. Madison hoped there was 'sufficient virtue'[8] among the citizenry to operate a republican government. He was worried that the likely division of the country into those with and without property, which he could see on the horizon, and which already existed to some extent, might overwhelm such virtue. Nevertheless, he said very little directly about citizenship. But it is possible that he gave such limited attention to the matter because he was not sure just how the necessary character of the citizenry might be fostered – at least without the kind of intrusion into the lives of the citizenry that the new republican regime was designed to prevent.[9]

Still, this leaves a substantial hole at the centre of the Madisonian constitutional design. If virtue was not in sufficient supply in the citizenry, how could citizens be relied upon through elections to choose the right law-makers? In particular, how would citizens be able to choose law-makers disposed toward deliberative ways of law-making and concerned with giving meaning to the public interest if they themselves lacked the capacities borne of experience that would enable them to judge these law-makers? However unsettling the thought, the citizens of a commercial republic would seem to need to be in their way as capable as their law-makers.

There is, however, another possibility. Madison may simply have thought that it would be sufficient for republican government if citizens were merely able to choose men of property as law-makers. Citizens would then need virtue, but of a very limited kind, and just enough to vote regularly for the most economically substantial of their fellow citizens.

But this does not solve the problem either. For it will either be the case that not all men of property can be relied upon to rise above a narrow conception of their own interests, and citizens will therefore need to be able to judge which ones can do so. Or, it must be the case that any man of property is as good as any other with regard to the broadness of their conception of the interests of the propertied.

The first possibility simply takes us back to the qualities necessary for citizens to judge their law-makers, where Madison is not a very expansive guide. The second flies in the face of much of what we know about the political behaviour of the propertied in popular regimes. The entire radical critique of popular government has argued that owners of productive assets regularly display the narrowest kinds of self-interest. The burden of this whole literature, confirmed by much empirical analysis, is that across a whole range of issues from the distribution of wealth and income to regulation of markets, those who control productive property cannot be relied upon either to take a large view of their self-interest, or to resist any easy identification of their own immediate well-being and the future of republican government.[10]

---

[8] James Madison, 20 June 1788, as quoted in Ann Stuart Diamond, 'Decent even though democratic,' in R. Goldwin and W. Schambra (eds), *How Democratic is the Constitution?*, p. 38.

[9] Cf. Plattner 'American democracy and the acquisitive spirit'.

[10] See the summing up of this literature in Stephen L. Elkin, 'Business-state relations in the commercial republic,' *Journal of Political Philosophy*, 2, 2 (1994), 115-39.

This view of the question, moreover, is not confined to the liberal and left side of the political spectrum but can also be found on the right. Here we have the panoply of arguments about rent-seeking and the use of public authority by particular interests to use other people's money raised through taxation to make their own lives comfortable.[11] We are thus entitled to wonder about the degree to which the owners of productive assets have, in fact, risen above a relatively narrow conception of their interests – not to mention whether they have been custodians of republican government.

The curious thing in all this is that Madison understood the dangers that a system of private property posed for republican government. It formed the basis for the most worrying kind of factional conflict in a republic, that between the propertied and the propertyless. In saying this, Madison implicitly conceded that the propertied could be just as much a faction as those without it. While the electoral system might prevent a minority from successfully pursuing factional schemes,[12] there remains the question of just what would prompt the propertied to enlarge their conception of their own interests. On this question, Madison is of less help than he might be.

Here is the crucial weakness in the Madisonian theory. He did not see that it was fundamental to the success of a commercial republic that the citizenry have the ability to distinguish those who would be public-spirited law-makers from hacks – there being no reason to assume that all men of property would fall into the first category. Moreover, even the most publicly-inclined men of property would need to be induced actually to act on their broad inclinations, in short to engage in deliberative ways of law-making aimed at giving concrete meaning to the public interest.

A Neo-Madisonian Theory of Political Constitution

The key to the constitution of a republican regime is an account of its public interest, the serving of which is the purpose of the institutions and dominant strata that give the regime direction. We must be able to say something substantive about this public interest to be confident that deliberatively-minded law-makers have something to deliberate about. More specifically, if we are to design a set of institutions whose workings will give concrete meaning to the broad dimensions of the public interest, we must know what they are. What these broad purposes call for in particular cases is a contingent matter and must be a product of the practical reasoning these institutions must foster.

What are the fundamental dimensions of the public interest? In answering, I will draw from Madison's discussion of a commercial republican constitution those features of the public interest that his analysis suggests, even if he himself was unwilling or unable to make them explicit.

---

[11] The canonical text is probably George Stigler, *The Citizen and the State* (Chicago, University of Chicago Press, 1975). See also the broad survey by Peter H. Aranson and Peter C. Ordeshook in Roger Benjamin and Stephen L. Elkin (eds), *The Democratic State* (Lawrence KS, The University Press of Kansas, 1985). See also my introductory essay in that volume 'Between liberalism and capitalism: an introduction to the democratic state'.

[12] Although even here there is reason to be uneasy about Madison's formulations. As Lindblom has argued, the privileged position of business operates outside of electoral control. See his *Politics and Markets* (New York, Basic, 1977).

If we follow Madison, one certain element of the public is that government should secure civil, political and property rights.[13] To do so is not simply a matter of subjecting government to strict limits, as if government itself were the enemy of the liberty that these rights define. To the contrary, the enemy of liberty is not government *per se* but tyrannical (or weak) government. Moreover, it may take considerable exertions of governmental authority to secure rights.[14] Thus, the problem for the public interest is to define the kinds of actions government must take to make rights a concrete reality in the day to day life of the society.

In addition, given Madison's concern for the prevention of factional rule, it seems plausible that he would be concerned about the extent of private power. Such concern is, of course, evident in contemporary arguments about powerful special interests, and particularly about business power. Popular government is just as much in danger from powerful private interests as it is from arbitrary actions by officials or majorities who bend public authority to their will. The public cannot only subvert the private but the private can corrupt the public.

Beyond these two aspects of the public interest, we may be reasonably certain that Madison at least acquiesced in Hamilton's judgment that law-making in the public interest must foster a commercial society. Commerce was to be the engine for the prosperity that he thought both valuable in itself and necessary for the stability of the republic.[15] At a minimum, this means that republican law-making should aim to promote material prosperity through an organization of wealth production that has a significant role for private ownership of productive assets and for markets.[16] On balance, law-making should support and encourage private ownership of these productive assets. Among other things, this means taking account of the fact that, if there is to be significant material prosperity, controllers of productive assets must have considerable discretion in how to deploy them. Without such discretion, they are unlikely to invest at a level that will promote significant and widespread material prosperity.[17]

Not only will controllers of productive assets need discretion, they will also need stability in the rules governing economic life. A central purpose of a commercial republic is wide-spread prosperity, and without stable expectations among asset-holders on the content of economic rules, this is unlikely to be achieved. Whatever else those with capital need, they need some sense of what the near-term future will bring. If they cannot form reasonable expectations about the near future, they cannot plan. And if they are even modestly rational, they will not then entertain even relatively small costs for such uncertain future gains.

[13] See *The Federalist*, no. 10; see also Nedelsky, *Private Property and the Limits of American Constitutionalism*, esp. ch. 5.

[14] *The Federalist*, no. 37. See also, Herbert Storing, 'The constitution and the Bill of Rights' in Robert Goldwin and William Schambra (eds), *How does the Constitution secure Rights?* (Washington, American Enterprise Institute, 1985).

[15] *The Federalist*, nos 11, 12 and 30.

[16] I here draw freely on my 'The constitution of a good society: the case of the commercial republic' in Karol E. Soltan and Stephen L. Elkin (eds), *The Constitution of Good Societies* (University Park, Penn State Press, forthcoming).

[17] See Lindblom, *Politics and Markets*, esp. ch. 13 and Adam Przeworski, *Capitalism and Social Democracy* (New York, Cambridge University Press, 1985), ch. 4. Cf. Elkin, *City and Regime in the American Republic*, ch. 7.

Stability of rules, however, cannot mean simply strengthening the ones that happen to exist at present. Those who run businesses are upholders of profits not competition, and they will naturally enough argue for the sanctity of the existing rules under which they have fattened their pocketbooks. Those businessmen who seek to innovate and those who have yet to appear on the scene may thus face considerable obstacles. Republican law-making, while it must certainly aim at promoting economic prosperity in the present time period, also must, if it is to promote long-term prosperity, enact laws that keep paths open for new businesses and new techniques. Republican law-making should aim at facilitating the commercial activity of all who have the means and desire to participate.

There is at least one other component of the commercial dimension of the public interest. A well-functioning commercial republic should be composed of a citizenry all of whose able-bodied members are able to secure at least modest levels of economic welfare through remunerative work. This extends the thought behind Publius' (Hamilton and Madison's) argument that a commercial society is necessary for republican government: the fruits of economic growth should not be available only to a few, and economic production should not be in the service of creating an oligarchy with the status of an aristocracy.[18]

The law of commerce in a republican regime is not a grant of wholesale power to government officials to promote widespread prosperity any way they choose. The means to be employed are limited by the components of the public interest – for example that prosperity is to be largely promoted through relying, for the most part, on private control of productive assets where controllers of these assets have considerable discretion in their use.

The law of commerce, moreover, is not law for the express purpose of promoting the fortunes of businessmen – at least not the fortunes of present ones to the exclusion of those to come, and not the fortunes of businessmen present or future to the exclusion of others who can help create wide-spread prosperity. More generally, law cannot be used as a means of creating a society built around inherited economic privilege if it is to be commercial republican law. It is in the service of republican government and is in this sense political law not economic law.

There is yet one additional dimension of the public interest. The central features of republican regimes are that they are regimes of limited powers where the limitations are defined by the manner in which rights are to be secured, private power regulated and a commercial society promoted. The purposes and the concomitant limitation on governmental power define the regime: if we wish for a republic we must value these concerns, and it is in their constitutive nature that the warrant is to be found for treating them as part of the public interest. Such purposes and limits, however, cannot exhaust the public interest. We can be reasonably certain that the ability to secure rights, to limit private power and to promote a commercial society through a limited exercise of public authority – that is, to set out a compelling account of the public interest –cannot be taken for granted. The kinds of institutions that are able to do so must not only be created but maintained, their foundations made secure.

---

[18] See the discussion in Elkin, *City and Regime in the American Republic*, ch. 6.

Otherwise said, if we desire a regime able to serve the public interest as I have defined it, we must also desire a regime whose institutions are capable of giving concrete meaning to its components: to desire the ends is to desire the means. It cannot be any other way. Unless the institutions that are to give concrete meaning to the public interest are well-suited to the task it cannot be served. The public interest of the regime includes, therefore, the creating and maintaining of the institutions that are authorized to give the public interest concrete meaning. The public interest thus has a reflexive component – it requires the active use of public authority to create and maintain the ability of authoritative institutions to reason about the meaning of the public interest.

It would be odd indeed if something like this were not part of the public interest of a republican regime, or if indeed it did not have any. What it takes to realize regimes is surely a considerable part of their public interest. Indeed it is difficult to see what else the public interest could consist of than the mix of regime purposes and the securing of the institutions that give the regime the ability to more or less successfully pursue those purposes.[19]

To determine what those institutions are for a republican regime, and how they are to work, would require extensive discussion of the competence of courts and legislatures and of the character of practical and legal reasoning. But if it is accepted that not all the work of defining limits on the exercise of public and private power can be done by courts – a point I will make in a moment – then some of the work must be done by the legislature. This, in turn, will mean that the legislature must be capable of reasoning about the content of the public interest – which leads to the question: what will enable the legislature to so act? A part of the answer is likely to be that the citizenry must have certain abilities or virtues, again a point that I will come to. Here I only want to say that the fostering of such a citizenry is an essential component of the public interest of a republican regime.

The problem for law-making in the public interest is to tie the exercise of governmental power to a conception of specific governmental purposes. By delineating those purposes the concept of the public interest that I have set out defines the appropriate exercise of political authority for such an active, limited government. Indeed, it is difficult to see how else, except through such a conception of the public interest, the ideas of active and limited government can be combined. In a well-functioning republican regime, at any given moment law-making gives specific meaning to the limits on governmental authority by giving firm definition to the public interest.

The public interest as I have defined it is capacious. A narrowly conceived one could hardly serve in any complex and heterogeneous society. But capacious does not mean empty. The public interest is broad enough to invite discussion and clear enough to indicate what kind of arguments are appropriate in defining its concrete meaning. Thus it is plain that arguments for the passage of a law that simply assert that it serves the interests of major constituencies are

---

[19] A parallel argument has been made by both Samuel Huntington and Bernard Crick. Huntington comments that 'the capacity to create political institutions is the capacity to create public interests' and 'the public interest is the interest of public institutions'. Samuel P. Huntington, *Political Order in Changing Societies* (New Haven, Yale University Press, 1968), pp. 24, 25. Crick says that the public interest is simply a way of 'describing the common interest in preserving the means of making public decisions politically'. Bernard Crick, *In Defense of Politics* (Chicago, University of Chicago Press, 1972), p. 177.

not arguments in the public interest, nor are arguments that all those affected by the law should receive something like equal benefits.

Thus, while there is no single right answer to the appropriate content of the public interest there are wrong ones. The public interest points to the kind of reasons that are to count in law-making. It is not then an empty phrase, invoked whenever we wish to argue for the use of public authority for reasons that are not in themselves likely to be convincing.

There is no presumption in my discussion of the public interest that it is free of internal conflicts. There will, for example, probably be conflicts between the discretion that asset-controllers need and the economic foundations of republican citizenship. Nor is there any presumption that there are no difficulties in giving concrete meaning to the public interest, or that the institutions that are to give it content will find it politically easy to do so. These are real difficulties, and designing institutions to meet them is a principal task of the theory of political constitution of a commercial republic.

Finally, the various elements of the public interest have such a status because they concern the defining purposes of a republican regime or because they are necessary to making the regime work in crucial ways. They are valuable then quite apart from whether their value is widely recognized by the citizenry. They are in the interests of citizens just to the degree they wish for a republican regime – even though they may be unable to say what that entails. These interests are then public interests not because they are held in common by the citizenry but because they are intrinsic to the workable commercial republican regime to which the citizens aspire. Republican government may be popular government but it certainly is not a simple majoritarian regime nor a regime that takes its bearings from what the people say they want at any given moment.

Republican Citizenship and the Regime's Social Foundations

I have argued that once an adequate conception of the public interest is set out, the rest of the constitutional design will fall into place – for we now have guidance on how governmental institutions must be organized. And once the institutional design is laid out, the features that a republican citizenry must have will also be apparent.

Given the public interest as I have defined it, how should republican law-making be organized? For a start, it must be deliberative in form. It is difficult to see how else the broadly defined public interest can be given meaningful expression. If law-making is anything other than deliberative – for example, organized around bargaining – the public interest can only be served by chance, as an accidental by-product of the bargaining. Similarly, if the broad contours of the public interest are to be given concrete meaning, this can only be accomplished through the exercise of practical reason, in short through deliberation.

Given the requirement of deliberation, and that the public interest includes securing a variety of rights and limiting the exercise of governmental power, it might be sensible for the people as constituent sovereign to deputize the Supreme Court and other courts to act as its agents – telling them what the concrete meaning of the public interest is, and when their agents chosen through elections violate it. Courts are good at deliberation and since the public interest defines limits on republican law-making, courts should be its principal custodian.

But unless it is supposed that the only limits that are worth caring about are ones that courts are likely to feel comfortable talking about, the legislature too must be capable of deliberative ways of law-making. Specifically, since the public interest includes promoting a commercial society with all that entails – even the staunchest defenders of courts as the principal custodian of the public interest will not find it easy to claim a strong competence for them here. The various dimensions of the public interest are, in fact, intertwined. For example, the question of the appropriate limits on the use of public power to promote or command private behaviour intersects with that of how best to promote widespread economic prosperity. Few will doubt that promoting prosperity is the province of legislatures rather than courts. If this is conceded, then so must the claim that the legislature must have a significant role in defining the limits on the exercise of public power.

Thus, in the effort to give concrete meaning to the public interest, consideration of the full range of its components must be undertaken not only by courts but by the legislature. We can go further and say that neither Court nor President can do their job in law-making unless they have as an interlocutor a legislature that can respond to arguments made by either of the other branches. A central problem then in the design of the American regime is how to ensure that the legislature engages in deliberative ways of law-making – not to the exclusion of other modes of law-making, but at least on those occasions when the public interest is at issue.[20] If the legislature is to do so, then representatives must be capable of arguing about how the dimensions of the public interest are to be brought to bear in particular choices.

How shall this be accomplished? It will help to think of the legislature as a school in which law-makers learn the arts of political reasoning. In thinking of the legislature in this fashion, it will be apparent that for the school to work properly it will require the right pupils, ones disposed to learn the arts appropriate to deliberative ways of law-making. Such pupils must of course be chosen by the citizenry, and this means that at the heart of the politics of a republican regime must be a citizenry capable of choosing the right sort of law-makers.

What sort of a citizenry must they be? In its most general form, the question is what will ensure that republican citizens are able to identify those who will see law-making as something more than an occasion for the assertion of particular interests. Two capacities are crucial: citizens must be able to judge whether those seeking office are inclined to deliberative ways of law-making in the service of the public interest; and they must be acquainted with the broad contours of the public interest. These are equally important since republican law-makers are not only to deliberate but to reason about specific matters, the

---

[20] It is not possible here to consider the content of such a distinction, but in a complex society, indeed plausibly in any modern society, there will be many matters that, for one reason or another – including some quite bad ones – become the subject of law-making but which have little bearing on the public interest of the regime. For such matters, it seems eminently reasonable to have them decided by various devices that simply aggregate whatever preferences law-makers – and, by extension, citizens – happen to have, including ones that are narrowly self-interested. But a significant part of law-making will indeed consider matters in which the content of the public interest is at stake, and it is here that deliberative ways of law-making are needed.

concrete meaning of the public interest. Here, however, I will only consider the citizenry's ability to judge whether law-makers are deliberatively minded – what I shall term the citizenry's public-spiritedness.[21]

Public-spiritedness is a disposition to give significant weight to the public interest. It is conspicuously not and probably cannot be what throwbacks to ancient republicanism such as Sam Adams and Benjamin Rush called for. Adams said 'a Citizen owes everything to the Commonwealth'[22] while Rush commented that every young man in a true republic must be 'taught that he does not belong to himself, but that he is public property'.[23] Public-spiritedness consists of the not very demanding belief that there *is* a public interest and that political life should devote significant effort to giving it concrete meaning.

As good a formulation as we have of the nature of public-spiritedness in a commercial republic is given by Judith Shklar:

> Active citizens keep informed and speak out against measures that they regard as unjust, unwise, or just too expensive ... Although they do not refrain from pursuing their own or their reference group's interests, they try to weigh the claims of other people impartially and listen carefully to their arguments. They ... serve their country ... by having a considered notion of the public good that they genuinely take to heart.[24]

I will only add that educating republican citizens to a concern for the public interest must be centred in local political life. Thus, a crucial part of the political constitution of the American regime must be a design for local government that, through carefully structured and wide-spread political participation, allows citizens to gain experience of giving concrete meaning to the public interest. Without the experience of deliberation citizens cannot reliably choose law-makers who are disposed to pursue deliberative ways of law-making.[25]

On the social basis of the regime, Madison teaches that a regime is not just composed of institutions, but is also rooted in a particular social strata whose self-interest is such that it can plausibly be expanded to encompass at least some aspects of the larger public interest. I have indicated that his reliance on the propertied as the social foundation for this self-interest is suspect.

Where then shall we look? It is worth considering the long-standing argument that for popular government to be successful it must be government rooted in the middle-class, and conducted with serious regard to their well-being. The argument can be sharpened by posing a series of questions. Will a confident and

[21] I have discussed how citizens might learn the broad substance of the public interest in 'Citizen and city: locality, public-spiritedness and the American regime' in Martha Derthick (ed.), *Local Self-Government* (Washington, The Woodrow Wilson Center of the Smithsonian Institution, forthcoming).
[22] Adams to Caleb Davis, 3 April, 1781. In Harry Alonzo Cushing (ed.), *The Writings of Samuel Adams* (New York, 1904–1908), vol. 4, p. 255.
[23] As quoted in Gordon Wood, *The Creation of the American Republic, 1776–1787* (New York, Norton, 1972), p. 427.
[24] J. Shklar, *American Citizenship: the Quest for Inclusion* (Cambridge, Harvard University Press, 1991), p. 5. Shklar goes on to say that what she calls 'ideal citizens' have 'no serious interests apart from public activity; they live in and for the forum'. She further comments that 'these perfected citizens are sometimes thought to be healthier and more fulfilled than people who are indifferent to politics, but there is little medical proof of such a proposition'. (p. 11).
[25] For a discussion of this whole matter see Elkin, *City and Regime in the American Republic*, esp. chs 8–9.

secure middle-class support the discretion that controllers of productive assets need if there is to be wide-spread prosperity through remunerative work? Can the middle class be induced to devote its political energies to seeing that the public interest is not reduced to giving controllers of productive assets what they say they need if they are to invest? More comprehensively, can the middle-class be reliably induced to give due regard to the foundations of the commercial republic in the activities of private controllers of productive assets while also being concerned to limit their discretion where it is necessary to serve the public interest? There are similar questions to be asked about other dimensions of the public interest. The general question is, can ways be devised that will expand and harness the self-interest of the middle-class such that they will be better custodians of the public interest than the holders of large-scale property have proved to be? And can a secure and confident middle-class make itself the centre of a majority coalition that will govern the American republic?

Conclusion

Most of the regimes that compose the democratic West are more statist in orientation, less worried about the limits of state power and more inclined to see the possibilities for its beneficent use than the commercial republic Americans aspire to be. The principal burden of political talk in such regimes falls, not on individual citizens or even on interest groups, but on the political parties whose proposals and counter-proposals, criticisms and replies are the principal stuff of day-to-day politics. Discussion of citizenship in these regimes generally revolves around citizens acting as voters who select which party shall rule, and the various kinds of benefactions and rights that citizens are entitled to. The idea of citizens as such – as opposed to citizens organized in and speaking through parties – playing a significant role in political life is not a major concern.

By contrast, a commercial republican constitution requires deliberative ways of law-making resting on the base of a citizenry with sufficient virtue to choose law-makers disposed and able to give concrete meaning to the public interest. It is in doing so that government in republican regimes is limited. The people limit their own rule by authorizing their agents, the branches of government defined by the constitution, to give concrete meaning to the public interest.

In a republican government the people must be a *self-limiting* popular sovereign. They must devise or have devised for them ways to limit their own rule so that popular government is not arbitrary and tyrannical. Here is the key to the kind of politics such regimes need, and thus to the design of their institutions and, more broadly, of their constitution. They need a self-limiting popular sovereign capable of practical reasoning. And the legislature must be a significant domain for its exercise: the legislature is where popular rule meets the problem of limits through an effort to define the public interest.

With these features of the political constitution in mind, friends of the American commercial republic must seek to repair the deficiencies in the Madisonian design. They must somehow continue the work that Madison helped to start – repairing what has declined, completing what has been left incomplete, and revising what was improperly designed at the beginning. They must do *in media res* what Madison (and his colleagues) did in the founding period. In the broadest sense, the great question is whether the people acting through the organs of self-reflection that they themselves have created (or at least consented to) can secure and strengthen the foundations of a commercial republican regime. This is a journey – a democratic journey – that has the quality about it of a self-levitating act. And being so precarious an exercise, there is no guarantee of success.

Republican government is a difficult taskmaster. It asks a great deal from ordinary people as citizens and when they become law-makers. The underlying tension in such a regime is the pressure to attend to the interests and problems of the citizenry without allowing the unlimited exercise of political power. This tension is not only real but necessary since the very promise of a republican regime is that it will pay due regard to both – being responsive to popular will and sensitive to why and how it should be limited.

Economical Constitutions

GEOFFREY BRENNAN AND ALAN HAMLIN

Introduction

The idea of an economical constitution is not self evident. The major task of this introduction must therefore be to offer and briefly defend a particular interpretation of this idea. The major task of the remainder of the chapter is then to provide an account of the primary constitutional mechanisms that may be employed within an 'economical constitution', the operating characteristics of these mechanisms, and the potential indirect and interaction effects associated with mechanisms of different types.[1] Our general purpose is to set out and recommend an economical approach to constitutional analysis which modifies the orthodox economic strategy in order to accommodate a range of concerns which, we believe, are important in the constitutional context. The orthodox economic approach's inability to address these concerns has led some non-economists to dismiss the economic approach altogether as an unsatisfactory basis for constitutional analysis. We believe that this dismissal is too hasty, although we concede that some economists' claims for the success of the orthodox economic approach have equally been too extreme. In this way we hope to suggest to economists that some revision of their basic approach is appropriate if they are to develop a fully rounded constitutional analysis, and to non-economists that the economic approach, thus revised, provides a powerful and appropriate basis for the analysis of constitutional design and reform.

A preliminary distinction to be made is that between an economical constitution and an economic constitution. An economic constitution is concerned with the constitutional and institutional structure of the economy and, perhaps, of economic policy. Thus, an economic constitution might specify the procedures and institutions involved in wage determination, or in the setting of interest rate policy. By contrast, the term 'economical constitution' is intended to refer to an economic approach to the general problem of constitutional design. It is not the domain of the constitution that is at issue, but rather the mode of argument used to analyse questions of constitutional design and the principles that are invoked to judge alternative constitutions.[2] An economical constitution, first and foremost, is a constitution that is derived

---

[1] We shall take for granted the general importance of the constitutional perspective in this chapter. We offer arguments in support of this view in G. Brennan and A. P. Hamlin 'Constitutional political economy: the political philosophy of *Homo economicus*?', *Journal of Political Philosophy*, 3, 3 (1995), 280–303. For related recent arguments which do not derive from an economic perspective see S. L. Elkin and K. E. Soltan (eds), *A New Constitutionalism* (Chicago, University of Chicago Press, 1993).

[2] Of course, an economical approach to constitutional design may involve an economic constitution, as in G. Brennan and J. M. Buchanan, *The Power to Tax* (Cambridge, Cambridge University Press, 1980), but equally an economic constitution may derive from non-economical arguments.

using the analytical apparatus and general approach of economics and the intellectual tradition it represents. In further establishing the idea of an economical constitution, we need to say a little more about both what we take to be included in the general domain of the constitutional, and the nature of the analytic and evaluative principles involved in the economical approach to constitutional design. We shall take each in turn.

By a constitution we mean to identify the set of institutions, procedures and practices which structure society, empowering and constraining the actions of agents. This is a deliberately broad interpretation of the constitution, and is certainly not limited to the idea of an explicit, written constitution even where such a document may exist. In particular, we would include within the constitutional domain social norms, conventions and other informal rules. We would also include rules which might be thought of as relating directly to social outcomes as well as the procedures and institutions which operate to generate in-period outcomes. The distinction between outcome and procedure orientated constitutional provisions may be illustrated by the contrast between a constitutional requirement for a balanced government budget, and a constitutional requirement for government tax and expenditure decisions to be made by a specified voting rule.

The general point here is that the range and form of the constitution should emerge from principled argument rather than from *a priori* stipulation. Of course, there are limits on what may be feasible, but beyond these limits, a constitution may lie anywhere on the continuum from the extreme case of an empty constitution – where there is essentially no attempt to structure society so that the resultant in-period situation is that of a state of nature – to the opposite extreme case of a fully constraining constitution – where the constitution attempts to foresee every possible social situation and prescribe the action of each agent so that all in-period decision making is pre-empted.

The normative stance adopted in the economical approach is based on a value theory that is both individualist and subjectivist; so that good is defined in terms of the achievement of individual ends – whatever they may be.[3] This is standard enough in welfare economic theory, but the shift from the in-period debate, which is the primary concern of welfare economics, to the constitutional debate reflects a shift from the traditional utilitarianism of welfare economics to the more contractarian stance of Constitutional Political Economy, where conceptual agreement amongst individuals is the appropriate test for evaluating alternative institutional arrangements.[4]

In terms of analytic method, the economical approach again builds on two relatively standard aspects of general economic methodology in a slightly non-standard way. The standard ingredients in this case are a mild form of methodological individualism, on which we will not comment further here,[5] and

---

[3] For further details of the points to be made in the next few paragraphs see Brennan and Hamlin, 'Constitutional political economy' and references therein.

[4] Conceptual agreement here is intended to reflect the idea that the contractarian criterion picks out those arrangements which no one could reasonably reject as a basis for informed and voluntary general agreement. See T. M. Scanlon, 'Contractualism and utilitarianism' in A. K. Sen and B. Williams (eds), *Utilitarianism and Beyond* (Cambridge, Cambridge University Press, 1982).

[5] For a discussion of alternative forms of methodological individualism which identifies the mild form relevant here see A. P. Hamlin and P. Pettit 'The normative analysis of the state' in A. P. Hamlin and P. Pettit (eds), *The Good Polity* (Oxford, Basil Blackwell, 1989).

a characterization of the motivational psychology of the rational individual, which will be the focus of some further comment since it is in this area that we wish to depart from what might be considered the economic orthodoxy.

Our characterization of the motivation of rational individuals portrays them as single-minded, not necessarily entirely selfish, and heterogeneous in their basic values and dispositions. The individual is single-minded in that the basic motivational structure of the individual agent is viewed as constant across institutional settings, at least in the short term. For example, agents do not shift from being selfish to being public spirited *simply* by virtue of changing the institutional setting in which they are placed. Of course, it is logically possible that institutions interact with the uniform motivational structure to produce different patterns of behaviour in different institutional settings, and such interaction may occur at a variety of levels. But changes in the social outcomes wrought by institutional change must be deduced from the analysis, not merely assumed as part of the axiomatic structure. Note that we do *not* intend that individuals should be seen as 'single-minded' in the sense that they have monistic value structures. We leave open the question of the content of individuals' values, and the possibility that their values may not be reducible to a single value. All that we intend by taking individuals to be single-minded is that their values and preferences, however complex their structure and whatever their detailed content, are not themselves institution specific.

Given our comment on the possibly complex structure of any individual's values, it should be clear that we make no presumption that the individual is entirely selfish. While self interest is taken to be a relevant aspect of motivation for all agents, it is not assumed to be the only relevant aspect.

If the abandonment of the essentially self-regarding nature of *homo economicus* identifies one way in which our approach departs from economic orthodoxy, our second departure involves the introduction of motivational heterogeneity, so that the structure of values, motivations and dispositions is taken to vary from individual to individual. Of course, even the most orthodox economist allows of some heterogeneity of tastes and preferences within a structure of self-regarding utility maximization. But the heterogeneity that we have in mind is much more radical than a simple variety of tastes. We wish to allow individuals to differ in their most basic values and dispositions, so that while some may be essentially self-regarding maximizers, others may be motivated by some particular conception of the public interest, and others may be disposed to act according to some particular conception of duty. In short, we wish to introduce a wide range of moral characters into an otherwise economic analysis.

Our reason for departing from economic orthodoxy in these ways is derived from a concern to extend the scope of economic analysis to include a range of ideas which are relatively familiar in the literature on constitutional politics and which seem to us to be central to any rounded constitutional analysis. Chief among these ideas are the Madisonian concerns[6] to view constitutions in terms of the design of institutions which strike a balance between the limitation of government powers, the expression of political opinion through processes of deliberation and representation which refine private opinions and select the most virtuous for office, and the maintenance of an environment which

---

[6] See the discussions by Richard Bellamy and Stephen Elkin elsewhere in this collection.

encourages individuals to participate in politics in an appropriate spirit. While an entirely orthodox economic analysis of constitutional design can easily recognize the first of these three elements, and can provide valuable insights into means by which power may be constrained, it must fail to provide an account of the second and third elements, since it cannot recognize the relevant categories. As a result, economists will tend to an unbalanced portrayal of the role of constitutions, while non-economists will tend to dismiss the economists efforts as missing the point. We believe that an economical approach to constitutions of the type outlined here may avoid both of these results.

Any economical approach to constitutional design begins with the study of alternative institutional structures as settings for individually rational action. Given that the value theory underlying the economical approach identifies collective benefit with the achievement of individual ends, it is clear that any mismatch between individually rational action and collectively beneficial outcomes must arise from the nature of the interaction between individuals. This is simply to say that in a Robinson Crusoe society of a single individual, private rational action must, trivially, also be socially beneficial. Once inter-actions are introduced, an additional element comes into play. Social outcomes are now determined in part by the structure of the interactions. Thus, whether a particular interaction promotes collectively beneficial outcomes or not is, in part, a matter of the specification of the rules of that interaction. These rules serve two distinct roles. The first role is to combine individual actions to produce social outcomes. But these same rules also act as the background conditions which allow the identification of individual rational action in that interaction. Different institutional rules will invoke different behaviour, and will also change the mapping from individual behaviour to social outcomes.

Interactions can usefully be divided into two broad classes, one in which individuals interact directly with one another to produce outcomes, and one in which the interaction is structured in such a way that the individuals act indirectly through appointed agents. This second class of interaction corresponds to the principal-agent structure, and we will focus most of our attention on such principal-agent structures, although much of what we say can also be applied to direct interactions which might be modelled in game theoretic terms.

Cutting across this distinction between principal-agent structures and direct interactions, several classes of institution may be identified by reference to the manner in which they structure interactions between individuals. We wish to pick out three such types of institutional mechanisms as being especially important, both because they illustrate the variety of institutional mechanisms at the disposal of the economical constitutionalist, and because we believe that these three mechanisms – acting individually or in various combinations – provide an analytic vocabulary which allows fruitful analysis of a very wide range of constitutional and institutional issues.

The institutional form most obviously associated with the economic approach to constitutional design is the market. Indeed, some commentators seem to suggest that the market is the only institutional form which might be supported by economical argument, so that the economical approach to constitutional design is taken to be no more and no less than an appeal for the further marketization of social life. By contrast, we wish to argue that economical arguments can pick out rather different institutional mechanisms in more general contexts. Economical arguments can point to a variety of institutional mechanisms which may act and interact in ways that are not normally associated with the market. Furthermore, we wish to argue that economical argument is not confined to a single vision of social and political life, but can make sense of a number of aspects of social life which might, at first sight, seem remote from economic ideas.

The institution of the perfectly competitive market is supported by (at least) three lines of argument, which we intend to distinguish so as to argue for (at least) three distinct classes of institutional mechanisms, each of which reflects a different aspect of the economical approach to constitutional design. The three lines of argument to be studied may be termed the sanctioning argument, the screening argument and the summative argument. The next three sections will elaborate on each in turn, before viewing possible interactions between the three types of institutional mechanism and offering some final comments.

Sanctioning Mechanisms

The sanctioning argument is perhaps the most obvious of the three to be considered and is probably what most people have in mind when they hear of the economic approach to institutional and constitutional design. It is certainly the argument stressed in the orthodox economic analysis of constitutions. Essentially, the sanctioning argument stresses the role of positive and negative private incentives in the decision calculus of individual agents, and so stresses the design of institutions which offer or reinforce such incentive structures. Examples of the economical analysis of institutional mechanisms that appeal primarily to the sanctions or incentives argument include the analysis of competitive democratic elections, and the range of models which stress the principal-agent structure of many political and social institutions.[7]

The basic strategy of all sanctioning mechanisms is to structure the inter-action between individuals in such a way that, for each individual who is party to the interaction, there is a positive correlation between the perceived private benefits accruing to the actor and the spillover benefits accruing to other individuals. This is no simple matter, not least because both the private and the spillover benefits associated with a particular action by a specific individual will often depend on the actions taken by others. Nevertheless, the broad strategy is clear enough. Within this broad strategy we wish to identify two forms of incentive mechanisms of particular relevance in a principal-agent setting, one based on *ex ante* competition and the other on *ex post* monitoring. Although these two will often work together, they work in rather different ways and in rather different circumstances.

The *ex ante* competition form of an incentive mechanism is most easily illustrated with a simple economic example. Suppose that a society must appoint someone to operate a fresh water spring which forms the only source of water to a community. Wary of the obvious threat of monopoly power and high water prices, the society allocates the right to operate the spring by a

[7] For a survey of economical models of the election process see P. J. Coughlin, 'Majority rule and election models', *Journal of Economic Surveys*, 3 (1990), 157–88. For an example of the analysis of a political institution in a principal-agent framework see B. R. Weingast, 'The congressional-bureaucratic system: a principal-agent perspective', *Public Choice*, 44 (1984), 147–92.

competitive auction, with candidates asked to bid for the right in terms of the price that they will charge for the water. The force of competition in this *ex ante* auction is to provide each bidder with a private incentive to reduce the price in an attempt to increase the probability of winning the operating licence. Under ideal circumstances, this type of *ex ante* competition will yield an outcome identical to the outcome that would be realized in a fully competitive market for water. But whether circumstances are ideal or not, the competition among bidders will tend to result in a lower price than would have prevailed in the absence of competitive tendering of this kind.

There are clear links from this simple story to the analysis of competitive elections, in which rival candidates offer commitments to the electorate in terms of specific policy platforms in an attempt to maximize their probability of election. Such a contest will, in ideal conditions, operate in much the same manner as a competitive market, with each candidate facing a private incentive to offer a platform that is collectively beneficial. But what are the 'ideal conditions' that are required for *ex ante* competition of this type to operate well? Most importantly for our present discussion, these conditions include the requirements that all relevant parties are reasonably well informed and that candidates are able to make credible commitments concerning their future actions.

The significance of the requirement for relatively full information can be illustrated in the context of our simple spring water example. If there is uncertainty about the true costs of operating the spring but all potential bidders have the same information and are risk averse, we would not expect bidders to be willing to offer prices as low as those that would emerge from a competitive market, since this would involve the risk of a loss. In these circumstances, prices (and profits) will be higher under *ex ante* competition than under market competition. However, if potential bidders have different expectations about the costs of the enterprise we might expect the bidder with the most optimistic view of potential profits to win the auction at a price that is below the competitive price and which involves losses to the firm – this is the idea of the 'winners curse'. As a final example of the potential impact of uncertainty or incomplete information, if there is uncertainty about the quality of the water to be supplied, and quality is costly to the operator, candidates may face an incentive to bid prices and quality down below the socially efficient levels in the *ex ante* auction. Of course, these difficulties with *ex ante* competition can be overcome in principle. Candidates might be offered some form of insurance against unforeseen cost variations; or candidates may be asked to commit to quality levels as well as prices. But complicating the structure in these ways is likely to introduce further difficulties.

The ability to commit to specified future action is also important in establishing the effectiveness of *ex ante* competitive mechanisms. If candidates cannot effectively commit themselves to future pricing policies, their promises will not be credible and will imply no real constraint on their post auction behaviour. If commitment is not possible, it may still be possible to generate the effect of *ex ante* competition through the discipline of continuous trading. Even if in a single auction of the type discussed the candidates will have no reason to honour their promised pricing policy, such a reason can be provided by repeating the auction at intervals. In this repeated version of the story, the winning candidate will have a reason to honour price pledges to the extent that any attempt to deviate from this strategy is expected to imply losing the licence at the next auction. Again this argument has a clear link to the analysis of elections, with the repeated nature of electoral competition reinforcing the incentive to deliver policies that are promised. We should also note that the commitment problem may be two-sided. In our example, it is not only the bidders that need to commit to pricing policies, but also the government which needs to commit to its side of the bargain by allowing the winning firm to operate that pricing policy without further intervention.

The alternative to *ex ante* competition as a source of appropriate incentive structures is *ex post* monitoring. Imagine a government agency (a civil service department, perhaps) populated by individuals presumed to be privately motivated. The task facing citizens is then to design an institutional structure which will ensure that the agency acts in the public interest. One obvious possibility is to construct a system of personal advancement and promotion within the agency which rewards activity of the relevant type. If individual activity can be monitored and rewarded in this way, it is clear that this institutional structure will act as an incentive mechanism with private and spillover benefits showing the required positive correlation. We require no public motivation on the part of the civil servants, indeed the more privately ambitious they are, the better the public performance of the agency. But we do require that monitoring is possible, and this in turn requires that we can distinguish 'good' actions from 'bad' actions; that we can associate actions with individuals; and that those that reward/punish are themselves appropriately monitored and rewarded. If any of these conditions breaks down, our ability to design and operate a satisfactory monitoring and incentive system will be reduced and, in the limit, destroyed.

Sanctioning mechanisms – whether based on *ex ante* competition, *ex post* monitoring, or some combination of the two – can be relatively subtle in their operation. They do not depend on the crude manipulation of personal rewards and punishments. Any shift in institutional structure may induce changes in the incentives facing agents operating within that structure. We provide a detailed analysis of an example in another essay[8] where the structure of the relationship between an elected legislature and an executive branch is studied to argue that the separation of these branches of government can be expected to shift the incentive structure in such a way as to reduce social benefits.

Although monitoring systems and competitive systems will operate well under rather different circumstances, there are clearly some circumstances under which neither can be expected to work well. Situations in which team work is important so that it is difficult to provide appropriate incentives at the individual level, or where the actions of individuals are not easily observed or easily identified as 'good' or bad' (as in the case of unobserved quality) provide examples of situations in which incentive based systems are unlikely to perform well. In these cases, and others like them, other mechanisms must be found to promote the public interest. But before turning to consider other mechanisms consistent with the economical approach to constitutional design, we must say something about the view of politics that is associated with the use of incentive based constitutional mechanisms, and about the motivational assumptions underlying their appeal.

---

[8] G. Brennan and A. P. Hamlin, 'A revisionist view of the separation of powers', *Journal of Theoretical Politics*, 6 (1994), 345–68.

The vision of politics associated with the sanctioning argument can be illustrated by the case of competitive popular elections.[9] There are two possible pictures here, both dependent critically on the idea that electoral competition effectively constrains rival parties. The first picture is an *ex ante* one. Here, rival parties or candidates offer policy platforms to the electorate as rival tenders for a contract. In the limit, such candidates will be totally constrained by the competitive process – the policy platform offered will leave candidates with no 'political profit', no discretion to adopt alternative policies of their own devising. Failure to fulfil the terms of the contract will lead to not being re-elected. Alternatively, the primary monitoring may be *ex post*. In this picture the ruling party may not be bound by a tightly specified *ex ante* contract, and may have discretion to act, but any failure to act totally in the citizens' interests and to be seen by the electorate to have so acted will again lead to losing the next election. In both *ex ante* and *ex post* cases, competition reduces and ultimately eliminates political rents. Parties must act in the relevant majority's interests as that majority conceives those interests. Politicians follow citizens' interest rather than lead or refine those interests. The object of constitutional arrangements under this vision of politics will be to secure the maximally competitive state of affairs. While this view of politics has much to commend it, it may miss important aspects of the constitutional problem by ignoring other dimensions of politics. We will return to this theme in the next section.

Finally, it is clear that the arguments underlying sanctioning institutions operate in a relatively parsimonious motivational setting. Incentive arguments are displayed most starkly against a background which assumes that all individuals are identically motivated and that this common motivation is purely self-interested – the classic world of *homo economicus*. This is both a strength and a limitation. It is a strength insofar as the argument relies only on some divergence between private motivations and public interests – we do not need to be specific about the precise content of either. Only if such a divergence is denied – so that we are in the somewhat idealistic realms of compliance theories in which everyone is assumed to be appropriately motivated by considerations of the public good – will the general form of the argument for sanctioning institutions be irrelevant. However the *homo economicus* assumption is a weakness in that we may come to think that sanctioning institutions are the *only* forms of institutions that may serve useful roles in improving social outcomes. The assumption of motivational homogeneity may distract attention from other institutional mechanisms which may have a role to play.

Screening Mechanisms

We do not always think of an election as an indirect means of choosing preferred policies or as a means of disciplining or monitoring politicians, and it does not always seem appropriate to reduce the discretionary power of a politician or official. The idea of representation, as opposed to delegation, captures the thought that an elected or appointed person is entrusted with discretionary power and allowed to display qualities of leadership and vision.

---

[9] For discussion of alternative visions of political process and their implications see G. Brennan and A. P. Hamlin, 'Rationalizing parliamentary process', *Australian Journal of Political Science*, 28 (1993), 443–57.

On first sight the economical approach to politics and to constitutional design can make little sense of this view of politics in which individuals are selected for positions of trust, but we wish to suggest that the relatively slight modifications in the background assumptions concerning individual motivations discussed above can provide the basis for an economical analysis of this aspect of politics which complements and enriches the discussion of sanctioning institutions.

This argument, which we term the screening argument, revolves around the idea of sorting agents into groups by reference to some underlying criterion, where the groups of agents may perform different institutional roles. Screening mechanisms have not been much emphasized in the economical literature on constitutional design to date,[10] and a part of our purpose here is to argue for their further study, but it seems clear that the idea of screening is central to many of our social institutions, including the procedures used to select individuals for particular positions such as judges and civil servants, where the idea of direct private incentive mechanisms seems inappropriate for one reason or another.

The basic idea is simple enough. If we drop the assumption of homogeneity of individual motivation, so as to allow for variety across individuals, we open up an argument for screening institutions. Screening and sorting mechanisms can be thought of as a means of operationalizing the economic principle of comparative advantage. In a standard economic example such as the labour market, individuals might be assumed to vary in their abilities and talents (even though in the standard models they will be assumed to share a common motivation). The principle of comparative advantage will then imply that each individual should specialize in that job in which her particular talents are best rewarded. A competitive labour market will act as a mechanism which effects such an allocation – sorting individuals into relevant occupational groups.

In the constitutional setting we would argue that, in addition to a distribution of skills and talents, we might wish to account for a distribution of motivations and dispositions – with some individuals being more self-interested while others are more public-spirited, for example. Whatever the details, the idea of a screening mechanism at the constitutional level would be to allocate individuals to social roles in which their dispositions, talents and motivations grant them a comparative advantage in terms of social benefits. To oversimplify we would seek to allocate roles which require trust and offer discretionary power to those who are relatively trustworthy and motivated by considerations of the public interest. We offer a formal model of this kind elsewhere.[11]

The first point to make here is that the simple idea of screening does not provide an account of a screening mechanism. It may be desirable to allocate individuals in one way or another across social roles, but we still need a mechanism which can achieve such an allocation (at least with some degree of accuracy greater than the random). In the economic case of the labour market, the relevant mechanism is a straightforward sanctioning mechanism. The income that an individual can earn in the job that matches her comparative

[10] In Brennan and Hamlin, 'Constitutional political economy' and G. Brennan and A. P. Hamlin, 'Economizing on virtue', *Constitutional Political Economy*, 6 (1995), 35–56, we have provided the beginnings of an analysis of such screening mechanisms in the constitutional setting.

[11] Brennan and Hamlin, 'Economizing on virtue', although the primary theme of that discussion concerns the possible feedback effects from institutional design to individual motivation – the possibility that institutions may undermine virtue.

advantage will be greater than the income on offer from alternative employment, so that the individual will have a private incentive to take up the most
socially productive role.

Such a simple incentive structure is unlikely to be useful in the constitutional
context since the roles which require trust and offer discretion are, by their
nature, likely to attract both the trustworthy and the untrustworthy, the one
attracted by the public benefits associated with the role and the other attracted
by the prospect of private benefits. This points to a general line of argument
which we term a 'currency effect'. Imagine a situation in which there are two
types of person, distinguished by their true motivational dispositions which are
unobservable. We wish to recruit persons into a role where one dispositional
type is more socially productive than the other. How can we ensure that the
relevant type is recruited disproportionately into the role when we cannot
observe the characteristic that distinguishes the types? If it is possible to
distinguish the types once they take up the role, it might be appropriate to
recruit at random and then dismiss the inappropriate type once they have
revealed themselves. Indeed, such a practice might deter inappropriate type
individuals from applying in the first instance. But in important cases it may be
difficult or costly or even impossible to distinguish types even *ex post* (notice the
connection here with the idea of *ex post* monitoring in the context of sanctioning mechanisms), and in these cases it will be necessary to attempt to screen
ex ante. A 'currency effect' is then an attempt to operate a differential incentive
mechanism which rewards the appropriate type of individual to a greater extent
than the inappropriate type. This is possible only because the two types have
different dispositions and so may value a given offer differently from each other.
If one had reason to believe that the appropriate type of individual were more
likely to value rewards paid in one 'currency' rather than another, then offering
the rewards in that currency would have the desired effect of making it more
likely that appropriate individuals would be recruited. Effectively the choice of
currency would provide an incentive for the appropriate type to reveal
themselves in a way that was reliable (that is, would not be subject to inappropriate individuals masquerading as appropriate in order to gain access to the
role), so that it would be possible to separate the types and allocate them to
increase overall social benefit.

Currency effects of this type might be in play when civil servants are offered
job security or social prestige and honours, rather than monetary reward. Or
when academics are offered research support rather than salary. Notice that this
argument for possible currency effects runs counter to the standard economic
argument for payment in cash rather than in kind, effectively by claiming that
in-kind payments can be used to discriminate between types of individuals.

Currency effects, then, are a form of screening mechanism that utilize
differential incentives. But not all screening mechanisms need involve such
currency effects. We might, for example, be able to screen by identifying an
observable characteristic of individuals that is correlated with the unobservable
characteristic of interest. This idea too is used in economic contexts to explain,
for example, the use made of certain educational qualifications as entry
requirements for jobs which make no use of the skills associated with those
qualifications. It is argued that the attainment of the educational qualifications
may be correlated with certain personal characteristics that are important in the
job but which are not directly observable either *ex ante* or *ex post*.

But screening effects can be negative as well as positive, and the recognition that institutional mechanisms may carry screening implications may also be important in identifying institutional failures as well as prospects for institutional reform. The possibility of 'adverse selection' is widely recognized in a range of economic models – the basic idea is that under a particular institutional structure there may be a tendency for individuals of different types to act differently and in ways which adversely affect the overall operation of the institution. A classic example is provided by insurance markets in which individuals may have private information concerning their own risks. If the insurance company cannot distinguish between individuals with different risk characteristics it can only charge everyone the same premium. But at this common price, only the relatively high risk individuals will find the insurance attractive, and so the market will adversely select the high risk individuals. Such a market may not be sustainable, and so a potentially important market may fail to exist. Notice again that the key point in this simple story is the existence of private information – or, to put the same point another way, the unobservable nature of some important individual characteristic.

Screening mechanisms may complement sanctioning mechanisms in several ways. We have already suggested that, in the case of currency effects, the introduction of the idea of screening extends the range of sanctioning mechanisms. But more importantly, screening mechanisms are capable of offering constitutional options in those circumstances where incentive based sanctioning mechanisms are weakest. This weakness may take either of two forms. At one level the weakness may derive simply from the failure of the conditions required for the operation of an incentive scheme; that is, there may be no basis for credible commitment, or no possibility for the discipline of continuous trading, or no opportunity for monitoring of individuals. But at a deeper level the weakness may come from the inappropriateness in some circumstances of the view that an essential task of a constitution is to limit the extent of discretionary power in the hands of delegates, and the recognition that in at least some circumstances it is more appropriate to think in terms of the empowerment of representatives. The circumstances in question will include the presence of screening procedures that reasonably command some measure of confidence.

Summative Mechanisms

The third line of argument to be identified – the summative argument –focuses attention on the aggregation of information or opinion. This line of argument is relatively familiar in both economic and political application and we shall have relatively little to say about it here. In the economic sphere perhaps the most famous example of a summative argument is Hayek's analysis of the market in terms of its use of information,[12] while the applications of a similar idea in the political and constitutional sphere include the 'jury theorems' of Condorcet, and the social choice theoretic view of voting as the aggregation of preferences.[13] In

[12] F. A. von Hayek, 'The use of knowledge in society', *American Economic Review*, 35 (1945), 519–30.
[13] K. J. Arrow, *Social Choice and Individual Values* (New Haven, Yale University Press, rev. ed., 1963); A. K. Sen, *Collective Choice and Social Welfare* (San Francisco, Holden-Day, 1970). For a collection of major contributions to the social choice literature, see, C. K. Rowley (ed.), *Social Choice Theory*, 3 Vols (Aldershot, Edward Elgar, 1993).

each case it is the ability of an institution effectively to aggregate across individuals that is of significance, issues of incentives and screening being relegated to minor roles.

In one sense, summative mechanisms are the most basic form of social institution – their aim is disarmingly simple – to aggregate directly from the individual level to the collective. However, the history of social choice theory tells us that this simple objective hides a plethora of difficulties. Attempts to 'simply' aggregate preferences, or opinions, or moral views into either social choices or social values are deeply problematic. But it is not these social choice theoretic problems that we wish to discuss here. Rather we wish simply to underline the idea that summative mechanisms relate most directly to direct interactions between principals rather than interactions displaying the principal-agent structure. To return to our central example of an election – if sanctioning mechanisms correspond to the selection of delegates and screening mechanisms correspond to the selection of representatives, summative mechanisms correspond most naturally to the idea of a referendum.

To underline the distinction between the issues raised by summation and those raised by the structure of the principal-agent relationship, we might note that politics (in all but its most dictatorial form) is crucially characterized by the existence of multiple principals. The social choice literature tells us that the move from single principal to multiple principals is problematic whenever principals have different perceptions of the actions the agent should ideally undertake. This problem can be avoided if we assume that all principals are identically motivated by a common view of the public interest, but this is to solve a problem by ignoring it. Even if the summation problem were solved, the principal-agent problem would remain; and to make sense of the principal-agent problem, the summation issue has to be tackled.

The issues at stake in a summative mechanism are, therefore, quite different from those we have emphasized in connection with either a sanctioning or a screening mechanism. While sanctions and screens might be seen as the opposite sides of a coin – the one concerned with restricting discretionary power in the hands of agents and the other concerned with allocating appropriate individuals into positions of discretionary power – summative mechanisms pre-empt discretionary power by making decisions directly and so making delegates and representatives unnecessary. Alternatively, we might think of summative mechanisms as operating at a stage after all questions of delegation and representation are institutionalized, and the topic is now final decision making among the set of delegates/representatives.

While we do not wish to suggest that summative institutional mechanisms are of less significance than either sanctioning or screening mechanisms, we will avoid the new issues raised by summative mechanisms and restrict ourselves to one or two further comments on the relationship between summative mechanisms on the one hand and sanctioning and screening mechanisms on the other.

Consider the classic problem of the prisoner's dilemma. This is a direct social interaction in which rational individuals will act in ways which defeat the public interest. The problem lies with the lack of correlation between the perceived private benefits of the alternative courses of action open to each individual and the associated spillover benefits to other players. In this sense, the prisoner's dilemma is an obvious example of a perverse sanctioning mechanism. But at the same time, since this is a direct social interaction and not a case of a principal-agent structure, we might also think of the interaction as an example of a (perverse) summative mechanism. Under this description, the rules of the interaction can be seen simply as rules by which we aggregate individual preferences into a social outcome.

It is also clear that we can imagine institutional solutions to a particular example of a prisoner's dilemma which rely on sanctions or on screens or on summative mechanisms. A simple sanctioning device would be to institute punishments for defection (or rewards for co-operation) which change the private payoffs in such a way as to establish the desired correlation between private and spillover benefits. A screening device might attempt to ensure that only individuals of a genuinely co-operative disposition encounter each other in the setting that would otherwise be a prisoner's dilemma. Finally, a summative device would attempt to change the aggregation rule so that, for example, the individuals could express their preferences over outcomes rather than their preferences over actions, and these could be the basis of the determination of the final outcome. These comments are intended only to reinforce the idea that in isolating the three identified institutional mechanisms we are identifying three distinct ways of viewing any particular social interaction.

Conclusion

In outlining our characterization of individual motivation we stressed the idea that individuals were to be conceived as 'single-minded', ruling out the possibility that individuals' characters depend directly on the particular institutional setting. In ruling out this direct institutional effect of dispositional character, we leave open the possibility of an indirect or feedback effect from institutional environment to dispositional character. Indeed, we see it as one of the key advantages of the approach we advocate that it can recognize and offer an account of such feedback effects.

What we have in mind is the possibility that a particular constitutional framework may induce dispositional characters of a particular type through time, either by some loosely evolutionary mechanism by which individuals adapt to their environment, or more overtly through learning, choice or education.[14] Such feedback effects may, of course, be either positive or negative. Some institutional frameworks may induce the types of character which support that institutional framework, while other institutional frameworks may undermine the characters on which they depend. In this way, some constitutions may be more stable than others. This understanding of the motivational stability of a constitutional order relates directly to the Madisonian idea of the maintenance of an environment which encourages individuals to participate in social and political life in an appropriate spirit.

As we have suggested, real social and political institutions do not normally conform to the ideal types of sanctioning institutions, screening institutions and summative institutions. Rather any particular institution or social interaction is made up of a blend of these three types of mechanism. Any social interaction can, therefore, be analysed in terms of its sanctioning, screening and summative

---

[14] See the analysis of the potential feedback effects from institutions which operate as sanctioning and screening mechanisms in Brennan and Hamlin, 'Economizing on virtue'.

properties and the interactions between these properties. The economical approach to constitutional design provides a framework within which all these aspects of social and political interactions can be recognized and analysed in a consistent manner and incorporated into an institutional recommendation that offers the best resolution of the underlying interaction. By focusing on the ways in which institutions structure the relationships between individuals, and by accommodating several views of political and social life, the economical approach to constitutional design offers a means of bringing together these alternative views of politics in terms of the study of the operating characteristics of the institutional mechanisms they recommend.

The fact that mechanisms of the three ideal types identified here can work together harmoniously – as in the case of the perfect market – might be taken to suggest that they always work well together. That is, that institutions of the three types can be mixed and matched in any combination to produce an economical constitution. This is not the case. A truly economical constitution must take care to account for potentially perverse interaction effects between institutions. A simple example will serve to illustrate the possibility of such perverse interactions. Imagine the role of a senior civil servant. We might seek to structure that role by use of sanctioning mechanisms or by means of screening mechanisms. Each approach is likely to yield imperfect results. In the case of sanctioning mechanisms it is unlikely that the actions of the incumbent can be monitored and evaluated sufficiently accurately to effect a fully efficient *ex post* incentive system, while it is equally unlikely that *ex ante* competition for the post can exert sufficient control. Similarly, it is unlikely that any practicable screening mechanism could ensure that the incumbent was disposed to act as the public interest requires. Nevertheless, it may be a mistake to believe that one can improve the constitutional position by invoking both types of mechanism, since, in this setting, they operate on very different principles. If the screening mechanism is employed it will only work to the extent that the incumbent is indeed trusted with the discretionary power associated with the role. But if this discretionary power is minimized by the use of sanctioning mechanisms, this will effectively also reduce the power of the screening mechanism to produce socially desirable outcomes. In short, the screening mechanism relies on the incumbent being given space in which to exercise discretion in the public interest, while sanctioning mechanisms operate by restricting such space. Of course, it is possible that a balance of screening and sanctioning institutions will be optimal, but it is equally possible (and perhaps more intuitive) that it is optimal to rely on just one type of mechanism – even if it is imperfect in operation – and discard the other. The economical approach to constitutional design is not predisposed to either solution, but does offer a coherent framework within which the choice and trade-off can be discussed.

The economical approach to constitutional design is sometimes taken to be narrowly committed to the increased marketization of social life, and sometimes taken to be narrowly committed to an analytic method which is insensitive to the complexity of social and political life. While we understand the origins of these views, we believe them to be false. We have argued that the real commitments of the economical method are to an analysis of institutions in terms of their impact on structuring the interactions between rational individuals, and that these commitments allow the economical constitutionalist to incorporate a much richer view of individual motivations and dispositions and, therefore, to recognize and analyse a wide variety of different institutional mechanisms and impacts – some of which might appear on the surface to be very remote from the caricature of narrow economic analysis.

Liberal Constitutionalism, Identity and Difference

JUDITH SQUIRES[1]

Introduction

Is there a tension between constitutionalism and democracy or is there an internal connection between the two? The answer of course depends on one's formulation of each of the concepts. The dominant voice of second-wave feminism could be argued to have assumed that a tension existed between democracy and constitutionalism, resulting in an endorsement of participatory democracy over liberal constitutionalism. In contrast to this position, and in keeping with the move to go beyond the binary thinking which characterizes so much current feminist writing, there now stands a significant body of feminist theoretical writing which could be read as endorsing democratic constitutionalism.

This body of feminist writing constitutes part of the broader 'politics of difference' literature which is primarily concerned to theorize what a recognition of 'difference' might involve in practical, political terms. I shall focus on the work of two difference theorists, Seyla Benhabib and Iris Young, who emerge from a feminist trajectory despite the fact that those advocating some form of difference politics do not confine themselves to a consideration of any particular difference in isolation from all others. Constitutionalism does not directly figure as a significant concern within this literature. Indeed, as with much of the recent writing on the 'politics of difference', the ontological and epistemological critique of liberalism is much more fully developed than is the positive political theory which might arise from taking difference seriously. However, I want to show that the distinctive attempts by Benhabib and Young to retheorize democracy in the light of a recognition of the significance of difference each results in an endorsement of proceduralism which involves an implicit appeal to a modified form of constitutionalism.

Democracy and Constitutionalism

Constitutionalism is often conceived in essentially liberal terms.[2] It is most frequently used, not only to mean 'the rules which establish and regulate the government', but also to cover some of the more substantive aspects of political liberalism such as systems of rights designed to protect individuals against the state, the philosophy of limited government, the universal application of rules

[1] Thanks to Richard Bellamy and Dario Castiglione for their patience, to Simon Thompson for his advice and to Richard Hobbs for his support.

[2] C. R. Sunstein, 'Constitutions and democracies: an epilogue' in J. Elster and R. Slagstad (eds), *Constitutionalism and Democracy* (Cambridge, Cambridge University Press, 1988), p. 327.

and so on. To endorse constitutionalism is consequently often perceived as an endorsement of many elements commonly associated with the liberal ethos: the atomistic rational agent whose existence and interests are ontologically prior to society; the belief that the ultimate worth of the individual is expressed in terms of political egalitarianism, conceived as negative liberty and formal rights; the separation of public and private spheres and the location of the political within the public; the transcendence of particularity and difference in the name of equality and universality; the endorsement of the priority of the right over the good and so on. But need we invoke this amorphous baggage of political liberalism when appealing to constitutionalism? Could we adopt a conception of constitutionalism that is not so firmly grounded in liberalism, and hence not 'naturally taken as antidemocratic'?

I shall take constitutionalism to comprise two key elements: rights provisions and structural provisions.[3] Rights provisions (safeguarding political rights, including the right to free speech, to vote, to associate and so on) are designed to fence off certain areas from majoritarian control. They operate as legal constraints upon the political process. The structural provisions of constitutionalism (such as the separation of powers, the representative system and so on) might be viewed as ensuring that government will act in the interests of the public at large, rather than those of self-interested representatives. Put rather schematically, we might claim that whilst structural provisions limit potential threats *to* democracy through the political process itself, rights provisions limit the dangers *of* democracy by expelling certain issues from the political agenda altogether.

Although there is a clear distinction to be drawn between these two elements within constitutionalism, it is nonetheless possible to argue that both pose a potential limitation on the operation of democracy. It could be argued that structural provisions are essentially antidemocratic in that the basic institutional arrangements specified may be changed only with extraordinary difficulty and are thus not subject to political revision, thereby insulating key issues from collective deliberation. Such an argument is put forward by those who advocate an agonistic politics understood as 'a site of resistance of the irresistible, a challenge to the normalizing rules that seeks to constitute, govern and control various behaviours'.[4] Those who adopt this vision of the political as performative and agonistic will necessarily view constitutionalism as antipolitical in that it is constative. For such theorists constitutionalism, in any form, carries no appeal.

However, for those theorists who do accept an institutionalized, bounded conception of the political, the concern is rather different. It is not the fact that structural provisions delimit the political that is of concern, but the current criteria upon which the delimitation is made. A key concern (as addressed within feminist and difference literature) is that representative mechanisms in particular function to exclude differences which ought to be politically recognized. It is the form (not the existence) of the boundaries that are subject to challenge, and it is the constitutional procedures governing representation that are the most obvious focus of concern to difference theorists.

---

[3] See Sunstein, 'Constitutions and democracies', pp. 327–9 for this distinction.

[4] See B. Honig, 'Towards an agonistic feminism: Hannah Arendt and the politics of identity' in J. Butler and J. Scott (eds), *Feminists Theorise the Political* (New York and London, Routledge, 1992), pp. 215–35.

This focus on the 'representational guarantee' within constitutions arises from the perception that current liberal constitutionalism does not, despite its rhetoric, allow for equal participation for all within the political body. Certain differences have been acknowledged by liberal democratic systems – yet these have been differences of interests and ideology, rather than identity. The differences that a polity deems politically pertinent will be a normative decision, reflecting and perpetuating the main political cleavages in society, whether language, class, race, centre-periphery or whatever. Hence the issue of *which differences* are to matter politically has always been particularly sensitive.

Based in a long-admired liberal commitment to tolerance, differences of identity have been claimed to be transcended in the political: firmly jettisoned from the public-political arena into the sphere of civil society. However, the 'cultural politics of difference' movements would have us question the assumed ethical and political desirability of the move from the illiberal discrimination on the basis of differences of identity to the liberal transcendence of identity differences. Those who argue for a 'politics of difference' contend in one way or another that liberal democracies have operated to deny differences of identity that ought to be recognized politically. Collective identities that are not amenable to erasure have not been 'recognized' and therefore validated.[5] Hence the concern regarding the structural provisions of the constitution, most notably those elements relating to representational guarantees.

To the extent that difference theorists focus upon the rights provisions of constitutionalism, it is to challenge the individualism implicit within their current formulation. For liberal constitutionalism has come to privilege the rights provisions of constitutions, and along with them the notion of individual legal persons as the bearers of rights. However, difference theorists would challenge those rights provisions within the constitution that are premised upon juridical and universalist assumptions whereby citizens are conceived of in abstract fashion, disembodied and transcendent of their particularities. They doubt a theory of rights that is so individualistically constructed can deal adequately with struggles for recognition. For in these struggles it is the articulation and assertion of collective identities that seems to be at stake.[6] The rhetoric of individual rights provisions is said to hinder the realization of a truly participatory democracy. As Habermas asks: 'Does not the recognition of cultural forms of life and traditions that have been marginalized, require ... some kind of collective rights that shatter the outmoded self-understanding of the democratic constitutional state, which is tailored to individual rights and in that sense is "liberal"?'.[7] Whilst sharing this critique of individual rights, difference theorists have developed conflicting alternatives: Iris Young's formulation of 'group rights' generating particular debate.

Concerned to realize some form of modified democracy – whether it be radical or discursive – difference theorists are turning their attention to the issue of constitutionalism. Their worry is that structural and rights provisions, as currently formulated, remove certain subjects (both issues and people) from public scrutiny and review, thereby working to exclude rather than recognize

---

[5] For discussion of this point see A. Phillips, 'So what's wrong with liberal democracy' in *Engendering Democracy* (Cambridge, Polity, 1991), pp. 147–68.

[6] J. Habermas, 'Struggles for recognition' in Amy Gutmann (ed), *Multiculturalism: Examining the Politics of Recognition* (Princeton, Princeton University Press, 1994), p. 107.

[7] Habermas, 'Struggles for recognition', p. 107.

difference. As we shall see, it is precisely this tendency which has led many feminists to critique constitutionalism. The question ahead of us then, is whether constitutionalism is so firmly embedded within liberalism that it cannot deal with the demands made by a politics of difference, or whether a politics of difference actually *requires* a form of constitutionalism to realise its goals. And, if it is the latter, how might the rights provisions and structural provisions be modified?

Feminist Challenges to Liberal Constitutionalism

Both the individualism of the rights provisions and the institutionalism of the structural provisions of liberal constitutionalism have been subjected to substantial critique by feminist theory and practice.[8] In this section I hope to show how developments within second-wave feminism worked to question both the philosophical foundations and the practical operation of liberal constitutionalism.

A critique of the rights provisions of liberal constitutionalism can be read from the ontological and epistemological critiques of abstract individualism and the ethic of justice. In its place a more situated theory of subjectivity and an ethic of care was asserted. The critique of the structural provisions of liberal constitutionalism was issued with the slogan 'the personal is political'. This slogan challenges the operation of both representative democracy and the public/private dichotomy and was used to advocate a more extensive and participatory democracy. I shall look briefly at these challenges, in order to depict the depth of scepticism regarding constitutional thinking which developed within feminist theory. I do this both to highlight how surprising the current constitutional turn within feminist theory is, and also to explain why it has come about.

Abstract individualism has been subject to such thorough and wide-spread critique within feminist writing that I shall simply take one manifestation of the challenge by way of example – the justice/care debate. This debate was initiated by Carol Gilligan's response to the work of Lawrence Kohlberg.[9] In criticizing Kohlberg's research into moral development on the basis that it privileged an 'ethic of justice' over an 'ethic of caring', Gilligan offered feminists a framework within which they might critique the individualism and universalism of liberal political institutions. As Benhabib later noted, 'Gilligan's critique of Kohlberg radically questions the 'juridical' or 'justice bias' of universalist moral theories'.[10] Contra Kohlberg, whose model of moral development assumed that the highest level of moral development involves the ability to abstract and universalize moral rules, Gilligan argued that we can distinguish between two ethical orientations: that of justice and rights on the one hand and

[8] Of course there has been a long and significant tradition of liberal feminism which has upheld the principles, if not the practices, of liberal constitutionalism. The strategy of this form of feminism has largely been about holding liberal institutions accountable to their own professed ideals: extending the rights provisions and amending the structural provisions of the day such that women might participate more equally within the institutions of the state and be recognized more fully as citizens. The challenges to liberal constitutionalism, however, emerge from another strand of feminist thought and practice.
[9] C. Gilligan, *In a Different Voice* (Cambridge MA, Harvard University Press, 1982).
[10] S. Benhabib, *Situating the Self* (Cambridge, Polity, 1992), p. 146.

that of care and responsibility on the other. The latter requires a contextuality, narrativety and specificity not valued in the former. Gilligan made the further claim that women were more likely to manifest the latter than were men, giving them a different – but not inferior – moral sense.

This debate, as played out in its polarized justice/caring form, has direct implications for the central feminist concern with the construction and policing of the public/private dichotomy, since the ethics of justice and caring are commonly perceived – by both critics and advocates – as mapping neatly onto the public and private spheres of liberal society.[11] The privileging of the ethic of justice over that of caring is interpreted as the celebration of the virtue of abstraction, generalization and universalization over the particular, contingent and embodied. These two ethics are deemed to have been constructed within the distinct public and private spheres of life respectively, and furthermore coincide with a male/female division (the nature of this mapping generating intense disagreement).

Whether one accepts the 'maternalists' claim of essential difference,[12] the standpoint claim of material/contextual difference, or a postmodern claim of contingent differences, it is repeatedly argued within feminist writings that we should distrust the 'neutral' universal paradigm as it serves either to exclude or assimilate women on the basis of this difference. It is argued that the state is constructed on the basis of abstract equality and serial individuals, whilst the domestic becomes the site for individuals who differ in essence and perform distinctive functions within a network of interdependent relations. These claims resulted in a widely held commitment to eroding the public/private dichotomy and extending the boundaries of the political to cover all aspects of life.

Such thinking informed much of the practice of the early Women's Movement, in terms of both the stress on solidarity and sisterhood, and in terms of organizational practice. Throughout the 1960s and 1970s feminists tended to be cynical about institutional politics and argued that women's energies should not be devoted to existing political institutions and electoral politics. Instead many within the Women's Movement advocated direct participation in women's autonomous organizations. These organizations aspired to be open to all, non-hierarchical and informal. Issues of participatory democracy became central, with great attention paid to organizational practice.[13] The explicit goal of a radical equality of participation for all women was pursued via mechanisms of rotating responsibilities, avoiding all hierarchies, validating personal experience as a mode of political expression. Seeking no collaboration with government these feminist groups repudiated the idea that change could be orchestrated from within formal arenas of political power and purposely stayed away. The slogan 'the personal is political', which arose to challenge orthodox definitions of the political, acted as a rallying cry for a whole generation of feminists and is

[11] For example see Benhabib, *Situating the Self*, p. 158.

[12] 'Maternalists' are committed to a conception of female political consciousness that is grounded in the virtues of women's private sphere – primarily mothering. Motherhood is put forward as the basis for a new conception of citizenship and the virtues of mothering claimed as a template for a more caring public life. For a critique of this perspective see M. Dietz, 'Context is all: feminism and theories of citizenship' in Chantal Mouffe (ed.), *Dimensions of Radical Democracy* (London, Verso, 1992).

[13] See, for a related emphasis, C. Pateman, *Participation and Democratic Theory* (Cambridge, Cambridge University Press, 1970).

often perceived to be the key statement of second wave feminism. The attempt to constitutionally rule certain issues as off the political agenda was thereby directly challenged. Both the foundations and the operation of liberal constitutionalism were subject to critique: abstract individualism and a rights-based ethic of justice were both jettisoned in theory; institutionalized politics and the clear demarcation of public and private spheres were both rejected in practice.

However, for many the experiences of the radical participatory democracy of the Women's Movement became paradoxical.[14] Although claiming to be open to all, women's groups were largely unrepresentative. The absence of formal structures often worked to create an insularity which left many women feeling excluded and silenced. The emphasis on participation was too demanding for those who were juggling many other demands on their time, and the lack of representative structures raised serious questions of accountability. As the tyranny of structurelessness became ever more evident, the structural provisions of constitutional frameworks for political action began to gain a renewed appeal.[15]

This appeal was consolidated by a number of other factors. Most notably, the assertion of commonality and sisterhood which had sustained the movement-based participatory politics of the Women's Movement became increasingly strained and prone to fragmentation. Although the Movement mobilized a sense of loyalty and belonging amongst its participants, this very cohesiveness worked to exclude those who did not conform to this particular vision of sisterhood. The idea of 'a different voice' was challenged by a plurality of heterogeneous 'others' who all claimed that this binarism failed to recognize the specificity of their identities. The nature and cause of such bitter fragmentation is now increasingly recognized and theorized from a post-structuralist perspective. Iris Young for instance, draws upon the Derridean notion of difference to argue that: 'The striving for mutual identification and shared understanding among those who seek to foster a radical and progressive political, can and has, led to denying or suppressing differences within political groups or movements'.[16] To demand such cohesion, she argues, is to deny the possibility of a fully inclusive citizenship and to appeal to an implicitly essentializing notion of identity.

The concepts of 'identity' and 'difference' have come to replace those of justice and caring as the dominant parameters for current feminist debate – with important implications for the discussion regarding constitutionalism. The previous polarization between justice and caring, based upon essential difference and giving rise to a distinctive female voice and mode of action, that confined debate regarding constitutions to a simple endorsement or rejection of the liberal model, has now crumbled, allowing for a more detailed evaluation of the various constituent elements of constitutionalism. As a result, we currently find within contemporary feminist political theory a more complex range of perspectives articulated in relation to the issue of constitutionalism. Recent feminist political theory has burst out of the liberal/radical taxonomy and now

[14] See A. Phillips, 'Paradoxes of participation' in *Engendering Democracy*, pp. 120–46.
[15] See J. Freeman, *The Tyranny of Structurelessness* (London, Dark Star/Rebel, 1970).
[16] I. Young, *Justice and the Politics of Difference* (Princeton, Princeton University Press, 1990), p. 312.

offers more nuanced evaluations of the various strengths and weaknesses of the complex facets of liberalism than has previously been the case.

Identity and Difference

In the wake of the practical developments of late modernity and the theoretical developments in post-structuralism, the issue of 'difference' has adopted a more heterogeneous and less essentialist form than was previously the case within many feminist writings. Much feminist theory has become concerned to theorize multiple differences and now forms a part of a broader kind of difference politics. Difference theorists and activists adopt a theory of subjectivity which is firmly critical of the classical liberal abstract individual and seek to positively and structurally recognize 'differences of identity' within our political structures rather than transcend them.[17] However, the perceptions of identity as authenticity and difference as dichotomous are also subject to substantial critique from this perspective.

Judith Butler, for example, has challenged the notion of authenticity, stating that: 'The foundationalist reasoning of identity politics tends to assume that an identity must first be in place in order for political interests to be elaborated and subsequently, political action to be taken. My argument is that there need not be a 'doer' beyond the 'deed', but that the doer is variably constructed in and through the deed'.[18] Such reasoning leads to a conception of political action, not as the formal representation of pre-formed group identities and interests, but as a performative enactment of identity. Hence, in the words of Butler: gender coherence 'operates not as a ground of politics but as its effect'.[19]

With these developments the process of decentring the subject is complete. But, taken to its logical conclusion, subjectivity is in danger of complete detachment from any social or psychic determination, becoming a mere point of intersection of the discordant 'discourses' which, in addressing and naming the subject, constituted it. The claim that there is no prediscursive 'I' has often been thought to undermine any sense of conviction in the emancipatory projects of modernity.[20] Resisting the categories and organizational structures of existing political systems, which serve to construct and constrain political identities in delimited forms, the ambition of some difference theorists has been to explode all boundaries, resist static categories and destabilize organizational structures with a view to exposing the radical contingency of identification. There seems to be little basis for a recuperation of constitutionalism here.[21]

In response to this potential voluntarism, other difference theorists claim that the important thing about identities is not to celebrate them and use them as a basis for political action, but to understand their formulation.[22] We need some

[17] C. West, *Keeping Faith* (New York and London, Routledge, 1993), p. 3.
[18] J. Butler, *Gender Trouble: Feminism and the Subversion of Identity* (New York and London, Routledge, 1990), p. 142.
[19] J. Butler, 'Gender trouble, feminist theory and psychoanalytic discourse' in L. Nicholson (ed.), *Feminism/Postmodernism* (London and New York, Routledge, 1990), p. 339.
[20] As Butler herself asks: 'if there is no subject, who is left to emancipate?' in '*Gender Trouble*', p. 327.
[21] For an example of the political ramifications of this position see Honig, 'Towards an agonistic feminism', p. 232.
[22] Benhabib, *Situating the Self*, pp. 161–2.

way of disentangling those differences that are inevitable from those that are chosen, and those that are simply imposed. Only then can we allow that the groups which deserve special resources to enable their active participation as citizens within the political arena are constituted neither by essential identities nor by any random collection of subjects who happen to come together. They may be both more contingent and more grounded than that.

One might summarize the trajectory of 'difference theory' thus: the initial feminist claim was one of essential binary difference which led to a rejection of the universalizing rights framework as androcentric rather than neutral; the form of political action arising from this perspective was a participatory democracy without formal mechanisms of membership, representation or accountability; the political project involved challenging the operation of the public/private dichotomy and extending the notion of the political. In contrast, a contemporary politics of difference perspective seeks recognition of multiple and contingent differences. The universalizing strategy of liberalism is still criticized as not dealing with difference, but the alternative now proposed is not one of solidarity and caring, but of antagonism and inevitable conflict. The political project is taken up with securing recognition of different identities within a single pluralist polity. For this one needs procedures. This is highly schematic, but serves to highlight the shift within difference thinking, and I hope serves to explain why the political agenda has changed accordingly.

The problem facing current difference theorists is that group identities and organizational structures are needed to construct the political. Consequently we are faced with an ethical question that will not go away: which differences do we want to inscribe within our political structures? We cannot avoid this issue altogether if we are to create and police the boundaries of a democratic political sphere. All political organizational structures are disciplinary strategies based upon power relations. This is inevitable. Yet much of the writings on difference offer no ethical basis from which to evaluate some structures as inferior/superior to others.

There have been crucial changes within the debate concerning difference – notably away from essentialism towards fluidity, from binary dualisms to multiple differences, away from discussion of 'women and men' to gendered diversity. Nevertheless, one central issue continually recurs: how to develop a politics of identity which both recognizes the precariousness of identity and its necessity. Is the politics of difference then just another manifestation of what Felix Guattari has called 'the dead-end of postmodernism'; the selling out of the emancipatory idea and embracing of a dangerous quietism? Or is it, as Lyotard would claim, the rejection of old ideologies and their replacement with new resistances? And what role, if any, does constitutionalism play in such a political vision? In order to address these questions I shall now turn to the work of Benhabib and Young and their attempts to rethink the political in the light of the theoretical developments surveyed above.

Recognizing Difference Politically

There is a tension between constituting political procedures (which inevitably posit some stability of identity and require exclusions of certain differences) and celebrating the fluidity of heterogeneous difference. It is a tension which has exercised the thoughts of most contemporary feminist political theorists, resulting in significantly disparate attempts at resolution. The spectrum of responses might include Bonnie Honig who opts for difference at the expense of procedures and rejects constative politics altogether; Benhabib who endorses the need for procedural mechanisms defining the boundary of the political, but grounds these in a discourse ethics which some perceive to be a telos of assimilation which ultimately seeks to transcend difference; Young who also endorses procedures for recognizing difference, but does so by proposing the institution of mechanisms for group representation which some argue leaves her endorsing group identities which themselves manifest the logic of identity; and finally Mouffe who endorses procedural mechanisms which are designed to allow for conflict between antagonistic identities within the political realm itself, but which are clearly non-neutral and require acceptance of a democratic 'grammar of conduct'. In each of these perspectives we find a shared tension between the ontological and the advocacy projects adopted: it is a tension stemming from an ontological position which understands identity as contextual and fluid and an advocacy position which recognizes the need for formal procedures of political recognition, necessarily working to freeze identity in some way. I shall focus on attempts of Benhabib and Young to resolve this tension.

Though Benhabib and Young's understandings of the nature and significance of 'difference' are in some ways in conflict, they share a common project to formulate a democratic theory based upon a revised understanding of subjectivity, and envisage democratic structures which would recognize difference more inclusively than has previously been the case. We find in their work clear, if distinct, critiques of liberal constitutionalism's ontological premises, but also endorsement of some variant of formal procedural democratic mechanisms which would appear to be in keeping with constitutional thinking. Each could be said to be reformulating the mode of argument used to analyse questions of constitutional design, advocating the replacement of liberal individualism with a politics of difference.

Benhabib's writings develop from a Habermassian model, which claims to offer the possibility of negotiating the issue of democracy and difference through an account of deliberative decision-making. Habermas argues for a proceduralist model of democracy, claiming that this would allow for the expression of difference in that it calls into question the republican move towards an ethical construction of political discourse. This discourse theoretical model insists on the fact that democratic will-formation does not draw its legitimating force from the previous convergence of settled ethical conviction, but from both the communicative presuppositions that allow the better argument to come into play in various forms of deliberation and the procedures that secure fair bargaining processes. In other words, Habermas takes the principles of conversation and applies them to the construction of democratic procedural mechanisms.

It should be noted that Benhabib has developed what she views as a feminist revision of Habermas's work in that she understands the procedural model as: 'an actual dialogue among actual selves who are both "generalized others" considered as equal moral agents, and "concrete others", that is individuals with irreducible differences'. In this, Benhabib develops the justice/caring debate into her own formulation of the 'generalized and the concrete other', which she argues reflects the dichotomous nature of modern political theory –

polarizing autonomy and nurturance, independence and bonding, the public and the domestic, and justice and the good life.[23] Her modification of the Habermassian model of procedural democracy is based upon the attempt to synthesize both justice and caring perspectives. She interprets Gilligan's work not as a wholesale rejection of universalism 'but as a contribution to the development of a non-formalist, contextually sensitive and postconventional understanding of ethical life'.[24] Universalism is interpreted by Benhabib procedurally, as a test of the validity of moral judgements, principles and maxims – applied equally to issues that Habermas (and Kohlberg) would want to distinguish as 'evaluative questions of the good life' and 'moral matters of justice'.[25] Benhabib's postconventional understanding of ethical life represents a revision of both the maternalist commitment to contextuality and Habermas's commitment to universalism, challenging the presumption that the ethics of justice and caring can be clearly located within distinct spheres of life. The feminist tradition of deconstructing the operation of the public/private dichotomy leads her to be suspicious of the move to locate the ethics of justice and caring within the public and private spheres.

The question, from the perspective of our concern with constitutionalism, is what difference, if any, Benhabib's proposed shift in focus from 'formal equality and reciprocity' to 'equity and complementary reciprocity' might make. Is it possible to modify constitutionalism such that it integrates a recognition of the importance of an ethic of caring as well as that of justice? Can constitutionalism survive an attempt to erode the dichotomy between the two, or is it fundamentally premised upon the separation of justice and caring, and the formal endorsement of the former only within the public sphere?

Given the nature of our enquiry, it is unfortunate that the reconstructive project – or how exactly the synthesis of the two perspectives might be realized in practice – is as yet not developed in any detail. But we do find an endorsement of a form of constitutional proceduralism which appears to combine the two ethics. For example, Benhabib writes: 'in democratic politics nothing is really off the agenda of public debate, but there are fundamental rules of discourse which are both constitutive and regulatory in such a manner that, although what they mean for democratic give and take is itself always contested, the rules themselves cannot be suspended or abrogated by simple majoritarian procedures'.[26] For Benhabib it is the 'rules of discourse' which provide the foundation for constitutionalism. Questions of justice and questions of the good life are thereby merged into a single endorsement of constitutional mechanisms.

This move has implications for Benhabib's understanding of the rights provisions of constitutionalism. This has particular significance in that one of our concerns, in exploring the possibility of modifying constitutionalism in the light of a politics of difference, must be the possibility of developing a non-individualistic conception of the rights provisions of constitutions: or, as Habermas put it, '. . . some kind of collective rights that shatter the outmoded self-understanding of the democratic constitutional state'.[27] It is Benhabib's

[23] Benhabib, *Situating the Self*, pp. 158–59.
[24] Benhabib, *Situating the Self*, p. 180.
[25] Benhabib, *Situating the Self*, p. 187.
[26] Benhabib, *Situating the Self*, p. 107.
[27] Habermas, 'Struggles for recognition', p. 113.

claim that discourse theory solves the tension between democratic politics and liberal guarantees of constitutional rights, for the meta-norms of discourse themselves provide for the autonomy of the individual moral conscience.[28] In this she is in accordance with Habermas who states: 'A correctly understood theory of rights requires a politics of recognition that protects the integrity of the individual in the life contexts in which his or her identity is formed'.[29] This proceduralist conception of rights posits an internal connection between private autonomy and citizenship recognition such that the rights provisions of a constitution could be justified with reference to the democratic aspiration of the structural provisions. 'Safeguarding the private autonomy of citizens with equal rights must go hand in hand with activating their autonomy as citizens of the nation.'[30] This argument reinforces the claim made elsewhere in this collection that a more developed concept of democracy is not only compatible with a strong system of rights but actually requires it.[31] This move would appear to be a highly significant one in the context of our project of modifying constitutionalism in the light of difference theory.

In majoritarian forms of democratic decision-making one of the key protections of individual differences is a set of rights which are constitutionally guaranteed and which may not be violated even by a decision of the majority. Benhabib (and Habermas) would have us ground these rights within the constraints of discourse itself. Benhabib claims both that basic rights are themselves essentially contestable and therefore presumably open to discursive vindication, and that they cannot be abrogated without suspending democracy itself, because these are the 'constitutive and regulative institutional norms of debate in democratic societies'.[32] This claim has caused some to argue that she cannot have it both ways: if they are contestable they can be abrogated; if they are not, their authority is grounded in something other than the discursive procedure itself.[33] Yet it is surely possible to distinguish between constitutional politics and normal politics whilst grounding both on the norms of deliberation. The significance of this move is that it serves to define constitutionalism as an essentially political project, whereby – contra the liberal model – constitutional provisions have no pre-political justification. There would be, in the words of David Miller, 'constitutional politics and not merely, as the liberal model would want, constitutional interpretation by judges'.[34]

To act democratically, according to Benhabib, is precisely to abide by the rules which govern an ideal speech situation. It is from these rules, ascertainable by reason, that we can derive both the structural and rights provisions of constitutionalism. But for many there is a serious question as to whether the ideal speech situation – which theorists of procedural democracy place at the centre of their model – can be neutral between different rhetorical styles and narratives forms. In other words, in prescribing organizational procedures, does this model assimilate crucial political differences? It is on this point that

---

[28] Benhabib, *Situating the Self*, p. 112.
[29] Habermas, 'Struggles for recognition', p. 113.
[30] Habermas, 'Struggles for recognition', p. 116.
[31] See Tony Prosser, 'Debating the British constitution' in this collection.
[32] Benhabib, *Situating the Self*, p. 106.
[33] See C. Gould, 'Diversity and democracy: representing difference', paper presented at the Conference for the Study of Political Thought, Yale, April (1994).
[34] David Miller, 'Citizenship and pluralism', *Political Studies*, 43 (1995), p. 449.

Benhabib finds a critic in Young who is concerned to reject the proposed merger of justice and the good life. She claims that concentration on the virtues of argument and the norms of deliberation is clearly exclusionary, working to silence or devalue the speech of subordinate groups. This claim has itself been subject to critique by those who do not share the post-structuralist perception of the power inherent within linguistic structures themselves.[35]

A second point of departure between Young and Benhabib is over their conceptions of community. Young claims that Benhabib posits a vision of community which reveals an understanding of social relations as 'the co-presence of subjects'.[36] The ideal is one of transparency of subjects to one another. This ideal, Young argues, submits to what Derrida calls the metaphysics of presence, which seeks to collapse the temporal difference inherent in language and experience into a totality that can be comprehended in one view.[37] This ideal of community denies the ontological difference within and between subjects. Hence, despite Benhabib's commitment to taking the perspective of the concrete as opposed to the generalized other, Young rejects her approach as being another denial of difference. To take such a vision of community as one's model for political arrangements does not purify politics, she argues, it avoids politics.[38] Benhabib responds that Young's claim – that mutual care and responsibility must presuppose a 'transparency' of understanding – is exaggerated: 'Young is not heeding the distinction between "consensus" and "reaching understanding"'.[39] The very commitment to conversation, she contends, suggests infinite revisability and indeterminacy of meaning.

Beyond the dispute between these particular theorists, the more general significance of these debates is the extent to which they serve to focus our attention upon the inevitability of antagonism,[40] and the extent to which linguistic structures embody power structures. If constitutionalism is to be understood as a product of political discourse, constitutional theory will need to make greater appeal to linguistic theory than has hitherto been the case.

What then does Young propose as her politics of difference? Like Benhabib, Young also claims that Gilligan's dichotomy between the ethics of justice and caring is homologous with the distinction between liberal individualism and community, and adopts the deconstructive strategy of undermining the fixity of such dualisms to claim that both have a common logic: each entails a denial of difference and a desire to bring multiplicity into unity.[41] Unlike Benhabib, however, Young does develop the detail of the practical arrangements advocated, rendering it somewhat easier to assess the implications of her critique of the liberal conception of democracy for constitutionalism.

Benhabib criticizes Young for celebrating all heterogeneity, opacity and difference in an undifferentiated manner.[42] On my reading, Young does

---

[35] See Miller, 'Citizenship and pluralism', pp. 445–6.

[36] Young, *Justice and the Politics of Difference*, p. 231.

[37] Young, *Justice and the Politics of Difference*, p. 98

[38] Young, *Justice and the Politics of Difference*, p. 233.

[39] Benhabib, *Situating the Self*, p. 197.

[40] See C. Mouffe, *The Return of the Political* (London, Verso, 1993) for discussion of the importance of recognizing the inevitability of antagonism in politics.

[41] Benhabib, *Situating the Self*, p. 307.

[42] See Benhabib who argues that she celebrates difference 'at the cost of belittling the importance of a coherent core of individual identity. Not all difference is empowering, not all heterogeneity can be celebrated.' *Situating the Self*, p. 198.

distinguish between politically pertinent and non-pertinent differences and cannot therefore be accused of celebrating all differences,[43] but I do not intend to dwell on this issue here. Rather I shall focus only on the issue of representation in her work.

Young quite clearly endorses constitutionalism itself: '... democracy must indeed always be constitutional; the rules of the game must not change with each majority's whim, but rather must be laid down as constraints on deliberation and outcomes, and must be relatively immune to change. Such rules should spell out basic rights that democratically arrived at decisions cannot violate, including economic as well as civil and political rights'.[44] Although profoundly critical of the principles of impartiality, merit and distributive justice, Young nonetheless endorses the rights provisions of a legally conceived constitutionalism as just constraints upon the operation of democratic decision-making.

The particular aspect of constitutionalism that Young endorses most forcefully is the aspect of representational guarantees. She claims that existing electoral and legislative processes are 'unrepresentative' in the sense that they fail to reflect the diversity of the population in terms of presence, leading her to demand that a certain number of seats in the legislature be reserved for members of marginalized groups. This call is made on the assumption that under-representation can be overcome only by resorting to guaranteed representation and that representing difference requires constitutional guarantees of group participation within the parliamentary system. Groups who have suffered oppression or disadvantage need guaranteed representation in order that their distinct voice be heard.

A politics of difference, she argues, requires the participation and inclusion of all groups via different treatment for oppressed or disadvantaged groups. This rejection of the assimilationist ideal is based in a belief that 'attachment to specific traditions, practices, language and other culturally specific forms is a crucial aspect of social existence'.[45] In this her argument is echoed by Charles Taylor's critique of 'difference-blind' theories which are in fact frequently (or possibly inevitably) a reflection of one hegemonic culture.[46] Young accordingly argues that a democratic public should provide mechanisms for the effective recognition and representation of the distinct voices and perspectives of those of its constituent groups that are oppressed or disadvantaged.[47]

What would constitute 'recognition' and a genuine openness to heterogeneity on Young's account? Intriguingly, she does not endorse a simple microcosm vision of representation, in the sense that representatives would be proportional to their numbers in the polity. She notes that: 'proportional representation of group members may sometimes be too little or too much to accomplish that aim'.[48] And continues: 'allocating strictly half of all places to women ... might be more than is necessary to give women's perspectives an empowered voice,

---

[43] See Young, 'Five faces of oppression' in *Justice and the Politics of Difference*, pp. 39–65 for a discussion of the need to positively recognize those social groups that have suffered 'oppression'.

[44] Young, *Justice and the Politics of Difference*, pp. 93–94.

[45] Young, *Justice and the Politics of Difference*, p. 163.

[46] C. Taylor, 'The Politics of recognition' in Gutmann, *Multiculturalism: Examining the Politics of Recognition*, p. 43.

[47] Young, *Justice and the Politics of Difference*, p. 183.

[48] Young, *Justice and the Politics of Difference*, p. 187.

and might make it more difficult for other groups to be represented'.[49] It would appear that Young is advocating neither the principle/agent conception of representation that is endorsed in liberal constitutionalism nor a *microcosm* conception of representation that one might expect from a difference theorist, but a *symbolic* conception.[50] In this context it is worth reflecting that, as Hanna Pitkin argues: 'since the connection between symbol and referent seems arbitrary and exists only where it is believed in, symbolic representation seems to rest on emotional, affective, irrational psychological responses rather than on rationally justifiable criteria'.[51] Any attempt to answer the question of whether political structures were 'representative', on this symbolic conception of representation, would be highly subjective, offering little basis for constitutional guarantees. Who might constitute the group whose subjective assessment of representativeness is to count politically? What would constitute 'recognition' in this symbolic sense and who would determine its fulfilment?

Given Young's critique of impartiality one must question whether there remains any basis for believing that a polity might secure mechanisms of (symbolic) representation that everyone, in all their diversity, feels to truly recognize their particularity. It is not clear whether recognition of difference requires that a group should be represented in proportion to its numbers in the population at large, or that there should be a threshold number of represent-atives, or whether representatives belong to one's group, or are merely elected by one's group. The problem facing Young's attempt to constitutionally guarantee the representation of difference within political structures is that when formalized into the structures of state-based representation, such a group-based representation can rigidify what are actually very fluid identities. It is for this reason that Young has been criticized for not being sufficiently attuned to the contingency of identity and thereby problematically conceiving politics as a process of dealing with already constituted interests and identities.[52]

In the context of reflections on constitutionalism we might summarize Young's contribution as an endorsement of a form of pure procedural justice. Justice, she argues, is the product of democratic deliberation, where that deliberation allows different voices to be heard within a heterogeneous public; the constitution and policing of such a heterogeneous public will require strong structural provisions; these provisions then become a precondition for demo-cracy itself. It is evident from this that the precise nature of the representative provisions is central to ensuring that the public is genuinely heterogeneous. A key aspect of her project is therefore to assert the need to modify the repre-sentational guarantees of constitutionalism and to do so in accordance with a politics of recognition rather than an aspiration to impartiality.

Reflecting generally on the impact of the theorizing of both Benhabib and Young on constitutional thinking, several points emerge. Without wishing to

---

[49] Young, *Justice and the Politics of Difference*, p. 188.

[50] See Robert Goodin's appeal to symbolic representation in 'Convention quotas and communal representation', *British Journal of Political Science*, 7 (1976), 255–72. See also Will Kymlicka's distinction between demands for proportional representation and 'threshold' representation *Multicultural Citizenship: a Liberal Theory of Minority Rights* (Oxford, Oxford University Press, 1995), ch. 7.

[51] H. Pitkin, *The Concept of Representation* (Berkeley and Los Angeles, University of California Press, 1967), p. 100.

[52] See Mouffe, *The Return of the Political*, p. 86.

overly synthesize their projects – we find in their work a clear assertion of the internal connection between constitutionalism and democracy. Constitutionalism is understood by both as a product of political discourse itself, rather than a legalistic constraint upon it. Both emphasize the dialogic nature of identification and recognition and accordingly emphasize the importance of bringing linguistic concerns to the fore in constitutional thinking. The theoretical basis for the rights provisions of constitutions are modified by each: Benhabib asserting the internal connection between private autonomy and citizenship recognition, Young developing a notion of 'group rights'. Finally, both stress the significance of the representational provisions of constitutions, thus focusing our attention more closely upon the criteria and form of representative structures.

Conclusion

I hope to have shown that there has been a turn within feminist theorizing which moves beyond both the dichotomous justice/caring debate and the binary participatory/representative models of democracy. I have taken Benhabib and Young as examples of theorists manifesting this trend towards the transcendence of such binary dualisms. I argue that this move takes place in no small part due to the ontological assertion of identity as contingent and the political recognition of the significance of plural differences. In the context of these debates about identity and difference, feminist theorists are developing models of democracy which assert the importance of procedural mechanisms of inclusion without assimilation.

As Anna Yeatman has noted: 'It is clear that a democratic politics of difference requires this post-ontological type of political community to commit itself to certain kinds of proceduralism'.[53] Given the centrality that proceduralism plays in these models of democracy, we witness a renewed concern in this literature to contemplate and modify the principles of constitutionalism. Benhabib offers renewed epistemological grounds for defending constitutionalism. Young attempts to modify its operation in the light of group rights claims. Both attempt to revise constitutionalism in the light of current practical and theoretical developments characterized by relativism and pluralism.

The project facing difference theorists is not then to dispense with political boundaries and celebrate all differences without qualification (as some of its critics suppose). Rather, the identity and boundaries of the political community are now subject to politics in ways which both destabilize any appearance of consensualist tradition and bring to light the historical artifice by which such traditions are constructed.

---

[53] A. Yeatman, *Postmodern Revisionings of the Political* (New York and London, Routledge, 1994), p. 89.

Designing Constitutions: the Political Constitution of a Mixed Commonwealth

ROBERT E. GOODIN[1]

The problem of a liberal commonwealth is how to control the abuse of power. The problem of a mixed commonwealth, in the sense in which I shall be using the term, is how to incorporate radically diverse social groupings in a way that would prove satisfactory to them all. The two problems sometimes overlap. Liberal universalists and cultural particularists find common cause in opposing racial or religious oppression, for example. Some of us even still aspire to subsume one within the other, finding some liberal accommodation to the problem of difference. But champions of difference, for their part, would insist upon the ultimate distinctiveness of the two sets of problems, maintaining the impossibility of all such liberal attempts at coming fully to terms with the problem of difference.

This is not the place to enter directly into that larger argument, beyond merely marking the fact that the argument is still arguable on both sides. (That is simply to say: taking the problem of difference sufficiently seriously to talk about it is not to concede that it must be taken so seriously as necessarily to preclude a universalist liberal solution.) Instead, what I intend do in this article is merely (1) to survey what sorts of constitutional accommodation can be made to problems of radical difference, (2) to notice the problems that arise in the structure of the larger constitution from those accommodations and (3) to draw some inferences from those problems about all such accommodation strategies.[2] If champions of difference suspect that in so doing I am obliquely arguing the liberal side of the issue which I purportedly leave moot, they are in a way quite right. Still, here as elsewhere, more progress is likely to be made obliquely, avoiding head-on clashes, entrenched positions and familiar battlelines.

What do Constitutions Constitute?

From 1789 forward, Peoples have purported to 'ordain and establish' constitutions for themselves. The bold language of preambles notwithstanding,

[1] This article forms part of a larger project. I am grateful for comments on this article, or interrelated portions of others, from Geoff Brennan, John Dryzek, John Ferejohn, Russell Hardin, Claus Offe, Bingham Powell, Cass Sunstein and participants at the Norwich workshop, particularly Steve Elkin, Alan Hamlin and Neil MacCormick and the editors of *Political Studies* and of this Special Issue.
[2] In so doing, I shall be drawing loosely on several of the chapters in R. E. Goodin (ed.), *The Theory of Institutional Design* (Cambridge, Cambridge University Press, 1996).

constitutions constitute The People just as they are constituted by them. Most trivially, constitutions circumscribe the borders of their intended geographic range of application thus determining populations within their catchment. Constitutions constitute a People and peoples, more subtly, by making some social groupings more salient (easier to organize, more useful to have organized) than others.[3] Occasionally, as arguably in America, constitutions even succeed in their grandest possible ambition: themselves providing a focus around which a People might self-consciously conceive itself.[4]

Such revisionism must be kept in its place, though. All those ways in which constitutions might constitute The People are important and too little acknowledged. Still and all, they are strictly limited. Political and economic constitutions alike typically can do something – but typically only a little something – to alter the sorts of people who operate within the institutions that they create. A political constitution must ordinarily content itself by and large with just providing a framework constituting the state and the government thereof, taking the social constitution as given.

At the same time, those constitutions rely for their proper functioning upon what sorts of people those are and what preferences and principles they harbour.[5] Political constitutions make certain crucial presuppositions about the sociological composition of the polity. They presuppose, if not exactly social homogeneity across the board, at least a certain homogeneity in the sorts of central principles which are internalized by all the major groups within the polity.

One way of putting the point is this. First-order disagreements over policy directions are the very stuff of politics. Any polity which experiences none is extraordinarily lucky – to the point of being extraordinarily suspect.[6] Coping with diversity at that level is precisely what the institutional designs of liberal democracy are all about. But beyond that surface disagreement must be a principled 'agreement to disagree', a principled agreement upon what procedures will be used to resolve those disagreements and a principled commitment to abide by those procedures in particular cases where they might work against one's first-order preferences.[7] Absent such principled agreement to

---

[3] Orlando Patterson tells a similar story about the differential organization of the Chinese on two Carribean islands presenting differential economic incentives for mobilizing the Chinese community along ethnic lines; see his 'Context and choice in ethnic allegiance: a theoretical framework and Carribean case study' in N. Glazer and D. P. Moynihan (eds), *Ethnicity* (Cambridge MA, Harvard University Press, 1975), pp. 305–49.

[4] Cf. R. M. Smith, 'The "American creed" and American identity: the limits of liberal citizenship in the United States', *Western Political Quarterly*, 41 (1988), 225–51.

[5] On some famous accounts, this is true even of the economic constitution of capitalist society. Fred Hirsch (*Social Limits to Growth* [Cambridge MA, Harvard University Press, 1976], part 3) suggests that capitalist economies can only work if people who maximize self-interest in their market dealings act in their political dealings on the basis of the public interest instead. People may well be just like that. (Indeed, there is good evidence suggesting that they are; see D. R. Kiewiet, *Micropolitics and Macroeconomics* [Chicago, University of Chicago Press, 1983].) But if so, that is despite rather than thanks to the market mode of economic organization; capitalist economies, in these ways, undermine rather than undergird the sociological preconditions of their own success.

[6] A. R. Zolberg, *Creating Political Order: the Party States of West Africa* (Chicago, Rand McNally, 1966).

[7] Philosophers are familiar with this proposition through discussions of Wollheim's paradox; R. Wollheim, 'A paradox in the theory of democracy' in P. Laslett and W. G. Runciman (eds), *Philosophy, Politics & Society*, 2nd series (Oxford, Blackwell, 1962), pp. 71–87. For empirical evidence, see J. W. Prothro and C. M. Grigg, 'Fundamental principles of democracy: bases of

disagree, collective decision-making is itself impossible – to paraphrase Locke, any given collectivity cannot move in two directions at once.[8]

Another more formal way of putting that point would be this. It is a familiar proposition from political sociology that cross-cutting cleavages serve to ameliorate social conflict. The logic of that observation rests on the fact that, in an environment characterized by fluid and shifting situation-specific alliances, no one wants to make permanent enemies. But – and this is the part of the story that standard political sociology misses – people's capacity to 'have a bob each way' in this manner depends crucially upon the willingness of their respective reference groups to let them do so. If instead those groups are intransigent, defining role expectations in a thoroughly all-or-nothing way, then anyone trying to do a little bit of one duty and a little bit of another would get no credit for either. Cross pressures may make individuals *want* to behave more moderately, but whether or not they *can* depends upon their various respective reference groups being willing to accept partial compliance as being better than none at all. Where the sociological facts of life are such that groups are not prepared to be tolerant in these ways, cross-pressures can do nothing to moderate the behaviour of individuals either.[9]

Yet another more sociological way to put the point is in terms of 'primordial sentiments' and ethnic loyalties.[10] It was a common claim, associated with post-colonial nation-building in Africa and Asia, that the arbitrary boundaries bequeathed the new nations by their colonial masters made no sociological sense. They constituted shotgun marriages of disparate tribes and groupings, having in common too little of a positive sort (and often too much of a negative sort: ancient grievances and historical animosities) to make for a stable state. All sorts of schemes – ranging from the creation of a new national language to the sponsorship of new national literatures – were cooked up for forming one from many.[11] But the thought then, confirmed now by the burgeoning nationalisms and ethnic cleansings of the post-Cold War period, was that a political constitution can provide a framework for governing a people as a single people only if they are willing to be so governed. Absent genuine social unity, or some principled commitment to live together despite diversity, there is no future for a socially mixed commonwealth.

In short, there is no particular reason to suppose that a political constitution itself can necessarily conjure up the social conditions which serve as preconditions for its own success. There are many things a constitution can do: it can prescribe equality for all in the eyes of the law; its electoral laws can be structured so as to encourage parties to appeal to members of other ethnic

---

agreement and disagreement', *Journal of Politics*, 22 (1960), 276–94; I. Budge, *Agreement and the Stability of Democracy* (Chicago, Markham, 1970); and R. Rose, *Governing Without Consensus* (London, Faber and Faber, 1971).

[8] J. Locke, *Second Treatise of Government*, ch. 8, para. 96.

[9] R. E. Goodin, 'Cross-cutting cleavages and social conflict', *British Journal of Political Science*, 5 (1975), 516–9.

[10] C. Geertz, 'The integrative revolution: primordial sentiments and civil politics in new states' in C. Geertz (ed.), *Old Societies & New States: the Quest for Modernity in Asia & Africa* (New York, Free, 1963), pp. 105–57.

[11] A. A. Mazrui, *Cultural Engineering & Nation-building in East Africa* (Evanston IL, Northwestern University Press, 1972). D. Apter, 'Comparative politics, old and new' in R. E. Goodin and H.-D. Klingemann (eds), *A New Handbook of Political Science* (Oxford, Oxford University Press, 1996), ch. 15.

groups as well to their own natural constituencies.[12] But all that is just to say that the constitution can lay down principles and invite people to internalize them. And it might so happen that the people actually go for it. They may come to regard the commonality of shared citizenship as of more importance than their diverse races, religions or social origins. They may come to regard the constitution's principles as their own, and act accordingly. If they do, the constitution will have succeeded in bootstrapping itself to sociological viability.

The point is not that that is impossible, just that it is so terribly contingent. It depends crucially on the way people happen to react to the appeals proffered by their putative constitution. Inevitably, at least in some places, they will not rise to the constitutional bait. For those cases, at least, constitutions inevitably will have to be framed in such a way as to cope with a constituency which is socially deeply divided.

Coping with Complexity: Structural Alternatives

Many ways have been tried, over the centuries, for coming politically to terms with problems of radical social diversity – problems of how to rule a set of groups which refuses to be ruled as one. Rather than surveying various particular devices that have been tried from time to time, I propose to proceed highly schematically.

Note from the outset, however, that this case is to be sharply distinguished from the more common one of simple social pluralism. Naturally, any polity contains a range of groups differentiated along various dimensions. Naturally, each of those groups has a distinctive range of interests which it wants protected and promoted. All of the ordinary structures of liberal political order are designed precisely to serve the purposes of a mixed commonwealth, in that more moderate sense. It is an open question whether those purposes are better served by unitary constitutions or by divided ones, by strong rights guarantees or by a robustly impartial state. But what is beyond questioning is that all those familiar mechanisms are responses to the fact of moderate social pluralism. Indeed, they would make no sense without it.

The sort of social diversity here in view is of a more immoderate form. The problem of radical social diversity of the sort I am considering arises in the case of groups which refuse to be ruled as one. They demand not only protection for their distinctive interests. Of course they want that as well. But even if there were some impartial and impersonal mechanism built into the liberal constitution that operated infallibly to protect their interests, that would not be enough for groups like this.

What these groups demand, most fundamentally, is constitutional recognition of their cultural distinctiveness. Their demand is for constitutional recognition, with the analogy to 'recognition' of independent states at international law being taken quite literally.[13] They demand that their proper names be

---

[12] Donald L. Horowitz commends the 'standard transferrable vote' on just those grounds; see his *A Democratic South Africa?: Constitutional Engineering in a Divided Society* (Berkeley, University of California Press, 1991), ch. 5.

[13] Though it is an open question, analytically, to what extent the domestic equivalent to international recognition is properly 'domestic' at all. But consider the precedent of American Indian tribes as 'domestic dependent nations' within American constitutional law. See 'Note: the Indian bill of rights and the constitutional status of tribal governments', *Harvard Law Review*, 82

written into the text of the constitution, with offices and prerogatives attached; they demand that their religion be named in the constitution, either as the official state religion or as one of the various religions granted official state recognition; and so on.[14]

The challenge thus posed by cases of radical social diversity is one of how to 'incorporate', quite literally, such insistently distinctive groups into the very structure of the political constitution.[15] There seem, at root, only two fundamental ways of doing so. One strategy is to assign each distinctive group a separate sphere within which it will enjoy autonomous decision-making power.[16] The other is for all decisions to be made collectively but to give all the distinctive groups veto power over those collective decisions.

The 'autonomous sphere' strategy manifests itself in several forms. Federalism represents the classic example of this logic, practiced on a geographical basis. (Apartheid, homelands and Indian reservations represent less happy faces of the same phenomenon.) But there are other variations, assigning each group authority over a specific set of people or activities or spheres of life. The way in which Church and state (canon and secular law) carved up authority over the world in medieval times is one example. The way in which self-governing guilds were given authority over all activities within a well-defined sphere is another.[17]

The veto-based strategy also comes in several forms. Calhoun's proposals for a system of 'concurrent majorities' being required to authorize governmental action – giving, in his case, the slave states a veto over federal policy in pre-Civil War America – is philosophically perhaps the most infamous.[18] But precisely such policies are formally institutionalized in the consociational

---

(1969), 1343–73 ; R. N. Clinton, 'Isolated in their own country: a defense of federal protection of Indian autonomy and self-government', *Stanford Law Review*, 33 (1981), 979–1068; and C. F. Wilkinson, *American Indians, Time and the Law: Native Societies in a Modern Constitutional Democracy* (New Haven CT, Yale University Press, 1987).

[14] C. Taylor, *Multiculturalism and 'the Politics of Recognition'* (Princeton NJ, Princeton University Press, 1992). J. Habermas, 'Struggles for recognition in constitutional states', *European Journal of Philosophy*, 1 (1993), 128–55. J. Tully, 'Constitutional demands for cultural recognition', *Journal of Political Philosophy*, 3 (1995), 118–40. An example of just such a constitution is that which Zionists wrote for Israel, on which see G. J. Jacobsohn, *Apple of Gold: Constitutionalism in Israel and the United States* (Princeton NJ, Princeton University Press, 1993).

[15] 'Incorporate' in the strong sense in which cities and communes and guilds were incorporated into the ruling structure of society in the middle ages, being specifically picked out by the constitution of the realm as agencies with rights of self-government and sovereign prerogatives of their own to exercise. On the medieval case, see H. J. Berman, *Law and Revolution: the Formation of the Western Legal Tradition* (Cambridge MA, Harvard University Press, 1983), ch. 12; on a modern revival, see G. D. H. Cole, *Guild Socialism Re-stated* (London, Leonard Parsons, 1920).

[16] Rights guarantees, whether for individuals or groups, are a manifestation of the same basic strategy, as I argue in R. E. Goodin, 'Structures of political order: the relational feminist alternative' in R. Hardin and I. Shapiro (eds), *Nomos XXXVIII: Political Order* (New York, New York University Press, 1995). The role of constitutions in guaranteeing fundamental rights is beyond the official focus of this article, which is strictly concerned with what Sartori calls their 'plan of government' aspect; G. Sartori, 'Constitutionalism: a preliminary discussion', *American Political Science Review*, 56 (1962), 853–64. But autonomous spheres within plans of government manifest many of the same problems as rights guarantees, of course, so I shall return to discuss the analogy briefly below.

[17] Berman, *Law in Revolution*, chs 7 and 12. Cole, *Guild Socialism Re-stated*.

[18] J. C. Calhoun, *A Disquisition on Government* (1853), reprinted in Calhoun (R. M. Lence, ed.), *Union & Liberty* (Indianapolis, Ind., Liberty Fund, 1992), pp. 5–78.

arrangements of the Low Countries and elsewhere.[19] Informally, the institutionalized veto given the geographically-apportioned upper house over the actions of the popularly-apportioned lower house has long served a similar function in the US, protecting rural interests from manufacturing interests and their contemporary analogues.[20] And of course at the international level, the original Charter of the United Nations granted veto powers to the five permanent members of the Security Council.

There are a familiar range of difficulties with each of these strategies. Some have to do with demarcation disputes. (What falls inside and what outside each group's autonomous sphere? What is it legitimate to veto and what not?)[21] Other difficulties arise from social change. The whole idea behind separate spheres or institutionalized vetoes is that we should try to mirror within the political sphere the social power relations found outside it. But political constitutions are enduring arrangements, capable of persisting far longer than the power balances thus embedded. (Who writing a new Charter for the UN today would give a Security Council veto to Britain and France but not Germany, to China and Russia but not Japan?)

On a more theoretical plane, there are further issues surrounding the logical coherence or moral justifiability of such arrangements. Vetoes are not just devices for self-protection but also constitute bargaining resources: in the former role, they may seem no more than institutional guarantees of Pareto efficiency; in the latter role, the scope for 'offensive vetoes' confers distributional leverage that is harder to justify on those or any other grounds.[22] Furthermore, consensual decision rules, whether consociational or veto-based or whatever, work from some baseline (typically, but not logically necessarily, the status quo); and movement from that baseline is permissible only with consent in the relevant form from relevant others. But there is no reason to suppose that that baseline would itself command universal consent, either, thus leading to a deep incoherence in that whole style of decision procedure.[23]

Those familiar problems, practical and theoretical alike, are all serious ones indeed. The ones to which I wish to call attention – theoretical of a kind, but

---

[19] A. Lijphart, *The Politics of Accommodation: Pluralism and Democracy in the Netherlands* (Berkeley CA, University of California Press, 2nd ed., 1975) and *Democracy in Plural Societies* (New Haven CT, Yale University Press, 1977). On links between consociationalism and federalism, see D. J. Elazar (ed.), 'Federalism and consociationalism: a symposium', *Publius*, 15 (no. 2) (Spring 1985), particularly contributions by Lijphart, Elazar, Duchacek and Steiner and Dorf.

[20] A. Hamilton, 'Federalist no. 59' [1788], in J. E. Cooke (ed.), *The Federalist* (Middletown CT, Wesleyan University Press, 1961), pp. 397–403.

[21] Even where veto powers are formally unconstrained, conventions typically grow up concerning their appropriate use. For an Australian example, the assent of the upper house is constitutionally required for passage of all legislation, including budgetary measures; but in the wake of the 1975 constitutional coup toppling the Whitlam Government, it is agreed by all parties that it is illegitimate for the Senate to bring down the government by 'blocking supply' (refusing to pass budget legislation); G. Sawer, *The Australian Constitution* (Canberra, Australian Government Publishing Service, 1988), p. 117. Or for a British example, the assent of the monarch is required to turn parliamentary enactments into law, but any monarch who dared to exercise that veto power today would precipitate a constitutional crisis that would herald the end of the monarchy as we know it: 'naturally', in the words of George Bernard Shaw's King Magnus in similar circumstances, 'I want to avert a conflict in which success would damage me and failure disable me' ('The Apple Cart', *Collected Works* [New York, William H. Wise, 1930], vol. 17, p. 212).

[22] B. Barry, *Political Argument* (London, Routledge and Kegan Paul, 1965), pp. 245–9.

[23] D. W. Rae, 'The limits of consensual decision', *American Political Science Review*, 69 (1975), 1270–94

with sharp practical consequences – are no more and no less serious. But they are in a way more important, calling into question a whole style of constitution making: constitution making by constitutional borrowing.

Second-Best Constitutions: the Need for Deep Revisions

There is a proposition in economics, less familiar elsewhere than it should be, called the 'general theory of the second best'. Simply stated, that theory says that a vision of what one would ideally like may not be a very good guide at all to the choice among non-ideal options where the ideal is unobtainable.[24] The best we can do, when the very best is impossible, may be something very different indeed.

This proposition has, as I have argued elsewhere, important implications for politics in general.[25] 'One person, one vote' is a valuable welfare-maximizing political principle in a polity where there are no 'persistent minorities'. Where there are, it leads instead to persistent oppression. Standard solutions involve devices such as entrenched rights or super-large majority requirements giving some groups of people more power than their numbers would warrant. The criteria for judging the success of such arrangements (their success, that is, in promoting the values which in a non-factionalized polity 'one person, one vote' is supposed to serve) lies not in how close they come to implementing the 'one person, one vote' rule but rather in how safely distant they are from that standard. If 'one person, one vote' is ideal under ideal conditions (the absence of factions and persistent minorities), the best political arrangements we can implement in a second-best world characterized by the presence of those phenomena is a system of entrenched rights and institutionalized vetoes the very point of which is to thwart the voting power of majority factions.[26]

Now, I want to argue that something very much like that is going to be the case with respect to schemes for separate spheres or institutionalized vetoes for dissenting groups in a radically mixed polity. The 'ideal' state of the world – anyway, the one presupposed by standard constitutional prescriptions – is one in which we all deliberate together, all making policies which are binding upon all in turn. Where the social preconditions for that do not exist, we are operating in what is in those terms a 'second-best' world. There is no reason to believe that the institutions we prescribe for that very different state of the world will be arbitrarily near those we would recommend for the ideal world. There is every reason to believe that they may be very different right across the board.

---

[24] More formally, suppose the ideal state of the world is characterized by three conditions {A, B, C}. If all three of those conditions cannot be attained, and the ideal world is therefore unobtainable, the second-best state of the world is not necessarily one in which more rather than less of those conditions are satisfied; that is to say, a situation displaying properties {A, B} is not necessarily better than one displaying {A} alone. Rather, the second-best situation might well be one displaying some systematic departure from *all* the conditions which characterize the ideal world. R. G. Lipsey and K. J. Lancaster, 'The general theory of second best', *Review of Economic Studies*, 24 (1956), 11–33.

[25] The discussion in this section draws heavily upon R. E. Goodin, 'Political ideals and political practice', *British Journal of Political Science*, 25 (1995), 37–56.

[26] On this tension, see particularly Jeremy Waldron's spirited attack on proposals for a British Bill of Rights: 'A right-based critique of constitutional rights', *Oxford Journal of Legal Studies*, 13 (1993), 18–51.

Talk about concurrent majorities and institutional vetoes, about federal enclaves and separate spheres, constitutes just such ameliorist approaches to the fact of social diversity, however. Those mechanisms are simply tacked onto otherwise standard-form constitutions, without any systematic reconsideration of the rest of those constitutions – constitutions which have been tailored for a very different ideal world or borrowed from a very different actual polity. That, of course, is just what the theory of second best warns us against doing unreflectively.

Furthermore, upon reflection there are reasons to believe that systematic revision might indeed be required right across the board in revising those standard-form constitutions for application to deeply divided societies. There is no reason to suppose that adjustment is required in the rules governing the legislature alone: institutionalized vetoes are well and good in blocking onerous legislation in the chamber itself, but something else is obviously needed to protect against similarly onerous exercises of executive authority or judicial discretion. There is no reason to suppose that solicitous respect for groups' autonomy within their separate spheres will suffice: something else is obviously needed to ensure similar respect for those groups' distinctive viewpoints in activities that by their nature transcend several spheres.

Now, many things follow from such reflections. The first, and most obvious, is that wholesale constitutional borrowing of the sort ordinarily practiced by drafters of new constitutions is ruled out or should be radically restricted in its scope. Reading across any large set of constitutional texts, it is striking how similar their language is; reading the history of any nation's constitution making, it is striking how much self-conscious borrowing goes on (often to the point of sending emissaries to call upon American supreme court justices and their overseas analogues).[27] Nothing I have said here militates against getting ideas from elsewhere, of course. But the theory of second best does militate against any wholesale borrowing of documents from elsewhere, with only marginal amendments to reflect local circumstance. It might sometimes work, but more often wholesale revisions will be required to make such amendments fit with the rest.

Second Thoughts on Second Best

Looking beyond that obvious lesson for constitutional borrowing of off-the-shelf models from elsewhere, further reflection on second-best constitutions for deeply divided societies might lead us to wonder whether that second-best solution is really viable, either. Try as we might to build constitutional Chinese walls around each group's sphere of authority, the separation can never be complete, guarantees of absolute autonomy never ironclad. For intransigent groups prepared to accept nothing less, a set of partially separate spheres will be utterly unsatisfactory – as unsatisfactory, and for much the same reason, as

---

[27] Texts are collected in A. J. Peaslee (ed.), *Constitutions of the Nations* (The Hague, Nijhoff, 2nd ed., 1956) and A. P. Blaustein and G. H. Franz (eds), *Constitutions of the Countries of the World* (Dodds Ferry NY, Oceana, 1976). Influences are traced in A. Rapaczynski, 'Bibliographic essay: the influence of US constitutionalism abroad', in L. Henkin and A. J. Rosenthal (eds.), *Constitutionalism and Rights: The Influence of the United States Constitution Abroad* (New York, Columbia University Press, 1990), pp. 405–62; stories of constitution writing are collected in R. A. Goldwin and A. Kaufman (eds), *Constitution Makers on Constitution Making: the Experience of Eight Nations* (Washington DC, American Enterprise Institute, 1988).

would be a system of partially checked powers on the liberal models discussed above. Unless groups which are unprepared to live together at the institutional level miraculously find some way of doing so at the meta-institutional level, the only recourse would seem to be separatism. Secession, though perhaps third best (at least from the perspective with which we started), may be the best that can be done in circumstances of radical social diversity.

There is a generic problem here, which similarly threatens rights-based solutions to problems of the abuse of power and discrimination at the individual as well as group level. Rights – like institutionalized vetoes and separate spheres – constitute an attempt to lock-in outcomes in situations where ordinary procedures of majoritarian democracy are not to be trusted. But inevitably there are things that cannot be locked-in in this way: things that straddle the rights or rightful prerogatives of several individuals or groups; or things which must, by their nature, be left to the discretion of those administering a policy or interpreting a rule.[28] In such situations, we have no recourse but to trust that the *spirit* of rights guarantees (etc.) will be respected, even where rights (etc.) literally cannot be.

That is not to say that the rights guarantees are otiose, that we do not need them against people who can be trusted to act well regardless and that we cannot effectively use them against those not so disposed. Rights are valuable reminders, even where they cannot be literally respected. The culture that grows up around the practice of rights, where they can be respected, usefully moulds people's responses to other situations where they cannot. Presumably, we would also find the same proving true of the other more political analogues of rights, such as institutionalized vetoes and separate spheres.

What that is to say, however, is that groups who are radically unprepared to live together without strong constitutional guarantees of the sort here in view are probably going to prove unable to live together even with them. Groups who are so distrustful of one another as to insist upon constitutional recognition of utterly separate spheres and utterly independent powers simply will not have the requisite resources to trust one another, where those institutionalized guarantees of autonomy break down and some sorts of joint decisions have to be made.[29] We cannot nail down everything in the constitution. Much must ultimately depend on trust. Groups which are so distrustful of one another as to require guarantees of their absolute autonomy to be written in blood in the constitution will not be able to muster the requisite trust; real world constitutions will not be able to muster the requisite guarantees.

What that, in turn, suggests is that there may be no constitutional solution to be found to the case of really radical social diversity. If the groups really feel that way about one another (rather than just pretending to, for strategic

---

[28] For a striking application to a very different sphere, see D. Gibson, 'User rights and the frail aged', *Journal of Applied Philosophy*, 12 (1995), 1–11.

[29] This is arguably the lesson to be learned from federalism in the communist regimes of eastern Europe, where ethnic tensions were exacerbated rather than eased by the imposition of federal structures without the internalization of federal principles or procedures; see R. H. Dorff, 'Federalism in eastern Europe: part of the solution or part of the problem?' *Publius*, 24 (1994), 99–114. The rhetoric of regional distinctiveness notwithstanding, newer demands for regional autonomy in western Europe seem to amount more to the politics of advantage than the politics of identity; cf. P. Piccone, 'The crisis of liberalism and the emergence of federal populism', *Telos*, 89 (1991), 7–44.

advantage), then there is little recourse but for them to secede and to form their own independent governments wholly separate from one another's. Where less-than-perfect guarantees of autonomy offered by the second-best solution of separate spheres and institutionalized vetoes prove insufficient to meet the demands of really intransigent groups who refuse to trust one another for any purposes whatsoever, this clearly seems the best option on offer.

Sometimes that genuinely does seem the right solution to the problem at hand.[30] Often it does not. Sometimes that is because the problem at hand seems to have been misrepresented, exaggerated for strategic advantage in constitutional wrangling. Other times, however, it is because even the third best may be pretty unviable. Secession is well and good for groups with sufficient resources to sustain an autarchic existence; for those whose plans and projects require the co-operation and collaboration of those that they shun, it is unclear what has been gained merely by recasting intranational disputes as international ones. And of course secession is not possible at all (or anyway, not without massive population relocations) in the vast majority of cases where the groups in question are geographically mixed rather than occupying discrete territories which can be constituted as separate states unto themselves.

The Economic Analogue

There is much the same need for trust, at some deep level, within virtually all our institutional structures – even those involved in ordinary commercial transactions. Our ordinary image of the business world is one of firms signing contracts with one another and standing squarely on their contractual rights vis-à-vis one another. But the reality of capitalist commercial relations is not at all like that. Macaulay's classic discussion of 'Non-contractual relations in business' quotes one businessman as explaining,

> If something comes up, you get the other man on the telephone and deal
> with the problem. You don't read legalistic contract clauses at each other if
> you ever want to do business again. One doesn't run to lawyers if he wants
> to stay in business because one must behave decently.

Another says, more succinctly, 'You can settle any dispute if you keep the lawyers and accountants out of it. They just do not understand the give and take needed in business.'[31] Commerce would be literally impossible if every buyer and every seller, every contractor and every subcontractor were constantly calculating how to cover themselves in a court of law.

The same is true of relations within as well as between capitalist firms. It is the essence of the principal-agent problem that much is inevitably done by others on your behalf, operating at some distance and minimal direct supervision, with information or talents that you inevitably lack. In these ways, notionally hierarchical relations turn into something much more nearly resembling bilateral bargaining relations.[32] Economists, assuming the worst, devote

---

[30] A. Buchanan, *Secession* (Boulder CO, Westview, 1991).

[31] S. Macaulay, 'Non-contractual relations in business', *American Sociological Review*, 28 (1963), 55–67, p. 61.

[32] Even in the most dramatic case of slavery, judging from A. L. Stinchombe's account of 'Freedom and oppression of slaves in the eighteenth-century Caribbean', *American Sociological Review*, 59 (1994), 911–29.

considerable attention to mechanisms for maximizing the extent to which agents' interests align with the principal's own, supposing that only in that way can agents be made to serve their masters. But organizational sociologists have long known that less taut management structures are more conducive to the sorts of good performance, even in terms of the masters' own goals.[33] And in any case, try as we will, the gap between principals' interests and those of their agents can almost never be closed completely. It is far better, given not only transaction costs of constantly monitoring compliance but also given the unforseen contingencies that inevitably arise and can never be protected against in advance, for a co-operative corporate culture to take the place of rigorously policed contracts of employment or exchange.[34]

The same, finally, is true of relations within the peak institutions – in the central exchanges – of the capitalist economy. Among them, the apparently quaint example of the Antwerp diamond exchange operating simply on the basis of a handshake among qualified dealers is perhaps the most famous. But upon closer investigation, it turns out that trading in the pits of all the most central exchanges of the international capitalist economy – places like the New York Stock Exchange and the Chicago Mercantile Exchange – works in much the same way. There are, of course, government agencies and self-regulatory bodies standing behind the handshakes. But much is, and in the context of a frenetic open-outcry market much must be done simply on the basis of trust.[35]

Within the firm, between firms and in the central exchanges of a capitalist economy, then, people must similarly be able to trust one another to some minimal extent for market mechanisms to work at all. Just as political relations between utterly untrusting groups seem impossible, so too do capitalist relations between utterly untrusting individuals. The institutions of the economic constitution of capitalism, just as those of the political constitution, presuppose some such minimal levels of trust. They are themselves incapable of generating that trust; they are themselves incapable of substituting for it.[36] If such trust is not already there, or cannot be conjured up by some other means, exchange relations themselves cannot be institutionalized. We must, in such cases, opt for some other altogether different design for the central institutions of the economy.

Conclusion

The upshot of my comments on the second best may seem painfully postmodern. They seem to suggest that in many (perhaps most) places things are different in ways that make a difference; and seemingly little differences in

[33] T. Burns and G. M. Stalker, *The Management of Innovation* (London, Tavistock, 2nd ed., 1966).

[34] D. M. Kreps, 'Corporate culture and economic theory', *Perspectives on Positive Political Economy* (Cambridge, Cambridge University Press, 1990), pp. 90–143. D. Gambetta, 'Inscrutable markets', *Rationality & Society*, 6 (1994), 353–68 and 'Godfather's gossip', *Archives Européenes de Sociologie*, 35 (1994), 199–223.

[35] W. Baker, 'The social structure of a national securities market', *American Journal of Sociology*, 89 (1984), 775–811. H. Leblebici and G. R. Salanick, 'Stability in interorganizational exchanges: rulemaking processes of the Chicago Board of Trade', *Administrative Sciences Quarterly*, 27 (1982), 227–42.

[36] Hirsch, *Social Limits to Growth*, part. 3. Cf. O. Williamson, 'The modern corporation: origins, evolution, attributes', *Journal of Economic Literature*, 19 (1981), 1537–68 and *The Economic Institutions of Capitalism* (New York, Free, 1985).

social circumstance can (and often do) make a big difference in the institutional and constitutional structures best suited to cope with them.

Certainly in all these ways my conclusions cut against the languid universalism of received Enlightenment theories of social order.[37] But, equally, my conclusions cut against the lazy relativism of certain forms of postmodernism, too.[38] There are indeed differences, which do indeed matter. Our theories and prescriptions ought be sensitive to those nuances. But those nuances can be incorporated into a larger theory: they can be seen as special cases of a larger explanatory pattern, as special applications of perfectly general principles and prescriptions. Recognizing particularity, and then reintegrating it into the general, constitutes the essence of the properly post-postmodern project in contemporary political and social theory.[39]

---

[37] Though it is worth noting that when men of the Enlightenment came to comment upon or indeed draft actual constitutions – whether for Poland or Corsica (in Rousseau's case) or the Carolinas (in Locke's) – they did so in ways highly sensitive to local circumstance. See J.-J. Rousseau, 'Considerations on the government of Poland and its proposed reform [1772]' and 'Constitutional project for Corsica [1765]', F. Watkins (trans. and ed.), *Jean-Jacques Rousseau: Political Writings* (Madison, University of Wisconsin Press, 1986), pp. 157–274 and 274–330.

[38] Many champions of difference, including the author of the most carefully worked-out application of these principles to actual legal cases, would concur in eschewing relativism even whilst also eschewing the 'totalizing' rhetoric of the rest of this passage; they would prefer instead to look at problems from all of the many particular points of view. For my part, I cannot see how we can integrate all these particular points of view without integrating them into some larger overall point of view (which need not of course correspond to any one of those particular ones). See especially M. Minnow, 'Justice engendered', *Harvard Law Review*, 101 (1987), 10–95 and *Making All the Difference: Inclusion, Exclusion and American Law* (Ithaca NY, Cornell University Press, 1990).

[39] S. Walby, 'Post-post-modernism? Theorizing social complexity', in M. Barrett and A. Phillips (eds), *Destabilizing Theory* (Oxford, Polity, 1992), pp. 31–52. O. O'Neill, 'Friends of difference', *London Review of Books*, 11, no. 7 (14 September 1989), 20–2.

Contributors

RICHARD BELLAMY has taught at the Universities of Oxford, Cambridge, Edinburgh and East Anglia and currently holds the established Chair of Politics at the University of Reading. His publications include *Modern Italian Social Theory* (1987), *Liberalism and Modern Society* (1992) and (with Darrow Schecter) *Gramsci and the Italian State* (1993). He has edited numerous collections of essays, most recently (with V. Bufacchi and D. Castiglione) *Democracy and Constitutional Culture in the Union of Europe* (1995) and *Constitutionalism, Democracy and Sovereignty: American and European Perspectives* (1996).

GEOFFREY BRENNAN is Director of the Research School of Social Sciences at the Australian National University. His main current interests are in rational actor political theory and public economics. He is the author with James Buchanan of *The Power to Tax* (1980) and *The Reason of Rules* (1985), and most recently with Loren Lomasky of *Democracy and Decision* (1993). He and Alan Hamlin are currently collaborating on a book on the analysis of liberal constitutionalism from a rational actor viewpoint.

DARIO CASTIGLIONE is Lecturer in Political Theory at the University of Exeter; and has been Visiting Research Fellow at the RSSS (ANU) and Visiting Scholar at ZERP (Bremen). His research interests lie in the history of political philosophy and theories of civil association, on which he has published in both English and Italian. Recent edited works include (with Lesley Sharpe) *Shifting the Boundaries. The Transformation of Languages of Public and Private in the Eighteenth Century* (1995) and (with R. Bellamy and V. Bufacchi) *Democracy and Constitutional Culture in the Union of Europe* (1995).

HOWARD CAYGILL is Professor of Cultural History and Sociology at Goldsmiths' College (London). His publications include, as co-editor, *The Faith of the New Nietzsche* (1993), and *The Kant Dictionary* (1995).

STEPHEN L. ELKIN is Professor of Political Science at the University of Maryland. He is Chair of the Executive Board to the Committee on the Political Economy of the Good Society (PEGS) and editor of the journal *Good Society*. He is the author of *City and Regime in the American Republic* (1987) and co-editor and contributor to *A New Constitutionalism* (1993) and *Constituting Good Societies* (1996).

LUIGI FERRAJOLI is Professor of Philosophy of Law at the University of Camerino and between 1967 and 1975 was a Judge and a founding member of Magistratura Democratica. He is the author of *Diritto e ragione. Teoria del garantismo penale* (2nd rev. ed., 1990), also translated into other languages and on which a volume of critical essays was published in 1993 (*Le Ragioni del garantismo. Discutendo con Luigi Ferrajoli*, edited by L. Gianformaggio). Recent works include *La sovranità nel mondo moderno* (1995).

ROBERT E. GOODIN is Professor of Philosophy at the Research School of Social Sciences at the Australian National University and editor of the *Journal of Political Philosophy*. He is, most recently, the author of *Utilitarianism as a Public Philosophy* (1995), and editor of a collection on *The Theory of Institutional Design* (1996).

ALAN HAMLIN is Reader in the Department of Economics at the University of Southampton. His main interests are in constitutional political economy and in ethics and economics. He is the author of *Ethics, Economics and the State* (1986), and editor (with Phillip Pettit) of *The Good Polity* (1989) and (with Sam Brittan) of *Market Capitalism and Moral Values* (1995). He is currently working on a book, with Geoffrey Brennan, on the analysis of liberal constitutionalism.

JEREMY JENNINGS is Reader in the Department of Political Science and International Studies at the University of Birmingham. He is the author and editor of three books and of numerous articles exploring political ideas and practice in France. He is presently writing a study of political thought in France since 1789.

NEIL MacCORMICK is Regius Professor of Public Law and the Law of Nature and Nations at the University of Edinburgh; Provost of the Faculty Group of Law and Social Sciences; and is currently a member of the ESRC. His work ranges over analytical legal theory, legal reasoning, and legal, moral and political philosophy. Current active interests include interpretation and reasoning in law, legal theory and the European Union, and constitutionalism, nationalism and the state. He has published and/or edited several books in these fields.

ISTVAN POGANY is Reader in Law at the University of Warwick. Recent publications include, as editor, *Human Rights in Eastern Europe* (1995). He is currently completing a book on the issue of restitution of property in Central and Eastern Europe and is engaged in research on minority rights in the area.

ULRICH K. PREUß is Professor of Constitutional and Administrative Law, and Director of the Center for European Law and Policy at the University of Bremen. He is a member of the Constitutional Court of the *Land* of Bremen, and has held visiting positions at Princeton, Bielefeld, the Institute for Advanced Study of Berlin and, as Volkswagen Professor, at the New School for Social Research of New York. He has published extensively on constitutional theory and the idea of citizenship in both English and German. Recent publications include *Constitutional Revolution. The Link between Constitutionalism and Progress* (1995).

TONY PROSSER is John Millar Professor of Law at the University of Glasgow. Recent works include (with Cosmo Graham) *Privatizing Public Enterprises: Constitutions, the State and Regulation in Comparative Perspective* (1991); and he is currently working on a book analysing the role of the utility regulators and a project on the responses of different legal systems to the new media and to media concentration.

ALAN SCOTT is Senior Lecturer in Sociology at the University of East Anglia. He is the co-author of *The Uncertain Science* (1992) and the editor of a forthcoming book on *The Limits of Globalization*.

JUDITH SQUIRES is Lecturer in Politics at the University of Bristol and editor of the journal *New Formations*. Recent publications include, as editor, *Principled Positions: Postmodernism and the Rediscovery of Value* (1994) and (with Erica Carter and James Donald) *Cultural Remix: Theories of Politics and the Popular* (1995).

JOSEPH H. H. WEILER is Manley Hudson Professor of Law and Jean Monnet Chair at Harvard University. He also serves as Co-Director of the Academy of European Law at the European University Institute. A collection of his essays on the European Union will appear in 1996 under the title of *The Constitution of Europe: Do the New Clothes Have an Emperor? and Other Essays on the Ends and Means of European Integration*.

Constitutionalism in transformation

Index

CONSTITUTIONALISM IN TRANSFORMATION: EUROPEAN AND THEORETICAL PERSPECTIVES